CONTRACT THEORY

STEPHEN A. SMITH
McGill University

OXFORD
UNIVERSITY PRESS

*This book has been printed digitally and produced in a standard specification
in order to ensure its continuing availability*

OXFORD
UNIVERSITY PRESS

Great Clarendon Street, Oxford OX2 6DP

Oxford University Press is a department of the University of Oxford.
It furthers the University's objective of excellence in research, scholarship,
and education by publishing worldwide in

Oxford New York

Auckland   Cape Town   Dar es Salaam   Hong Kong   Karachi
Kuala Lumpur   Madrid   Melbourne   Mexico City   Nairobi
New Delhi   Shanghai   Taipei   Toronto
With offices in
Argentina   Austria   Brazil   Chile   Czech Republic   France Greece
Guatemala   Hungary   Italy   Japan   South Korea   Poland   Portugal
Singapore   Switzerland   Thailand   Turkey   Ukraine   Vietnam

Oxford is a registered trade mark of Oxford University Press
in the UK and in certain other countries
Published in the United States
by Oxford University Press Inc., New York

© Stephen A. Smith 2004

The moral rights of the author have been asserted

Database right Oxford University Press (maker)

Reprinted 2007

ISBN 978-0-19-876561-5

To Susan

Preface

This is a book about the law of contract, in particular the common law of contract. Like most books about contract law, its primary aim is to help readers better understand that law. But it differs from the usual contract textbook in that rather than trying to set out in an orderly fashion the rules of contract law, it tries to set out in an orderly fashion propositions about the underlying nature of, and justification for, those rules. The focus of this book, in other words, is contract theory rather than contract doctrine.

Questions of the following kind will therefore be addressed. What, if anything, is the justification for enforcing contracts? Is it the value of promoting social welfare or the importance of protecting individual rights? How are contractual obligations like or unlike the obligations imposed by the law of tort and unjust enrichment? Are they promissory obligations or obligations to compensate those whom we have induced to detrimentally rely upon us? What function, if any, does the common law doctrine of consideration fulfill? Why do common law courts rarely order contract breakers to perform their contracts?

In addressing these questions, this book has two aims. The first is to help readers better understand the existing literature on contract theory. This aim will be pursued primarily by identifying and comparing the key arguments found in that literature. Another way of describing this aim is that the book seeks to develop classificatory schemes for theories about contract law. The need for such schemes seems clear. While scholars, judges, and lawyers have been writing about contract theory since at least the time of the ancient Greeks, the amount of published contract theory has grown exponentially over the last seventy-five years, and especially over the last twenty-five years. Thus, just as there was a need at the turn of the last century for textbooks that placed the existing common law rules into a manageable, intelligible schema, there is now a need to do the same with the ever growing body of theory about those rules.

The book's second aim is to make a substantive contribution to contract theory. This book is not just *about* contract theory; it also *does* contract theory. Thus, in addition to classifying and describing theoretical positions, I also evaluate those positions. Moreover, I frequently propose new arguments—or revise old ones—where I conclude that the existing arguments are inadequate. This alludes to another way, aside from the focus on theory, that this book is different from books about contract doctrine. Throughout the common law legal world, the main body of contract doctrine is relatively well settled, and has been so since at least the beginning of this century. We can speak, at least in broad terms, of *the* common law of contract. Indeed, for many purposes, we can speak of the law of contract without even differentiating between common law and civil law. But we cannot speak of *the* theory of contract. There is no single theory of contract that is universally accepted; rather there exists a variety of mutually exclusive theories, with few elements in common. Indeed, scholars often debate whether a particular argument or position even qualifies as a theory of contract (as opposed to, say, a theory of unjust enrichment law, or a theory about what contract law *should* look like). The reader who looks to this book for *the* theory of contract will therefore be disappointed. This is not to say all theories are equal. In this book, I reject many theories, while supporting others. In the end, however, because there is little consensus as to the best theory of contract, studying contract theory mainly entails learning about competing theories.

Format of the book

Most contributions to contract theory can be placed into one of two broad categories. The first category is composed of 'general theories', by which I mean theories that attempt to explain the basic idea of contractual obligation and, by implication, contract law as a whole. An example would be the view that contracts are rights-based promissory obligations. The second category is composed of 'particular theories' or theoretical accounts of particular substantive contract law doctrines, such as offer and acceptance, consideration, and so on. An example of a particular theory is the idea that consideration is essentially a formal requirement; a second example is the idea that the rules on mistake and frustration are best understood as rules of contract interpretation.

General theories and particular theories are, of course, linked. General theories have implications for understanding particular substantive doctrines; conversely, the explanation of substantive doctrines has implications for general theories of contract. A complete theory of contract will therefore explain both the basic concept of contractual obligation and each of the specific doctrines that make up the law of contract. But the distinction between general and particular theories is important for the organization of a book on contract theory. For example, such a book might be organized exclusively around general theories (e.g., a chapter on 'contract as promise', a chapter on 'contract as induced-reliance', and so on) or it might be organized exclusively around particular theories (e.g., separate chapters on offer and acceptance, consideration, remedies, and so on).

In this book, I adopt a third, mixed approach: both general and particular theories are used as organizing concepts. The format is as follows: Part I consists of a single chapter focusing on methodological issues. More specifically, this chapter examines the general criteria for identifying and evaluating contract theories. The discussion of substantive contract theory begins in Part II; in this part, the most important general theories of contract are described and evaluated. Finally, in Part III, particular theories dealing with the main substantive doctrines of common law contract —offer and acceptance, consideration, breach, and so on—are examined.

In discussing particular rules and doctrines some exposition of the law is necessary, but this will be kept to a minimum. Readers are presumed to have, or to be acquiring, a basic knowledge of the common law of contract. Fortunately, exhaustive knowledge of the law is not generally necessary for my purposes, given that most contract theory focuses on the core rules of contract law.

A final point is that while this book focuses on the common law of contract, in particular the English common law, much of what is said applies equally to the civil law tradition. Indeed, many of the theoretical arguments discussed in this book were drawn from, or influenced by, civilian thinking about contracts. It is often said that studying other legal systems makes us more aware of what is unique or special about our native system. But teaching contract law in a faculty in which the common law and civil law traditions are taught together in a unified way, has shown me that such study can also make clear how much is shared between legal traditions, particularly at the level of underlying principles. I have tried to reflect that experience in this book.

Acknowledgements

I began this book while I was a Fellow of St. Anne's College, Oxford University, and completed it in my present position, as a member of the Faculty of Law, McGill University. Oxford and McGill provided both the opportunity and the inspiration to write this book, and I owe a great debt to both institutions. The faculty members and students at both universities also had a significant influence on my approach to the book's subject matter. My experiences at Oxford and McGill, and my move from one to the other during the course of writing, have shaped my thinking and, of course, this book.

I also owe debts to many individuals. A number of colleagues, at McGill, Oxford, and elsewhere, read chapters of this book and provided helpful comments: Dennis Klimchuk, Roderick Macdonald, Yves-Marie Morissette, Eric Posner, Ruth Sefton-Green, Shauna Van Praagh, Jane Stapleton, and Richard Sutton. Other colleagues were kind enough to discuss with me — often at great length — many of the book's ideas; the list is too long to name them all here, but special thanks go to Timothy Endicott, Mark Gergen, Daniel Jutras, Nicholas McBride, Ewan McKendrick, Peter Benson, and Lionel Smith. Finally, a number of McGill students provided invaluable assistance as editors, researchers, and critics: Didier Frechette, Adam Kramer, Eric Mendelson, and Bryan Thomas. Three students, in particular, deserve a special mention for helping to bring the book to completion: Finn Makela, Toby Moneit, and Jeff Roberts.

The research and writing of this book were facilitated by grants from the Social Sciences and Humanities Research Council of Canada and The Foundation for Legal Research.

Stephen A. Smith

Montreal, Canada
August 15, 2003

Summary Table of Contents

Detailed Table of Contents

Table of Cases

Table of Statutes

Table of Regulations

PART I

Methodology

Part I of this book is comprised of a single chapter focusing upon methodological questions raised by the study of contract theory. More specifically, the chapter focuses on two questions: (1) what qualifies as a 'contract theory' (for the purposes of this book), and (2) how are theories of contract evaluated? Consideration of methodological issues is logically prior to consideration of substantive contract theory arguments, but readers who have little familiarity with either contract theory or legal theory generally may find that the abstract issues raised in Chapter 1 are more accessible if they have sampled some of material covered in Parts II and III. The overview provided in Chapter 2 may be useful in this regard.

I

What is Contract Theory?[1]

What is contract theory? How would we recognize a 'theory of contract' if we were to come across one? And if we found a theory of contract, how would we know it was a good theory? Abstract questions such as these are familiar in books on general jurisprudence (books about the nature of law and legal systems generally),[2] but they are less common in books that focus on a substantive area of law. In part, this is the case because such questions are indeed ones of general jurisprudence. Similar questions could be posed, and similar answers given, with respect to criminal law theory, tort theory, constitutional law theory, or just legal theory generally. A second reason these questions are not common in books on substantive law is that they are complex and there is little agreement about the answers.

But a book about contract theory cannot ignore such questions entirely. 'Theory about contract theory' is important, first, because of the risk of arguing at cross-purposes; if we are not clear what we mean by contract theory, we may end up comparing the theoretical equivalents of apples and oranges. Many disagreements between supposedly rival theories of contract are of exactly this kind: the theories do not so much disagree as have different aims. An historical account of the genesis of the consideration doctrine, for example, has different aims from, and so is not a rival to, an argument for abolishing the consideration requirement.

A second reason that theory about contract theory is important is that many of the deepest differences in contract theory rest on disagreements, often unarticulated, about the criteria for assessing theories. For example, the popular idea that the basic purpose of contract law is to promote economic welfare or 'efficiency' (the 'efficiency theory' of contract) is sometimes rejected on grounds that efficiency is an unattractive moral principle (4.1.5) or that economic principles are foreign to legal reasoning (4.1.6). But advocates of efficiency theories often regard objections of this sort, even if true, as beside the point; all that matters, they say, is whether the

---

[1] I discuss some of the issues raised in this chapter in Smith (2000).
[2] e.g. Hart (1994); Dworkin (1996).

theory is consistent with what judges actually do. Whatever position is taken, it should be evident that the debate is not about whether an efficiency theory fits with this or that particular legal rule. Rather, it is a debate about what qualifies as a good theory. One view holds that a good theory should show the law in a morally appealing light and should be internal to the law; the other view holds that such considerations are irrelevant.

The primary aims of this chapter, then, are to indicate what is meant by 'contract theory' in this book and to identify possible criteria for assessing contract theories. By way of illustration, but not in order to reject a theory from further consideration, I will also note some implications for particular theories of adopting these criteria.

1.1. WHAT IS CONTRACT THEORY?

It is sometimes thought that legal theory, including contract theory, is anything written about the law that is not 'doctrinal' or 'black letter' law. Theory, in this view, is everything other than the sort of scholarship exemplified in traditional legal textbooks. The term 'theory' is indeed broad, but whatever words are used to describe the various kinds of non-doctrinal contract law scholarship that exist, such scholarship is not all engaged in the same project and so cannot usefully all be compared. (Moreover, some of what goes on in traditional contract textbooks *does* count as contract theory). 'Things written about contract law', like 'things written about airports', is not a coherent subject, at least for scholarly purposes. Thus, we need to explain, or at least to stipulate, what the term 'contract theory' means when it is used in this book.

Broadly speaking, four types of accounts are possible of any area of the law: (1) historical, (2) prescriptive, (3) descriptive, and (4) interpretive. Historical accounts seek to explain how and why the law has developed the way it has; they reveal the law's causal history. For example, an explanation of modern contract law as the product of changing forces of production in the 18th and 19th century is an historical account,[3] as is an explanation of modern contract law as the product of medieval scholars' concerns for Aristotelian notions of virtue.[4]

Prescriptive accounts of the law are accounts of what the law should be: of the ideal law. An argument that contract law should promote

---

[3] See Horowitz (1977).   [4] See Gordley (1991).

economic efficiency is a prescriptive account, as is an argument that the consideration rule in contract law should be eliminated.

Descriptive accounts, as the name suggests, aim to describe the law as it is now or as it was at a certain time. When lawyers explain contract law to their clients, they are typically engaged in a descriptive exercise, and most textbooks on contract law are, in large part, descriptive accounts.

The fourth type of account, an interpretive account,[5] is the main focus of this book; 'theories of contract', in the sense intended in this book, are interpretations of contract law. Interpretive theories aim to enhance understanding of the law by highlighting its significance or meaning. As I explain in more detail below, this is achieved by explaining why certain features of the law are important or unimportant and by identifying connections between those features—in other words, by revealing an *intelligible order* in the law, so far as such an order exists. For example, the idea that the rules on consideration, mistake, and remedies are evidence that contractual obligations are rights-based promissory obligations, is an interpretive theory. So too is the idea that these rules are best explained on the basis that contract law's fundamental purpose is to promote economic efficiency. If either of these claims is true, it reveals an intelligible order in the law—it helps to 'make sense' of the law—and thereby helps us better understand it.

In saying that the primary concern of this book is with interpretive theories, no criticism of historical, prescriptive, or descriptive accounts of the law is intended. They are simply different projects. Moreover, these projects clearly are relevant to, and sometimes overlap with, the interpretive project. This is why, in practice, nearly all interpretive theories include historical, prescriptive, and descriptive elements.

More specifically, historical accounts obviously provide valuable clues as to how the present law should be understood.[6] If we know that, as a matter of historical fact, law-makers have long been motivated by the belief that contracts are promises, we have a strong hint that contemporary contract law might be explained best by a contract theory that regards contracts in the same way. Similarly, if we know the judges in a pivotal case were bribed by the winning side, we might think it unlikely that the

---

[5] In legal scholarship, the idea of interpretation is often associated with Ronald Dworkin's work (1985). The above definition is broadly consistent with Dworkin's use of the term, but as I explain below, it does not commit one to endorsing Dworkin's particular understanding of interpretation.

[6] Examples of scholarship in which historical arguments are used to support theories of modern contract law include Gilmour (1974), Atiyah (1979), and Gordley (1991).

case's ratio could be supported by any morally appealing principle. It must be stressed, however, that an historical account, however complete, is not the same thing as an interpretive account of the law. History only provides clues to the answers that the interpreter seeks. What an interpreter is trying to understand—to interpret—is the law, not what motivated the judges who made the law.

The relationship between prescriptive and interpretative accounts is complex. At one level, it is similar to the causal relationship that exists between historical and interpretive accounts. Among the factors that influence law-makers are their views about whether proposed legal rules are morally justified. Those views may, of course, be wrong, but it seems likely that in most cases they are at least related to whether the rules are, in fact, morally justified. It is a reasonable starting assumption (but no more) that the actual law bears some relation to good law. Stated differently, moral arguments play an indirect role in historical accounts of law, and historical accounts, as explained above, play an indirect role in interpretive theories. Whether the link is stronger than this—whether as *a matter of principle* it counts in favour of an interpretive theory in that it reveals the law to be morally justified—is a different and more difficult question to which I return below.

Considered from the opposite perspective—from the perspective of what an interpretative account of contract can do for a prescriptive account—the link between interpretation and prescription is clear. Before attempting to reform the law, reformers must understand the law that they are planning to reform. Indeed, once the theoretical foundations of the law are understood, it is usually a short step to suggesting reforms of that law. It is primarily in this way that reform proposals are examined in this book.

Finally, descriptive accounts are obviously important for doing interpretive legal theory. Descriptive accounts provide the data that the interpreter is trying to interpret. But it must be stressed that there is no sharp break between description and interpretation; the difference is a matter of degree. A purely descriptive account would be entirely useless, if not impossible. It would amount to little more than a randomly collated list of data. This is why all textbooks engage in interpretation to some degree; for example, all textbooks impose an order or schema on the material they discuss. Consistent with this conclusion, many of the arguments discussed in this book were first raised in contract law textbooks.

1.2. FOUR CRITERIA FOR ASSESSING THEORIES OF CONTRACT

By a 'theory of contract', therefore, I mean an interpretive theory as defined above. But what makes a particular interpretive theory of the law a good one? What are the criteria, in other words, for evaluating interpretive theories? This is the most difficult of the methodological questions faced by legal theorists. It is rarely addressed explicitly in contract theory scholarship, although no theorist can avoid taking a position, explicitly or not, on the answer.

In what follows, I will suggest that four criteria are of particular relevance in assessing contract theories: (1) fit, (2) coherence, (3) morality, and (4) transparency.

1.3. FIT

The most obvious criterion for assessing interpretive theories is whether they fit the data they are trying to explain.[7] A theory 'fits' if it is consistent with, and supported by, the relevant facts. With respect to contract law, those facts include (at a minimum) a group of legislative or precedent based legal rules and a set of decisions.[8] For example, the rule that liability for breach of contract is ordinarily limited to the value of the promised performance is a contract law fact. So too is the decision in *Tito v Waddell*[9] that the defendant must pay only nominal damages despite having deliberately breached a contract. Now, consider the rather implausible suggestion that the primary aim of contract law is to punish wrongdoers. As an interpretation of contract law, this suggestion scores poorly on the fit criterion because, *inter alia*, it is not supported by the above rule and decision.

What qualifies as contract *law*?

The first, and in many ways the most difficult, question raised by the fit criterion is not about fit *per se*. Rather, the question is this: what counts as contract *law*? Legislation and judicial decisions clearly are sources of law in a common law legal system. But what of things like custom,

---

[7] e.g. Dworkin (1995) 65–68.
[8] On a broad definition of 'facts' the criteria of morality and transparency discussed below could also be subsumed within the fit criterion. The explanation of the morality and transparency criteria is essentially that a good theory should take account of the 'fact' that, from the internal perspective, law is a morally justified, transparent practice.
[9] [1977] Ch 106.

community standards, trade practices, industry norms, and morality generally? The special case of 'morality' is examined below in a discussion of the morality criterion. As for other 'social norms', this book adopts the traditional and still orthodox position that such norms are legal norms only insofar as they have been explicitly or implicitly incorporated or used as such by recognized legal authorities—by courts, legislatures, and other authorized law-making bodies.[10] Fundamentally, then, law for the purposes of this book is 'state law'.[11]

The main implication of adopting this orthodox view of what counts as law is that certain kinds of 'law and sociology' contract scholarship turn out to be of relatively minor importance for the purposes of this book. I refer here in particular to empirical studies about how contracts are made and the role that contract law does or does not play in structuring commercial transactions.[12] From the perspective of this book (and from the perspective of most law and sociology scholars), such scholarship typically provides a theory or account of the *behaviour of contracting parties* rather than a theory or account of *contract law*. Aside from its intrinsic merits, sociological work of this sort may, of course, provide valuable information for scholars doing contract law theory. Many contract theories make assumptions about the effects of legal rules or about contracting parties' knowledge of legal rules. Sociological studies may prove or disprove these assumptions. But an explanation of contracting practices is not contract theory because the facts it seeks to explain are not contract *law* facts.

What qualifies as *contract* law?

A second difficult question raised by the fit criterion is this: what counts as *contract* law? Assuming we know what *law* is, it is still necessary to

---

[10] e.g. Hart (1961); Raz (1994) 21–238.

[11] This definition is consistent with believing that social norms play a greater role in determining contracting parties' *behaviour* than does state law. The reason for focusing on state law is not that it is important (though it is), but rather that it has certain distinctive features. In particular, state law claims, and to a significant degree must achieve, authority over all citizens. It should also be noted that focusing on 'state law' is not inconsistent with holding that judges are motivated by norms other than those they articulate in their judgments. The distinction drawn above is not between 'law in action' and 'law in the books' (on which I say more below), but between the behaviour of legal officials and the behaviour of contracting parties. Finally, the focus on state law does not deny that many legal standards require courts to incorporate social norms on a regular basis (for example, 'reasonableness' standards might be understood in this way), nor does it deny that when courts create new law they often do so by endorsing a pre-existing social norm.

[12] e.g. Macauley (1963).

determine which legal rules and decisions are the legal rules and decisions that a theory of *contract* law must explain in order to apply the fit criterion. Of course, one of the aims of an interpretive theory is to provide an answer to this question. But interpreters cannot get started without a pre-interpretive view, however rough, of the data that they wish to interpret.[13] An interpretation is an interpretation of *something*.

Contract law theorists rarely discuss this issue explicitly. But attention to the approach that nearly all of them implicitly adopt reveals an important methodological point. Contract law—pre-interpretation—is rightly regarded as that which people familiar with the law (lawyers, judges, legal scholars) take to be contract law. The parameters of contract law, and also the identification of what is central and what is peripheral to contract law, are determined by the consensus of those familiar with the law. Indeed, this 'consensus method' can never be avoided completely, since it is a general feature of communication and argument. Most disagreements about contract theory are founded on agreements (typically implicit) about what needs to be explained. For example, an argument as to whether a particular case is a contract case would be incoherent unless the disputants shared a prior consensus regarding certain cases to which the word 'contract' could be applied.

The consensus method is usually sufficient to establish which rules and decisions count as part of contract law for the purposes of starting an interpretive inquiry. But in some cases the conclusions suggested by this method are incomplete. More specifically, in respect of certain rules, there is no consensus as to whether they are part of contract law. For example, some lawyers consider estoppel part of contract law; others consider estoppel part of tort law or another non-contractual source of obligations. This and similar debates—of which there are many—are the inspiration for much contract law scholarship. Fortunately, perfect agreement on the relevant facts is not required for an interpretative inquiry to be possible. It is enough that there exists reasonable consensus on the core elements of the subject (and what counts as 'core' is itself established by consensus). Indeed, one of the aims of interpretive inquiries is to suggest how borderline cases should be classified. Of course, it cannot always be assumed that the required degree of consensus around the core actually exists. This is an empirical question. But in respect of contract law, at least, the necessary consensus exists; it is reflected in the broadly similar view of contract law found in nearly all contract law textbooks.

---

[13] Dworkin (1985) 65–68.

What qualifies as a theory of *contract* law?

Consistent with the above observations, an interpretation of contract law may legitimately conclude that certain rules which are, by consensus, regarded as part of contract law, should be regarded either as exceptions or as belonging to another area of the law—in other words, that the existing consensus is wrong. The grounds for such a conclusion are that the consensus is inconsistent with the best interpretation of the rest of contract law, in particular, it is inconsistent with the best interpretation of the core rules and decisions. That such conclusions will sometimes be reached is inevitable. It would be astonishing if every aspect of an institution that was created by innumerable individuals acting over hundreds of years fitted together into a seamless web.

But acknowledging this possibility raises a further difficult question: how much of what is commonly understood as contract law can be characterized by a theory as an exception, or as foreign to, contract law, while maintaining that the theory is still a theory of *contract* law? Is contract law absent the doctrine of consideration still contract law (see 6.3 for a positive answer)? In answering this difficult question, I suggest we have little choice but to adopt again the consensus approach that is adopted when determining what facts provisionally make up contract law. That is, we must rely on the experience of lawyers and others familiar with contract law to tell us when we have gone too far.[14] A theory of contract fails the fit criterion if it rejects as an exception or as misclassified so much of contract law that those familiar with the law would not recognize what remains as 'contract' law (though such an account might qualify as a good theory of *something else*—as I discuss below).

Of course, some 'contract' theorists argue explicitly that the very idea that there exists a distinct thing, however defined, called 'contract law' is mistaken. Thus, some theorists have concluded that most, or even the entirety, of what lawyers have traditionally understood as contract law is better regarded as a part of tort law.[15] The arguments underlying such conclusions (assuming they are sound) are typically consistent with the distinction between core and the periphery adopted above. Those advocating such conclusions typically adopt the consensus method; what distinguishes such scholarship is that it argues that, in order to understand

---

[14] See Weinrib (1995) 8–11.

[15] This is arguably the conclusion of Gilmore (1974), and with some qualifications, Atiyah (1986) 10–57. Of course, some scholars also argue that what is currently called contract defies any kind of rational explanation, contractual or otherwise. I discuss this possibility in the next section.

contract law, one must broaden the scope of the inquiry (and hence the scope of the core) to a larger category, such as 'obligations' or 'private law'. The outcome is not, strictly speaking, a theory of contract law — such scholarship denies that 'contract law' is a meaningful category — but it is a theory that, if persuasive, explains the data that theories of contract law claim to explain.

Finally, it needs to be acknowledged that the relationship between fact identification and theory production suggested by the consensus method, whereby the theorist first gathers the provisional facts (here legal rules and decisions) and then, after developing an interpretive theory, returns to those provisional facts and 'reorders' them, is an overly simplistic description of the interpretive approach.[16] No sharp line divides fact identification and theory production: interpretive exercises are a constant back and forth between theory and facts. A theorist's understanding of which facts are relevant is continually revised by the theorist's attempts — which themselves are continuously being revised — to understand those facts.

1.4. COHERENCE

A second criterion by which contract theories may be assessed is coherence.[17] Two versions of this criterion may be distinguished. According to the less-demanding version, a theory satisfies the coherence criterion to the extent that it presents contract law as consistent or non-contradictory. According to the more demanding version, mere consistency is not enough. This version states that theories should also be evaluated according to the extent that they show contract law as a unified system.

It is understandable that both versions of the coherence criterion regard consistency as a virtue of a good theory. A theory that reveals the law as inconsistent is less successful at achieving what was described earlier as the basic goal of interpretation: that of revealing an intelligible order in the law. Consistency in the sense of non-contradictoriness is a basic requirement of intelligibility.

The additional requirement found in the more demanding version of the coherence criterion — that the theory shows contract law to be coherent in the sense of being unified — is more controversial. Contract law is unified if all of its constituent parts flow from a *single* master idea or

---

[16] e.g. Finnis (1980) 3–18, Dworkin (1986) 65–68.

[17] On coherence as a standard for assessing theories see generally: Raz (1994) 277–325 (rejecting coherence) and Weinrib (1994) 29–46 (supporting coherence).

principle. For example, the idea that the entirety of contract law is based on promoting the value of efficiency is, in this sense, (perfectly) coherent; the same can be said of the view that all of contract law is based on a principle of enforcing promises.

Strong arguments can be made for and against adopting unity as a criterion for assessing contract theories. On the one hand, the interpreter's goal of making *a* practice intelligible seems inconsistent with regarding the underlying foundations of that practice as strongly heterogeneous. Insofar as the relevant practice merits a single label or title—for example 'contract law'—then it must be supposed that the different parts of the practice are related to one another in some way. A theory of contract law that revealed it to be a hodge-podge of entirely unconnected rules would make the name 'contract law' unintelligible; such a theory must suppose that what we now call 'contract law' should be regarded as more than one thing. This latter conclusion is, of course, a possible outcome to an interpretive inquiry about contract law—but it is not one that many contract theorists have adopted. Most contract theorists are rightly suspicious of interpretations that are radically inconsistent with lawyers' understandings of the terms they use. If the term 'contract law' is widely used, it seems reasonable to start, at least, with the presumption that the term is useful and meaningful (but this can only be a presumption).

On the other hand, human actions, including law-making actions, may be perfectly intelligible even when they are not unified in the sense just described. We rightly query individuals when their behaviour reveals them to be acting inconsistently: to the extent they act inconsistently, their behaviour is less intelligible. But this is not the case for individuals who act upon a plurality of different, though not inconsistent, reasons. Unless one assumes (as few people do) that all reasons for acting can, in the end, be reduced to a single master principle, it is accepted as perfectly intelligible, indeed appropriate, that people act for different reasons in different situations. Charity is an appropriate response to certain kinds of situations; in another situation, courage may be appropriate. Neither charity nor courage, however, seems reducible to the other, or to a third master value. The same must be true of legal systems. For example, certain aspects of a legal system might best be explained using the idea of sympathy, while other parts might be explained using the idea of fairly allocating risks. Let us take an example closer to our concerns: there is no reason to suppose that the basis for invalidating restrictive covenants is the same as the basis for invalidating prostitution contracts—or that either of these rules can be explained on the same basis that orders of specific performance are explained. I conclude, then, that a requirement of perfect unity seems not only unattainable in practice, but also inappropriate in theory.

Taken together, the above considerations suggest that coherence in the sense of unity is an appropriate criterion for contract theories only if it is applied in a relatively undemanding form. More specifically, to explain why contract law merits the title of 'contract law', a good theory must show that *most* of the core elements of contract law can be traced to, or are closely related to, a single principle. Consistency aside, nothing further is demanded by the coherence criterion.

1.5. MORALITY

The third criterion for assessing interpretive theories of contract is a moral criterion. Together with the transparency criterion discussed next (with which it shares many features), the morality criterion plays a critical role in assessing general theories of contract. As we shall see in Chapters 3 and 4, the most important distinctions between the leading theories of contract is not how well they fit the law, or whether they portray the law as coherent, but how they score on the morality and transparency criteria.

The morality criterion exists in what I shall call weak, moderate, and strong versions. Disagreements between legal scholars about the meaning and significance of the morality criterion—which are widespread if not always explicit—are essentially disagreements about which of these versions is appropriate. The strong version is perhaps the easiest to understand. It holds that a theory of law is better if it portrays the law in a morally appealing light, that is, if it portrays the law as morally justified. At the other extreme, the weak version of the morality criterion holds that it is enough that a theory explain why legal actors might claim, sincerely or not, that the law is morally justified. Finally, the moderate—and most complex—version of the morality criterion holds that a good theory must explain the law in a way that shows how legal actors could sincerely, even if erroneously, believe the law is morally justified. I discuss each of these versions below. But first it is necessary, by way of background, to explain why morality matters at all in assessing contract theories.

1.5.1. MORALITY AND LAW'S SELF-UNDERSTANDING

The different versions of the morality criterion are essentially different responses to the fact that the subject matter of legal theory—the law—is a human practice. To understand a human practice—to make it intelligible—it is necessary to understand what the participants in the practice think they are doing. In other words, it is necessary to understand how the practice is regarded internally. Suppose a social scientist is trying to understand—to interpret—the 17th century medical practice of blood-letting. An account of blood-letting might focus purely on the physical act of blood-letting and on the physical consequences produced by blood-letting. Such an account might conclude that the practice of blood-letting, which turned out to be a poor medical technique, was basically a practice for making sick people sicker. In purely medical terms, this account is not inaccurate, but as an interpretation of the *meaning* of blood-letting it is missing something. It completely ignores 17th century doctors' beliefs that the point of blood-letting was to improve their patients' health. Although the practice was not in fact beneficial, it was presented as beneficial and presumably was understood by participants to be beneficial. A complete account of blood-letting should take account of this feature of the practice.

In the same way, to understand the human practice of law, it is necessary to take account of how law is understood from the inside—by legal actors. More specifically, it is necessary to understand legal actors' public or 'legal' explanations of what they are doing. Because it is the public institution of the law, and not the inner minds of legal actors, that a legal theory seeks to interpret, the theorist is interested in how legal actors explain what they are doing when they are acting as legal actors. The relevant evidence of this understanding is found in judicial reports, parliamentary debates, and lawyers' arguments in courts—rather than, say, in judges or legislators' personal diaries or in psychological assessments of their motives.

'Legal actors' are those who participate officially in making and applying the law. These include, in particular, judges and legislators, but also lawyers and others. As a shorthand, and to emphasize that it is the public or 'legal' explanations of such actors that is my concern, I will refer to their understanding of the law as 'law's self-understanding' or the 'legal system's self-understanding'. Of course, not all legal actors explain the law in the same way, even when they are acting in their legal capacity. For example, different judicial decisions may explain a particular rule in different ways. But the very broad views about law that I discuss below are widely shared. Indeed, it is an important part of the concept of law that it is regarded by legal actors (in their official capacities) in the ways described below. A system in which legal actors did not express these views would probably not be regarded as a legal system.

One fundamental feature of law's self-understanding is that it presumes a close link between law and morality. More specifically, laws are understood, from the inside, as providing morally good or justified reasons to do what the law requires. From the internal perspective, it is considered *wrong*, and not merely foolish, irrational, or contrary to self-interest to disobey the law. Most legal rules are of course accompanied by sanctions (broadly defined), but the sanction is not the reason we are meant to follow the rule: we are meant to follow it because it stipulates what is appropriate ('good', 'right') conduct.

Another way to state this point (which I will frequently adopt) is to say that law is understood internally as a *legitimate* authority. A legitimate authority is a person or institution whose requests that we act in a certain way are good reasons to do so. In the case of law, these 'good reasons' mean good *moral* reasons to so act, as opposed to self-interested or prudential reasons (such as fear of punishment). In other words, a legitimate authority is a morally justified authority. It is a defining element of a legal system that it claims authority. This claim or self-understanding is one of the distinctions between a legal system and the commands of a gunman writ large: both the gunman and the legal system ask for compliance, but only the latter presents its claims as morally justified.[18]

Since at least the publication of H.L.A. Hart's *The Concept of Law*,[19] there has been broad, if not quite universal,[20] agreement amongst legal theorists that law's self-understanding (an aspect of what Hart called 'the internal perspective on law') is a feature of law that legal theories must take into account. Furthermore, there has been general agreement that a central feature, if not *the* central feature, of that self-understanding is law's claim to authority—the claim or belief that law is morally justified. In this minimal respect, what may be called the 'morality thesis'—the idea that legal theory must somehow take account of law's claim to authority—is widely accepted. It is when theorists turn to consider what is required in order to 'take account' of law's self-understanding, and in particular law's claim to authority, that disagreements arise. The three versions of the morality criterion identified above are different views of what is required to take account of the claim to authority.

---

[18] Hart (1994) 79–99; Raz (1994) 210–20.

[19] Hart (1994).

[20] Non-believers include Kelsen (1979), 'Scandinavian realists' such as Ross (1968) and Olivecrona (1939), and 'behaviouralists' such as Schubert (1979).

1.5.2. THE WEAK VERSION (CONSPIRACY THEORIES)

The weak version of the morality criterion holds that a legal theory must explain why law claims authority but it regards any kind of explanation as, in principle, sufficient. More specifically, a good explanation need not show that the law is actually authoritative, or even that it could plausibly be thought by insiders to be authoritative. In this view, a good explanation might be completely external to the real or supposed truth of the claim to authority.

The standard imposed by the weak version of the morality criterion can be illustrated by considering the (rather implausible) idea that contract law is a tool for systematically exploiting the poor for the benefit of the rich. If nothing more were said, this 'theory' would not satisfy even the weak morality criterion. The theory does not explain why law is regarded as a legitimate authority in law's self-understanding. That the law exploits the poor is, by definition, not a good explanation on its face for why the law claims authority. Anyone who understands the meaning of 'exploiting the poor' and who also claims that law is a legitimate authority is conceptually confused about what counts as a justification for authority. Faced with such an account of the law, law's claim to authority is unintelligible.

But it is possible to imagine an expanded version of an 'exploitation' theory that could satisfy the weak version of the morality criterion. For example, it might be asserted that legal actors are not sincere when they claim that law possesses authority. It might be further argued that they make this claim because, although they do not believe it (or perhaps do not care whether it is true), they are rich themselves and think the law's exploitative aims will be better achieved if the exploited do not realize what is happening. In this view, law's claim to authority is part of a conspiracy by legal actors to delude others as to the nature of law.

Conspiracy explanations of law's claims to authority are genuine explanations, but they are difficult to take seriously. No one doubts that judges and other law-makers occasionally dissemble, but as a general explanation for features of law that have evolved over centuries through the efforts of countless individuals, conspiracy explanations are unrealistic. It is just not plausible to suppose that legal actors are involved in a mass conspiracy.

Conspiracy explanations appear to be the only category of explanation of law's claim to authority that satisfy the weak version of the morality criterion without, at the same time, also satisfying the moderate version. None of the most important theories of contract—and none of the theories discussed in detail in this book—satisfy only the weak version.

1.5.3. THE STRONG VERSION

The rejection of conspiracy theories and of weak accounts of law's claim to authority generally is clearest in those who adopt the strong version of the morality criterion.[21] According to this version, taking account of law's claim to authority means attempting to justify, so far as possible, that claim. On this view, a good theory of law ought to show that the law *is*, in fact, morally justified. In the words of Dworkin, perhaps the best-known proponent of the strong version, '[a] successful interpretation must not only fit but also justify the practice it interprets.'[22] A legal interpretation must thus engage in substantive moral argument. On the basis of such an approach, it has famously been argued by Dworkin that efficiency theories of law should be rejected. The moral foundations of such theories, Dworkin argues (for reasons I discuss in 4.1.5), are morally unappealing.

The basic idea underlying the strong version is that intelligibility and truth are closely related. Recall that the goal of an interpretation is to try and make sense of the data being interpreted, that is, to reveal an intelligible order in that data. In respect of law's claim to authority, that claim will be more intelligible, the strong version holds, insofar as it is shown to be true. A claim that 'the law is justified' just makes more sense—it is more intelligible—insofar as the law actually is justified. The claim makes sense because it is true.

More specifically, according to this view, our ideas of what 'makes sense' cannot be separated, at least in the case of law, from our ideas of what makes 'morally good' sense. In practice, this means that to properly understand a self-reflective human practice, such as the law, the theorist must join in that practice, and hence attempt, as far as possible, to explain the practice in the same way that the practice explains itself.[23] The theorist need not duplicate law's self-understanding exactly—it is part of that self-understanding that the law may be mistaken in parts—but the more that is justified the better the explanation.

The main objection to the strong version of the morality criterion is that, although intelligibility and truth may be related, they are,

---

[21] Influential supporters of the strong version include Dworkin (1986) and Weinrib (1995).

[22] Dworkin (1986) 285.

[23] 'This book takes up the internal, participants' point of view; it tries to grasp the argumentative character of our legal practice by joining that practice and struggling with the issues of soundness and truth participants face': Dworkin (1986) 14. '. . . [N]ot only does an internal account orient itself to the features salient in legal experience, but it also understands those (and other) features as they are understood from within the law': Weinrib (1995) 11.

fundamentally, distinct concepts. More specifically, a statement, claim, or belief may be intelligible even if it is false. As applied to law, the objection is that a theory of law that reveals law's claim to authority to be false does not thereby make law's claim to authority unintelligible. The claim may be wrong, but it can still be intelligible. A statement such as 'purple is very tasty' is not intelligible. It is unintelligible not because it is false—the adjectives true and false are meaningless here—but because it is conceptually confused. It is nonsense. By contrast, a statement such as 'apartheid is morally justified' is false, but intelligible. We may disagree with the statement but we can understand what someone means by expressing such a view, and why they might come to support it, false though it is. We could imagine having an argument about whether apartheid is justified—though we cannot imagine arguing about whether purple is tasty. It follows that if our aim is to understand the law—to make it intelligible—the strong version's requirement of explaining the law in a way that shows the law's claim to authority to be true is unwarranted. The version conflates accounts of what the law *should be* (the goal of a *prescriptive* theory) with accounts of what the law *is* (the goal of an *interpretive* theory).

For this reason, the strong version of the morality criterion is, in my view, unpersuasive. But I acknowledge that the issue is a difficult one, and that the above objection is too briefly explained to convince committed adherents of the strong view. It also must be acknowledged that, in practice, most contract theorists are very concerned to show not just that their theory fits the law, but also that it justifies the law *and* that it justifies the law better than the alternatives. Most, but not all, contract theorists write as if they accepted the strong view.[24]

1.5.4. THE MODERATE VERSION

The moderate version of the morality criterion holds that a good legal theory should explain the law in a way that shows how the law *might be thought to be* justified even if it is not justified. In other words, such a theory must show how legal actors could sincerely, though perhaps erroneously, claim that the law was morally justified.

The idea underlying the moderate version of the morality criterion was introduced in the previous section. In criticizing the strong version, I explained that the goal of making a human practice intelligible does not require that participants in the practice be shown to be correct in what

---

[24] e.g. Fried (1981); Atiyah (1981); Barnett (1986); Gordley (1991); Posner (1997).

they think. It only requires that the practice be explained in a way that shows the participants are not incoherent or insincere when they say what they do. To give a non-legal example: a person who says that all cats are brown has made an incorrect ('not justified') claim. Yet it is possible to make perfect sense of what that person has said if it is known that the only cats he has ever seen are brown cats or that he suffers from a peculiar kind of colour-blindness. The statement is incorrect ('not justi-fied'), but it is still intelligible. The same applies to statements made about the law, including the claim that law is an authority. According to the moderate criterion, we can perfectly understand—render intelligible—such a statement even if it is incorrect, so long as we can explain how it might be made sincerely.

Functionalist explanations

There are two kinds of explanations about law's claim to authority that could satisfy the moderate criterion without also satisfying the strong criterion. The first, a 'functionalist' explanation, supposes that legal act-ors are controlled by external forces that are typically unacknowledged and unknown. We could imagine a functionalist version of the 'exploit-ative theory of contract law' described earlier. For example, it might be argued, following certain Marxist ideas, that law's claim to authority in an exploitative legal order is an inevitable by-product of the system of pro-duction in a capitalist society.[25] In this explanation, the legal actors are not aware of the reasons that inform their understanding of the law. The actor thinks he is making a claim because the claim is his own belief; in reality, his claim merely reflects the nature of the forces of production of the capitalist society that surrounds him.

Functionalist explanations have a long pedigree in the social and nat-ural sciences,[26] and cannot be dismissed out of hand.[27] But for good reasons they are relatively unpopular in contemporary legal scholarship. On the one hand, the factual assumptions underlying functionalist explanations, like the factual assumptions underlying conspiracy explan-ations, seem implausible. Functionalists claim not merely that legal

---

[25] See Hunt (1996).   [26] e.g. Hempel (1965); Abrahamson (1978).
[27] Broadly speaking, functional explanations explain a state of affairs by appealing to its role in a system—that is, its function. Thus a feminist functionalist might explain the existence and nature of the institution of marriage by appealing to its role in maintaining patriarchy. Similarly, an ecologist may use a functionalist approach to explain the existence of specific organisms in an ecosystem by reference to the role they play in it. Functionalism is a broad and diverse methodology and it is not my intention here to advance a particular view of it. For our purposes, only a general understanding of the approach is required.

officials are mistaken in thinking their claim that law is morally justified is true; they further claim officials are mistaken in thinking that their own beliefs had anything to do with why they made this claim. On the functionalist view, legal officials suffer from a collective and deep false consciousness. Given the number, variety, and sophistication of the actors involved in making law's claims to authority, the suggestion that these actors have all wildly misunderstood the reasons with which they explain the law is prima facie implausible. Moreover, insofar as a plausible explanation for how legal officials could be so deluded can be provided, the explanation is too strong. If the hidden forces that drive the development of the law work as successfully and covertly as the explanation suggests, the obvious question is why are those defending the explanation—and everyone else for that matter—not subject to the same or similar types of unconscious forces.[28] Functionalism, at least in its stronger versions, is self-defeating.[29]

Moral explanations

The second kind of explanation that is capable of satisfying the moderate criterion without also satisfying the strong criterion is one showing that the law is—or might plausibly be thought to be—supported by recognizably 'moral' principles. Insofar as the law is, or could be thought to be, supported by recognizably moral principles, law's claim to authority is intelligible. It is intelligible because we have satisfactorily explained why legal actors might claim that the law is actually justified. The explanation is that the actors believe the relevant principles both fit the law and morally justify it.

It is important to recognize that there are two ways that a theory of this second kind might fail to actually justify the law. First, the theory might show that, while the recognizably moral principles that it identifies could plausibly be *thought* to underlie the law, that they do not actually underlie the law. In effect, the theory is claiming that the legal actors have made a (mere) mistake.[30] For example, the theory might suggest that law's claim to authority would be justified on efficiency grounds *if* the behaviour of

---

[28] On the problems of false consciousness, see MacKinnon (1995) esp. n. 5.

[29] For different, and (if successful) stronger criticisms of functionalism, see Dworkin (1986) 12–13 and Weinrib (1994) 3–8.

[30] Certain versions of feminist and other 'critical' legal theories explain the law in this way. These versions do not object to the (liberal) values that are said to underlie the law (for example, liberty or equality), but they hold that legal actors are (empirically) mistaken in thinking that these values are in practice realized by the law: Gutmann (1980).

contracting parties was influenced by threats of damage awards. But the theory might go on to say that the claim is unjustified because it turns out that, as a purely empirical matter, the behaviour of contracting parties is not so influenced. This theory satisfies the moderate criterion because it is understandable—intelligible—that a legal actor might mistakenly think that contracting parties are so influenced. It is not necessary to resort to conspiracy theories or functionalist accounts to explain this kind of mistake: it is just an ordinary mistake, the kind that people make all the time. The only limitation on such explanations of why the law lacks authority despite claiming it, is that they cannot suppose that legal actors are systematically mistaken in their empirical beliefs about how the law operates. Short of adopting a conspiracy or functionalist explanation of apparent 'mistakes', it is just not plausible that legal actors can be systematically mistaken about the law.

The other reason a theory that satisfies the moderate criterion might not provide a persuasive justification for the law is that the recognizably moral principle that the theory identifies is not a good or justified moral principle. The adjective 'moral' in the phrase 'recognizably moral principle' refers to a certain *kind* or *type* of principle; it is not an endorsement or justification of the principle. In broad terms, a principle is moral if it is the kind of principle that could sensibly be advanced in a moral argument. So far as the moderate version of the morality criterion is concerned, the test, then, is not whether the proposed principle is a good one, but whether it is the kind of principle that someone could intelligibly adopt in defence of law's claim to authority. Consider, for example, a claim that punishing innocent persons is justified whenever doing so significantly decreases the murder rate. Many people do not agree with the 'utilitarian' principle on which this claim is based. In their view, punishing the innocent is wrong, and it is wrong regardless of whether or not it leads to the greatest overall happiness. But whatever its merits, the utilitarian principle just identified is clearly recognizable as a moral position. It is possible to engage in a moral debate with someone who holds this position, even if one disagrees with it profoundly. By contrast, if I were to argue that punishing the innocent is justified in certain circumstances because this is what I was taught to believe all my life, or because this is what I was told in a dream, or because this would make the law more aesthetically pleasing, I would not be relying on a moral principle.

In terms of contract theory, the main implication of adopting the moderate version of the morality criterion, thus understood, is essentially negative: adopting the moderate version excludes one possible reason for rejecting utilitarian, and especially efficiency-based utilitarian, explanations of contract law. Some legal theorists (notably Dworkin)[31] argue that the alleged moral defects of utilitarianism are a sufficient reason for rejecting efficiency-based and other utilitarian interpretations of the law. If the moderate morality criterion is adopted, this objection cannot be sustained. Regardless of whether utilitarianism provides morally unappealing foundations for contract law, utilitarian principles clearly are recognizable as moral principles, and thus utilitarian theories clearly satisfy the moderate version of the morality criterion. This is not to say that all possible contract theories will pass the moderate version: for example, the imaginary 'exploitative' theory of law described earlier does not pass. The idea that the rich should exploit the poor is not merely a bad moral principle, it is not a moral principle at all.

What qualifies as a 'moral' principle?

On the assumption that functionalist explanations of law's claim to authority are unconvincing, the moderate version of the morality criterion requires then, that good theories show that the law is, or could be thought to be, supported by recognizably moral principles. I have given some examples of 'moral' and 'non-moral' principles above, but it might well be asked whether there is a general test for determining what counts as a 'recognizably moral principle'. This difficult question is similar to the 'what counts as contract law' question that I examined when discussing the fit criterion. The general approach to answering it is also the same: a moral principle is one that is regarded as moral by the consensus of those familiar with the practice of making moral arguments.

Easy cases for this test involve principles that are conceptually of entirely the wrong kind. For example, principles framed in terms of human physiology, or early childhood experiences, or the structure of capitalism, are not moral principles. They may have implications for how people act, but they are not moral principles because by themselves they say nothing about what ought to happen, or about what is good or bad.

More difficult to classify are principles that adopt normative language ('ought', 'good', etc.), but that are alleged not to be moral because, essentially, they lie too far from the ideal view of what morality requires. Consider, for example, a theory that justifies the law on the grounds that the law ought to serve the exclusive interests of one class or of one gender. It seems clears that any conclusions as to whether this theory provides a

[31] Dworkin (1986) 288–95.

moral justification at all will be influenced by one's views about what would provide a *good* moral justification. More specifically, the idea of promoting one class or gender exclusively is arguably too far from the ideal of what truly *ought* to happen to qualify as a recognizably moral justification. Exactly how close a purported justification must be to an ideal justification in order to qualify as recognizably moral is, of course, a difficult question. But fortunately for our purposes, a precise answer is not needed. There is a broad gulf in contract theory scholarship between those theories (relatively few in number) that explain law in purely non-moral terms, and those that try to show the law as morally justified. The former, such as Marxist and certain versions of feminist theories of law, do not purport to provide anything that might be regarded as a justification of the law, and they seem incapable of doing so on even a fairly broad definition of what counts as a moral theory. The latter category of theories—which reduce, essentially, to versions of rights-based and utilitarian theories—turn out, by contrast, to offer justifications of the law that fit comfortably within leading traditions of moral theory; they easily satisfy any plausible test of what counts as a recognizably moral theory.[32]

1.5.5. SUMMARY RE THE MORALITY CRITERION

The differences between the weak, strong, and moderate versions of the morality criterion can be illustrated by returning to the example of the 17th century practice of blood-letting. Although doctors' claims that they were curing the sick are not moral claims, they are claims about the justifiability of what they were doing, and so can be analysed in a similar way. A weak explanation of this practice might suggest that doctors were engaged in a massive fraud (perhaps in order to get more patients) when they claimed they were curing illness by blood-letting. By contrast, an explanation that would satisfy the strong version would have to show that blood-letting did actually cure illnesses in the way the doctors claimed. Finally, an explanation that would satisfy the moderate morality criterion might suggest that, while the general aim of the practice was to cure the ill,

---

[32] Proponents of the strong morality criterion can, of course, point to this link between ideal moral theory and the concept of a 'moral' theory for support. Specifically, it may be argued that if we are willing to classify a theory as not recognizably moral because it is too far from the ideal of what morality requires, then we ought to take the further step of ranking theories according to how close they are to the ideal. Every move closer to an ideal moral theory makes a theory more of a 'moral' theory and hence makes law's claims to authority more intelligible. I do not think this step needs to be taken—as I have said, I believe we can safely regard a theory as moral even if not the best moral theory—but the distinction is admittedly a fine one.

and that while it was genuinely, if wrongly, believed that blood-letting was consistent with this aim, the practice was not a particularly effective cure.

Consistent with the arguments I made above on behalf of the moderate morality criterion, discussion of the moral foundations of the contract theories examined in this book is limited, for the most part, to determining whether those foundations are recognizably moral foundations as opposed to whether they are the best possible moral foundations. It is worth adding, however, that the rights-based promissory theory that is favoured in this book does not depend on rejecting the strong version of the morality criterion. To the contrary, the theory satisfies this criterion as well or better than the alternatives.

1.6. TRANSPARENCY

The fourth and final criterion for assessing interpretive theories of contract is transparency.[33] Though less studied by legal theorists than the previous criteria, it is equally, if not more important, in assessing contract law theories. In particular, the transparency criterion turns out to be critical when comparing rights-based theories to efficiency theories and other utilitarian theories.

The transparency criterion evaluates contract theories according to how well they account for what may be called the 'legal' or 'internal' explanation of contract law. As I noted when examining the morality criterion, the law, which is a self-reflective human practice, possesses its own self-understanding. One aspect of that self-understanding is the claim discussed above that the law is morally justified. My concern here is with a second aspect of law's self-understanding, which is the claim that law, and more specifically legal reasoning, is transparent. Law is transparent to the extent that the reasons legal actors give for doing what they do are their real reasons.[34] By contrast, law is not transparent if the real

---

[33] The most thorough (and nearly the only) discussion of transparency as a criterion for assessing private law theories is found in Weinrib (1995) Chapter 1.

[34] For example, suppose that a state agency announces that it will award construction contracts to the lowest tender. The agency is acting transparently if it actually awards contracts to the lowest tender. On the other hand, if the agency awards contracts only to contractors who are related to state officials, it is not acting transparently. A second example concerns the doctrine of consideration. Insofar as courts that purport to apply this doctrine focus on whether contracting parties exchange or agree to exchange something of value with each other, the courts are acting transparently. But if, as some critics contend, courts routinely 'invent' such exchanges in order to enforce agreement arrangements for quite different reasons (e.g., reliance, fairness, or promoting a valuable activity), then they are not acting transparently.

reasons are hidden. That law is understood, *from the inside*, as transparent is clear: law-makers, and in particular judges, give reasons for acting as they do and those reasons are presented as their real reasons. The report of a legal decision is not presented as mere window dressing; it is meant to explain why the plaintiff did or not win.

In broad terms, to *account for* law's claim to be transparent a legal theory of the common law must, *inter alia*, take account (in a way yet to be specified) of the reasons that judges give for their decisions.[35] For example, a satisfactory explanation of *White v Bluett*,[36] the 19th century case in which a court refused to enforce a father's promise to discharge his son's debt in exchange for the son agreeing to stop complaining, must take account of the court's explanation that the agreement was invalid because it lacked consideration. Similarly, an explanation of contract damages must take account of judges' stated aims of putting plaintiffs, so far as money is able, in the positions they would have been in had their contracts been performed.

But what does it mean to 'take account' of legal explanations of the sort just described? As with the morality criterion, there exist weak, moderate, and strong versions of what it means to take account of law's claim to transparency, and thus of what it means to take account of the actual reasons that law-makers provide. Briefly, the strong version holds that a good theory of law will portray legal practice as in fact transparent; in other words, the explanation the theory gives of the law will support the explanation that legal officials give. At the other extreme, the weak version of the transparency criterion holds that it is enough that a theory explain why legal actors might claim, sincerely or not, that the law is transparent. Finally, the moderate, and I will suggest most plausible, version of the transparency criterion holds that a good theory must explain the law in a way that shows how legal officials could sincerely, even if erroneously, believe the law is transparent.

I will examine each of these versions of the transparency criterion separately. The examination is brief as the relevant issues are similar to those considered in my discussion of the morality criterion.

---

[35] The criterion of transparency is most easily understood in the context of a common law legal system in which the historically primary law-makers—judges—provide public reasons for their rulings. In principle, the criterion of transparency applies equally to civilian legal systems, and to legislative sources of law generally, although care must be taken in identifying the internal or legal viewpoint in respect of these legal sources. To mention just one difference: an analysis of the internal legal viewpoint in civilian systems would place significant weight on legal treatises.

[36] (1853) 23 LJ Ex 36.

1.6.1. THE WEAK VERSION

According to the weak version of the transparency criterion, *any* explanation of law's claim that legal reasoning is transparent is sufficient. In particular, a satisfactory explanation need not show that law is transparent or even that it could sincerely be thought to be transparent. A good theory could reveal the claim to be a deliberate falsehood.

By way of illustration, consider the idea that the rules on duress are best explained on the ground that they promote efficiency. If nothing more is said, this explanation does not satisfy even the weak transparency criterion. It fails because it offers no explanation for why the courts, in deciding duress cases, reason using concepts like consent and autonomy, and do not mention efficiency or anything remotely similar. Such an explanation leaves law's claim to transparency unintelligible. The concepts of consent and efficiency are, on the ordinary understanding of their meaning, different *in kind* and not just degree. Consent is not understood as merely a subsidiary aspect of efficiency.

An expanded efficiency-based interpretation of duress could, however, satisfy the weak version transparency criterion. This would be the case if the interpretation explained why, consistent with the relevant conception of efficiency, judges might be expected to announce reasons that (on the surface anyway) appear unrelated to efficiency. For example, it might be argued that judges misrepresent the reasons for their decisions because they think the public is more willing to accept decisions based on the relatively neutral and widely shared value of consent than decisions based on the more politically charged value of efficiency. On this variant of a conspiracy theory, judicial reasoning is a sham. Though such a theory is far-fetched, it is nevertheless valid according to weak version criteria because it explains why judges might present the law as transparent.

Conspiracy theories appear to be the only category of explanation of law's claim to transparency that do not also satisfy at least the moderate version of the transparency criterion. But as with conspiracy explanations of law's claim to authority, conspiracy theories of law's claim to transparency are difficult to take seriously, at least if offered as general explanations of that claim. Particular instances of judges consciously misrepresenting their reasoning process undoubtedly exist, but it is just not plausible to suppose that the vast corpus of legal reasoning, which was created by countless individuals over centuries, is all the result of a mass effort by judges to misrepresent what they are doing.

1.6.2. THE STRONG VERSION

The strong version of the transparency criterion holds that a good theory must show law's self-understanding to be true. It must show, that is, that the arguments judges employ determine the actual results of cases.[37] A good explanation of duress, therefore, must show that concepts like consent and autonomy actually explain the results of the cases.

Adopting the strong version of the transparency criterion does not mean that a good explanation must simply replicate what judges have said. If this were the case, then adopting the strong version would make legal *theory* impossible: theorists would be restricted to doing exactly what judges do. What the strong version requires is that the theorist's explanation of the law, which explanation may, and normally will be, at a more abstract or theoretical level than the legal explanation, leads by logical steps to the court's reasoning. The theorist's explanation of the law must show why the legal concepts employed by a judge are an appropriate way of expressing in practice the broader concepts that the theorist argues underlie the law. A good theory, on this view, works through, rather than around, judicial reasoning.

But why suppose that the legal explanation is correct? The most plausible reason is the same one that was offered in defence of the strong version of the morality criterion: the interpreter's goal of making the law (and thus law's self-understanding) intelligible is better achieved if the claim to transparency is shown to be true. True statements are more intelligible than false statements. But as I explained in discussing the strong version of the morality criterion, this linking of intelligibility and truth seems unwarranted. A false statement or belief may be perfectly intelligible so long as a plausible explanation is given for holding the statement or belief.

---

[37] There appear to be relatively few committed supporters of the strong version of transparency criterion. Certain textbooks stand out for their attempts to justify, or at least to remain consistent with, the judicial explanation of rules and cases, e.g., Treitel (1995). For the most part, such texts are intended to be descriptive rather than interpretive projects. Certain of Ernest Weinrib's theoretical writings appear to support the strong version of the transparency criterion. For example, he writes: '[N]ot only does an internal account orient itself to the features salient in legal experience, but it also understands those (and other) features as they are understood from within the law' (1995) 11. But Weinrib's substantive work on tort theory is more consistent with the moderate version.

1.6.3. THE MODERATE VERSION

The moderate version of the transparency criterion holds that a good legal theory should explain the law in a way that shows how judges could sincerely, even if perhaps erroneously, believe that the reasons they give for deciding as they do are the real reasons. This approach rejects both the idea that judges are engaged in a conspiracy to mislead and the idea that judicial reasoning must be correct. Stated in positive terms, the idea underlying the moderate version is that a false, but sincere, claim is perfectly intelligible so long as a plausible (i.e., non-conspiracy-based) explanation is given for that claim.

As was true in respect of the morality criterion, there are two ways that a theory could satisfy the moderate version of the transparency criterion without at the same time necessarily satisfying the strong version. The first is by adopting a functionalist explanation of law's claim to transparency. A functionalist approach supposes that judicial reasoning is the result of external, and typically unknown, forces that cause judges to reason as they do. A functionalist efficiency-based account of duress, for example, might explain that, although judges think their decisions are motivated by concepts like consent, in reality judges are mere cogs in a socio-evolutionary process, whereby inefficient rules are inevitably eliminated over time. The same socio-evolutionary process could be used to explain why judges continue to reason using irrelevant concepts like duress: judges reason in this way because rules that are based directly on a concept like efficiency are too difficult to apply or, alternatively, are unlikely to be accepted by other judges or citizens (4.1.6).

For reasons explained in my discussion of functionalist explanations of law's claim to authority, functionalist explanations of law's claim to transparency are vulnerable to obvious objections. In particular, it seems implausible, in light of their training and sophistication, that all or even many judges are in the grips of a collective false consciousness—and if it were plausible, then it seems likely that legal theorists would be in the grip of similar forces.

The other way of satisfying the moderate transparency criterion that does not necessarily satisfy the strong criterion is to explain the law using concepts that are recognizably 'legal' (or at least using concepts that, though more abstract than standard legal concepts, work *through* recognizably legal concepts in their explanation of particular rules and decisions) even if those concepts are not the same legal concepts that were employed by judges.[38] I will call this kind of explanation an *internal* or *legal* explanation. In those cases in which the theorist's internal explanation differs from the judicial explanation, the explanation for this difference—and hence for law's claim to transparency—is simply that those offering the judicial explanation are mistaken. By offering an internal explanation, the theorist is acknowledging that the judicial explanation is the right *kind* of explanation. The judicial explanation is in the right ball park, as it were. In particular, no assumption is made or implied that the judiciary is engaged in a fraud or is in the grip of an unseen force. They simply made a mistake, which is understandable (and hence intelligible).

Short of accepting a conspiracy or functionalist approach, only an internal explanation seems capable of reconciling law's claim to transparency with the possibility that judicial explanations of the law are wrong. Insofar as a theorist's explanation of the law reveals the law to be based on concepts that are external to legal reasoning—on concepts, in other words, that are not just different from those that the judge did use but from those that the judge *might* have used—then the law's belief that its reasons were real reasons is not just mistaken, but conceptually confused (and hence not intelligible). An external explanation of the law supposes that judges are not even in the right ball park. For this to be explicable, either a conspiracy or functionalist explanation of legal reasoning must be accepted.

The above argument in favour of internal ('legal') explanations over external ('non-legal') explanations clearly assumes that it is possible to distinguish internal explanations from external explanations. Is this assumption reasonable? Some scholars have argued that legal reasoning is indistinguishable from ordinary moral or political reasoning.[39] Certainly, there is no bright line distinguishing legal from non-legal arguments. The practice of law is too large and varied. It is, moreover, an ever-changing practice: the concept of what counts as a possible legal argument

---

[38] The important point here is that, like the strong version of the transparency criterion, the moderate version does not require that a good theory remain at the (relatively low) level of abstractness found in judicial reasoning. An explanation is 'legal', in the sense used here, if it leads logically to concrete rules that are recognizably of a legal kind. An abstract account satisfies this test if it works *through* (rather than around) the kind of reasoning that judges engage in. This kind of explanation is found in what are sometimes described as mainstream or orthodox legal theories, which explain the law using concepts of individual rights and duties. A leading example in contract theory is Fried's *Contract as Promise* (1981).

[39] e.g. Kennedy (1976; 1986).

evolves over time. Ideas that were once discussed only in law schools often eventually find their way into legal judgments.

But the conclusion that the border between legal and non-legal is blurred and moving does not mean that it can never be usefully employed. The existence of law schools is predicated on the belief that legal reasoning is different from other modes of reasoning. As first year law students quickly learn, there exists a characteristic mode of legal reasoning, in which only certain types of arguments are acceptable. For example, the fact that the defendant in a breach of contract case once assisted the plaintiff may be a good reason for criticizing the plaintiff's decision to sue, but it is not the sort of reason a judge would adopt for refusing the plaintiff's claim. Learning to 'think like a lawyer' is essentially learning to distinguish legal from non-legal arguments.

It follows that the test for determining which kinds of explanations are legal explanations—and thus satisfy the moderate criterion—is one we have already encountered: an explanation is legal if it is recognized as such by the consensus of those familiar with law. One way of implementing this test is to ask whether the theorist's explanation is of the sort that, once translated into concrete concepts, could be accepted by a court, even if no court has yet done so. In other words, just as moral principles are the kinds of principles raised in moral arguments, so too legal explanations are the kinds of explanations raised in legal arguments. Some cases are easy. For example, the idea that the doctrine of duress is properly understood as part of the law of unjust enrichment rather than part of contract law is a recognizably legal explanation of duress. Although this explanation is different from the contract based explanation of duress that is given, or at least assumed, by most judges, it explains duress using recognizably legal ideas. By contrast, the idea that duress is best understood as, say, a reflection of male hegemony does not satisfy the moderate transparency criterion. 'Male hegemony' is, at the current time anyway, not a recognizably legal concept, nor can it be described as merely a more abstract articulation of such a concept. The concept of male hegemony is foreign to legal reasoning.

For the purposes of assessing general theories of contract, the main significance of the above arguments concerns the status of various examples of what can be described loosely as 'legal realism' scholarship.[40] Broadly defined, legal realism—probably the most influential approach

---

[40] On legal realism generally, see Leiter (1995). Seminal realist scholarship includes Frank (1931) and Cohen (1935). My definition of legal realism is intentionally broad.

to legal scholarship in the 20th century, at least in North America—is the view that judicial reasoning obscures, rather than reveals, the true basis of a legal decision. Some scholarship fitting within this broad definition, such as Fuller and Perdue's famous explanation of the 'expectation' measure of damages as a proxy for the 'reliance' measure, would probably satisfy the moderate transparency criterion.[41] That the law should protect reliance is not the official judicial explanation for contract damages, but it is the sort of explanation that courts *could* recognize.

But other examples of realist scholarship arguably do not satisfy the moderate version of the transparency criterion. In particular, and as I explain in more detail in Chapter 4, efficiency theories of law arguably do not pass the moderate version. Efficiency-based explanations character-istically explain the law using concepts that are foreign to legal reasoning. The efficiency-based explanation of damages for breach of contract, for example, is essentially that damages are incentives to promote future efficient behaviour. This explanation is flatly inconsistent with the legal view that damages are remedies, meaning that they are intended to rem-edy a past harm. This difference is not merely one of terminology or of degree; it is a difference in kind. The legal explanation focuses on the rights and duties of the litigants, the efficiency explanation focuses on the incentives for future behaviour of contracting parties generally. To be sure, we sometimes find examples of courts using explicit or implicit efficiency-based reasoning. Arguably, such reasoning is becoming more common as economic analysis of law filters through law schools to the courts. But in the main areas of private law, this kind of efficiency-based reasoning is not employed by the courts.[42]

A similar observation could be made in respect of various other examples of 'law and . . . scholarship': law and sociology; law and anthro-pology; law and feminist theory.[43] The kinds of explanations of legal rules offered in such scholarship are typically, though not invariably, external

---

[41] Fuller and Perdue (1936). I use the example of Fuller and Purdue with hesitation as Fuller was critical of what I describe above as the 'stronger' realist projects found in self-described realists such as Frank (1931) and Cohen (1935). Fuller clearly is not a realist in the classic mould. His article with Purdue shares, however, the realists' general aim of debunking judges' own accounts of what they are doing.

[42] This is not to deny that courts often try to understand the behaviour of firms and individuals using economic models of behaviour (albeit usually without adopting technical economic terminology). By 'this kind of efficiency-based reasoning', I mean reasoning that regards *private law* as a tool for promoting efficient behaviour: see generally 4.1.

[43] For concise accounts of leading examples of such scholarship, see Patterson (1996) Chapters 20, 27–31.

to legal explanations of the rules. Examples might include the explanation of a legal rule in terms of society's need for scapegoats or as a consequence of historically hierarchical gender relations. Explanations of this sort are different in kind, not just in degree or in levels of abstraction, from legal explanations.

It follows that if the moderate version of the transparency criterion is accepted, a large amount of contemporary legal scholarship scores poorly on one of the criteria for assessing interpretive theories of contract. In my view, this is sufficient reason to reject the *interpretations* of contract law offered by such scholarship (though some such theories, in particular efficiency theories, will nevertheless be examined in considerable detail later in this book). Of course, this is not to say that such scholarship has no role to play in thinking about law. To the contrary, it plays a crucial role in evaluating the law and in considering legal reforms. If one believes that the law should promote, or at least not harm, efficiency or gender equality, then it is obviously important to know whether the law does this. But addressing this question is a different project from that of interpreting the law.

1.7. LAW IN THE BOOKS AND LAW IN PRACTICE

Closely related to the issue of transparency is a distinction that is often drawn by legal scholars between 'law in the books' and 'law in practice'. The law in the books refers to legal rules as they are presented in law reports, argued in the courts, and summarised in orthodox textbooks; the law in practice refers to how the law works 'in reality'. What I will call the 'gap thesis' claims that there is a significant difference or gap between the law in the books and law in practice. I have already considered some examples of this thesis, but it merits a separate discussion.

At least three versions of the gap thesis exist: explanation scepticism; rule scepticism; effect scepticism. Each version is examined below, but the primary focus will be on rule and effect scepticism.

Explanation scepticism

Explanation scepticism is the view that the judicial explanation of legal rules is not the true or real explanation. For example, Fuller and Purdue's argument that the standard 'expectation' measure of contract damages can be understood as protecting the promisee's interest in not being made worse off as a result of relying on a promise, rather than the promisee's interest in the performance of the promise, is an explanation sceptical interpretation. I mention explanation scepticism here for completeness, but as it has already been discussed (under the heading of the transparency criterion), I will say nothing more about it.

Rule scepticism

A second version of the gap thesis, which also finds its roots in the work of the American realists and their latter-day followers, claims not just that there is a difference between the legal and the true explanation of judicial rules, but also that there is a difference between the judicial expression of legal rules and how (and whether) those rules are *applied*. In other words, there is a difference between what judges *say* they are doing and what they are *actually* doing.

In its extreme form, rule scepticism holds that legal decisions are determined by the psychological make-up and emotive inclinations of judges rather than by any rule-based reasoning process, legal or otherwise.[44] A caricature of this extreme view holds that what a judge had for breakfast is more important in determining how they will decide a case than the legal rules. In its more moderate and plausible form, rule scepticism accepts that there are rational explanations for judicial decision-making, but it argues that those explanations are different from the official rule-based explanations. An example of rule scepticism is the claim that although common law courts say that a valid contract requires an exchange of consideration, in practice courts invent or make up consideration whenever (for other good reasons) they want to enforce a contract that is lacking consideration.[45]

A good theory of law obviously must take account not just of what judges say they are doing, but also of what they are actually doing. A theory of law that ignores how the law is applied in practice is ignoring that law is meant to operate in the real world. But the extent to which such gaps exist is, of course, an empirical rather than a theoretical question. Moreover, it is a difficult empirical question because it typically cannot be answered in respect of any particular rule without a detailed analysis—usually going beyond the official reports—of numerous decisions from all levels of courts. Analyses of this sort are outside the scope of this book, but I try to take account of them where they have been done. Overall, this book does not adopt a general position on rule scepticism: in respect of certain rules I think it is warranted, in respect of

---

[44] e.g. Frank (1930) 100–20.   [45] Atiyah (1986) 179–243.

others it is not. But it is fair to say that a position of strong rule scepticism is rarely adopted.

As with explanation scepticism (to which it is closely related), a rule-sceptical account of law that satisfies the transparency criterion must explain *why* there is a difference between what judges say they are doing and what they are really doing. It follows, again, that accounts that are strongly rule sceptical, in the sense of replacing legal rules with non-legal considerations, typically score poorly against even moderate versions of the transparency criterion. Insofar as an explanation supposes that the 'true' rule is of a completely different *kind* from the purported rule, it usually renders the legal or internal perspective on law unintelligible—and to this extent is a less successful interpretation.

Effect scepticism

A third version of the gap thesis, made famous in contemporary scholarship by the 'Wisconsin school' of law and sociology,[46] focuses on how legal rules affect citizens. The theme of effect scepticism is that assumptions allegedly made by law-makers—and by legal theorists for that matter—about the effectiveness of legal rules are not borne out by the facts. In particular, such scholarship typically claims that contracting parties pay little attention to strictly legal considerations when they form and perform contracts, and, similarly, that legal remedies are of little practical relevance when contracts are broken.[47] The behaviour of contracting parties is said to be influenced not by legal rules, but rather by things like bonds of trust, social norms, concern for reputation, and crucially, bargaining power (for example whether one party is a monopolist).[48]

To the extent that it is true, the effect scepticism version of the gap thesis is significant for interpretive inquiries, though in a more limited way than is sometimes assumed. No plausible theory of contract supposes that citizens are always guided by legal considerations when they create and perform contracts. That a lawsuit, in practice, is a last resort, and that other non-legal factors are crucial in determining parties' behaviour, is, in broad terms, compatible with all the leading theories of contract. For example, the idea that promises are morally binding and thus should be enforced by the courts is consistent with a promisee waiving that right or

---

[46] e.g. Macauley (1963); Macneil (1980). For an overview of this scholarship, see Gordon (1985).

[47] e.g. Macauley (1963).   [48] e.g. Macauley (1963); Hurst (1964) 285–423.

deciding that the costs of litigation are not worth the price of a law suit. The legal theories discussed in this book are theories not about how citizens act, but about the law that applies in those (rare) cases in which disputes are brought before courts.

But while the practical irrelevancy of law, if true, is not a general objection to interpretive legal theory, it may count against certain kinds of interpretive theories. More specifically, the conclusion that law has little practical relevance may be a clue that it is not performing the tasks that certain theories suppose it is performing. Efficiency theories, for example, view contract law as a system of incentives and disincentives for promoting efficient behaviour; remedial orders are regarded as threats or inducements aimed at *future* contracting parties. If remedial orders have little influence on contracting parties' behaviour, such an account is less convincing (though it still might qualify as the best explanation: see 4.2.2). In general, studies of how people respond to legal rules are important when assessing theories that explain law on the basis of the incentives it provides.[49]

As with rule-scepticism, effect-scepticism raises difficult empirical issues. To establish that the factual assumptions on which the law appears to be based are faulty, legal theorists must become social scientists, getting their hands dirty in the real world in which contracts are made. Legal theorists have shown even less enthusiasm for this task than they have shown for pursuing the kinds of inquiries necessary to support a rule-sceptical or explanation-sceptical account. Again, although this book can do little to fill this void, I try to take account of such work where it has been done. In general, my conclusion is that such work is more significant for scholars interested in law reform (prescriptive legal theory) or in contracting behaviour than it is for scholars doing interpretive legal theory. Many interpretive theories make no assumptions about the effects of legal rules on contracting behaviour. Those that do, like efficiency theories, make assumptions that are, by and large, reasonable (at least in the context of specifically contractual behaviour: 4.1.7).

---

[49] But it should be kept in mind that a theory of law may be valid even if the factual assumptions on which it is based are false. It is perfectly understandable—intelligible—that law-makers might make factual mistakes. Thus, an efficiency theory might be the best account of contract law even if the law fails to promote efficiency, say because citizens are not rational. The conclusion that contract law would be consistent with the goal of promoting efficient behaviour *if* people were rational tells us something important about contract law. Lacking a better alternative account, a reasonable conclusion is that contract law is best explained as an imperfect attempt to promote efficient behaviour.

1.8. CONCLUSION

The most general lesson to be taken from this chapter is that disagreements between contract theories are often disagreements, typically unarticulated, about the appropriate criteria for evaluating contract theories. The main purpose of this chapter has been to identify possible criteria, to explain the different ways in which they have been understood, and finally, to argue in favour of certain conceptions of those criteria.

More substantively, I explained that this book is concerned with interpretive theories of contract law. An interpretive theory is a theory that helps us to better understand the law by illuminating the significance of, and connections between, its different parts. As such, interpretive theories are linked to, but different than, historical, prescriptive, and descriptive theories. Interpretive theories are assessed according to: (1) how well they fit the rules and decisions that make up contract law, (2) how coherent they are, and (3) how well they explain the way that legal actors themselves explain what they are doing. The third criterion can be subdivided into two parts: (1) how well does the theory explain law's claims to authority (the claim that law is a legitimate or morally justified authority), and (2) how well does the theory explain law's claim to transparency (the claim that legal reasoning is meaningful)?

A further distinction was drawn between weak, moderate, and strong versions of what is required to explain the above claims to authority and transparency. The weak versions hold that any explanation is sufficient, even if it shows legal actors to be insincere in their claims. The strong versions hold that a good explanation of the law will show that the law's claims to authority and transparency are actually true, that is, that the law is actually morally justified and that the reasons alleged to motivate decision-making actually do motivate decision-making. Finally, the moderate—and, I argued, most persuasive—versions state that a good explanation must show that the law's claim to authority and claim to transparency might be thought to be true (even if they are not in fact true). This can be done either by advancing a functionalist explanation or, more plausibly, by advancing an interpretation that shows legal actors to have been mistaken. To fit within the latter approach, an interpretation of the law must propose a normative justification for the law that is recognizably 'moral' (in order to make sense of law's claim to authority) and must explain the law in terms that are recognizably 'legal' (in order to make sense of law's claim to transparency).

A final observation is that the preceding account of the different criteria for assessing contract theories may give the impression that the theorist's task is impossible. Contemporary contract law is the product of innumerable individuals acting over hundreds of years. How could such a creation possibly possess an intelligible order of the kind required to satisfy the above criteria? This objection would indeed be fatal if one were to reject contract theories unless they satisfied perfectly the criteria of fit, coherence, morality, and transparency. But these criteria are not thresholds. Instead, they are standards against which a theory may be assessed as better or worse than the alternatives.

PART II

General Theories of Contract

Part II focuses on general theories of contract. 'General theories' are theories that aim to explain the basic concept of contractual obligation and, by implication, most of the main features of contract law. Chapter 2 provides a broad map, or schema, for classifying such theories. Chapters 3 and 4 then examine different general theories from the perspective of, respectively, an analytic question about the nature of contract law and a normative question about the justification for contract law. Detailed discussion of particular contract law topics, such as offer and acceptance, consideration, mistake, and so on, is left for Part III.

2

Introduction to General Theories: Classification and Overview

This chapter and the two that follow are devoted to examining general theories of contract law. General theories, in the sense intended here, are theories that purport to explain the basic concept of contractual obligation and, by implication, most of the main features of contract law. They are theories of 'contract law' in its entirety. The idea that contractual obligations are rights-based promissory obligations is a general theory, as is the idea that contractual obligations are efficiency-based induced-reliance obligations. By contrast, the idea that the rules on frustration are best understood as a subset of the rules governing the interpretation of contracts is not a general theory; it is a theory about a specific feature of contract law.

General theories of contract law and theories about specific features of contract law are, of course, linked. General theories are tested, in part, by assessing how well they explain the various doctrines that make up contract law. In similar fashion, theories of particular doctrines are informed by, and assessed in the light of, general theories. A complete picture of the world of contract theory requires that both the general and the particular be examined. Nevertheless, the distinction between general theories and theories about particular doctrines is a useful one. There is a danger, when considering general theories, of getting bogged down in details—of failing to see the proverbial forest for the trees. To understand clearly the basic idea of contractual obligation, it is sometimes necessary to step back from individual rules and doctrines, and to consider contract law as a whole. In addition, many of the most important objections to certain general theories are general objections in the sense that they focus on general moral or methodological features of the theory in question. For example, the claim that efficiency theories rest on implausible behavioural assumptions (4.1.7) and the claim that promissory theories are inconsistent with the harm principle (3.1.4) are general objections in this sense. Neither is tied to alleged

defects concerning how the theory explains a certain doctrine or set of doctrines.

In a similar way, if one examines individual contract law doctrines exclusively from the perspective of general theories there is a danger of never getting beyond foundational questions. Referring again to the forest metaphor: it is often unnecessary, and sometimes unhelpful, to have the entire forest before one's mind when trying to say something interesting about a particular tree. This is certainly true of contract law doctrines; many explanations of specific contract law doctrines are independent of this or that general theory of contract. Some turn out to be inconsistent with all general theories, for others the opposite is the case. For example, the suggestion noted a moment ago—that the rules on frustration are really an aspect of contract interpretation—could, in principle, be adopted by all of the general theories of contract examined in this book.

General theories then, can usefully be examined separately from the detailed analysis of individual contract law rules and doctrines that takes place in Part III of this book. Prior to beginning this examination, however, it will be helpful to have a general idea of the terrain before us. To avoid both repetition and inappropriate comparisons we need to know, in broad terms, which general theories are alike and which are different. In other words, we need a map of contract theories. The primary purpose of this chapter is to provide such a map. Like all maps, the one developed here will highlight certain features of the terrain, while flattening or ignoring others; a map that reproduces everything is of little use. The complexities and qualifications disregarded in this simple map will be made to appear in later chapters.

2.1. TWO QUESTIONS FOR CONTRACT THEORY

It would be convenient if contract theories could be classified on the basis of a single criterion. Something like: does the theory regard contracts as self-imposed obligations or as obligations that are imposed by law? It would then be possible to neatly line up all theories according to how they answered this question. Unfortunately, contract theories are more complex than that. The main lesson of this chapter—and one of the main lessons of this book—is that contract theories, at least insofar as they are complete theories, address two quite different sorts of questions, and so must be categorized according to two criteria. Failing to distinguish between these questions is probably the most common source of confusion in contemporary discussions of contract theory.

The first question that a complete theory of contract must answer is an *analytic* question about the nature of contractual obligations. The second question is a *normative* question about the justification, if any, for contractual obligations. Each question is discussed separately below. Following this, I explore how the questions are related. Finally, there is an inquiry as to what is left out of a schema on contract theory that is organized along the lines that I propose.

2.2. THE ANALYTIC QUESTION

The analytic question is a 'what' question. It asks: what are the essential characteristics of a contractual obligation? Specifically, how is a contractual obligation like or unlike the obligations given legal force by tort law, unjust enrichment law, the law of trusts, and so on?[1] Another way of describing the analytic question is that its answer tells us what sorts of events give rise to a contractual obligation and what the content of the obligation thus created is.[2]

Most contract theories can be placed into one of three broad categories (or a mixture of these categories) according to how they answer the analytic question. According to the first category, *promissory* theories,[3] contractual obligations are promissory obligations or another closely related

---

[1] A different approach is to identify contract law with a particular sphere of human activity. Thus, Hugh Collins states that: 'The law of contract states the fundamental legal rules governing market transactions': (1997) 1. But the connection between contract law and any particular sphere of human activity seems a weak one. With respect to Collins' suggestion, for example, consider that non-contract law rules are frequently applied to market transactions (e.g., tort rules on misrepresentation), while contract law rules are frequently applied to non-market transactions (e.g., agreements between spouses).

[2] Strictly speaking, these two issues (what events give rise to contractual obligations; what is the content of a contractual obligation) are distinct, and thus there exists *two* analytic questions about contract law. The questions will be discussed together, however, because (as will become clear below) the answer to one is invariably the flip-side of the answer to the other. For example, promissory theories regard contractual obligations as triggered by promises *and* regard their content as an obligation to do what one has promised. Admittedly, good arguments can be made for why, *in practice*, a court should separate these two issues (some of which I examine when considering reliance theories in Chapter 3). But at the level of principle, the cause and content of a contractual obligation are closely linked.

[3] The plural 'theories' is important because the label 'promissory' describes only one aspect of a complete theory of contract. In addition to the analytic question, a complete theory must also answer the normative question—and (as I explain in a moment) labeling a theory as promissory does not tell us how the theory answers that question. It would therefore be more accurate (but more time-consuming) to refer to promissory theories as 'promissory answers to the analytic question'. The same observation applies to reliance and transfer theories.

kind of voluntary obligation, such as an agreement-based obligation.[4] This understanding views contractual obligations as essentially self-imposed: the obligation is created by communicating an intention to undertake that same obligation. The obligation thus created is regarded as a duty to do what was undertaken—in other words, as an obligation to perform a promise. Promissory theories provide the traditional, and probably still the orthodox, answer to the analytic question about contract law.

Reliance theories make up the second category of responses to the analytic question. As the name suggests, these theories regard contractual obligations as amounting to reliance-based obligations. More specifically, a contractual obligation is regarded as an obligation to ensure that those who rely upon us are not made worse off as a result. In contrast to the will-based understanding supplied by promissory theories, reliance theories therefore regard contractual obligations as imposed-by-law.[5] In this understanding, a contractual obligation may arise when one person induces another to rely, even if the former did not intend to undertake an obligation. It follows that reliance theories regard contract law as closely related to, if not actually a part of, tort law. In each, obligations are imposed on persons because of what they *do* (e.g., driving a car, making a reliance-inducing statement) and not because of what they have *intended*.

The third, and at present least well-known, answer to the analytic question about contract law is provided by *transfer* theories.[6] These theories suppose that the beneficiary of a contract has a right to the performance of a future act, which right has arisen and is owing because the other party handed over or gave that right (*transferred* it) to the beneficiary (similar to what happens when a contractual right is 'assigned' to another party). As such, transfer theories (unlike promissory ones) do not understand the right in question to have been created by the contract. Rather, the right arises because it has been transferred to the beneficiary in the same way that a tangible piece of property—let's say a watch—might

---

[4] e.g. Fried (1981). The label 'promissory theories' is, strictly speaking, too narrow for a category that includes theories that regard contracts as agreements. But possible alternatives—'self-imposed obligations theories' or 'voluntary obligations theories'—are linguistically awkward. The label 'will theory' might seem appropriate, but it is liable to mislead as it arguably covers both intentional acts that *create* rights (promises, agreements, vows) and intentional acts that *transfer* rights (the transfer of a contractual right).

[5] This is not to say that the legal enforcement of promissory obligations is accomplished without the intervention of 'the law'. The point of the distinction is that reliance theories regard the obligations that contract law upholds as originating not in an undertaking (however defined), but rather in a decision by the courts or the legislature that in such and such circumstances a duty ought to exist.

[6] e.g. (with certain qualifications) Barnett (1986); Benson (2001).

be transferred. Unlike a watch, though, the transferred right is intangible. Moreover, the duty that is created after the transfer is not a negative one such as, 'don't interfere with the watch'. Instead, it is a positive one that commands performance of an action. Loosely stated, the imperative might be: 'you transferred that right to performance to me, and it's mine now—so give it to me'. As such, the transferor has an obligation not to interfere with the right of the transferee to receive her performance. Therefore, just as occurs with reliance theories, the 'contractual' obligation collapses, here into the tort obligation that requires one to respect another's rights.

The promissory, reliance, and transfer theories of contract are essentially different views about how to categorize contract law. Determining what sorts of events give rise to contractual obligations and what is the content of a contractual obligation determines where contract law fits within private law. Each group of theories thus gives a different answer to the question of what makes contract law *contract* law. If contractual obligations are promissory, then contract law is an autonomous category of legal liability. On the other hand, if contractual obligations are reliance-based, then it is more likely that they are closely related to (if not actually a part of) tort law or another non-promissory basis of liability. In this view, contract law as a distinct category disappears—a conclusion argued for explicitly by certain defenders of reliance theories.[7] Finally, if it is transfers that give rise to contractual obligations, it is the legal categories of property and tort that should apply. Property rules would logically inform the transfer of the right (as occurs with the regulating of gifts, testamentary dispositions, etc.), and would oversee the formation of the contract. As for the rules of contract liability, we would look to the law of tort.

Describing the analytic question as giving rise to what are essentially classificatory issues might be thought to diminish its importance. Nothing could be further from the truth. Just as our knowledge of the natural world is explained primarily through classificatory schemes (e.g., mammals/canines/bull dogs), so too our knowledge of the law is explained through classificatory schemes. It is, of course, appropriate to argue about what labels are adopted, about what goes where, and even about the entire basis of a classificatory schema (e.g., 'legal' schemes as opposed to, say, schemes based on economic or sociological criteria).[8] But to argue against

---

[7] e.g. Gilmore (1974).
[8] My reason for adopting a 'legal' classification scheme rests on a distinction between internal and external explanations that is defended in 1.5–1.6. See also Smith (2000).

legal classification *per se* is like arguing against legal knowledge. It should also be kept in mind that classification is practically significant in law. Most obviously, if courts fail to relate like to like, and to distinguish unlike from unlike, they may fail to achieve the most elementary requirement of justice: treating like cases alike. Moreover, even scholars who purport to be solely interested in normative issues cannot avoid taking a position on analytic questions. To state, for example, that contract law is, or should be, informed by a certain normative principle assumes that we know what qualifies as contract law—which is an analytic question. Finally, classification is critical in ensuring the efficient dispensation of justice: if a judge knows that a particular case is a contract case rather than a tort case, the judge will also know, without further thought, that a large number of consequences follow more or less automatically. Without categories, judges must decide every case from first principles. The same applies to the lawyer or citizen trying to learn the law. In short, categories matter very much for both the understanding and the practice of law.

2.3. THE NORMATIVE QUESTION

In addition to answering the analytic 'what' question, a complete theory of contract must also answer a justificatory or normative 'why' question. The normative question, simply stated, is this: why give legal force to contractual obligations? Stated in broader terms, the question is: why have a law of contract? What is the justification, if there is one, for maintaining this institution? Answering the analytic question does not answer this normative question, at least not in any straightforward way. A conclusion that contractual obligations are, for instance, promissory obligations does not tell us why promises should be legally enforced, or if they should be enforced at all. Perhaps promises should be regarded as creating at most only moral obligations, akin to obligations to give to charity. As we shall see (3.1.4), many contract theorists reach exactly this conclusion.

Most contract theories can be placed into one of two broad categories according to the answers they give to the normative question: utilitarian theories or rights-based theories. *Utilitarian* theories justify contract law on the ground that it promotes utility, broadly defined. Theories that justify contract law in terms of its beneficial effects on welfare, wealth, autonomy, close relationships, or any other (alleged) aspect of human well-being are utilitarian theories in the broad sense in which the term is used here.[9] The essence of a utilitarian theory of contract law, so under-stood, lies not in a particular understanding of utility—of the 'good'—but in the theory's view that contract law is essentially a vehicle for *promoting* the good, however defined.

The best known and most developed utilitarian theories of law are 'efficiency' theories. Efficiency theories regard contract law as an instrument for promoting the overall welfare, subjectively understood, of society's members. In this view, the justification for contract law is that it makes people better off in terms of how they themselves understand the notion of 'better off'. Efficiency theories of contract are therefore closely linked to the traditional version of utilitarianism, which evaluates actions according to how much happiness, or preference-satisfaction, they produce.[10] Other utilitarian theories that I discuss more briefly regard contract law as promoting closer social relationships, a particular distribution of wealth, or conditions favourable to the achievement of individual autonomy.

The second category of answers to the normative question is found in *rights-based* theories. These theories justify contract law on the basis of individual rights. In this view, contractual obligations are grounded in respect for individual rights, and contract law gives legal force to such rights by enforcing them directly or by attaching legal consequences to their infringement. Insofar as the latter approach is taken, contract law is seen as giving force to contractual rights through a scheme of corrective justice—understood here in the broad sense of a duty to repair harms that one has caused. An order of damages, in particular, is justified on the ground that *this* defendant, having infringed *this* plaintiff's right to the performance of a contract, has a duty in justice to compensate the plaintiff. The conclusion that a damages order would increase social welfare (perhaps by establishing incentives for future contracting parties to act in welfare maximizing ways) is therefore irrelevant in this approach.

In principle, rights-based theories of contract can be further distinguished according to how they understand the rights that contract law upholds. In practice, though, nearly all rights theories regard contractual rights as classically individualist or 'negative-liberty' rights. In other words, contract rights are rights to non-interference with person, property, or liberty. As for the content of contractual rights—whether it is a

---

[9] I therefore use the term in its contemporary sense in which utility is equated with 'the good': e.g. Brandt (1979).

[10] Bentham (1789); Mill (1861).

right to performance, or compensation, or whatever—the answer provided by rights-based theories depends on which answer is given to the analytic question discussed earlier. But the most common and (I will argue) the most plausible rights-based view regards contractual rights as rights to the performance of a promise.

Rights-based theories of contract law remain the traditional and, at least among legal actors, the orthodox way of answering the normative question about contract law.[11]

2.4. THE LINK BETWEEN THE ANALYTIC AND NORMATIVE QUESTIONS

The main reason for distinguishing analytic from normative questions is that the answer to one does not determine, at least in a straightforward way, the answer to the other. Thus, two theorists might agree that contracts are promises, but then disagree as to whether the justification for enforcing promises is utilitarian or rights-based.[12] Similarly, two theorists might agree that contractual obligations are justified on rights-based grounds, but then disagree as to whether those obligations arise from promises, reliance, or transfers. In short, any combination of answers to the respective questions is possible in principle.

Of course, one could examine each of the six possible combinations individually. The disadvantage to this approach, aside from significant repetition, is that we might fail to recognize how ostensibly different theories are alike in important ways. As we shall see, all utilitarian theories, whether they regard contracts as arising from promises, reliance, or transfers, share certain strengths and weaknesses, as do all rights-based theories. Similarly, the merits and demerits of, respectively, promissory, reliance, and transfer theories are, to a large extent, the same regardless of whether the theory in question is joined to a rights-based or a utilitarian approach to the normative question.

A further advantage of separating analytic questions from normative questions will be seen when we turn, in Part III, to explanations of particular contract law doctrines. The theoretical issue raised by a particular doctrine is often exclusively, or at least primarily, either analytic or

---

[11] See, in particular, Charles Fried's *Contract as Promise* (1981). Note that Fried's view that contracts are promises is not what makes his theory rights-based: promissory obligations are often defended on utilitarian grounds.

[12] For promises, see Atiyah (1981) 1–122. For reliance theories, see Fuller and Perdue (1936).

normative. The primary issue raised by the rules on specific performance, for example, is the significance of these rules for why contracts are enforced—a normative question. With respect to the rules on estoppel, on the other hand, the primary issue is the significance of these rules for understanding the events that give rise to contractual obligations—an analytic question. Separating analytic and normative questions at this stage makes issues of this kind easier to understand.

All this said, it must be kept in mind throughout that there are obvious and important connections between analytic and normative questions. To provide a justification for contractual obligations, it is necessary to know what sort of a thing a contractual obligation is. A justification justifies something: the substance of the 'something' is the focus of the analytic question. Just as the analytic question informs the normative one, the reverse is also true—at least if one accepts the argument in the previous chapter that a good theory of contract must account for the law's claims to be morally justified (1.5). Assuming this argument is persuasive, the list of possible answers to the analytic question must be limited to the kinds of obligations that might plausibly be considered *moral* obligations—ones that a law-maker might sincerely think the state is justified in enforcing.

The link between analytic and normative questions is arguably even stronger than this. Although the best known answers to the analytic question are prima facie open to both utilitarian and rights-based justifications, in practice scholars who defend particular answers to the analytic question also hold that, in the end, there is only one good justification (the justification they defend) for the obligation they have identified. For example, Charles Fried, whose answer to the analytic question is that contracts are promises, argues that although both utilitarian and rights-based justifications for promissory obligations exist, ultimately only a rights-based justification works.[13] In principle, such an approach must be correct: the best theory of contract will answer both the analytic and normative questions and it will tie its answers together in such a way that they cannot be separated.

For these reasons, it is impossible to maintain a rigid distinction between analytic and normative questions, and no attempt to do so will be made in what follows. But the distinction is a useful one for explanatory purposes—or so I hope to show.

---

[13] Fried (1981).

2.5. THEORIES NOT ACCOUNTED FOR

Not all contract theory scholarship can be placed into the classificatory schema described above, even when 'contract theory' is understood (as it is here) as referring exclusively to 'interpretive theory' in the sense explained in the previous chapter. For one thing, while a complete theory of contract should answer both the analytic and the normative question, not everyone who writes about contract theory attempts to answer both questions. Theories developed by such scholars are partial, but they are not for that reason wrong.

A second body of contract scholarship that does not fit into the schema is scholarship that aims to provide what I shall call 'fairness explanations' of the law. Fairness explanations focus on how contracting parties' abilities to rely upon their strict legal rights are allegedly limited by the law's concern for values such as altruism, co-operation, good faith, substantive fairness, inequality of bargaining power, and unconscionability. Such scholarship is not located on the map because it does not aim to provide a *general* theory of contract, as defined above. More specifically, it does not attempt to answer the analytic or normative questions that are the core concerns of general theories. Rather than providing theories of the nature of, or justification for, contractual obligations, such scholarship attempts to explain certain limits on contractual obligations. For example, a concern for substantive fairness may be a reason *not* to enforce an agreement; but it is not a reason *to* enforce an agreement. Thus, while I examine limits on the force of contractual obligations at various points in this book (mostly in Part III, particularly Chapter 9), this is not my primary concern at this stage. For the present, the issue is why those obligations exist in the first place, and what their characteristics are.

Finally, there exist three kinds of theories that do provide answers to the analytic and/or normative questions, but whose answers do not fit into my schemas. The first are what may be called 'sceptical theories'. Sceptical theories suppose that no sensible answer, or perhaps only a negative answer, can be given to either or both of our questions.[14] On this view, what is known as 'contract law' has no real meaning or justification, and any attempt to find or impose order on 'contract law' is a hopeless task.

A second kind of theory that does not line up neatly with my categories is a mixed theory. A mixed theory contains elements from different

---

[14] While this is a theoretical possibility, it is difficult to find real-life examples. Certain scholarship falling within the critical legal studies school might qualify: e.g. Unger (1983).

categories of answers. It might, for example, contain both promissory and reliance answers to the analytic question and/or both rights-based and utilitarian responses to the normative question.[15] A theory that suggests that some contractual obligations are promissory and others are reliance-based is mixed, as is a theory that regards the justification for contract law as resting upon both individual rights and promoting efficiency.

It might be thought that mixed theories would be attractive to contract theorists, as such theories can draw on the strengths, while ignoring the weaknesses, of competing unitary theories. But for reasons explored in the previous chapter (1.4), most contract theorists view mixed theories as a distinctly second-best solution. Recall that one reason for this is that part of what it means to be theoretical is to abstract from the particular — to be general. The more elements a theory contains, the more it resembles description, as opposed to interpretation. A second reason is that the theorist's aim to make the law intelligible — to reveal a meaningful order in the law — is, by definition, less easily achieved if, as is common in mixed theories, the theory shows the law as containing inconsistent elements (1.4). The same is true, albeit to a lesser extent, if a theory shows the law to contain multiple foundations.

Clearly, neither mixed nor sceptical theories can be rejected out of hand. They are both potential candidates for the best interpretation of contract law. Nevertheless, they shall not occupy the departure point of my inquiry. Instead, I shall start by considering whether and to what extent unitary, non-sceptical, answers can be given to the analytic and normative questions. Other, more complex, possibilities will be considered when I find — as I will — that unitary theories cannot account for everything. Much of this later discussion will take place in Part III.

The third and last category of theories that do not fit into my schema is a miscellaneous category. Theories in this category provide non-sceptical unitary answers to the analytic and normative questions, but those answers do not refer to promises, induced reliance, or transfers, or to rights-based or utilitarian moral principles. Clearly, such theories are logically possible. Promises, induced reliance, and transfers do not exhaust the range of events that might give rise to legal obligations. Similarly, there exist moral principles that cannot be described as either

---

[15] Fuller and Perdue, for example, justify reliance-based obligations on both utilitarian and rights grounds: (1936). Mixed answers to the analytic question are found in many efficiency theories of contract: e.g. Goetz and Scott (1980).

utilitarian or rights-based. That said, it is difficult to think of a significant *general* theory of contract that fits into this category.[16]

Thus, again, these alternatives will not occupy the departure point for my inquiry, especially in Part II's discussion of general theories. Their primary usefulness is in helping to explain certain limits on the scope of contractual obligations. As such, they are discussed primarily in Part III.

2.6. CONCLUSION

This chapter presents a classification scheme—a map—for distinguishing between different general theories of contract. The chapter's main substantive argument is that general theories should be classified according to how they answer two questions: an analytic question about the nature of contract law and a normative question about the justification for contract law.

With respect to the analytic question, a further distinction was drawn between: promissory theories, which regard contractual obligations as promises or another kind of self-imposed obligation; reliance theories, which regard contractual obligations as obligations to ensure that those whom you induce to rely are not made worse off; and transfer theories, which regard contractual obligations as obligations to respect rights transferred between parties. A further distinction was also drawn with respect to answers to the normative question. In this case the distinction is between: utilitarian theories, which justify contract law on the basis that it promotes utility (broadly defined), and rights-based theories, which justify contract law on the ground that it gives legal force to individual rights. Significantly, it was argued that while the analytic and normative questions are related, particular examples of general theories may (and in practice do) defend different combinations of answers to these questions (e.g., rights-based promissory theories, utilitarian promissory theories, rights-based transfer theories, and so on). Finally, it was noted that while there exist sceptical theories, mixed theories, and theories based on concepts that do not fit within any of the categories just described, the focus of this book, in the first instance anyway, is upon

---

[16] One possibility might be James Gordley's idea that contract law is best explained on the basis of Aristotelian virtues of liberality and commutative justice: (1991). But while I cannot defend the claim here, it is suggested that insofar as Gordley's theory is meant to provide a positive justification for contractual obligations (rather than only a reason for *limiting* their scope), it disaggregates into a mixture of utilitarian and rights-based justifications.

theories that fit within this chapter's map. The primary focus, in other words, is upon the unitary, non-sceptical answers to the analytic and normative questions described above.

The next two chapters examine in more detail these answers.

3

The Nature of Contractual Obligations: The Analytic Question[1]

In the previous chapter, I suggested that contract theories should be categorized according to how they answer two basic questions about contract law: (1) an analytic question about the *nature* of contract law, and (2) a normative question about the *justification* for contract law. I also argued that in respect of the answer they give to the analytic question, most contract theories can be placed into one of three broad categories (or combination thereof). *Promissory* theories regard contractual obligations as obligations that have been created by the parties through promises or a related kind of self-imposed obligation, such as an agreement. *Reliance* theories regard contractual obligations as being imposed by the law in order to ensure that those whom we induce to rely upon us are not made worse off as a consequence. Finally, *transfer* theories regard contractual obligations as obligations to respect property-like rights that have been intentionally transferred (not created) between contracting parties.

In this chapter, I examine in more detail each of these answers to the analytic question. The general aim is to determine what, if anything, is distinctive about contractual obligations—how are contractual obligations different, if indeed they are different, from other kinds of legal obligations? Another way of describing this inquiry is that it seeks to establish where contract law should be located on the larger map of private law. If contractual obligations are promissory obligations, contract law is properly understood as an autonomous category of private law. On the other hand, if contractual obligations are reliance-based or arise from transfers, then contract law should be understood as part of, or at least closely related to, other categories of private law such as tort or property law.

The answers to the analytic question identified above were developed, at least in their contemporary versions, largely in response to perceived

[1] This chapter draws on Smith (2000b; 2001).

defects in the alternatives. I begin, therefore, by exploring the traditional view that contracts are promises. A significant part of this exploration will focus upon the most important objection to that view, which I call the 'moral' or 'harm principle' objection. Next, I examine, but ultimately reject the reliance and transfer theories that were developed in response to this objection. In the final section, I conclude that while none of the three views examined can explain all of contract law, promissory theories offer the best account of its core features.

Three general points should be kept in mind. First, the chapter focuses on the general strengths and weaknesses of the theories described above. Detailed discussion of contract law rules and doctrines is left until Part III. Second, the answers to the analytic question discussed here are presented, at least in the first instance, as unitary explanations of the entirety of contract law, at least so far as the analytic question is concerned. Of course, few legal scholars suppose that a unitary explanation can account for the entirety of contract law. Indeed, some of the best known expositions of the theories discussed below are found in scholarship that explicitly defends mixed answers to the analytic question (for example, explaining certain rules using promissory theories and other rules using reliance theories).[2] Nevertheless, the strengths and weaknesses of the various answers to the analytic question are most easily understood if those answers are presented first as unitary explanations.

Third, and finally, it is important to keep in mind that while I will refer to the promissory, reliance, and transfer *theories* of contract, these theories are not 'complete' theories of contract. As the previous chapter suggested, a complete theory of contract must answer both the analytic and normative questions. The label 'promissory' or 'reliance' or 'transfer' tells us how a theory answers the analytic question, but that label does not determine, at least in any simple fashion, the answer to the normative question (2.4). For example, both rights-based reliance theories and utilitarian reliance theories are possible. The use of the plural in discussing promissory, reliance, and transfer *theories* is meant to allow for this possibility. At the same time, because the analytic and normative questions are, in the end, linked—a single complete theory of contract will answer both questions—it is not possible to avoid normative issues entirely in this chapter. In particular, it is not possible to evaluate either promissory or

[2] e.g. Fuller and Perdue (1936); Atiyah (1981).

reliance theories properly without examining certain *moral* objections to such theories.[3]

3.1. PROMISSORY THEORIES

The traditional and still orthodox view of the nature of contractual obligations is that they are self-imposed *promissory* obligations. In the 19th century, theories supporting this view were called 'will theories',[4] expressing the idea that contracting parties 'willed' their obligations upon themselves. In this book, I refer to such theories by the contemporary, if somewhat narrower, label of 'promissory theories'. Aside from having a convenient set of cognates ('promise', 'promisor', 'promisee'), the term 'promissory' properly emphasizes that contracts are regarded in this view not just as the products of intentional acts (i.e., of the 'will'), but as the product of acts expressing an intention to undertake an obligation. The label promissory therefore emphasizes that contractual obligations are obligations that are *created* by the parties—that they are, in other words, 'voluntary' or 'self-imposed' obligations.[5]

Strictly speaking, a promissory theory of contract is different from a theory that regards contractual obligations as arising from agreements. Though both promises and agreements are voluntary obligations, a promise binds only one person, the promisor, while an agreement binds two persons (insofar as it is an agreement to do or not do something). Consistent with this distinction, scholars who regard contractual obligations as self-imposed often refer to contracts (which normally bind two persons) as agreements rather than as promises. In this book, I do not generally distinguish between promises and agreements. Unless otherwise indicated,[6] the term 'promissory obligations' refers also to 'agreement-based obligations'. Likewise, the term 'promissory theories' refers also to 'agreement-based theories' of contracts. The reason for this approach is in part linguistic—the English language lacks a single word for 'promises and agreements'—

---

[3] There are two main differences between the treatment of moral issues in this chapter and the next. First, for the most part the distinction between rights-based justifications and efficiency-based justifications—which is the theme of the next chapter—is not relevant in this chapter. Second, moral issues are examined in this chapter only insofar as doing so assists in answering the analytic question.

[4] On the history of the will theory, see Atiyah (1979) 405–408.

[5] As will become apparent later, this qualification is crucial in distinguishing promissory theories from transfer theories.

[6] The distinction between promises and agreements is significant primarily in understanding the intricacies of offer and acceptance: (Chapter 5).

and in part substantive in that the distinction between promises and agreements is not generally significant when evaluating general theories of contract. As I hope to show, the strengths and weaknesses of both promissory theories and agreement-based theories are broadly similar.

To assess promissory theories of contract, it is necessary first to be clear about what a promissory obligation is, and how it is created. My aim here is not to offer a moral justification of promissory obligations, but simply to explicate the ordinary understanding of how promises are made and their role in practical reasoning. That done, I then consider whether contract law fits this conception and finally, consider an important methodological (or 'moral') objection to promissory theories.

3.1.1. THE CONCEPT OF A PROMISSORY OBLIGATION

A promise is created by communicating an intention to undertake an obligation. Each element of this description speaks to a different aspect of the ordinary understanding of promising. *Communication* is necessary because while it is possible to, say, make a vow to oneself, a promise must be made to another person or persons (by a promisor to a promisee). Second, the communication must express a genuine *intention* to undertake an obligation. The intention requirement is consistent with the ordinary view that it is not possible to make a promise by mistake or inadvertently or without knowledge of the concept of promising.[7] Finally, the communicated intention must be an intention not merely to perform a particular act, but to *undertake an obligation*. An intention to give a friend a ride is not a promise to give the ride, no matter how firmly that intention is expressed. Phrases such as 'I promise' or (depending on the context) 'I agree', 'I will', or 'I shall' are the usual ways of communicating the requisite intention to undertake an obligation.

The promissory obligation that is created by expressing the requisite intention is to do the very thing that is promised. If I promise to paint your house, my promissory obligation is to do just that—to paint your house. The force or character of this obligation is best understood using Joseph Raz's notion of exclusionary or pre-emptive reasons for action.[8] A promise pre-empts or excludes other considerations for action: it provides both a reason to do what is promised *and* a reason to ignore other reasons for and against doing what is promised. Thus, a promise does not simply create an additional reason or consideration that the promisor

[7] It may be possible, however, to be mistaken about the *content* of a promise. I discuss this difficult issue later in this chapter and (in more detail) in 5.2.1 and 8.1.1.

[8] Raz (1972; 1977; 1982).

should take into account when deciding what to do. This can be contrasted with the reasoning that occurs when one decides *whether to make* a promise in the first place. In the latter instance, external considerations (such as the price of paint in the 'paint your house' example above) are equally legitimate. Once a promise is made, however, it becomes both the primary and exclusive reason for action. This is not to say, of course, that promisors always treat their promises as exclusionary reasons for action: the point is rather that this is how promises are meant to be treated.

A final observation is that promissory obligations, thus understood, are distinct from reliance-based obligations.[9] Although most promises induce reliance, it is perfectly possible to make a promise without inducing reliance or even wanting to induce reliance.[10] Likewise, promissory obligations are not dependant on whether, or to what degree, the promise induced reliance. On the conventional understanding, a promise cannot be withdrawn simply because the promisee has not yet relied upon it: the promise binds from the moment it was made. The converse also applies— it is possible (and common) to induce reliance without making a promise. Thus, it is perfectly sensible to say 'I firmly intend to do X, but I warn you I am not promising to do X'.

3.1.2. THE PROMISSORY EXPLANATION OF CONTRACT LAW

Assuming that promises are to be understood in this way, the next question is whether contract law can be explained using a promissory model. To begin, do promissory theories fit the rules and decisions that make up the law of contract (recall that the 'fit' criterion requires the theory to fit the data which it explains: 1.3)?

The 'fit' issue is often employed by promissory theories' detractors. Their complaints shall be addressed, but it is first more important to recognize that promissory theories provide a prima facie natural explanation for many areas of contract law. The popularity and persistence of such theories is largely a result of their close connection with certain central features of contract law.[11] In particular, promissory theories pro-

---

[9] For a contrary view, see McCormick (1972); Scanlon (1990).

[10] For example, I might say 'I promise to do X, but you would be better off not to rely on me doing X' if I know that I am unreliable or want you to become self-reliant.

[11] Perhaps the clearest evidence of this popularity is that lawyers, judges, and scholars in common law systems traditionally refer to contracting parties as 'promisors' and 'promisees'; even critics of promissory theories typically adopt this language. In this respect, contrast the analytically neutral terminology of 'creditor' (of the relevant obligation) and 'debtor' (of the relevant obligation) that is adopted in many civil law jurisdictions.

vide a prima facie natural explanation for four central features of contract law: (1) freedom *to* contract, (2) freedom *of* contract, (3) the remedies of specific performance and expectation damages, and (4) privity of contract.

Freedom to contract

Freedom *to* contract refers to what is arguably the most basic requirement for establishing a contractual obligation: that the person obliged *undertook* to do something. On the orthodox understanding, and stripped to their bare essentials, the rules on offer and acceptance provide that in order to create a contractual obligation one person must undertake (agree, promise, offer) to do something for another person. A mere statement of fact or of intention to act, though it sometimes gives rise to non-contractual liability (e.g., for negligent misstatement), does not give rise to a contractual obligation. Freedom to contract means that individuals are free to enter contracts or not to enter contracts.

Thus understood, freedom to contract is consistent with regarding contractual obligations as promissory obligations. Promises, unlike statements of fact or mere statements of intention, communicate an intention to undertake an obligation. The rules on offer and acceptance can therefore be understood as a means of identifying what types of communication constitute a promise.

Freedom of contract

Freedom *of* contract refers to the idea, fundamental in the orthodox understanding of contract law, that the *content* of a contractual obligation is a matter for the parties, not the law. The first rule of contractual interpretation is to look to what the parties have actually said or written. A contractual undertaking 'to pay Ann £100' is interpreted not as an undertaking to pay Ann the 'fair price' or the 'efficient price' or the 'standard price' but as an undertaking to pay Ann the specified price, namely, £100. Freedom of contract in this sense is also consistent with regarding contracts as promises. The content of a promise, on the ordinary understanding, is determined by the content of the undertaking that the promisor communicated, and as such is prima facie within the control of the promisor.

Remedies

The standard remedies for breach of contract—specific performance and payment of compensatory damages—also appear, at least at first instance, consistent with regarding contracts as promises. Specific performance is an order to do the very thing that the promisor promised to do. As for damages, the standard measure of contract damages— 'expectation' damages—seeks to place the injured party, so far as money can do it, in the position that he or she would have been in had the contract been performed. In other words, the injured party is awarded the financial value of the *promise*. Moreover, neither remedy depends, in principle anyway, on external considerations such as the promisee's reliance; the promisor is simply ordered to perform the promise or to pay its equivalent value.

Privity of contract

Finally, privity of contract (the idea that contractual obligations are binding only on the contracting parties) is also consistent with regarding contracts as promises. The privity rule is consistent with this view because promissory obligations are personal obligations. A promise is created by communicating an intention to undertake an obligation *to someone*—the promisee—and the obligation thus created is in principle owed to that person alone.[12]

3.1.3. FIT OBJECTIONS TO PROMISSORY THEORIES

The four features of contract law described in the preceding paragraphs mesh well with promissory theories, providing the latter with greater 'fit criterion' legitimacy. That said, anyone with more than a passing knowledge of contract law will recognize that promissory theories' boast of fitting the law is subject to numerous qualifications. I turn, then, to examine the main 'fit objections' to promissory theories. My exploration of these objections—six in total—summarizes arguments developed in more detail in Part III. So as to avoid distracting the reader with too many intra-textual references, footnotes directing the reader to the relevant section of the book accompany each heading.

The objective approach[13]

One objection that is often made to promissory theories is that they are inconsistent with the objective approach that the common law adopts for

---

[12] See Smith (1997b). Certain common law legal systems have departed from the traditional privity rule, including recently, the United Kingdom: see the *Contracts (Rights of Third Parties) Act* 1999. But all still accept (as do civil law regimes) that, in general, contractual obligations bind only the contracting parties.

[13] See 5.2.1 and 8.1.1.

determining the existence and content of a contractual obligation. Critics say that this objective approach shows that contract law aims to enforce not those obligations that parties *intend* to impose upon themselves, but instead those obligations that parties outwardly *appear* to intend to impose upon themselves.[14]

This is arguably the most significant fit objection to promissory theories. I supply two rejoinders to it. The first (and perhaps less convincing) of these counter-arguments attempts to reclassify the court's objective approach as either a part of tort law or a different, reliance-based part of private law. According to this view, it is only in cases in which the defendant actually (or 'subjectively') intends to make the relevant promise that the defendant can be held liable on contractual grounds, properly understood. If the defendant does not have this intention, but nonetheless gave the outward or 'objective' appearance of having such an intention, her liability is properly understood as extra-contractual. In essence, the defendant has made a misrepresentation. She is therefore liable not because she made a contract (which requires a promise and so an intention to promise), but because she gave the appearance of so doing, thereby inducing the plaintiff to rely.

This response defends the promissory model of contract law, but only at the cost of removing from that body of law a rule (the 'objective test') that has long been considered central. More significantly, this response fails to explain why courts hold defendants who (in this view) only appear to make a promise to the same obligations as defendants who have actually made a promise. If the former case were truly an instance of extra-contractual reliance-based liability, we would expect both assessments of liability and of the measure of damages to depend on the plaintiff's reliance. But courts subject both defendants who 'subjectively' intend to bind themselves and parties who (only) give the appearance of having such an intent to the same rules. In other words, courts treat parties who (in this view) only appear to have made a promise as if they have actually made a promise.

A second, and I will suggest, more convincing response to the objective approach objection draws a distinction between the kind of intention required *to make* a promise and the kind of intention that matters in *determining the content* of a promise. This response accepts, consistent with the orthodox account of promising, that subjective intentions are what count in determining whether a promise was made at all: a promise

---

[14] e.g. Gilmore (1974) 41–45; 8.1.1.

cannot be made without intending to make a promise. The response asserts, however, that the *content* of a promise is, on both the ordinary and philosophical understanding of promises, determined objectively. In interpreting a promise, as in interpreting normal communications, the aim is not to determine what the promisor intended, but what the promise actually *meant*—which is determined 'objectively'. If this view of promising is correct, as I conclude in Chapters 5 and 8, the objective approach is inconsistent with promissory theories only insofar as it applies to the intention *to make* a contract. And this inconsistency, I further conclude, is relatively minor, particularly since it appears that courts do not consistently adopt an objective approach when assessing intentions *to enter* contracts.

Simultaneous transactions[15]

A second possible fit objection to promissory theories is that they are unable to account for everyday transactions such as buying from a vending or ticket machine, making a purchase in a store, or taking a bus. In these and other 'simultaneous exchanges' it is often impossible to find anything resembling a promise or an agreement. Putting money into a machine, handing over goods, getting on a bus, etc., are all intentional acts. But in most such cases at any rate, the parties do not agree or promise or undertake to do anything. Rather, they simply do something (e.g., hand over money, get on the bus, etc). How, then, can such contracts be reconciled with a promissory theory of contract?

The short answer, I suggest, is that they cannot be reconciled with such a theory. To be sure, some transactions that appear simultaneous involve implicit promises (though often only by one of the parties). But not all such transactions can be explained away on this basis. This conclusion leaves the defenders of promissory theories with two options. The first is to abandon the exclusive focus on promises, agreements, and other kinds of voluntary obligations, and instead to explain contract law as the body of law that deals with all acts expressing an intention to change one's normative relations with others. Under this definition, contract law would govern, in addition to promises and agreements, all consensual intra vivos and inter vivos transfers of property. This is an intriguing suggestion, but it can be criticized on the basis that it improperly groups together two distinct interests—an interest in controlling property and an interest in undertaking obligations. Self-imposed obligations, as I hope

[15] See 5.2.2.

I have made clear, possess a number of distinct features. Prima facie, they should be governed by distinct rules.

The second option, which is the option I defend in Chapter 5, is that promissory theorists should accept the implication of the above conclusion, namely, that simultaneous transactions are not contracts. Simultaneous transactions do not involve promises (or any other kind of self-imposed obligation), and so are not properly governed by rules designed for promises. Instead, such transactions should be regarded as non-contractual transfers of property. They should be grouped, in other words, together with executed gifts and wills. The result of this reclassification would be to shift a numerically large number of exchange transactions out of contract law. But in conceptual terms this admission is not significant. The common law has long recognized that certain transfers (e.g., completed gifts) are not contractual transfers.

The bilaterality of contracts[16]

A third possible fit objection to promissory theories is that promises are essentially unitary acts, yet contracts are bilateral. Both an offer *and* an acceptance are required to create a contract. Moreover, in a typical contract this process creates obligations for both parties.

The main response to this is that it is an objection to promissory theories only if they are defined narrowly as theories that focus exclusively on promises in the strict sense. It is not an objection to promissory theories defined more broadly (as I do generally in this book), so as to include theories that regard contracts as other kinds of self-imposed obligations, in particular, agreements. An agreement (in the performative sense with which we are concerned here[17]) is created when *two or more persons* agree to undertake interdependent obligations.

Admittedly, some theorists have argued that the offer and acceptance model is consistent with regarding contracts as promises in the strict sense. Their argument is that in the conventional understanding, a promise is not binding until communicated and accepted.[18] But even if this

---

[16] See 5.2.3.

[17] The non-performative sense of agreement is 'agreement in judgment' (e.g. an agreement that a painting is beautiful).

[18] Charles Fried defends this position using the example of a group of population control enthusiasts who, having picked his name at random out of the telephone book, send him postcards in which each promises not to produce more than two children. As Fried observes, there is 'something strange in the proposal that all of these people are now under an obligation *to me* to limit the size of their families': (1981) 41.

point is accepted, it is not clear how a (narrow) promissory model can explain the fact that most contracts create, at the same moment, *obligations* on both contracting parties. Even assuming that it takes two persons to *make* a promise, the resulting promissory obligation is incurred by just one of the persons. The suggestion that contracts are pairs of conditional promises is no answer to this objection. The two promises cannot each be conditional on the other: neither promisor would have an obligation to commence performance.[19]

Insofar as the bilaterality of contracts poses a puzzle for promissory theories (understood here in the broad sense), the puzzle is to explain why the law enforces agreements, but not (with certain exceptions — see 5.2.4) mere promises. Except for the requirement of mutual obligation, agreements and promises have the same structure and are created in the same way. Each is a self-imposed obligation that is created by communicating an intention to undertake an obligation. Each gives rise to obligations to do the thing promised or agreed to. The reasons for enforcing each are therefore likely to be broadly similar.

There is no easy answer to this question. The best explanation would appear to be that the bilaterality of contracts is more a consequence of the consideration rule than of any deep distinction between promises and agreements. Except for the special case of offers to enter unilateral contracts (5.2.4), a 'promise' that is given in exchange for consideration necessarily becomes (part of) an agreement. If I promise to give you £100 in exchange for your promise to give me your bicycle, the end result, if you 'accept', is not two promises but a mutual agreement. Of course, it may then be asked why the consideration rule exists — but this is a different issue (that I discuss below).

I conclude, then, that the bilaterality objection is not so much a reason for rejecting promissory theories (in the broad sense), as a reason for rejecting an exclusive focus, in such theories, on promises (in the narrow sense). The discussion above also suggests (though I have not yet fully defended the point) that while contracts may be better described as agreements than as promises, this distinction is not fundamental when explaining the law. What matters is not whether contracts are agreements or promises, but whether they are self-imposed obligations. The bilaterality objection does not speak to this issue, and therefore is not fatal to promissory theories.

---

[19] On the concept of agreement and its relationship (in contractual settings) with promises, see Penner (1996) 333–34.

Consideration[20]

The connection just mentioned between the bilaterality of contracts and the consideration rule leads to a fourth possible fit objection to promissory theories, which is that promissory theories cannot account for this rule. Nothing in the concept of promise suggests that a promise is any less a promise if it is not given in exchange for the promisee doing or promising to do something (as required by the consideration rule). That the consideration rule appears to be consistent with regarding contracts as agreements is no answer to this objection, because, as I just noted, there is nothing in the difference between agreements and promises that explains why only the former should be enforced.

The only plausible response to this objection, I suggest, is to accept that the consideration rule cannot be explained as flowing from the idea that contracts are self-imposed obligations. This leads us to ask how damaging this admission is for a promissory theory. If the consideration rule can be explained in a way that shows it as flowing neatly from a reliance theory, a transfer theory, or any other theory of the nature of contractual obligation, then it clearly poses a significant problem for promissory theories. But as I explain in Chapter 6, none of the plausible explanations of the consideration doctrine satisfy this test. Briefly, the consideration rule appears best explained on one of three grounds: (1) it is a form requirement (like the requirement of a seal), (2) it is a mechanism for keeping the law out of non-market transactions, or (3) it is an historical anachronism. The second and third of these explanations are inconsistent with all three leading answers to the analytic question. By contrast, the first explanation (which is the explanation I ultimately defend)—that the consideration rule is a form requirement—could be adopted by any of these answers. Formalities are justified, in broad terms, on the basis that they facilitate the expression and proof of contracting parties' intentions (6.1). As such, while they are not *required* by reliance, transfer, or promissory theories, they are not inconsistent with the substantive sources of liability that are the focus of these theories.

Mistake, frustration, and discharge for breach[21]

A fifth possible fit objection to promissory theories is that they are unable to account for the rules providing that contracts may be set aside on the

---

[20] See discussion in 6.3.   [21] See 8.3, 9.3, and 9.4.

grounds of mistake, frustration, or breach. The idea underlying this objection is that, by allowing contracts to be set aside on these grounds, courts are ignoring the parties' promises. If promissory theories are correct, the objection goes, contracts should be set aside only on conditions provided for by the parties' promises.

This objection correctly assumes that, from a promissory perspective, the only prima facie acceptable explanation for setting aside a valid contract is that the parties' agreement explicitly or implicitly stipulated such a result. A promise that was made on the basis of a mistaken assumption about past facts or about what would happen in the future is still a promise. But the question—a difficult one—is whether cases in which mistake, frustration, or breach is successfully pleaded are actually inconsistent with enforcing promises. Clearly, the contracts in such cases do not explicitly provide for the results reached by the courts. It also seems clear that in most such cases the parties were not thinking, when they entered their contract, about what should happen if it turned out that they were mistaken or if circumstances changed in the future. On a narrow or traditional approach to contract interpretation, this means that the parties did not stipulate the result reached by the court—and thus that the court is not merely applying their agreement. But if a broader and (I shall argue in Chapter 8) more plausible approach to interpretation is adopted, then many—some might say all—decisions in which contracts are set aside for mistake, frustration, and discharge can be explained as flowing from the parties' intentions. Properly understood, the definition of interpretation is more expansive than that which the objection uses to derive its argument. In this understanding, when we make promises and agreements (and other communications), we intend many things that we have not said nor even thought about: communication is grounded on a web of unspoken and usually unconsidered assumptions about how things should function in the world. It follows that it is often perfectly appropriate for a court to conclude that contracting parties intend that their agreement should not bind if certain factual assumptions are false, if circumstances change, or if a breach was committed—and this is true even if they never mention or even think about those assumptions during negotiations.

On the other hand, to the extent that successful pleas of mistake, frustration, and discharge for breach cannot be explained as a matter of interpretation (my view is that a limited number of cases cannot be so explained), they admittedly cannot be explained by a promissory theory. But when this happens, they also cannot be explained by any of the other leading answers to the analytic question. Concepts such as 'fundamental error' or 'radical change of circumstances', which are invoked in non-promissory explanations of these rules, do not flow from ideas of protecting reliance or respecting rights transfers. Like consideration, these notions are reasons for limiting the scope of obligations that are first explained on other grounds. Thus, to the extent that mistake, frustration, and breach pose a difficulty for promissory theories, they pose a difficulty for all the leading answers to the analytic question.

Implied-in-law contractual terms[22]

A sixth and final possible fit objection to promissory theories is that they cannot account for the many terms that are implied into contracts not as a consequence of interpreting the parties' intentions ('implied-in-fact' terms), but as a matter of law ('implied-in-law' terms). For example, the *Sale of Goods Act* stipulates into contracts of sale a variety of terms, such as that goods be of satisfactory quality. As such, this objection amounts to a similar but more robust variation of the objection regarding mistake, etc. that was raised in the previous section.

In considering this objection, it is important first to note that not all implied-in-law terms pose the same challenge to promissory theories. In particular, the many non-mandatory terms that aim merely to replicate terms that would normally be implied as a matter of fact into the agreements are, at most, only mildly inconsistent with promissory theories of contract. Insofar as parties do not state otherwise, it is reasonable to conclude that they tacitly agree to this kind of implied-in-law term. The primary challenge is raised by mandatory implied terms, and in particular by mandatory terms that are intended explicitly to protect one of the parties (or third parties). Common examples include terms implied by statutes into employment contracts or certain categories of consumer contracts.

Terms of this kind are only rarely explicable on the basis that they merely confirm or replicate the terms that the parties would, in any event, have agreed upon. Moreover, even if certain mandatory terms can be explained on this basis, they are still inconsistent with promissory theories because they cannot be waived by the parties. Mandatory implied terms expressly override and contradict what the parties have promised insofar as this is inconsistent with such terms. Finally, it should be noted that mandatory terms pose a difficulty for promissory

[22] See 8.4–8.5.

theories even in cases in which the parties are aware of the terms and do not wish to override them. Such theories cannot explain *why* the terms exist: implied-in-law terms are not required by promissory theories. In this respect, the existence of mandatory implied-in-law terms shows, at a minimum, that promissory theories are incomplete. Other concepts, for example, fairness must be introduced to explain theiro existence.

For these reasons, I conclude in Chapter 8 that the existence of certain implied-in-law terms either cannot be explained satisfactorily by promissory theories or are flatly inconsistent with promissory theories. This is an important concession, but it is not, I think, fatal to promissory theories. The most significant implied terms are well known by contracting parties and tacitly agreed to. Furthermore, a similar concession must again be made by the other leading answers to the analytic question about contract law. Although implied-in-law terms are consistent with the general idea (found in reliance theories) that contractual obligations are imposed by law, in practice such terms rarely protect reliance. As for transfer theories, their concept of an intentional transfer is similar to a promise in respect of implied-in-law terms. Thus, as was true of mistake, frustration, and discharge for breach, insofar as implied terms suggest a limit on the scope of promissory theories, they also suggest a limit on the scope of other leading answers to the analytic question.

Conclusion

My brief survey of various fit objections to promissory theories suggests that, while promissory theories cannot explain the entirety of contract law, none of the fit objections are fatal to a promissory theory. Certain objections can be avoided by adopting an 'agreement' version of a promissory theory, others by using a more sophisticated notion of promising (or of agreement), and still others by accepting that not all that we think of as contract law is properly regarded as contract law. The remaining objections do not argue for a different general answer to the analytic question about the nature of contract law. Rather, they suggest that *any* unitary answer to the analytic question—promissory or non-promissory—cannot account for the entirety of contract law.

Seen in this light, it is not surprising that, while promissory theories are often criticized in the ways just described, the most important objection to promissory theories is not a fit objection. It is to this objection that I now turn.

3.1.4. MORAL OBJECTIONS TO PROMISSORY THEORIES

The most important objection to promissory theories of contract is an essentially moral objection. In discussing this objection, I touch upon normative questions of the kind that are the main focus of the next chapter. The objection is nonetheless appropriately examined here because it is directed at a particular answer to the analytic question, and because it can be made from the perspective of either of the normative theories that are examined and contrasted in the next chapter (rights-based, utilitarian).

Stripped to its essentials, the moral objection is that it is illegitimate for the state to enforce promises *qua* promises, and thus the state must be doing something other than enforcing promises when it enforces contracts.[23] It is for this reason, say the objectors, that promissory theories supply an inappropriate answer to the analytic question.

The reason it is said to be illegitimate for the state to enforce promises *qua* promises is that doing so is inconsistent with the 'harm principle'. This foundational principle of modern liberalism (defended, though not always under this name, in both utilitarian[24] and right-based moralities)[25] holds that it is illegitimate for the state to interfere with an individual's liberty unless that individual has harmed, or is about to harm, another individual.[26] Enforcing promises *qua* promises is said to be inconsistent with this principle because a promissory obligation is fundamentally an obligation to benefit another rather than an obligation not to harm another. The obligation to do what you have promised to do arises (as we have seen) regardless of whether the promisee has relied—and thus arises regardless of whether non-performance will leave the promisee in a worse position than he was in before the promise. Lon Fuller and William Perdue made this point by observing, famously, that awarding a disappointed promisee the value of the promised performance ('expectation damages') is a 'queer kind of compensation', in that it compensates promisees for something they never had.[27] According to the 'harm principle objection', enforcing promises, is like enforcing a duty to give to charity, albeit the duty is owed to a specific person. Keeping a promise,

---

[23] The objection has been articulated in slightly different forms by e.g. Fuller and Perdue (1936), Atiyah (1979), Raz (1982), Benson (1996).
[24] Mill (1859).   [25] Kant (1797) 196.
[26] The harm principle was first articulated in its modern form in Mill (1859).
[27] (1936) 53.

like giving to charity, is praiseworthy—but a failure to do so should not in itself, be of concern to the law.[28]

An example may help illustrate the harm principle objection. Suppose I telephone a landlord who is advertising a holiday cottage for rent, and we agree that I will rent the cottage next month. Ten minutes after making the agreement, and before the landlord has relied on my call (e.g., by turning away other bookings or beginning to prepare for the rental), I call the landlord again, informing him that I have changed my mind. Should I be legally bound to my initial promise? According to the harm principle objection, I should not be bound. The landlord has not been harmed by my change of mind; he is in the same position he was in before the phone call (aside from having wasted a few moments talking to me). To be sure, the landlord may be disappointed that I have retracted my promise. But disappointment is not harm. I may be disappointed if I fail to win a lottery I have entered, but no one would suppose that I have been harmed by losing.

For those who accept the harm principle and the above characterization of promissory obligations, it follows that the state should not be involved in enforcing promises *qua* promises. The state should become involved with promise-breaking only when promise-breaking coincides with the breach of a non-promissory obligation not to harm another, and then only because of the breach of the non-promissory obligation.

At this point, it might be asked if objections to promissory theories based upon the harm principle are even relevant. Why, after all, should it be damaging to an *explanation* of the law (an answer to the analytic question) that the law is portrayed as doing something morally illegitimate? Why should we prefer, for categorical purposes, that the law is acting in a morally justified way? This difficult methodological question was addressed in Chapter 1. I will not repeat that discussion here other than to reiterate that from certain respectable perspectives it matters very much whether an explanation of the law is consistent with moral principles (1.5). Moreover, the moral objection can be expressed as a matter of consistency with other parts of the law.[29] Admittedly, the law enforces

---

[28] Thus, Raz writes: 'It follows from the harm principle that enforcing voluntary obligations is not itself a proper goal for contract law. To enforce voluntary obligations is to enforce morality through the legal imposition of duties on individuals. In this respect it does not differ from the legal proscription of pornography': (1982) 937.

[29] Consistency matters because, as I explained in 1.4, understanding a social phenomenon like the law is a matter of finding an intelligible order in that phenomenon. Insofar as a theory supposes that similar parts of the law adopt inconsistent principles, this goal is less fully achieved.

certain clear obligations to benefit others; for example, the obligation to pay taxes. But private law obligations to benefit others are rare, and the uncontroversial instances that exist (for example, duties of disclosure in insurance contracts) are recognized as exceptions to the rule.

Fried's defence of promissory obligations

The appeal of promissory theories thus turns, to a significant extent, on whether the moral objection can be rebutted—on whether it can be shown, that is, that breaking a promise actually does harm the promisee. If this can be shown, then it is more plausible to conclude that the law upholds promissory obligations. The best known contemporary defence of such a position is found in Charles Fried's *Contract as Promise*.[30] Fried summarizes his argument as follows:

> There exists a convention that defines the practice of promising and its entailments. This convention provides a way that a person may create expectations in others. By virtue of the basic Kantian principles of trust and respect, it is wrong to invoke that convention in order to make a promise, then to break it.[31]

Fried's defence is unpersuasive. In essence, his argument is that promises become legal obligations because the institution of promising is governed by a societal convention. Promises create obligations to perform, in this view, because they are conventionally understood to create such obligations. For Fried, the act of invoking, but then disregarding, this convention amounts to a wrong—where 'wrong' means the breach of a duty that the law may legitimately enforce. The underlying flaw in Fried's argument is the idea that societal conventions should be legally enforced. A convention may very well reflect the beliefs and expectations of a societal majority (and in this way be relevant in applying otherwise grounded legal duties), but that is hardly adequate justification to give a legal sanction to that convention. Consider the convention that requires dinner guests to bring a gift for the host. If a guest decides to disregard the convention, the host may very well be insulted or disappointed, but no one would presume them to have legal standing to enforce the convention. That an action is understood as wrong *by convention* is just another way of saying that most people think it is wrong. To respect the harm principle, the state must still ask whether the action is *in fact* harmful. As such, moral outrage and indignation (such as that felt by our dinner host in the face of a breached convention) do not qualify as legally enforceable duties

---

[30] (1981) Chapter 2.   [31] Fried (1981) 17.

because they are not harm for the purposes of the harm principle. Instead, what matters for the purpose of law is whether individuals' rights have actually been infringed.

The failure of Fried's argument helps to explain why the harm principle objection is emphasized by critics of promissory theories of contract. Nevertheless, Fried's book, *Contract as Promise*, remains the most sophisticated and complete defence of a promissory theory to date. This leaves us with two possibilities: either a defence of promissory theories that can rebut the harm principle must be found, or an alternative answer to the analytic question must be given. My own view, which I defend in the following subsection, is that the harm principle objection can be rebutted. After presenting that defence, I will examine the alternative answers to the analytic question provided by reliance and transfers theories.

Rebutting the moral objection: The link between contract and property

To avoid the harm principle objection, a promissory theory must explain why a promisee can fairly be regarded as *owning* a right to the promisor's performance of the promised act. If the promisee owns this right, then non-performance resembles other ordinary harms to the promisee's property rights. But furthermore, in order to qualify as a promissory theory of contract, the theory must explain why that right is a right *created* (rather than *transferred*) by a promise. In short, the account must explain how, by making a promise, it is possible to create, at the very moment of promising, a present right to the performance of a future act.

As we have seen, the harm principle objection to promissory theories denies this possibility. According to this objection, it makes no sense to suppose that simply by uttering certain words ('I agree to deliver this pen to you tomorrow'), I can create a right (to have a pen delivered tomorrow) where none existed before. Promissory theories of contract appear to involve a sleight of hand, whereby something is created out of nothing.

An important first step in understanding the harm principle objection is to recognize that part of its force derives from the fact that contract law's closet neighbours are usually thought to be categories of *obligational* law, in particular, tort law. According to any plausible interpretation, tort law (and its obligational cousins) is concerned with the protection of already existing rights and not with the creation of new rights. The legal rights to our persons, our property, and our liberty that tort law protects do not (so far as tort law is concerned) depend on our doing certain acts to create such rights. We may, of course, waive such rights under the law of torts, but, and unlike in promissory theories' account of contract law, no positive act is required for these rights to come into existence. Viewed from the perspective of tort law, then, promissory theories do indeed seem unorthodox.

The view of contract law's place within private law is altogether different, though, if we overcome the assumption that contract law's closest neighbour is tort. If we can do so, a new picture will be created and a better understanding of contract's place in private law will emerge. This is exactly what occurs if we resituate contract law alongside the law of property.[32] The subject of property law, as presently understood, comprises a hodge-podge of rules whose strongest connection is often historical rather than conceptual. But at the conceptual level, one of property law's fundamental tasks is to determine how and when property rights are *created*.

Unlike other rights that come into the world with the presence of our bodies, property rights, historically, did not just appear—they were *created*. In other words, first ownership of things happens by individuals doing particular acts to create property rights. Traditionally, these acts were used in the service of the acquisition of unoccupied land, animals, or things on land. Today, such actions more often centre upon intangible goods (as occurs with intellectual property). In either case, though, the implication is the same: private individuals act to create legally enforceable rights *where none existed before*. And more importantly for our purposes, this phenomenon accords with a central element of promissory theories, namely, that promissory obligations are obligations that are *created by* the promise.

To draw an analogy between contract law and (part of) property law is, of course, not to rebut the harm principle objection. A substantive argument is needed to explain how and why doing the acts that constitute a promise can create new rights. But the analogy is important, first, in order to dispel the assumption that contract law, when viewed on a promissory model, is prima facie odd. Viewed from the perspective of the broader private law (and not merely from the perspective of

---

[32] The historical link between contract and property (primarily via the law of debt) is made clear in Ibbetson (1999).

obligational private law), the promissory model of contract has close relatives. The second reason the analogy is important is that it strongly suggests that contract theorists looking to develop promissory models should look to property theory for inspiration rather than tort theory. (The significance of tort theory, in this view, arises only once we turn to thinking about how contract law rights, once created, ought to be protected.)

Intrinsic justifications for promissory obligations: The 'special relationship' theory

With these observations in mind, I turn now to consider how the idea that promises are capable of creating new rights might be defended. There exists a wide range of possible explanations, but I will argue that the most promising are what may be called *intrinsic* (or 'non-instrumental') justifications. An intrinsic justification of promising regards the act of making and performing a promise as intrinsically important, as valuable in and of itself. Different intrinsic theories offer different suggestions as to why promising is valuable, but perhaps the most plausible suggestion is that promise making and promise keeping are constitutive elements of a close relationship.[33] This suggestion derives from the observation that, when a promise is made, the promisor is meant to treat the promisee differently from other people. As I explained above (using the notion of 'exclusionary' reasons for action), a promisor is meant to regard the promisee's interests as superior to (or 'excluding') all others' interests. In contrast to the normal situation, in which everyone's interests who may be affected by what we do are regarded as equal, the only interest that the promisor is meant to take into account (exceptional circumstances aside) are the promisee's interests. The significance of this is that treating the promisee's interests as special in this way can help to create or to sustain a close relationship between the promisor and promisee. Where a promise is made and kept, the parties are placed in a close relationship of trust, and that relationship is respected.

The attractiveness of the 'special relationship' account of promising is that it explains not just why promises are valuable, but also why they create exclusionary reasons of action. Indeed, in this view the exclusionary nature of promissory obligations is not a detriment to the theory, but a requirement of it. The special relationships that promises create will be created *only when* promises are regarded as creating exclusionary reasons

---

[33] Smith (2000b).

for action. Take away the exclusionary nature of promissory reasons, and the special relationship will not exist. If it were acceptable to break a promise where doing so would promote a greater overall good—say when breaking a promise allows the promisor to promote a number of valuable relationships—then no promise could foster special relationships. In every case, the promisee would know that his interests were not treated in the special way that they are treated under an exclusionary reason model of promissory obligations.

The intrinsic justification for promissory obligations just described can be contrasted with the leading alternative—an instrumental justification. According to the instrumental justification, making and performing a promise is valuable because it promotes a different and *distinct* good, such as maximizing welfare, wealth, autonomy, or trust. Thus, the best known instrumental account justifies promissory obligations on the basis that, by facilitating mutual co-operation and reliance, they enhance individuals' welfare, broadly defined.[34] The main difficulty faced by instrumental accounts of promising is how to explain why promises create exclusionary reasons for action. This feature of promising raises a difficulty because there are situations in which welfare (or trust, autonomy, etc.) seems better promoted by breaking a promise than by keeping it.[35] If Jane really does need my money more than Ann, then if I am trying to promote general welfare, it would seem I should give my money to Jane, notwithstanding my promise to give it to Ann.

The standard response to this objection points to the instrumental value of having *general* rules.[36] General rules, it is said, save time or save us from making errors when our judgment is impaired by lack of information or by emotions, and so on. Applied to promising, the argument is that the overall good is better promoted if, in practice, promises are treated as creating exclusionary reasons for action, since in most cases, keeping a promise is indeed instrumentally valuable. This response clearly cannot be rejected out of hand. But particularly in the case of promising, where the very point of the institution is to create exclusionary reasons for action, it seems forced. An instrumental theory explains as accidental or contingent that which is usually thought to be a defining element of promissory obligation. Another way of making this point is that instrumental explanations of promising are not consistent with how promising is regarded internally by those making promises (on the

---

[34] Hume (1739) Book III, Part II, sec. V; Mill (1979) Chapter 5; Sidgwick (1874) 443.
[35] See Fried (1981) 15–16.   [36] e.g. Sidgwick (1874) 428–38, Hare (1981) 1–43.

importance of this criterion, see 1.6). Participants in the practice of promising think it matters in principle that promises are kept.

For these reasons, an intrinsic justification along the lines just described appears the best way to justify promissory obligations. Even if other intrinsic justifications might be possible, the important point is that only an intrinsic justification of promising can explain, in a straightforward manner, why promises create exclusionary reasons for action. An intrinsic theory makes central that which the practice of promising itself makes central.

Thus understood, promissory obligations may legitimately be enforced by the state. A promissory obligation is not an obligation to benefit another, but rather an obligation to satisfy a duty that is created by the promise and that is owed, as a matter of right, to the promisee. The promisor is meant to treat the promisee's interest in the promised action in the same way as the promisee's interest in his property or person. In each case, the promisee's interests must be regarded as special, as excluding considerations of general welfare or personal advantage when deciding whether to respect those interests.

To be sure, part of the explanation of promissory duties is that close relationships (or whatever other intrinsic good is thought to be promoted by promising) are a good thing. If a promisor's duty was a duty to promote or protect this 'good' then it would indeed be inconsistent with the harm principle. The state would then be restricting liberty in order to promote a good rather than to prevent harm. But state enforcement of promissory rights is not done *in order* to promote a particular good. In the account of promissory obligations given above, the good of close relationships is part of the story of why such obligations exist; but the obligations themselves are specific obligations owed to particular persons. This is the distinctive feature of the intrinsic explanation of promising: the intrinsic value of promises is obtained if and only if promises create obligations that are owed to particular individuals. It is wrong, according to the intrinsic account, to break a promise, and the wrong is a wrong done to a particular individual. It follows that, while the good that promises create is *part* of the justification for state enforcement, when the state enforces promises it does so not to promote that good but to ensure that individuals do not wrongfully harm other individuals.

The explanation just described has a further advantage in that it accords with the everyday understanding of promissory duties. More specifically, promising is widely recognized as a useful institution. Furthermore, it is generally understood, in the everyday sense, that promissory obligations are owed to particular persons and not to society in general. To break a promise, is to wrong a particular person or people. And, not coincidentally, this same view is found in thinking about property rights—both in scholarly and everyday thinking. It is generally agreed that if a system of property rights were not generally valuable, in the sense of grounded in some conception of the good (welfare, self-fulfillment, autonomy, etc.), then individual property rights would not be valid.[37] But it is also recognized that property rights are rights owed to particular individuals: the prohibition against theft is one of the clearest examples of a rule that is supported by the harm principle. Thus, for property rights, as for contract rights, the good of the general institution is part of the explanation for why the state enforces the relevant rights—but the rights remain rights in the classic (individualist) sense.

Understood in this way, promises are fairly understood as creating rights to the performance of the promised act. It may still legitimately be asked whether such rights should be enforced by the legal system. But the question now is not whether these rights are of the right structure or form. Instead, it is whether they are of sufficient weight or whether they are overridden by other considerations. And there is nothing in the general story of how promises create rights to suggest that promissory rights should generally be regarded in either of these ways (though *certain* promissory rights might be so regarded).

To summarize: according to the version of the promissory theory defended above, contract law is like property law in that it is fundamentally about the creation, rather than the protection of rights. Both contract and property specify ways in which rights can be created where none existed before, and both delineate the scope of those rights. Furthermore, each justifies those rights, in part, because of the role they play in helping us to lead valuable lives. Contract law allows people to create rights to performance. This is valuable because of the intrinsic value of such obligations in creating special relationships and thus in achieving valuable lives. But in enforcing such rights, the state is enforcing duties that are owed to particular individuals rather than duties to promote the good of special relationships or any other social good.

Before completing my defence of promissory theories, I stated that the failure of Fried's defence to the harm principle objection left us with two options: either find a better defence of promissory theories or jettison such theories in favour of a different answer to the analytic question

---

[37] See Waldron (1988).

about contract law.[38] It remains to be seen whether the second option provides a viable alternative. It is to this question that I now turn.

3.2. RELIANCE THEORIES

The response of most contract theorists to the objections to promissory theories discussed above has been to develop non-promissory theories of contract. Two categories of such theories are examined in this chapter. The first, and better known, is that of reliance theories. Reliance theories have a long historical pedigree,[39] but their popularity in modern times can be traced to Fuller and Perdue's 1936 article, *The Reliance Interest in Contract Damages*,[40] and to later work by Patrick Atiyah[41] and Grant Gilmore.[42] But none of these writers attempted to develop a comprehensive reliance theory of contract,[43] so my references to a 'reliance theory' should be understood as referring to a model rather than to a theory adopted in full by one scholar or by a group of scholars. In particular, it should be remembered (for reasons I hope will become clear) that no scholar has ever argued that a reliance theory can explain the entirety of contract law.

Notwithstanding what I have just said, the basic idea underlying reliance theories is familiar to most lawyers: contractual obligations are obligations to ensure that others whom we induce to rely upon us are not made worse off as a consequence of that reliance. An example helps to illustrate how the 'reliance interest' (to adopt Fuller and Perdue's terminology) may be injured in contractual situations. Suppose that a vendor agrees to provide a lathe for a buyer's factory in exchange for £1,000 paid in advance. The buyer's payment of the £1,000 is induced by the

---

[38] One implication of my defence of the first option is that contract law is an autonomous body of law linked to the law of property. If this is correct, then some detail needs to be added to this classification, which I will do in the final section of this chapter.

[39] Atiyah (1981; 1979).   [40] (1936).   [41] (1979; 1981).   [42] (1974).

[43] Thus there is no equivalent in the reliance literature to Fried's *Contract as Promise*: (1981). Fuller and Perdue's article, *The Reliance Interest in Contract Damages*, is the best known defence of the importance of reliance in contract law, but as the title suggests the article's focus was upon explaining damages rather than expounding a general theory of contract. Moreover, it is unclear to what extent the author's believed they were advancing a general theory of contract based on reliance as opposed to merely broadening the traditional promissory theory (see Smith (2001)). In later work, Fuller gave equal, if not more, prominence to ideas traditionally associated with promissory theories: (1941). A more complete exposition of a reliance theory is found in Atiyah's scholarship, though here too no comprehensive statement exists; Atiyah developed the idea in bits and pieces over years and his ideas evolved considerably. A survey of contemporary work on reliance theories is found in Barnett (1996).

vendor's agreement to make and deliver the lathe. If the vendor then fails to deliver and also keeps the money, the buyer will be in a worse position than he was prior to paying the £1,000: the buyer will have suffered a 'reliance loss' of £1,000. Significantly, the reliance interest may be at risk even if no payments are made under a contract. Consider that our lathe-buyer is likely to have incurred other costs in preparing his factory for the expected arrival of the lathe—perhaps by retrofitting his factory to accommodate it. Of further significance, the buyer has probably also incurred 'opportunity costs' in reliance on the contract. In this context, opportunity costs would represent profits the buyer would have realized had he (successfully) bought the lathe from another vendor.[44]

It is incontrovertible that contracts typically induce reliance and that breaches of contract typically leave those who have relied worse off than before they contracted. The question is whether such reliance is the key to explaining contract law—as reliance theories assert—or whether it is merely the by-product of an obligation justified on other grounds. In addressing this question, I begin by examining two issues: the preconditions for reliance-based contractual liability, and the content of a reliance-based contractual obligation. Following this examination, I then consider whether the basic idea of reliance-based liability is morally sound, and, finally, whether it fits with the various doctrines that make up contract law.[45] Throughout the discussion, a significant part of the analysis will amount to exploring the degree to which reliance-based liability can be disentangled from promissory liability, and from liability for telling a falsehood. In theoretical terms, the task for reliance theories is to find a conceptual space lying in between the duty to keep a promise and the duty to tell the truth. If it is not possible to find this space, this 'home' for reliance, then reliance-based liability will collapse into either promissory liability or liability for misstatement. The former leads back to the

---

[44] Fuller and Perdue, as well as Atiyah, argued that in addition to the reliance interest, the 'restitution interest' was important in explaining contract law. This is an interest in reversing unjust enrichments—say my interest in recovering property that I transferred to you by mistake or on the basis of a failed agreement: Birks (1985). The restitution interest clearly may be at risk when a partially completed agreement is breached. But a 'restitutionary theory' is not plausible as a general answer to the analytic question since many claims for breach of contract are made by parties who have not performed. It is also worth noting that insofar as benefits are transferred under a broken contract, a claim for the value of those benefits could be made on the basis of the reliance interest (as defined above).

[45] Thus, references to reliance-based 'liabilities' or 'duties' should be understood as leaving open the question whether such liabilities and duties actually exist in either morality or law.

orthodox view of contracts as promises, and the latter to a view that cannot account for more than a tiny number of contract law rules.

The preconditions for reliance-based liability: The analogy to negligent misstatement

What are the pre-conditions that might give rise to a reliance-based liability? To begin, it is important to determine what condition(s) *beyond mere reliance* might give rise to such a duty. Of particular importance, in this regard, is the question of whether a *promise* is a necessary precondition of reliance-based liability. If a promise proves *not* to be a necessary element, the question then arises as to how to identify which type of reliance-inducing acts are actually relevant to contract law.

The terminology of promisors and promisees that is used throughout Fuller and Perdue's article, and in most of Atiyah's work, suggests that these authors regard the making of a promise as a necessary condition for the creation of a reliance-based duty. But such a position—when it is adopted as a matter of first principle[46]—is difficult to defend. More specifically, if the aim of contract law is to protect the reliance interest, there seems to be no good reason why reliance that is induced without a promise should be ignored. If a purchaser tells a manufacturer that it intends (but does not promise) to double its orders next year, the manufacturer may rely on that statement, for example, by refitting for larger volume production. From the perspective of protecting reliance, it should not matter, at least in principle, that this reliance was induced by a serious statement rather than a promise.

If it is then accepted, as I think it must be,[47] that in principle reliance-based duties (assuming they exist) can arise without promises, the next question is: what kinds of statements, promissory or otherwise, give rise to reliance-based duties? In addressing this question, two observations come to the fore. Firstly, a reliance theory of *contract* must focus upon statements of intention *that are not carried through*, and not upon

---

[46] The proviso is important because (as I explain later) it may be justified in practice to restrict reliance-based liability to cases in which reliance is induced by a promise.

[47] It might be thought that one reason to limit reliance-based liability in principle to cases in which reliance is induced by a promise is that the making of a promise is ordinarily understood to preclude the promisor from changing her mind. But if it is accepted that, by promising, a promisor gives up the right to change her mind, then changing one's mind after making a promise is wrong full stop, regardless of reliance. This wrong cannot be described as letting someone down who has relied, since it will already have been established that reliance matters only *if* it is wrong to change your mind. Yet if it is wrong to fail to do what one has promised to do, then the case is made for promissory liability, pure and simple.

statements that are (merely) false. False statements (represented by concepts such as fraud or misrepresentation) are only rarely germane to breach of contract situations. A breach of contract typically arises through inadvertence or a change of mind, not because of untruthfulness.

The second observation is that something more than the mere foreseeability and the reasonableness of reliance must be required in order to support a reliance-based duty. No advocate of reliance-based liability would suppose that if I say that I intend to teach contract theory next year and then do not teach it, I should be legally liable to students who reasonably and foreseeably relied on this statement. Clearly, something more is needed.

To begin to determine the content of this 'something more', a useful analogy can be drawn with the law of negligent misstatement. Ever since *Hedley Byrne & Co Ltd v Heller and Partners Ltd*[48] introduced liability for negligent misstatement into English law, English courts have been addressing the question of the scope of liability for relied-upon statements. It is true that they have done this in the context of claims based on false statements of fact, rather than claims based on statements of intention that are not carried through. But in terms of scope of liability, the underlying issues appear similar, if not identical. Reliance on a weather forecaster may be both reasonable and foreseeable, but it has never been supposed that a forecaster should be liable for negligent misstatement if a forecast is carelessly made. 'Something more' is required for a claim in negligent misstatement to succeed. In broad terms, the approach of English courts to identifying this extra factor has been to ask whether and how the relevant parties' relationship differs from that of weather forecasters and their listeners—whether, that is, the parties are joined by special ties. This approach also seems appropriate when assessing a claim for reliance-based contractual liability.[49] In each case, liability requires that the parties be in a relationship sufficiently close or 'proximate' so as to find not only that *this* plaintiff has relied on *this* defendant, but also that the defendant was responsible for that negligence.

The above paragraph suggests that advocates of a reliance-based theory of contract look should look to the law of negligent misstatement as a means of determining which preconditions would give rise to contractual liability. In negligent misstatement cases, courts have looked for the existence of a 'special relationship' or an 'assumption of responsibility'. The factors that establish a special relationship or an assumption of

---

[48] [1964] AC 465 [*Hedley Byrne v Heller*].   [49] See in particular, Spence (1999) 25–65.

responsibility are subject to debate, but the following list conveys the general idea:[50] (1) Was reliance foreseeable? (2) Was reliance by the particular plaintiff foreseeable? (3) Was reliance reasonable, in the sense that it would be rational for someone in the plaintiff's general position? (4) Was the statement made for the purpose of inducing the plaintiff to rely? (5) Did the defendant give assurances to the plaintiff that it was appropriate to rely? (6) Did the defendant disclaim responsibility in any way? (7) Did the parties have a prior relationship? (7) Was the plaintiff dependant on the defendant? One difference between this test for negligent misstatement and any such test that might exist for liability in respect of unfulfilled statements of intention is that factor (4)—was the statement made for the purpose of inducing the plaintiff to rely?—should play a greater role in establishing reliance-based contractual liability. This is because the essence of a reliance-based duty is that we should not let people down whom we have *induced to rely*.

Those familiar with the law of negligent misstatement will know that the test established by the above list is far from precise. But as has been true in respect of negligent misstatement law, efforts to fine tune the list are unlikely to lead to a significant increase in precision. The imprecision is not the result of scholarly inattention, confused thinking, or the complexity of the subject matter: it is a structural feature of this kind of test. Unlike the test for, say, establishing the existence of a promise, which presents a syllogistic series of 'yes/no' questions ('was there a communication?' 'did it express an intention to undertake an obligation?' and so on), the test for establishing a reliance-based duty presents a list of 'considerations', each of which is to be 'taken into account' in arriving at an overall conclusion. It involves 'all-things-considered' reasoning rather than syllogistic or rule-based reasoning. And the same is true of any attempt to determine a 'reliance answer' to contractual liability. Further study into the nature of reliance-based duties would almost certainly lead to an expansion and refinement of the above list of considerations; but it would remain a list of considerations in the sense just described.

The *content* of reliance-based duties: The duty to reimburse

The foregoing account of the possible preconditions for a reliance-based duty leads to obvious questions about how these preconditions might translate into legal rules and whether those rules are consistent with the

---

[50] *Hedley Byrne v Heller*; *Caparo Industries plc v Dickman* [1990] 2 AC 605.

formation rules in contract law. I will address these questions below. But I want to turn now to the second of my preliminary organizing issues, that dealing with the *content* of a reliance-based duty.

Assuming that a reliance-based duty arises in the circumstances just described, what is this duty a duty to do? Here again the main issue concerns the distinction, if any, between reliance-based liability and promissory liability. More specifically, the main issue is whether a person subject to a reliance-based duty should be regarded as being under a duty to do what she said she would do (as is the case for promissory duties) or instead only under a duty to reimburse the relying party for his reliance. Expressed in contract law terms, is a reliance-based duty a duty to perform the (allegedly) primary contractual obligations described in the contract, or is it only a duty to pay for reliance losses? In a contract of sale, is the seller's obligation to deliver the promised goods—or an obligation to reimburse the buyer's reliance costs if the goods are not delivered?

Advocates of reliance theories have written in detail about secondary contractual obligations (remedies),[51] but they have said little about how reliance theories understand primary contractual obligations. Their silence suggests that they accept the traditional contract law view that the primary contractual duty is a duty to do what you have said you would do. But this view is difficult to reconcile with the conclusion that statements of intention, and not just promises, can in principle give rise to reliance-based contractual liability. Insofar as contracts are formed by promises it makes sense to regard a contractual duty as a duty to perform the primary contractual obligation: a promise binds the speaker to do what he said he would do. But insofar as contracts are formed by statements of intention (including, but not limited to, promissory statements of intention), it seems inconsistent to regard contractual duties as duties to do what one said one would do. A statement of intention is normally understood as reserving to the speaker the right to change his mind. That is why we distinguished promises from statements of intention; only the former is understood to bind speakers to do what they said they would do. This distinction is illustrated by situations in which speakers explicitly contrast promises and statements of intention. If I say to my students 'I intend to teach contract theory next year, but I am not making a promise', my reason for distinguishing between what I intend to do and what I promise to do is to reserve to myself the right to change my mind. I am saying to my students 'you do not have a complaint against me if I change my mind'. This remains the case no matter how

[51] e.g. Fuller and Perdue (1936).

firmly the statement of intention is expressed. I still reserve the right to change my mind even if I say that 'I really, really intend to teach contract theory next year, but I do not promise'.

It might be thought that, regardless of a speaker's intentions, it is appropriate, from the perspective of a reliance-based theory, to bind a speaker to do what he said he would do if the preconditions for reliance-based liability are satisfied. Such a situation should not be problematic for a theory that regards contractual obligations as imposed-by-law and not self-imposed. But this disregard of a party's intention cannot, in practice, be absolute. No advocate of reliance-based liability would suggest, for example, that courts should ignore contracting parties' attempts to limit or exclude liability. Consistent with my account of what could be the preconditions of reliance-based liability, a statement excluding liability for reliance-based losses is effective in precluding reliance-based liability. The exclusion clause negates the existence of the necessary close relationship by showing that the relying party was not justified in holding the speaker *responsible* for the consequences of his reliance. The significance of this is that the same must be true of the message that is expressed when a speaker makes a mere statement of intention rather than a promise. Communicating a mere statement of intention rather than a promise is like communicating a special kind of exclusion of liability clause: the speaker is telling the listener that she is reserving the right to change her mind. The point of using non-promissory language when expressing an intention to act is specifically to communicate that the speaker is not bound to do what he said he would do.

For reliance-based duties to be consistent with the 'right to change one's mind', then, they cannot be understood as duties for reliance-inducing persons to do what they said they would do. That duty, if it exists, is a promissory duty. The only plausible way of understanding a reliance-based duty, therefore, is as a duty *to reimburse* the reliance costs of those who rely on you *in case* you do not do what you said you would do. The primary contractual duty is a conditional duty: *if* you do not do what you said you would do, *then* you have a duty to pay to the relying party a sum equivalent to their reliance costs.[52] Changing your mind is

---

[52] Thus understood, a reliance-based duty resembles the duty articulated in the famous American tort case of *Vincent v Lake Erie Transportation Co*, 24 N.W. 221 (Minn 1910). The defendant had tied his boat to the plaintiff's dock during a storm, thereby damaging the dock. The court held that the defendant had not committed a wrong by tying his boat, but that nonetheless he had a duty to pay the plaintiff for the damage to the dock. The defendant's duty was not a duty to keep his boat away from the dock, but rather a duty to pay for the repair of the dock *if* he used the dock and caused harm thereby.

not itself a breach of a duty, but if you do so after inducing another to rely, you then have a duty (assuming the other preconditions of liability are satisfied) to ensure that the other is not left worse off as a result. In my lathe example, the vendor's contractual duty is thus not to deliver the lathe. Instead, it is to reimburse the buyer for his reliance in terms of money paid, costs of refitting his factory, and gains foregone by not pursuing alternative opportunities to buy a lathe.[53]

To conclude: a reliance-based duty arises when a reliance-inducing statement is made in the context of a close or 'special' relationship. Properly understood, the content of the duty is not to 'perform the promised action' but rather to reimburse the other party for her reliance costs in cases in which the promised action *is not performed*. Thus interpreted, a reliance-based duty is distinct from both a promissory duty and a duty to tell the truth. I turn now to consider whether this duty is morally plausible and whether it fits with the law of contract.

3.2.1. MORAL OBJECTIONS TO RELIANCE THEORIES

Scholarly discussion of reliance theories has focused on whether reliance theories fit the law. Before looking at this issue, however, I want to ask the same *moral* question of reliance theories that their defenders ask of promissory theories: is it legitimate for the state to protect induced reliance *qua* induced reliance? Most of the literature on reliance-based liability assumes an affirmative answer. This assumption, I argue below, is questionable at best.

A useful way of approaching this difficult issue is to ask whether reliance theories are vulnerable to the same harm principle objection that was directed at promissory theories. Recall that according to the harm principle objection, it is illegitimate for the state to enforce promises *qua* promises because a promissory duty is essentially a duty to benefit another rather than a duty not to harm another. It might be thought that reliance theories are immune to this objection. A person who has relied to his detriment on another's statement of intention is worse off as a result if the intention is not carried through. In my lathe example, the buyer is

---

[53] It further follows that a reliance theory regards *damages* for breach of contract not as compensation for losses incurred by reliance costs, but as 'compensation' for the plaintiff not receiving reimbursement from the defendant. 'Compensation' is within quotation marks because it can be argued that from a reliance perspective, an order of 'damages' is actually specific performance of the second disjunct of the reliance-based obligation. The order directly enforces the defendant's (alternative) primary duty to reimburse.

left worse off, as compared to his pre-contractual situation, by the amount of the £1,000 that he paid to the vendor for the undelivered lathe. The harm that a reliance-based contractual duty seeks to avoid, therefore, seems no different than the harm that tort duties in misstatement seek to avoid. As such, it would seem that the state is prima facie justified in enforcing a law of contract that claims to protect reliance.

But the analogy to misstatement law is misleading because a reliance-based duty is not actually a duty to *avoid* or *prevent* reliance-based harms or losses. As I explained above, a reliance-based duty is a duty *to reimburse* another for reliance costs that the other person was induced to incur. Insofar as it makes sense to speak of a reliance 'loss', therefore, that loss is not what was spent in reliance, but the amount that was not *received* by way of reimbursement from the defendant. And any compensation that is paid is not compensation for the plaintiff's 'reliance', but compensation for the defendant's failure to pay to the plaintiff a sum equal to that reliance. The distinction is a fine one, but it is crucial in assessing whether the state is justified in enforcing reliance-based duties. A reliance-based duty is not fundamentally a duty to ensure that others are not made worse off; it is a duty to pay money to persons who have, through no fault of the person subject to the duty, become worse off as a result of their reliance. Viewed from this perspective, a reliance-based duty looks very much like a duty to benefit another; more specifically, it looks like a duty to benefit those who have been induced to rely to their detriment. To adopt the same analogy used when critiquing promissory theories, the reliance-based duty is akin to a charitable duty, albeit it is owed only towards those whom have been induced to rely. A theory based on the idea of enforcing such a duty is prima facie vulnerable to the harm principle objection.

One possible response to this moral objection vis a vis reliance theories is that it ignores a crucial moral difference between promissory and reliance-based duties: promissory duties are triggered merely by uttering certain ritual words ('I promise . . .') whereas reliance-based duties are triggered by inducing others to rely to their detriment. Thus, while promises *qua* promises do not materially change anything in the world—they are just words—reliance-inducing statements, by definition, lead to a material change in the world. It follows, according to this view, that if you have made a reliance-inducing statement (and assuming the other preconditions described above are satisfied) you are *responsible* for the change that ensued. And because you are responsible—even if not blameworthy—it is fair to impose upon you a duty to nullify the detrimental effects of that change.

The idea that by doing a blameless act one can become responsible for another's welfare is not unfamiliar.[54] For example, we have both a moral and a legal duty to care for children that we bring into the world. Similarly, if I knock someone over by accident, spilling their groceries onto the pavement, I have a moral duty both to apologize and to help pick up the groceries, even if I was not at fault. Examples of traditional private law duties of this sort are more difficult to find. One famous example is the duty enforced in the American tort case of *Vincent v Lake Erie Transportation Co.*[55] In *Vincent*, the court held that a ship's owner had a duty to reimburse a dock owner for damage resulting from the owner's (blameless) decision to use the dock without permission in a storm.

Again, however, the analogy is imperfect. The beneficiaries of the duties in the above examples are not responsible for the events that gave rise to the duty (being born, being knocked over, having one's property damaged). By contrast, the beneficiaries of reliance-based duties are at least partly responsible for their situation. If the beneficiaries of reliance-based duties had not *chosen* to rely, they would not have incurred reliance costs. Having chosen to rely (and keeping in mind that reliance-based duties can in principle arise without promises), they are in a different moral position from persons who bear no responsibility for their vulnerability or loss.[56] Looked at from the defendant's perspective, it appears unfair to hold the defendant liable for the consequences of changing her mind, given that she never made a promise. In Fried's words, 'why should my liberty be constrained by the harm you would suffer from the disappointment of the expectations you choose to entertain about my choices?'[57] That a reliance-based duty is a duty to reimburse rather than a duty to perform does not alter this conclusion. A duty to reimburse constrains our ability to change our mind because it makes us responsible for the consequences of so doing. In effect, we are at the mercy of another's actions.

Those who support reliance-based liability often turn to hypothetical examples to show that, while it may be difficult to explain the moral foundations of reliance-based duties, such duties are supported by ordinary and widely-shared moral intuitions. But the difficulty with this way of

---

[54] Honore (1988).   [55] 24 N.W. 221 (Minn 1910).   [56] Fried (1981) 11.
[57] Fried (1981) 10.

defending reliance-based duties is that the more compelling the example, the more plausible is the counter-argument that the relevant reliance-inducing statement is actually a promise. Consider an example suggested by Neil McCormick: a person walking along the cliff edge of a bay spots a swimmer in trouble below; the walker lowers a rope ladder, which the swimmer swims towards, thereby eliminating the only other possibility of saving himself by swimming to a beach in the next bay.[58] The walker, having induced the swimmer to detrimentally rely upon him, is now under a duty, McCormick suggests, not to pull up the rope. McCormick's conclusion that the walker has a duty not to pull up the rope seems plausible. But is this a case of a reliance-based duty or of a promissory duty? Recall that it is possible to communicate an intention to undertake an obligation—to promise—without actually saying 'I promise'. For McCormick, who believes that promises *are* reliance-based duties, the answer is that the duty is both promissory and (therefore) reliance-based. But if promissory duties and reliance-based duties are distinct, as I have argued, then one must decide which type of duty this (or any similar case) illustrates. The answer is not clear, but that McCormick thinks this is a promise illustrates how hard it is to find a distinct conceptual space for reliance-based duties. Indeed, it is difficult to think of a case in which it is clear both that the preconditions for reliance-based liability are satisfied *and* that no promise was made. In every case in which a speaker says explicitly 'but I am not making a promise', the close relationship needed for reliance-based liability seems to be precluded by the making of that statement. The necessary 'assumption of responsibility' is absent; the speaker is telling listeners that they rely at their own peril. Yet unless it is possible to find at least some instances in which a mere statement of intent, rather than a promise, is sufficient to ground a reliance-based duty, the conclusion must be that such duties are in truth promissory.

It is suggested that the lowering of the rope in McCormick's example *is* a promise. The walker has communicated, albeit implicitly, an intention to undertake an obligation, namely, not to withdraw the rope. More generally, it is suggested that *every* case that appears to support a reliance-based duty can more plausibly be explained as an instance of a promissory duty. (Not coincidentally, the same argument is often made in respect of

---

[58] McCormick (1972).

liability for negligent misstatement).[59] In other words, I conclude that there is no moral space for reliance-based liability that does not overlap that already covered by promissory liability and liability for falsehoods. But I acknowledge this issue is difficult, and that it will continue to be a matter for debate for the foreseeable future.[60]

Before leaving this topic, it should be noted that there is a connection in respect of the issues just discussed between so-called reliance-based liability and liability (or lack thereof) that is allegedly based on principles of good faith, unconscionability, estoppel, and certain other classically 'equitable' duties.[61] In respect of each of these principles, part of the reason legal scholars debate their value is that, like reliance-based liability, it is not clear that they express distinctive moral principles. It can be argued, with some justification, that standard legal concepts such as promise-keeping, not telling lies, duress, etc. can account for the cases that those defending such principles say are explained by them (see 5.4, 6.3.5, 8.3.5, 9.2). Furthermore, the moral principles underlying these ideas are, in broad terms, similar to those underlying reliance-based liability. Duties based on ideas of good faith and unconscionability, like reliance-based duties, are said to arise in situations in which one person becomes responsible for the welfare of another. They are responsible despite not having made a promise to that person to be so responsible or having committed any other wrong as wrong is usually understood — say by telling a lie. The responsibility arises, again to speak broadly, because one party is in some way dependant on the other. It therefore seems likely — though I cannot defend this claim here — that insofar as good faith, unconscionability, and reliance-based duties are defensible, such defence will rely on broadly similar notions. It also follows that those who are comfortable with expansive understandings of good faith and unconscionability are likely also to be comfortable with reliance-based liability.

---

[59] The original source is Lord Devlin in *Hedley Byrne v Heller* 465, 529. See generally, Howarth (1995) Chapter 6.

[60] At a minimum, those who support reliance-based duties need to think carefully about the moral foundations of their positions. In this respect, legal scholarship mirrors scholarship in moral theory. Moral philosophers have investigated the link between promises and reliance, but largely ignored the significance of reliance *per se*: e.g. McCormick (1972), Scanlon (1990).

[61] For example, fiduciary obligations.

3.2.2. FIT OBJECTIONS TO RELIANCE THEORIES

Reliance theories of contract therefore raise significant moral questions. But the most common objection to reliance theories is not that they are inconsistent with morality, but that they are inconsistent with a number of central features of the law. The discussion below focuses on three such features: (1) formation rules, (2) performance rules, and (3) remedial rules.

The formation objection

Perhaps the most important fit objection to reliance theories is that reliance is not part of the test for contractual liability, as that test is normally understood. The rules on offer and acceptance do not establish contractual liability on the basis of failure to take account of induced reliance. Instead, of course, these rules look to whether an offer to do something has been accepted. A promise or an agreement, not reliance, appears to be the prerequisite for contractual liability.

At first blush, the 'formation' objection to reliance theories seems decisive. On closer inspection, however, the issue is more complex. Although the offer and acceptance rules are not direct tests for reliance, they can plausibly be viewed as a proxy for a test that does just this. Nearly all agreements that meet the offer and acceptance requirements will, in practice, induce reliance. The courts could, of course, test for such reliance directly by asking the plaintiff to introduce evidence of her reliance. But such a requirement raises difficult evidentiary issues, especially since reliance in contract settings is often 'negative' reliance, in the form of the 'opportunity cost' of not pursuing alternative opportunities. It can be difficult to prove this kind of reliance. On this basis, it would not be unreasonable for the law to make a blanket assumption that agreements induce reliance.

Furthermore, statements that satisfy the offer and acceptance rules are the *kind* of reliance-inducing statements that reliance theories should care about. In my account of the preconditions for reliance-based liability, I suggested that reliance-based duties arise, broadly speaking, when the relevant parties are in a 'close' or 'special' relationship. I also noted that the test for establishing such a relationship is necessarily imprecise, involving the balancing together of many factors. Given this imprecision, it can be argued that the law ought to use indirect, but clear, proxy tests for establishing the necessary close relationship. From the perspective of a reliance theory, the offer and acceptance rules can be regarded as doing just this: they are a proxy for tests that directly assess the 'closeness' of parties' relationships. If parties have gone through the offer and acceptance process, the necessary special relationship will normally exist. The offer and acceptance process ensures that the parties have made contact, know about each other, are serious, know reliance is likely, have given assurances, and so on. Of course, the offer and acceptance rules are not a perfect test for special relationships—for example, sometimes it is not reasonable (absent the law) to rely even when an offer is accepted, and vice versa (because it is unlikely the offeror will perform). But given the need for bright-line rules, they can reasonably be defended as a second-best test. The alternative of directly applying the various criteria listed earlier would leave the law too uncertain.

Three other aspects of the formation rules support the reliance theories' position that induced reliance is the key to contractual liability. First, the test for establishing offer and acceptance is an objective test: the courts are concerned not with what a contracting party 'truly' or 'really' intended, but with how a reasonable person would understand what was intended. In my earlier discussion of promissory theories, I queried whether all aspects of the offer and acceptance rules are objective, and I added that an objective test is not necessarily inconsistent with promissory liability. But whatever the merits of those suggestions, an objective approach clearly is consistent with a reliance theory.

Second, there are certain formation rules in the common law that explicitly require courts to take reliance into account. In particular, it is normally thought necessary to establish reliance in order to make a plea in estoppel.[62] Third, and finally, under the reforms that various common law countries, including the United Kingdom, have enacted to overturn the privity of contract rule, reliance by a third party is one of the triggers for contractual liability to that party.[63]

I conclude, therefore, that despite first appearances, reliance theories are able to explain contract law's formation rules.

The performance objection

The second main fit objection is that the *content* of a contractual obligation is different from that supposed by reliance theories. According to orthodox contract law doctrine, a contracting party's primary obligation

---

[62] I say 'normally' because this point is sometimes disputed, particularly with respect to American law: e.g. Farber and Matheson (1985); Yorio and Thel (1991).
[63] *Contracts (Rights of Third Parties) Act 1999.*

is to do what he said he would do. According to reliance theories, a contracting party's primary obligation is to reimburse the other party for his reliance losses in case what was promised was not done. Breach of contract, in this view, is established by showing that the duty to reimburse was not performed.

But as was true in respect of the formation rules, the difference between these two accounts of contractual obligation may be more apparent than real. A duty to reimburse may be different in principle from a duty to pay damages upon breach, but in practice they look identical. Each requires the payment of a sum of money equal to the relying party's loss (issues regarding the *quantum* of damages are discussed under remedies). If follows that, insofar as a plaintiff is claiming damages for breach of contract, the plaintiff in practice will not have been reimbursed as required according to a reliance theory (or at least the plaintiff must think this is the case). Leaving aside claims for specific performance (discussed below), every time a plaintiff proves breach of contract both the reliance theories' concept of breach and the orthodox view of breach are established. In short, the reliance theorist can argue that, while judges say a contractual duty is a duty to perform, in practice this duty is enforced only in cases in which the defendant has both failed to perform *and* failed to reimburse the plaintiff.

The remedies objection

The third and probably best known objection to reliance theories is that they are inconsistent with the common law's remedies for breach of contract. According to reliance theories, the remedy for a breach of contract should be an order to pay a sum of money equal to the *reliance* costs of the plaintiff. But according to orthodox contract law, the remedy for breach of contract is either an order to do what the defendant said he would do (specific performance) or, more commonly, an order to pay 'expectation' damages (defined as the value, in monetary terms, of the contracted-for performance).

The 'remedies' objection to reliance theories was the focus of Fuller and Perdue's article. Their response, which focused solely on awards of damages, was similar to the explanation just given of the formation rules: expectation damages are a proxy for what the courts really care about, which is reliance damages. Fuller and Perdue defended this conclusion by observing that in most commercial contracts the plaintiff relies by, *inter alia*, not entering a similar contract with a different contracting party. That is to say, if the defendant had not agreed to the contract, the plaintiff would have contracted with someone else. Since in a competitive market these other potential contracts would normally be on similar terms as the contract that was made with the defendant, the plaintiff's reliance loss will normally be equal to the profit he would have made on the main contract. Thus, 'negative' reliance, in the form of not taking up alternative opportunities, will be equal, in the usual case, to expectation damages. Expectation damages can therefore be explained by reliance theories on the basis that they award to plaintiffs the (reliance) value of foregone opportunities.

As Fuller and Perdue acknowledged, the 'foregone opportunities' theory does not explain why expectation damages are awarded for contracts made in non-competitive markets—defined here as markets in which the contracted-for goods or services are not available on reasonably similar terms from someone else. In such cases, it cannot be assumed that the plaintiff's foregone opportunity is equal to the value of the promised performance, because we cannot point to a similar contracting opportunity that the plaintiff passed over. Nonetheless, Fuller and Perdue's theory can account for awarding expectation damages in such cases on the grounds that the administrative and evidential costs of a more finely tuned rule are too high. It is not easy for courts to determine if markets are competitive. Moreover, the conclusion that the plaintiff could not have made an identical contract with another party does not mean that he did not forego other money making opportunities. The plaintiff might have invested the money or resources he devoted to the contract with the defendant in a different, but equally lucrative, venture. Proving the alternatives, and then establishing the profits that they would have generated, will again, raise difficult evidential issues.[64]

The common law rules on specific performance are more difficult to explain from a reliance perspective. Admittedly, in one respect these rules fit well with a reliance theory. The rule that damages are the primary remedy fits with the reliance theories' view that a contractual duty is not a duty to perform but rather a duty to reimburse for reliance expenditures. Orders to pay damages may be regarded, in this view, as either the specific enforcement of the duty to reimburse or as compensation for failure to perform that duty. In either case, the content of the order required by the reliance theory will resemble the 'damages' orders that courts routinely

---

[64] It has also been argued, in particular by Atiyah, that although courts purport to award expectation damages regardless of whether the contract was made in a competitive market, they actually award reliance damages in cases in which it is clear that reliance damages differ significantly from expectation damages: Atiyah (1995) 456–64.

make. The difficulty for reliance theories is to explain why specific performance is *ever* ordered. Specific performance is an order to do something that, according to reliance theories, defendants did not have a duty
to do in the first place. In a contract of sale, for example, the vendor is not
under a duty (in the reliance view) to deliver the goods—his duty is only
to reimburse the purchaser if he fails to deliver. So why do courts sometimes order delivery? To be sure, the value of performance is typically
equal to reliance costs (for reasons explained above). But the classic cases
in which specific performance is ordered—a contract for the sale of a
unique good—are precisely the kinds of cases in which it is most likely
that the value of performance will not equal reliance. By definition, alternative suppliers do not exist with respect to contracts for the sale of
unique goods—and so the plaintiff cannot complain that he passed by an
opportunity to make a similar contract. Awarding specific performance of
a contract of sale of a unique good is therefore likely to overcompensate
the plaintiff for his reliance loss.

Other fit objections

In addition to the formation, performance, and remedies objections just
discussed, a number of fit objections that were directed at promissory
theories apply equally to reliance theories. In particular, and as I
explained above, the consideration doctrine and, depending on how they
are interpreted, the rules on mistake, frustration, and discharge pose
difficulties for reliance theories as much as for promissory theories. To be
sure, the consideration rule would fit neatly with a reliance theory if it
required that each party actually do something or refrain from doing
something in exchange for the other's consideration: consideration would
be equivalent to reliance. But the standard way of fulfilling the consideration doctrine is not by actually doing something, but by *promising* to do
something. As regards doctrines such as mistake, frustration, and discharge, insofar as these are understood as based not on the interpretation
of a contract but rather on a concern for fairness or some other external
value, they again do not seem accounted for by a reliance theory. Instead
they must be viewed as limits on the scope of the reliance principle.

With respect to this last group of fit objections (and for that matter,
the other fit objections), the point is made by certain advocates of reliance
theories (particularly Atiyah) that regardless of what courts *say* they are
doing when applying the rules on consideration, mistake, etc., that in
practice they care very much about the existence and extent of reliance.
As regards the consideration doctrine, in particular, Atiyah has argued

that courts do not always apply the orthodox test of benefit to the promisor or detriment to the promisee.[65] Rather, courts find or do not find consideration for a variety of other reasons, notably whether the party seeking relief relied on the contract. Similarly, the courts are said to be more likely to set aside a contract for mistake or frustration if the parties have not relied on it.

Summary of fit objections

The reliance theories' explanation of why contract law is best understood in terms of reliance-based duties can be summarized in two statements. The first is that many of the core contract law rules—offer and acceptance, breach, remedies—are proxies for an unstated concern for reliance. The second is that contract law rules are not applied neutrally, but rather are manipulated or ignored with the aim of ensuring that detrimental reliance is protected.

Summarized in this way, the reliance theories' explanation of contract law invites two general observations. The first is that the detailed analysis of a large number of decisions that would be required to properly assess the second argument is beyond the scope of this book. My own view, which I only report here without defending, is that while stronger versions of this claim are implausible, there is some truth in the claim that judges care about reliance more than they say they do. Indeed, given the intuitive attraction of reliance-based liability, it would be strange if judges did not sometimes take reliance into account.

The second observation is that both of the above arguments—that many rules are proxies to protect reliance and that these rules are manipulated to protect reliance—proceed on the assumption that the judicial or 'legal' explanation of contract law is misleading. It is misleading, according to reliance theories, because judges do not explain the offer and acceptance rules, the breach rules, the remedies rules, etc. on the basis that they protect reliance. What judges say is that these rules are designed to identify and enforce promises or agreements.

Whether this divergence between the 'legal' or 'internal' explanation of the law and the reliance theory's explanation of the law matters when evaluating reliance theories turns on methodological issues that I discussed in Chapter 1 (1.6). Without going over that discussion here, it is suggested that even for scholars, like myself, who worry about such divergences, the divergence between the legal explanation and the

[65] (1986) 187–99.

reliance theory's explanation is not especially significant. Reliance theories are different only in degree and not in kind from the sort of explanation that courts routinely give. Indeed, in a different context—that of the law on negligent misstatement—the importance of protecting reliance *is* the internal explanation of the law. In this respect, the account that reliance theories offer of the law is similar to the unjust enrichment-based explanation of many legal rules that was given prior to the official recognition (only recently in England) that unjust enrichment is a source of law. That is to say, it is the kind of explanation that courts might, over time, come to accept. It follows that unlike, say, Marxist, feminist, or even efficiency theories of law (see 1.6), reliance theories are not strongly external to legal reasoning.

For these reasons, I conclude that the most important criticism of reliance theories is an essentially moral criticism: reliance theories are not grounded in a distinct and compelling moral foundation. It is this lack of a solid moral foundation, I suggest, that makes the attempts by reliance theories to explain away contract law's apparent indifference to reliance seem strained. Taken together, these concerns about the moral foundations and about how well reliance theories fit the law are sufficient reasons, I conclude, to reject reliance theories as general answers to the analytic question about contract law.

3.2.3. A RESIDUAL ROLE FOR RELIANCE THEORIES?

Notwithstanding the above conclusion, reliance theories might be useful in understanding *parts* of contract law. If—and this is a big if—the general idea that reliance-based duties are valid legal duties is plausible (meaning that, contrary to my conclusion above, they express a distinct and compelling moral principle), then *certain* contract law rules might be best explained in terms of a concern for induced reliance. Obvious candidates include the doctrine of estoppel and the objective test of formation. Accordingly, in Part III of this book I consider reliance-based interpretations of a number of particular rules.

Locating reliance-based liability in the map of private law

Assuming, for the sake of argument, that the idea of protecting reliance is a valid basis for at least some legal obligations, a final question raised by reliance theories is this: where do reliance-based obligations belong on the map of private law? Are they contractual or tortious or something else? On the assumption that it is possible to defend *a* general theory of contract, the conclusion must be that reliance-based duties are not contractual. For example, if contracts are best understood as promises (as I conclude below), a non-promissory reliance-based duty is not contractual. Legal rules should be classified according to the interests they protect, and promissory and reliance interests are different.

But neither can reliance-based duties be assimilated easily into the mainstream of tort law (i.e., the tort of negligence). Tort obligations, for the most part, are essentially negative obligations not to harm others in certain ways—for example not to harm others by driving carelessly or by manufacturing a defective product or by giving bad advice. Reliance-based duties, by contrast, are best understood as essentially positive duties to do something—to reimburse reliance costs—*for* other persons (which is why they are morally controversial). The wrong is not inducing reliance, but rather failing to reimburse another for costs they incurred because of the reliance you induced.

Reliance-based duties (insofar as they exist) must, then, be considered separate from both mainstream tort duties and contractual duties. Whether this means they constitute a distinct category of legal obligation is difficult to say. I suggested earlier that reliance-based duties closely resemble duties based on concepts of good faith (understood here to include notions such as abuse of rights and unconscionability). Reliance-based liability might, then, be regarded as just one aspect of the broader concept of 'good faith'.

3.3. TRANSFER THEORIES

For the reasons just given, most contemporary critics of promissory theories regard reliance theories as explaining, at most, only a small part of contract law. Certain of these critics have turned to a third approach to answering the analytic question about contract law; what I have called the 'transfer theory' of contract.[66] The origins of transfer theories can be traced back to at least Hugo Grotius,[67] but their central tenets are less known and developed than those of promissory or reliance theories. Even more than reliance theories, the category of transfer theories must be understood as representing a model or broad approach rather than a comprehensive position that can be ascribed to any individual or group of

---

[66] Barnett (1986); Benson (1995; 1996).

[67] Grotius (1625) Book II, Chapter XI. On the historical origins of transfer theories, see Benson (1996) 42.

scholars.[68] Nonetheless, transfer theories make a significant contribution to our understanding of contract law—and this is true even if, as I shall suggest, they are ultimately unpersuasive as a general answer to the analytic question.

The idea underlying transfer theories is simple: a contract is a transfer of rights. As Peter Benson observes, transfer theories analogize a contract to the 'widely recognized and simple model of completed gifts and exchanges'.[69] Suppose that I give you my watch as a gift. From the moment that I physically transfer the watch to you, you own the watch (assuming the transfer was voluntary, etc.). No promise, reliance, or other act is necessary to effect the transfer of rights to the watch: it is enough that I intended to transfer the watch to you and that you intended to receive it. If I then try to interfere with your ownership of the watch, say by trying to take it back, I will commit a tort, if not a crime. Transfer theories of contract suppose that the same process happens in an ordinary executory contract. The only difference, an important (and conceptually difficult) one, is that what is transferred is not existing rights to a physical object, but existing intangible rights to the performance of future acts.[70] Thus, the legal significance of a contract in which I undertake to deliver to you my watch next week (say in exchange for you undertaking to pay me £50) is that *from the moment of contracting* I have transferred a right— that I already own—to you.[71] That right is not the right to the watch—I still own the watch—but rather the right to the performance of a future act (my delivering the watch to you). Our contract transfers to you an intangible, but real, right to that performance. Transfer theories, therefore, regard contracts in the way lawyers typically regard assignments of contractual rights. An assignment is the transfer of an existing contractual right. A contract, according to a transfer theory, is the transfer of an existing performance right.

It is tempting, but misleading, to regard transfer theories as providing new foundations for promissory theories of contract. It is true that, like promissory theories, transfer theories regard contracting parties as

---

[68] The most complete exposition of a transfer theory is found in Barnett (1986), but the position defended in Benson (1995) and, especially, Benson (1996; 2001) is closer, though not identical, to the model examined in this chapter.

[69] Benson (1995) 319.

[70] Benson (1995) 319. In his most recent work, Benson argues that the rights transferred in a contract are the rights to an actual thing and not to the performance of an act: (2001). For reasons I explain below, this version can explain only a small part of contract law.

[71] '. . . [C]ontract law concerns enforceable obligations arising from the valid *transfer* of entitlements that are *already vested* in someone' (emphasis added): Barnett (1986) 297.

'owning' rights to the performance of the relevant contractual undertakings. Moreover, in each theory, a contractual right is a right that the other contracting party do the very thing that she said she would do. But there is a fundamental difference in the way that each theory explains how contracting parties come to own these rights. In transfer theories, the explanation is that the contract brings about the transfer of an already existing right. A contractual transaction, in this view, concerns dealings with things that the parties' *already own* or have rights to. By contrast, it is of the essence of a promissory explanation that it regards contracts as creating *new* rights. Promissory rights (assuming they exist) are rights *created* by a promise. Indeed, it is this feature of promising—that it permits rights to be created where none existed before—that is the very reason promissory obligations are regarded by some critics as unsuitable for legal enforcement.

3.3.1. MORAL OBJECTIONS TO TRANSFER THEORIES

Transfer theories are not vulnerable to the harm principle objection that was directed at promissory theories and reliance theories, nor to any other obvious moral objection. If I transfer a right to performance to you, you *own* this right; if I fail to perform, I have interfered with your property rights. In a transfer theory, breach is viewed, 'not merely as failing to confer a benefit to the promisee in virtue of their contract, but as interfering with what already belongs to the promisee in virtue of their contract'.[72] Depending on the mental element involved, that interference is either a tort or a crime. According to transfer theory, then, failing to perform a contract harms another, just as forcibly taking back a watch that I have given away harms the recipient of my gift. The liberty to alienate property rights, and the duty not to interfere with property rights thus acquired, are basic to most moral and legal theories.

3.3.2. FIT OBJECTIONS TO TRANSFER THEORIES

Turning to questions of fit with contract law, the validity of a contract, according to a transfer theory, should be determined in the same way that that the validity of a transfer of a physical asset is determined. The test is not whether a promise or agreement was made, but whether the transferor and transferee intended to make the transfer. The rules of offer and acceptance are, of course, not typically expressed using the language of transfer. But the concept of 'agreement' that is usually invoked when

---

[72] Benson (1996) 42.

explaining the rules can plausibly be understood as a test for a (mutual) intention to transfer. An 'agreement' can refer to either of two quite different things. An agreement may be an agreement to do something. This *obligational* sense of agreement is the sense that promissory theories of contract assume offer and acceptance rules establish. But an agreement can also be an agreement in fact. For example, we can agree that a painting is beautiful or—closer to our concerns—agree that you own a certain piece of property. This *factual* sense of agreement, which does not involve creating obligations, is the sense of agreement that transfer theories suppose offer and acceptance rules seek to establish. A contract is an agreement that certain rights previously owned by the transferor are now owned by the transferee. This story fits the model of offer and acceptance closely enough. Indeed, the words 'offer' and 'acceptance' seem appropriate to explain a transaction that is analogous to a transfer of physical property. It makes sense, linguistically, to 'accept' an 'offer' to hand over a physical object. (From the perspective of promissory theories, by contrast, this language sounds awkward.) For the same reason, transfer theories have a ready explanation for why it takes two persons to make a contract. For a transfer to take place, both the transferor and the transferee must intend to bring about the transfer.

In other respects, a transfer theory's explanation of contract law is similar to the explanation give by a promissory theory. Each theory regards contracting parties as under obligations to do the very thing they said that they would do, and each determines the scope of those obligations according to the intentions of the parties. It follows that, as with promissory theories, transfer theories have a ready explanation for the main features of contract remedies: if the plaintiff owns the defendant's performance, then expectation damages and specific performance are appropriate remedies. If you steal or break my property, it is right that you should give me back my property or compensate me for its full value.[73] It also follows that, as with promissory theories, transfer theories have more difficulty explaining the various limits on the existence and scope of contractual obligations that are imposed by the law (e.g., consideration, the objective test for formation, mistake, frustration, and implied-in-law terms).

---

[73] A difficult question that I do not address here is whether transfer theories are consistent with regarding contractual rights as personal rather than proprietary. Prima facie, it would seem that if a contract is viewed as the present transfer of an existing right, contractual rights should be regarded as proprietary—with the normal implications for remedies.

3.3.3. CONCEPTUAL OBJECTIONS TO TRANSFER THEORIES

The preceding paragraphs provide only the briefest sketch of how a transfer theory fits contract law. But as with promissory theories, it seems unlikely that issues of fit will be decisive in assessing transfer theories. In any event, the most important objection to a transfer theory is a *conceptual* objection. The main issue raised by transfer theories is not whether they are consistent with the nature of morality or with the nature of law, but, instead, whether they are consistent with the very nature of rights.

The conceptual objection to transfer theories is that it is not possible for contracting parties to do what such theories suppose they are doing when they make a contract. More specifically, the objection is that the rights that transfer theories suppose are transferred by contracts do not exist prior to the making of contracts. Contracting parties do not own rights 'to the performance of a future act (by them)', which they can then transfer to another party. Of course, each of us possesses what Wesley Hohfeld called a liberty right to do or not do various acts in the future,[74] which right encompasses the kinds of acts involved in performing contracts. I have the right to give or not give you my watch next Thursday. But a contract in which I agree to deliver my watch to you next Thursday cannot be regarded as transferring that liberty right to you. What you own after our contract is made (if you own anything) is not the right to decide at some point in the future what I am going to do next Thursday. Instead, what you own is the right that I deliver the watch to you next Thursday. For transfer theories to make sense, then, what I must be transferring to you at the moment of contracting is not the liberty to determine what I will do in the future, but a right to demand that I deliver the watch next Thursday. But I do not own this right. At the moment, all that I 'own', in respect of my actions next Thursday, is the right to decide what I will do next Thursday. I do not own 'the right that I do something' in the future: all my ownership rights are liberty rights.

In recent work, Benson has responded to the above objection by arguing that the right that is transferred by a contract is not a right to the performance of a future act, but instead, the right to the very *thing* promised in the contract.[75] The thing promised, he adds, 'may be either an external object of some sort or service'.[76] This response, however, is vulnerable to the same objection I made above. Except for contracts to sell

---

[74] Hohfeld (1913).   [75] Benson (2001).   [76] Benson (2001) 135.

a specific object, a contracting party does not own, at the moment just prior to contracting, rights to the 'things' that this response assumes are transferred by a contract. Leaving aside whether it makes sense to speak of a service as a 'thing', we cannot own, at the present moment, something which does not yet exist. My contractual agreement to paint John's house next Friday cannot be regarded as transferring to John my right to 'the painting of John's house next Friday' because I did not, at the moment just prior to contracting, 'own' anything resembling 'the painting of John's house next Friday'. What I 'owned', if I owned anything in this regard, was a liberty right to do or not do various things next Friday, painting included. It is not clear how one could even describe the kind of right that is supposedly transferred in this view. Should I say 'I hereby transfer to John the right to my painting of John's house next Friday'?

3.3.4. CONCLUDING REMARKS

For these reasons, a transfer theory is unpersuasive as a general theory of contract law. If a promisee owns the rights to the promisor's performance, it must be because the contract has created — not transferred — those rights. That said, transfer theories may be valuable in explaining certain aspects of the law of contract that cannot easily be explained other models. In particular, transfer theories prima facie provide the best explanation of contracts of simultaneous exchange, for example purchases from vending machines or (most) sales across a store counter (5.2.2).

The final question to address before leaving transfer theories is whether such transactions should be regarded as contractual. Is 'transfer' part of the law of contract? Consistent with what I said above about the place of reliance in the map of private law, and assuming again that a promissory theory is ultimately accepted as the best general theory of contract law, the answer must be no. Although both transfers and promises involve acts of will, they are distinct concepts because only promises create obligations. The reasons for allowing persons to transfer rights are different from the reasons (such as they are) for allowing people to create new rights and, more generally, to create binding obligations with other persons. Currently, the common law places most of the rules that deal with transfers (e.g., gift, inheritance, and so on) in the law of property. These rules are, however, distinct from those property law rules that define how property rights are originally created and what is entailed by such rights. For this reason, I suggest (although I cannot pursue the suggestion here) that 'transfer' should be regarded as a distinct category of law, standing alongside contract, tort, property, and unjust enrichment.

3.4. CONCLUSION: REDRAWING THE MAP OF PRIVATE LAW

My survey of contemporary contract theories started with the orthodox view that contracts are promises or some other form of self-imposed obligation. At first, this view appears to be inconsistent with the principle —fundamental both in law and in morality—that the state should not enforce private law obligations to benefit others. I then provided a new defence to this harm principle objection, and suggested that it should be measured against the alternative of choosing a different answer to the analytic question.

The best known alternative view—which holds that contractual obligations are obligations to ensure that others whom we induce to rely are not made worse off—also seems vulnerable to moral objections, not to mention fitting awkwardly with various core features of contract law. A second alternative view, which regards contracts as transfers of existing rights, is morally unimpeachable, but it appears conceptually confused in assuming that we own the kinds of obligational rights that this view supposes are transferred by contracts. My overall conclusion, therefore, is that promissory theories provide the best answer to the analytic question about contract law.

A prominent aspect of my defence of promissory theories of contract is the claim that contract law is an autonomous body of law, distinct from tort law and other branches of private law. In closing, I want now to add some details to that claim. What is distinctive about contract law, on a promissory theory, is that it represents a method of creating new rights where none existed before. It follows that the distinctively contractual parts of (what is now called) contract law are the rules specifying how contract rights are created—namely the contract formation rules of offer and acceptance, consideration, intent to create legal relations, and so on. It further follows that contract formation rules are (as I have already suggested) akin to the rules in property that specify how new property-like rights are created. Each specifies the acts that are required to create a particular sort of right, and the content of the right thus created. Property (in this narrow sense) and contract (understood here as comprised of essentially formation rules) should, I suggest, nonetheless remain as distinct legal categories because the nature of the acts specified and the nature of the rights thus created are different. In property, the relevant acts, in broad terms, are those indicating an intention to control or possess a thing (broadly defined), whereas in contract the relevant acts are those indicating an intention to undertake an obligation. In terms of the nature of the right created, in property it is control over an inert thing (tangible or intangible). In contract, it is the right to the performance of a future act.

Turning to the rules dealing with infringements of contractual rights, a strong argument can be made—again following the property analogy—for classifying the breach rules as part of tort law (a view I defend in more detail in Chapters 10 and 11). To fail to perform is regarded in promissory theories as harming the promisee's property-like right to the performance of an act. Thus, in the same way that theft and negligent damage to property are not considered part of the law of property, non-performance should not be regarded as part of contract law. The one difficulty with this view is that the duty to perform a contract is different from other tort law duties in that it is a duty to do something for a particular person. For this reason, it probably makes sense to regard contractual duties as akin to, but not identical with, normal tort duties—in the same way that formation rules are regarded as akin to, but not identical with, formation rules in property law generally. The structure of the duties are the same in each case, but their content is sufficiently different to merit keeping them separate.

As for remedial rules, the promissory account described above has nothing special to say about how remedies for breach of contract should be classified. It is worth noting, though, that for the same reason that contract duties should be regarded as closely similar to tort duties, remedies for breaches of those duties should also be regarded as closely similar (a conclusion I defend in Chapter 11).

It remains only to reiterate that nothing in the preceding story entails the implausible conclusion that a promissory theory can explain everything currently labelled as 'contract law'. As I noted when discussing reliance and transfer theories, significant parts of what is now called 'contract law' may be explicable only on the basis of a concern for recognizing transfers of already existing rights or (less plausibly in my view) for protecting reliance. A promissory theory of contract law does not deny such accounts, though it does suggest that rules that can only be explained on the basis of recognizing rights transfers or protecting reliance ought to be reclassified as lying outside the domains of contract law. In addition, I have also observed that certain rules are difficult to explain on the basis of any general answer to the analytic question. For the most part, such rules limit the type or scope of obligations otherwise recognized, rather than provide positive reasons for establishing an obligation. The rules on consideration and various mandatory implied-by-law terms are prominent examples, but other significant features of contract law such as mistake, frustration, and duress might also fit into this category.

The promissory theory of contract law that is left after these admissions is both of limited ambition, in that it classifies as non-contractual significant aspects of existing contract law, and of significant complexity, in that it acknowledges that no single principle animates the entirety of what remains contract law. Whether it merits the title of a promissory 'theory of contract' is a matter on which reasonable people may disagree, but my own view is that enough of the core of contract law is explicable to justify the title.

4

The Justification of Contractual Obligations: The Normative Question

Alongside the analytic question discussed in the previous chapter, a complete theory of contract must also address a normative question. That question, simply stated, is this: what justification, if any, exists for contract law? This normative question must be addressed because contract law (like other parts of the law) presents itself as normatively justified. A contract is understood, at least from the legal perspective, as creating an *obligation*—something that you *ought* to do. To understand this normative feature of contract law, we need to understand whether, how, and to what extent, contract law is, in fact, justified. The contrast theorist seeking to find an intelligible order in the law must determine, in other words, whether the law's claim to be justified is intelligible (1.5). In addition, the normative question is important for the practical reason that individuals found to have breached contracts may have their property seized or even be imprisoned (in the event that they disregard a court order to fulfill or remedy a contractual obligation). It goes without saying that it matters very much whether state coercion is justified, whatever its legal basis.

As I noted in Chapter 2, most answers to the normative question about contract law fall into two main categories. One category is comprised of what were described as utilitarian theories of contract. A contract theory is utilitarian, in the very broad sense that I use this term, if it justifies contract law on the basis that contract law promotes utility—understood here as any conception of, or aspect of, human well-being, whether it be increased wealth, welfare, autonomy, closer relationships, etc. According to this view, contract law promotes utility (however defined) by establishing incentives for people to act in 'utility-promoting' ways or (less importantly as it turns out) by supporting judicial orders that command individuals directly to act in utility-promoting ways (say by ordering that an object be transferred to a person who values it more than the current owner). Different versions of utilitarian theories can be distinguished by, *inter alia*, what they regard as the 'good' thing that contract law promotes.

The best known and most important group of utilitarian justifications of contract law, 'efficiency' theories of contract, regard contract law as promoting the 'welfare', subjectively understood, of all members of society. Other utilitarian theories justify contract law on the ground that it promotes closer social relationships, a particular distribution of wealth, or conditions favourable to the achievement of individual autonomy.

The second category of answers to the normative question is found in rights-based theories of contract. Rights-based theories justify contract law on the ground that contract law vindicates or upholds citizens' rights. According to this view, contractual obligations are obligations not to infringe the rights of others, and contract law gives force to such rights either directly, by ordering that they not be infringed, or indirectly, by enforcing duties to repair losses caused by rights-infringements. In principle, rights-based theories can be distinguished according to how they understand the rights that contract law protects, but in practice, the most important examples of rights-based theories all regard contractual rights as classical 'negative-liberty' rights to non-interference with one's person or property.

In assessing utilitarian and rights-based theories, my approach (as in the previous chapter) is to present them in the first instance as unitary explanations of the entirety of contract law. After examining these theories separately, I then consider theories that purport not merely to be qualified versions of these answers to the normative question, but instead to incorporate a (coherent and rational) mixture of the two answers. These 'mixed' theories suppose that some parts of contract law are justified on utilitarian grounds and other parts justified on rights-based grounds—and that there are good reasons for the distinction. Of course, some scholars believe that contract law cannot be justified at all, either because its foundations are immoral or (what is more commonly asserted) because it is founded on a morass of competing, if not contradictory, principles. I do not consider this view as an answer *per se* to the normative question, but throughout the chapter it remains in the background as the default position.

Two further points should be kept in mind. The first is a reminder that the normative question discussed in this chapter cannot be separated neatly from the analytic question discussed in the previous chapter. In particular (and as I have discussed before: 2.4), to determine whether and how contractual obligations are justified, we need to know what kind of a thing a contractual obligation is; for example, whether it is a promissory obligation or a reliance-based obligation or a simple transfer of property.

Thus, in the same way that my analysis of answers to the analytic question required me at times to consider normative issues (e.g., the harm principle objection to promissory theories), my analysis of answers to the normative question will entail consideration of analytic issues from time to time.

The second point is that we should not be surprised if a 'knock-down' argument cannot be made on behalf of either utilitarian or rights-based justifications for contract law. The debate between these opposing justifications mirrors a debate in moral philosophy that has been going on for centuries, if not millenia.[1] The argument between those favouring utilitarian justifications for punishment and those favouring rights-based justifications, for example, has gone on for as long as scholars have reflected about the merits of punishment. While I ultimately defend rights-based theories, the purpose of pointing out this debate is to show that no answer to the question 'why enforce contracts' is likely to appear so persuasive as to command universal acceptance.

4.1. UTILITARIAN THEORIES: EFFICIENCY THEORIES

Utilitarian theories justify contract law on the ground that contract law promotes human well-being or 'utility', broadly defined. In analysing such theories, I will focus primarily on the best-known and most influential category of such theories, efficiency theories. The other categories of utilitarian theories, which I discuss briefly at the end, have not been developed to the same extent as efficiency theories, nor had the same influence as efficiency theories on how lawyers think about the law. Moreover, the strengths and weaknesses of other utilitarian theories are, in broad terms, similar to the strengths and weaknesses of efficiency theories.

Efficiency theories of contract, in the sense intended here, are theories that regard contract law as an instrument for promoting efficient behaviour. Efficiency, as I will explain in more detail, is understood on a cost-benefit model: an action, rule, or whatever is efficient if its benefits outweigh its costs. The metric for assessing costs and benefits in efficiency theories of contract law can be described in different ways, but the

---

[1] But not always using these terms: related contrasts include those drawn between the right and the good, consequentialism and non-consequentialism, deontological and teleological, and instrumental and non-instrumental.

most common, and also the most useful metric, is the satisfaction of individual preferences—typically called 'welfare' (thus efficiency theories might also be called welfare-maximizing theories).[2] Understood in this way, the notion of welfare is comprehensive; it 'incorporates in a positive way everything that an individual might value—goods and services that the individual can consume, social and environmental amenities, personally held notions of fulfillment, sympathetic feelings for others, and so forth.'[3]

In principle, efficient behaviour might be promoted by courts *ordering* individuals to act in efficient ways, but in practice efficiency theories regard the law as promoting efficiency by establishing *incentives* for efficient behaviour and disincentives for inefficient behaviour.[4] Thus, remedies are explained not on the basis that they promote efficiency directly—the payment of damages, for example, is not itself efficient—but rather on the basis that they promote efficiency indirectly, by giving future contracting parties incentives to act efficiently.

A legal rule or decision is efficient, then, if it promotes behaviour of a kind that leads to an overall increase in the satisfaction of individual preferences—of human welfare. The claim of efficiency theories of contract is that contract law rules and decisions are efficient in this sense.

Efficiency theories are often described as 'economic' theories of contract. When used in context this label is unobjectionable, but it is not adopted here in order to keep clear the distinction between (what I call) efficiency theories and (what is usually called) 'economic *analysis*' of law. Economic analysis of law is fundamentally a methodology or approach to examining the law rather than a theory *of* law. In broad terms, economic analysis of law is practised by anyone who assumes that individuals respond to incentives and who then thinks about law in terms of the incentives it establishes. The connection between economic analysis of law and efficiency theories of contract is that someone who defends the latter will almost certainly do so using the former. But the reverse is not always true. Analysing the law using economic methodology is consistent with denying that law is, or should be, efficient. When the label 'economic' is used in this (more appropriate) sense, then, there is no economic *theory* of contract—there is only an economic methodology or approach to thinking about contract.

---

[2] For an argument that 'wealth' is the appropriate metric, see Posner (1998) 27. The distinction between wealth and welfare is not significant in my analysis.

[3] Kaplow and Shavell (2001) 980.   [4] Crasswell (2001).

4.1.1. EXCHANGE AND THE ROLE OF CONTRACT LAW

Arguably the most fundamental idea underlying efficiency theories of contract law is that if two persons make a voluntary exchange the exchange will make each better off, and is therefore efficient. If I give you my cow in exchange for your horse, the presumption is that I value your horse more than my cow and that you value my cow more than your horse. Since 'better off' is defined in terms of satisfying individual preference, the transaction makes both of us, and by extension, society generally, better off.

Significantly, the presumption that voluntary exchanges are 'mutually beneficial', and hence efficient, does not deny that non-voluntary transfers of resources may also be efficient. If the state forced me to give you my cow and you to give me your horse, then, assuming the facts were otherwise unchanged, and assuming that being forced is not in itself a source of disutility (as distinct from any disutility we suffer from losing our animals), the same efficient result would be achieved. The transfer might also be mutually beneficial if you simply took my cow without asking and left behind your horse. Indeed, the transfer might be efficient — even though not mutually beneficial — if you took my cow without leaving behind your horse. If the benefit that you gained from my cow was greater than the loss that I suffered by losing the cow, the transfer would be an example of an 'efficient theft'.

The example of efficient theft shows that the criterion of efficiency adopted by efficiency theories is what economists call 'Kaldor-Hicks' (or cost-benefit) efficiency.[5] A rule or decision is Kaldor-Hicks efficient if its benefits outweigh its costs (measured in terms of efficiency); more strictly, a rule or decision is Kaldor-Hicks efficient if the gains made by those who benefit from the rule are greater than the losses incurred by anyone who might be harmed by the rule. The definition is important to keep in mind since in much economic work, including much economic work on contracts, the concept of efficiency employed is the stricter notion of 'Pareto' efficiency. An act is Pareto-efficient (also called Pareto-improving) if no one is made worse off and at least one person is made better off; trade-offs between one person's gains and another's losses are not allowed. Pareto-efficiency is favoured as a standard by many economists since it does not require the complex (some would say impossible) interpersonal comparisons of welfare required to assess Kaldor-Hicks

---

[5] On the different concepts of efficiency used by economists, and their significance for law, see Coleman (1980).

efficiency. To determine if a rule is Pareto-efficient, it is sufficient to ask if everyone did, or would, agree to it.

It might be thought that contract law is amenable to an efficiency-based justification that adopts the Pareto definition of efficiency. As I just noted, it is a basic assumption of efficiency theories that voluntary exchanges are mutually beneficial—which means they are Pareto-efficient. Efficiency theories of contract law, however, are theories of contract *law* rather than theories of contractual transactions. The 'acts' that are being assessed are actions by courts—the making of rules, the handing down of individual decisions, and so on. Few, if any, legal rules or decisions, contractual or otherwise, satisfy the Pareto standard. There will always be people who would prefer that the rule in question did not exist; the rules against fraud, for example, do not benefit good liars. For this reason, although the concept of Pareto-efficiency can be used to explain why voluntary exchanges are desirable, and why the law might want to encourage such exchanges, it cannot be used to justify contract *law* itself.

The example of efficient theft also shows that the efficiency-based argument in favour of voluntary transactions is not an argument about the importance of liberty in principle. The argument is grounded, rather in practical concerns about the likelihood of involuntary transactions leading to efficient results. In principle, thefts can be efficient. The problem, from an efficiency perspective, is that in practice there is a serious risk thefts will not be efficient—because most thieves do not care whether their victims' losses are offset by their own gain (and even if they did care, the information needed to determine if the theft was efficient would be difficult to obtain). Moreover, a rule that permitted 'efficient thefts' would lead potential victims to expend considerable resources protecting their property. The efficiency-based explanation for the criminal prohibition of theft, therefore, is that individuals should be discouraged from refusing to bargain in situations in which bargaining is possible. Thieves are punished, in other words, for attempting to avoid the market. As for state-ordered transfers, from an efficiency perspective the problem here—even assuming that government actors act with proper motives—is essentially informational. No central authority has ever had, or seems likely ever to have, information sufficient for it to be certain that commanded transfers will be efficient. Personal preferences are just that—personal—and even if it is possible in theory for them to be known by government actors, their volatility and sheer number make it unlikely that any central authority could know individuals' preferences well enough to distribute resources efficiently. The macroeconomic arguments in favour of markets over command economies thus link up with the microeconomic arguments in favour of voluntary transactions.

The likelihood that mutual exchanges will be beneficial, together with the practical difficulties associated with achieving efficient transfers by other means, lead, then, to a presumption in efficiency theories in favour of voluntary transactions. But what is the role of contract law in this story? Nothing said thus far answers this question. Exchanges and other types of voluntary transactions may, and do, happen all the time without contract law. If I go to the marketplace and give you £100 for a book on your stall table, we have exchanged property. The validity of this transaction assumes a system of property rights and rules for transferring such rights. But assuming that no promises, undertakings, or representations are made, simultaneous exchanges of this sort can happen without a law of contract.

From an efficiency perspective, the main economic function of contract law is to assist transacting parties who face difficulties associated with *non-simultaneous* transactions. Stated differently, contract law facilitates *deferred exchanges*. An example is useful here. Suppose that you agree to build me a boat in exchange for £10,000, payable in advance. Absent a law of contract, there is an obvious risk that, having received the £10,000, you will renege on our deal and pocket the money. Of course, you might perform—you may be worried about your business reputation or about extra-legal means of enforcement (think of deals among mafiosi) or you may just think it would morally be wrong to renege.[6] But it is clear that what economists call 'opportunism'—taking advantage of another's vulnerability—is a risk. Given this risk, I may decide it is not worth entering into what would otherwise be a mutually beneficial arrangement (even if, unknown to me, you would have performed). The risk of opportunism persists, note, even if we devised a different method of payment; for example, payment on delivery. Payment on delivery would leave both of us vulnerable. You cannot be sure that by the time the boat is built I will not change my mind. I might also demand a lower price at the last moment, attempting to exploit the fact that you now have a custom-made boat that will be difficult to sell to anyone else. And from my perspective, I still cannot be sure that you will build the boat. Moreover, if it is important to me that the boat be ready by a certain date, there is a risk that, once the date approaches, you will raise your price in the knowledge that I have no time to find an alternative builder.

[6] e.g. Macauley (1963); Ellickson (1991); E. Posner (2000).

The fundamental role of contract law from the perspective of efficiency theories, then, is to ensure that the kinds of concerns described above do not prevent parties from entering mutually beneficial deferred exchanges. From an efficiency perspective, the law enforces contracts in order to protect individuals who enter into deferred exchanges. By this means (and others described below) the law facilitates the making of such contracts.

The efficiency-based explanation of contract law's main features

The various rules that make up the law of contract can be analysed from the above perspective. Thus, the purpose of contractual 'validity' rules, according to efficiency theories, is to identify the kinds of agreements that are likely to be mutually beneficial. In broad terms, a proposed transaction is likely to be mutually beneficial if the parties agreed to it, and did so voluntarily and on good information. The rules on offer and acceptance, duress, misrepresentation, undue influence and, subject to my comments below, mistake and frustration, are therefore regarded by efficiency theories primarily as means to ensure that contracts are voluntary and informed agreements.

As for the 'content' of a contract, the basic rule that contract law should give effect to the intentions of the parties is explained on the basis of the assumption that contracting parties typically know best what is in their own interests. Significantly, the process of implying (non-mandatory) terms into contracts is also defended by efficiency theories, essentially on the ground that contract law promotes efficient behaviour by filling out incomplete contracts. The argument here is that it is costly (and probably impossible) for parties to write a 'complete contract', that is, a contract that describes their obligations exhaustively and in respect of all possible eventualities. The law is therefore seen as facilitating efficient contract-making by providing contracting parties with a set of default terms that they can rely upon to fill the gaps in their contracts as needed. If the parties do not like the default terms provided by the law, they can stipulate different terms. But the law does not require contracting parties to engage in the economically wasteful and exchange-discouraging activity of trying to write complete contracts.

Of course, the law's provision of default terms—which terms, according to most efficiency theories, are found not just in the basic rules of interpretation but also in rules governing mistake, frustration, discharge, and even remedies—is efficient only if the *content* of the terms themselves is efficient. The claim that their content is efficient has been

defended in a number of ways. A brief survey of these ways is illustrative of the different approaches that efficiency theories can take to explaining particular legal rules. The survey will also provide evidence for a point I make below when evaluating efficiency theories, which is that taking into account *all of the factors* that are relevant to assessing efficiency is extremely difficult.

To begin, 'direct' explanations account for the efficiency of default rules on the basis that the actions they require (or do not require) are themselves efficient. For example, a term implied into a contract of sale to the effect that delivery must happen during normal business hours could be justified on the ground that delivery outside of business hours normally involves additional costs, and so is inefficient. The implied term is therefore efficient because it requires that delivery take place at an efficient time. A second kind of direct explanation supposes that implied terms are efficient because they mimic what the parties would have stipulated had they been able (costlessly) to create terms in their contract to govern the situation in issue. Thus, in my delivery example, the implied term that delivery must happen in business hours might be defended on the ground that this is the term the parties would have included had they negotiated this issue. Yet a third kind of direct explanation supposes that the law does not actually 'impose' terms at all, but rather just gives effect to the genuine, but unexpressed, intentions of the parties. In this view, the courts are giving effect to implied-in-fact terms when they impose default terms. If this accurately describes what courts do, then the efficient result will be achieved for the same reason that voluntary exchanges generally are efficient—the parties know best what is in their own interests.

Direct explanations of default terms defend such terms on the basis that they give contracting parties incentives to *perform* their contractual obligations efficiently. By contrast, 'indirect' explanations account for the efficiency of default terms on the ground that they facilitate efficient *contract-making*. In this view, the existence and content of default terms makes the (efficient) practice of contracting more attractive. Each of the three variants of direct explanations described above can be reframed as an indirect explanation. Thus, the argument can be made that the content of default terms is efficient because, by enforcing terms that require parties to act efficiently when performing contracts, or that mimic what the parties would have stipulated, or that express the parties' genuine but unexpressed intentions, the law facilitates contracting. People are more likely to enter contracts, according to this view, if they know that the terms the law imposes will satisfy one of these criteria because these are the criteria they would have agreed to themselves.

A better understanding of efficiency theories of contract law requires a shift from the sort of general observations made above to more specific arguments about particular legal rules. It is characteristic of efficiency theories that they offer highly detailed explanations of specific areas of contract law. Of course, an examination of every such explanation would require a separate book. Fortunately, such a task is not necessary because the strengths and weaknesses of efficiency-based justifications for contract law are broadly similar regardless of which rule is being considered. The discussion below focuses upon the area of contract law that has attracted the greatest attention of efficiency theorists: contract remedies.

4.1.2. REMEDIES FOR BREACH OF CONTRACT: THE EFFICIENT BREACH THEORY

In principle, there are two ways that remedial orders might be used to promote efficiency; and thus two ways in which efficiency theories might explain such orders. First, remedial orders might be used to order individuals to behave in ways that *directly* increase welfare. To take a simple example: a court might order Jane to deliver a car in her possession to Susan, on the basis that Susan will obtain more welfare from the car than will Jane. In this example, the required act (delivering the car) directly increases welfare because the result of the act (Susan owning the car) increases the level of welfare in the world (because Susan obtains more welfare from the car than Jane). Second, remedial orders might be used to create incentives for individuals so that *in the future* individuals will act in ways that (directly) increase welfare. Thus, a court might order a defendant who had engaged in inefficient behaviour to pay a sum of money to the plaintiff, on the basis that this would discourage individuals from behaving in a similar way in the future. The literature on efficiency theories of contract does not always distinguish these two ways of promoting efficiency, but in practice most theorists explain the law on the basis of the second method—that remedies establish efficient incentives.[7] The reasons for this choice are discussed in 11.2. Here, I focus on explaining the substance of the incentive-based perspective.

In describing the efficiency-based explanation of remedies, it is convenient to begin by examining the basic or 'simple' version of this explanation. Following popular usage, I will label this explanation the 'efficient

---

[7] Craswell (2001).

breach theory'.[8] Complicating factors will be introduced later, when I consider objections to this simple explanation.[9]

The idea underlying the efficient breach theory is that it is sometimes efficient for parties to not perform their primary contractual obligations— and that the remedies available in law facilitate non-performance in exactly such cases. Recall that a basic assumption of efficiency theories is that voluntary exchanges are normally mutually beneficial. If you consent to buy my bicycle from me for £100, you must think that my bicycle is worth more than £100 to you, and I must think the bicycle is worth less than £100 to me. Performing an agreement to exchange is normally efficient, therefore, because the outcome is that the bicycle is transferred to someone who values it more than she values what she gave up, and vice versa. But this conclusion does not always follow. You may have forgotten that you had a perfectly good bicycle stored in your basement. Or I may not have realized when I made the agreement that shortly afterwards I would be offered a job that requires a bicycle. In such cases, one or both of us may come to regret our decision—and if we do, the presumption that the contemplated exchange is efficient can no longer be supported. Rather, the breach of the agreement appears to represent efficient behaviour.

Regrets about entering a contract are not uncommon because contracting parties often have imperfect information about the past or the future. In the famous case of *Tito v Waddell*,[10] the inhabitants of Ocean Island granted mining rights to British Phosphate in 1941 in exchange for a fee and a promise to replant the island to its original state. British Phosphate mined the land, but before it had begun to replant, intensive bombing (during WWII) left the island permanently uninhabitable. The islanders were moved to another island 1,500 miles away. On these facts, and assuming the islanders did not place a very high non-tangible value on their previous home being replanted, replanting the island would have been inefficient. Replanting would have cost more than it was worth to the islanders or to anyone to whom the islanders might have been able to sell the island. Another way of making this point is that had the contracting

---

[8] Birmingham (1970); Barton (1972).

[9] One complicating factor that I ignore is the question of whether remedies are best understood as specifically enforced default terms of the contract or, instead, as obligations that are external to the contract that courts impose on parties who have breached the terms of their contracts. Nothing substantive appears to turn on the distinction. In this chapter, I follow most efficiency-based analyses of remedies in adopting the latter approach.

[10] [1977] Ch 106.

parties known in advance about the bombing and relocation, they never would have bargained for the replanting clause. Thus, the efficient breach explanation concludes that the efficient outcome in this case is for the contract to be breached.

In *Tito*, breach is said to be efficient because the *value* of performance fell dramatically. The more typical situation in which breach is said to be efficient is where the *cost* of performance, whether in direct costs or opportunity costs, has risen. Suppose a farmer agrees to sell 100 barrels of grain to a merchant. The grain costs the farmer £25 a barrel to grow and is worth £50 a barrel to the merchant, so the contract price will be somewhere between £25 and £50 a barrel, say £40. The contemplated exchange appears efficient. But suppose further that, before delivery happens, a second merchant, who values grain at £75 a barrel, offers the farmer £60 a barrel for all his grain. The efficient outcome now is for the second merchant, who places the highest value on the grain, to end up with the grain. This outcome can be achieved by the farmer breaching his contract with the first merchant, and then selling the grain to the second merchant.

The conclusion that the efficient breach theory draws from examples such as these is that it is sometimes efficient for contractual obligations not to be performed. The next question is how a legal system concerned about efficiency should respond to this conclusion. One possibility would be to expand the defences of mistake and frustration so that contracting parties would be able to set aside contracts they later regretted. The law could say, in effect, that a contract that ceases to be efficient at the time of performance is no longer binding. The difficulty with this approach is that people might be dissuaded from entering and relying upon contracts because they would worry that their contracts would later be worthless. From the perspective of contracting parties, one function of a contract is to assign to one or the other party the risk that circumstances might change.

Another possibility would be to design contract remedies in such a way as to promote breaches in those cases in which it was efficient. According to the efficient breach theory, this is the method the law has adopted. More specifically, the law is said to foster efficient breaches by making damages, not specific performance, the primary remedy, and then by setting damages at the value of the promised performance. If specific performance were the primary remedy, contracting parties could be forced to perform when it was inefficient to do so. The islanders in *Tito*, for example, could have obtained an order forcing British Phosphate to replant. By making damages the primary remedy, the law effectively gives contracting parties the choice of performing or paying damages. Holmes expressed this feature of the common law in his famous remark that 'the duty to keep a promise at common law means a prediction that you must pay damages if you do not keep it—and nothing else'.[11] As for the measure of damages, the idea here is that by setting damages at the value of the promised performance ('expectation damages') the law internalizes the costs of breach to breaching parties, thereby giving contracting parties an incentive to perform when, but only when, it is efficient to do so. Specifically, if damages were assessed at less than the expectation measure, there would be an incentive to breach in some cases in which breach is not efficient (when the cost of performance is less than its value). For example, if damages were assessed at £50 for the breach of a promise that cost £100 to perform, but that is valued by the promisee at £200, then the promisor will have a financial incentive to breach—even though performance clearly is efficient. By contrast, if damages were more than the expectation measure (for example, if punitive damages were awarded in contract) then parties might be dissuaded from breaching in cases in which the cost of performance is greater than its value. If the mining company in *Tito* faced the threat of paying punitive damages for its contemplated breach, then, assuming the amount of damages were set sufficiently high, it might have performed rather than have to pay such damages.

Finally, the efficient breach theory's explanation of those rare cases in which specific performance *is* ordered is basically that sometimes it is too difficult (and thus too costly) to assess damages.[12] This would be the case where loss cannot be assessed without evaluating a promisee's subjective or non-market preferences—as with the breach of a contract to deliver unique goods or the breach of a contract to transfer title to land (land historically being a form of unique good). These are, of course, exactly the kinds of cases in which specific performance is awarded in the common law.

Thus described, the theory of efficient breach nicely illustrates four general features of efficiency-based explanations of contract law. First, efficiency-based explanations often provide seemingly neat explanations of legal rules that appear difficult to explain on more traditional accounts. In respect of remedies, for example, an efficiency theory explains why damages and not specific performance is the presumptive remedy in

---

[11] Holmes (1897) 462.   [12] Kronman (1978).

breach of contract cases. Furthermore, an efficiency account of contract explains why a deliberate breach does not attract the sort of penalties (criminal or punitive) that usually attend other purposeful wrongs. In short, certain features of contract law no longer appear to be inconsistent or puzzling when efficiency (and not rights) is recognized as foundational.

The efficient breach discussion also casts light upon another feature of efficiency theories. Such theories make strong assumptions about human behaviour—in particular, assumptions about how individuals will react to material incentives. Efficiency theories suppose not only that the law represents a structure of incentives, but also that contracting parties will behave in accordance with these incentives (such as those provided by remedies).

The third and most obvious characteristic of efficiency theories (as illustrated by efficient breach) is that they justify the law in terms of the aforementioned incentives. The justification for 'remedies' is not to remedy the harm caused to the plaintiff by the defendant's wrongdoing. Instead, it is to provide incentives to other potential contracting parties to act properly (efficiently) in the future.

Finally, the above explanation illustrates the significant difference between how efficiency-based theories explain legal rules and how 'internal', or legal, explanations explain those rules. Holmes was a judge as well as a scholar, but judges do not typically describe contractual obligations as disjunctive obligations to perform or to pay damages. On the contrary, judges maintain that there is an *obligation* to perform a contract. A breach of that contract is described as a wrong—and this is the case even when, as in *Tito*, the efficient breach theory says that breach is desirable. Moreover, damages are understood from the legal perspective in exactly the way that they are described—as *remedies* for past wrongs.

In the next section, I examine each of these characteristic features in more detail by considering four objections to efficiency theories. I will continue to use the efficiency-based explanation of contract remedies as a test model, but it is important to keep in mind that nearly identical observations could be made about efficiency-based explanations of other contract law rules.

4.1.3. FIT OBJECTIONS

Perhaps the most common criticism of efficiency theories (as described above) is that economic reality is more complex than such theories assume. Once this complexity is taken into account, it is said, the theory does not fit the law nearly so well as first appears. We will examine this criticism using the above explanations of specific performance and damages as examples.

Specific performance

Consider the (admittedly basic) efficient breach theory's explanation of specific performance. As economists themselves have pointed out, it may be questioned whether a presumptive remedy of specific performance would actually encourage wasteful performance. This is because if performance of a particular contractual obligation is indeed inefficient, the relevant contracting parties will have incentives to renegotiate or 'bargain around' a rule of specific performance so as to reach the efficient result.[13] In other words, inefficient performance would not actually happen. Thus, in the *Tito* case described above, it is unlikely that granting the islanders the right to demand specific performance would have resulted in the mining company wastefully replanting the island. Assuming that the court had the facts correct—namely, that replanting cost far more than it was worth to the islanders—it would have been in both parties' interests to reach an agreement whereby the islanders waived their right to replanting, in exchange for the company paying them a sum of money in between the cost of replanting and the value of replanting. A payment within this range would leave both parties better off than if performance happened. Given the possibility of making a mutually advantageous bargain, economic theory suggests that the parties, or more likely their lawyers, would have made a deal.

The same reasoning can be applied to the grain example, above, in which a farmer vendor who was contractually obliged to sell his grain to one merchant receives a higher offer from a second merchant. A rule that specific performance is the primary remedy need not lead to an inefficient outcome in this case. The farmer could use a portion of the profits he would make from selling at a higher price to the second merchant to pay the first merchant to waive his rights to performance. Moreover, even if the original contract of sale were performed, the efficient result could still be achieved; the first merchant could resell the grain to the second merchant. If the second merchant does indeed value the grain more than the first merchant, such a deal would leave both of them better off. Thus, they would have an incentive to conclude just such a bargain.

---

[13] This is one application of the 'Coase theorem'—the idea that individuals have an incentive to bargain around (apparently) inefficient legal rules: Coase (1960).

The possibility of renegotiation or resale following an order of specific performance does not establish that a presumptive rule of specific performance is efficient, but it does make it more difficult to determine which presumptive remedy—damages or specific performance—is more efficient. In theory, the relevant resources can end up in the control of the party that values them most under either remedy. Given this possibility, the efficiency of damages as compared to specific performance turns on a range of factors not yet discussed. Three such factors are examined below.

One factor is the 'transactions costs' associated with each rule; these represent the costs, in money, time, or other resources associated with any renegotiation or resale. These are real costs that must be accounted for by any efficiency theory. The lower such costs are, the more efficient the outcome (everything else being equal). In cases like *Tito*, in which the reason that performance is inefficient is that the value of the performance has dropped, the transactions costs associated with a rule of specific performance will typically be greater than those associated with an order of damages. If damages are ordered, then in the typical case the parties should, in principle, need no further dealings (meaning that they incur no further transactions costs—but note the factor of litigation costs discussed below). By contrast, an order of specific performance would typically lead to further transactions costs as the efficient outcome can be achieved only if parties negotiate a deal whereby the promisee waives the right to specific performance. Thus, a damages rule seems the more efficient for such cases. But in sales of goods cases (such as our grain example), in which the reason performance (appears) to be inefficient is that a third party values the goods more highly, it is less clear which rule results in lower transactions costs.[14] Given that either the seller or the buyer can resell the goods to the third party, the answer depends on which of them is able to make such a sale at the lower cost. Typically, sellers are better placed to do this, because they are in the business of selling. But it is possible that the original buyer would be better placed— for example if she is a broker. As such, it is possible that a rule awarding specific performance might yield more efficiency in such cases than one awarding only damages. Overall, however, consideration of transactions costs would appear to support granting damages as against specific performance.

---

[14] If the contract involves a service that is desired by a third party, then the previous analysis applies because a service cannot be resold once it has been performed.

A second relevant factor when assessing the efficiency of specific performance as compared to damages is the dispute resolution costs associated with each rule. These are the court and litigation costs borne by the state and the parties. Again, these are real costs, and so must be accounted for in an efficiency analysis. This factor generally argues in favour of specific performance as a presumptive rule. The reason is that ordering specific performance is usually straightforward, whereas assessing damages is not. With respect to specific performance, the only question the court needs to ask is whether performance is possible. But a damages order requires that the courts engage in the often difficult task of calculating the plaintiff's loss. As well, if contracting parties are aware that specific performance is the presumptive rule, then, assuming that breach is established and that specific performance is desired and possible, there is little reason for the parties to even go to court. The legal outcome is clear.

A third, closely related factor, which again argues in favour of a rule of specific performance, is that courts may underestimate the full costs of breach when assessing damages. Well-known evidentiary difficulties associated with determining losses and (a related point) legal limits on the recovery of non-pecuniary and consequential losses may lead courts to undercompensate victims of breach. The likelihood of undercompensation then leads, according to the logic of the efficiency-based explanation of damages, to the encouragement of inefficient breaches. Of course, following an undercompensatory damages order (or in anticipation of such an order) the parties could strike up a new contract, thereby ensuring that the efficient performance occurs. But this step introduces additional transactions costs. Ordering specific performance avoids the possibility of undercompensation (and, for that matter, overcompensation) entirely.

The end result of taking into account these and other considerations I have not mentioned,[15] is that it is difficult to say whether a presumptive rule of damages or a presumptive rule of specific performance is the more efficient. From an efficiency perspective, each rule has advantages and disadvantages. In theory, these advantages and disadvantages could be weighed against one another to determine the optimal overall rule. But in practice this is extremely difficult, if not impossible, to do because of the difficulty of attaching figures to the relevant costs. A quick glance at the

---

[15] For example, the effect of the chosen remedial rule on decisions such as whether to enter a contract at all, who to contract with, how much to spend in reliance on expected performance, and how much to spend on precautions against breach: Craswell (1988; 2001).

economic literature on this topic over the last twenty-five years confirms this conclusion. The number and sophistication of the articles debating the respective merits of damages and specific performance is matched only by the lack of consensus as to which remedy is more efficient.[16]

Damages

The above discussion focused on the efficiency of awarding specific performance for breach of contract. A similar story can be told if we examine more closely the efficient breach explanation of the *measure* of damages awarded in contract. We have seen that awarding victims of breach compensation for the value of a promised performance appears prima facie an efficient rule. The measure of 'expectation damages' internalizes the costs of breach to the promisor, so that the promisor has an incentive to breach when, but only when, the cost of performance is more than the value of performance. Again, however, the full story is more complex than this. The above explanation focuses solely on the effects of damage awards on contracting parties' decisions to perform or not (the 'breach' decision). But a host of other decisions are also affected by the measure of damages awarded.[17] To determine if a particular measure of damages is efficient, therefore, it is necessary to consider its effects on these other decisions. In particular, it is necessary to consider whether the current rule internalizes the costs of these decisions to the relevant party (in the same way that it internalizes the costs of the breach decision). As I explain below, the rule appears not to do this. The end result is that it is unclear whether the measure of damages currently awarded in contract law promotes efficient behaviour.

One additional decision that is affected by the measure of damages awarded is what may be called (albeit awkwardly) the 'contract' decision. This is the decision to enter a contract in the first place (by making an offer and receiving an acceptance). Recall that in my initial explanation of the efficiency theory, I noted that, from an efficiency perspective, the basic function of contract law is to facilitate contracting—which is another way of saying that its basic function is to facilitate the contract decision. I further noted that the primary way this is done is by protecting persons who enter contracts from the losses that they might suffer if the other party reneges on the agreement. The significance of this for the efficient breach theory is that such protection is achieved by awarding not

---

[16] A sample includes Kronman (1978), Schwartz (1979), Bishop (1985), Mahoney (1994).
[17] See generally Craswell (1988; 2001).

expectation damages, but *reliance* damages. Reliance damages are equal to the costs incurred and profits foregone (from entering a different, but comparable, contract) in reliance on a contract. As such, they fully compensate for the loss suffered as a result of *entering* a contract—and so fully protect those who enter contracts. Moreover, granting more than reliance damages (i.e., granting expectation damages) is inefficient from this perspective. A rule of reliance damages internalizes to each party the costs of her or his respective contractual promise (i.e., her offer or acceptance). If a contractual promise is not performed, the promisor must bear the losses caused to the other party by virtue of that promise. Expectation damages, by contrast, require that the promisor pay a sum *greater* than the value of the losses caused by her promise. So far as the contract decision is concerned, a rule of expectation damages therefore has the effect of dissuading some parties from entering beneficial contracts. Another way of making this point is that the measure of damages applied to 'defective' contractual promises should be the same tort measure that is applied generally to statements that provide defective information (i.e., misstatements). From the perspective of the contract decision, a contractual promise is regarded (in efficiency theories) as a way of conveying potentially valuable information.[18] As such, the measure of damages for the promise being defective should be the same as the measure for defective statement of fact—reliance damages.

A second type of behaviour that efficiency theories must take into account when evaluating the efficiency of expectation damages is the amount of reliance that contracting parties invest in a promised performance (the 'optimal reliance' decision). With respect to this decision, the difference between the efficient measure of damages and the measure awarded by law is even more significant. Recall that promisees often rely on promises because doing so increases the value of the promised performance—which is efficient. From an efficiency perspective, then, the law should establish incentives for promisees to incur the optimal amount and type of reliance on promises. This, of course, has implications for the type of damages that should be awarded. As the law currently stands, a party may carelessly rely in situations when she knows that the promise is unlikely to be performed; she may do this because she is safe in the knowledge that she will receive her expectation damages regardless of her squandered reliance. Such behaviour is inefficient, but there is nothing in the current measure of damages to deter it.

---

[18] Goetz and Scott (1980).

To dissuade such behaviour, the measure of damages should actually be set at zero. This is the efficient rule because it internalizes to the relying party the costs and benefits of her decision to rely.

What are the implications of the above discussion? We have seen that an expectation measure of damages is efficient vis a vis the breach decision, but, at the same time, there are other decisions that will be affected by damage awards for which this measure is not efficient. There is no single measure of damages that will promote efficient behaviour with regard to *all* of these decisions. This conclusion does not mean that there is no measure of damages that will create the most aggregate efficient behaviour—in theory, it might well be that expectation damages produce the most efficient aggregate behaviour (if it could be proved, say, that the breach decision overwhelms all others). But making the necessary calculation is complex to say the least. I doubt that such a calculation has or even could be attempted. As was true in respect of the specific performance/damages issue, the necessary quantitative data is missing.

Conclusion regarding fit objections

The above discussion illustrates a general truth about efficiency theories of law: when the economics of the law are taken seriously, it is difficult to say conclusively whether or not the current rules are efficient. This is an important criticism of over-ambitious efficiency theories of the law. But it is not, in my view, a decisive objection to efficiency theories. Although it may be difficult to show definitively that contract law or even particular bits of contract law are efficient, it is just as difficult to prove the reverse. Moreover, even if the rules of contract are not the *most* efficient possible rules, they clearly do promote efficiency as compared to a regime of no contract law. Both specific performance and damages orders are more efficient than a rule of no remedies for breach. In broad terms, the existence of contract law undeniably facilitates the practice of making mutually beneficial exchanges.

Consistent with this conclusion, the leading critics of efficiency theories have, for the most part, not relied on the fit objection; indeed, some critics of efficiency theories acknowledge that such theories fit the law well.[19] I turn, then, to examine the other main objections to efficiency theories.

---

[19] Dworkin (1985) 284–85.

4.1.4. THE 'UNREALISTIC ASSUMPTIONS' OBJECTION

A second common objection to efficiency theories of contract law (and to economic analysis of law generally) is that they are based on unrealistic assumptions about human behaviour.[20] In particular, it is said that they are based on unrealistic assumptions about people's rationality and self-interest. As we have seen, efficiency theories regard contract law as a system of incentives designed to produce efficient behaviour. It is thus a central assumption of efficiency theories that people will change their behaviour in response to incentives. More specifically, it is an assumption of such theories that people will rationally pursue their own self-interest (bearing in mind that 'self-interest' can be defined very broadly).[21] The theory of efficient breach, for example, appears to be based on an assumption that contracting parties will not perform if the cost of performance is greater than damages.

That people do not consistently act as rational maximizers of their own self-interest is undeniable; indeed, economists rarely controvert this point. Many contracting parties will not contemplate breaching a contract, even if it would be in their self-interest to do so, because they believe that they have a moral obligation to perform. Similarly, psychological studies have demonstrated time and again that individuals are prey to irrational modes of reasoning. One example is the 'sunk cost' fallacy—continuing on a course of action simply because one has invested heavily in it.[22]

But is a conclusion that humans are sometimes irrational or moralistic fatal to efficiency theories of contract law? I suggest that this is not the case for two reasons. First, the assumption that individuals are rational maximizers of their own self-interest seems relatively robust when applied to *contractual* behaviour. As compared to behaviour that is the subject of tort law or criminal law, contractual behaviour is more likely to be self-interested and rational. In the common law world, contracts are exchanges, and most exchanges are commercial in the broad sense of the term. Indeed, contracting parties are frequently companies, which are

---

[20] Elster (1993); Ellickson (1989).

[21] Polinsky (1983) 10. A further assumption is that individual preferences are exogenous, by which is meant that they are not affected by the legal system. This is an important assumption: if what individuals desire is determined by what the law sanctions, it would be unsurprising, but not very interesting, to find that the law is efficient. But outside perhaps of illegal contracts, the assumption of exogenous preferences seems robust when applied to contract law.

[22] Thaler (1991); Kahneman and Tversky (1984; 1986).

required by corporate statute to act for profit. And even if they were not so required, they would likely go out of business if they failed to act in a self-interested rational manner.

The second, more important reason that the unrealistic assumptions objection is not fatal to efficiency theories of contract law is that efficiency theories do not require that everyone, or even the majority of people, act in a rational, self-interested fashion. It is enough that a significant number of people act in this way. An efficient legal system will look broadly the same regardless of whether the behaviour of 25% or 100% of the population is affected by incentives and disincentives. If the behaviour of 75% of the population is impervious to incentives, then, from the standpoint of promoting efficiency, the people in that 75% should be ignored as there is nothing that can be done to induce them to act efficiently. So long as the 25% respond to incentives—and on the reasonable assumption that there is no other way a legal system can induce the non-responding 75% to act efficiently—the rules can be said to promote efficient behaviour (if the correct incentives are provided). Of course, it is unlikely that the point of an entire system of law is to influence the behaviour of only a small percentage of the population. Faced with this conclusion, we might well ask whether a different explanation of the law exists. But the mere fact that a significant number of people do not react efficiently to incentives does not prove that an alternative explanation exists.

4.1.5. THE MORAL OBJECTION

The third and probably best-known general objection to efficiency theories of law is that they rest on unappealing moral foundations. Efficiency theories, it is alleged, do not provide an answer to the normative question about contract law because they do not actually provide a *justification* for contract law. For some scholars, notably Ronald Dworkin, this is sufficient reason to reject such accounts.[23]

Of course, it may well be asked why it matters at all whether a theory of law reveals the law as resting on immoral or amoral foundations. If our goal is to understand the law rather than defend it, why should it count against an explanation that it does not justify the law? The answers— both positive and negative—that have been given to this question were discussed in some detail in the discussion in Chapter 1 of the criteria for assessing theories (1.5). I will not go over that discussion here, except to

---

[23] Dworkin (1985) 286–95; see also Coleman (1982; 1988).

reiterate that on certain (though not all) plausible views it counts in favour of an interpretation of the law that it shows the law as morally justified or, more weakly but more plausibly, that it shows the law as resting on foundations that could be considered by some people as morally justified. According to the latter view, which I defended, it counts in favour of a theory of law that it offers a justification for the law that is recognizable as a *moral* justification. Insofar as the proposed justification is recognizably moral, the theorist will have succeeded in rendering intelligible a central feature of law, namely its claim to be justified.[24]

As we have seen, a legal rule or decision is efficient if it promotes behaviour of a kind that leads to an overall increase in the satisfaction of individual preferences. The moral foundations of efficiency, thus understood, are, in broad terms, utilitarian, in the classic or traditional sense of that term.[25] In classical utilitarianism, the good is understood as the satisfaction of the preferences or desires of all the individuals in society — usually described as the maximization of utility. Both classical utilitarianism and efficiency theories therefore evaluate actions according to whether they increase overall well-being, as well-being is understood by the individuals who make up the relevant society.

It follows from the above that the standard moral objections to efficiency theories are similar to the standard moral objections to classical utilitarianism.[26] Two such objections are examined below: the distributive justice objection and the rights-based objection.

The distributive justice objection

The distributive justice objection states that efficiency theories are indifferent to the distribution of welfare; all that matters on an efficiency account is the total welfare enjoyed by the society. Moreover, in practice, welfare is measured in efficiency theories in purely financial terms, specifically in terms of 'willingness to pay'.[27] The efficient breach theory, for example, assumes that efficiency is achieved when goods end up with those who value them most — which value is determined by the amount that people are willing to pay for those goods. Understood in this way, the overall welfare of a society made up of 100 persons will be the same regardless of whether each person has £1 or one person has £100 and the

---

[24] I note also that some defenders of efficiency theories, notably Richard Posner, have thought it important to defend the moral foundations of such theories: Posner (1981) Chapters 3 and 4, Posner (1990) Chapter 12.

[25] Bentham (1789); Mill (1861); Miller (1987) 530–33.

[26] On which, see Smart and Williams (1973).   [27] Posner (1998) 12–77.

rest nothing. On the same reasoning, if an overfed wealthy person is willing to pay £5 for a loaf of bread while a starving poor person can only pay £1, welfare will be maximized by giving the loaf to the wealthy person.

The distributive justice objection to efficiency theories of law is a significant one. But its force is greatly weakened insofar as our focus is limited to efficiency theories of *contract law*. This is the case because, even assuming that distributive justice matters, this value seems better achieved through forms of state action other than contract law, in particular through taxes and transfers.[28] Contracting parties can and do bargain around, or otherwise thwart, contract law rules that attempt to achieve redistributive goals. The standard example is rent control legislation. As has frequently been pointed out, rather than redistributing wealth between landlords and tenants, rent control legislation in practice typically leads either to run-down apartments, hidden charges, or to landlords simply switching their investments to more profitable uses.[29] A second example is the imposition of mandatory product warranties. Insofar as such a rule is adopted for redistributive aims, producers can frustrate this goal simply by raising their prices. The only effective way to stop behaviour of this sort is to regulate not just a contract's terms, but also the choice whether to contract at all—in other words, to take the activity out of the realm of contract law entirely. The conclusion suggested by these observations is that distributive goals are better solved through taxes, transfers, and other non-contractual schemes.

The rights-based objection

The most significant moral objection to utilitarian theories, including efficiency theories, is that they fail to take individual rights seriously.[30] Objectors to utilitarianism argue that a preoccupation with the 'overall' good of society may lead to the individual being abused or disregarded. Classic examples may be found in criminal law, such as when an innocent person is punished in order to prevent a riot. Such a result is so repugnant, critics claim, that any overall justification that permits such behaviour is no justification at all. In contract law, the examples are less dramatic, but the objection is the same. According to an efficiency theory, the purpose of remedies for breach of contract is not to force wrongdoers to remedy their wrongdoing, but rather to send a signal to future

---

[28] For a contrary view, see Kronman (1980)   [29] Trebilcock (1993) 4–6.
[30] Rawls (1971) 27, 29, 185–89; Dworkin (1978) 184–205.

contracting parties. The underlying motive is thus the same as in the utilitarian theory of punishment: the defendant is sanctioned in order to induce others to behave properly. This is illustrated most clearly by cases in which a party is required to pay damages following an *efficient* breach. According to efficiency theories, contracting parties who breach inefficient contracts have acted properly—they have done the efficient thing. Yet they are still required to pay damages.

A standard rebuttal to the innocent party objection is to state that, while in principle utilitarianism allows for punishing the innocent, in practice this is very unlikely to happen. This is the case, continues the rebuttal, because punishing the innocent would bring the whole legal institution into disrepute, thereby causing it to fall or at least to be less effective. Thus, the rebuttal concludes, there are good utilitarian reasons to prevent innocents from being punished. Such a response might be effective in the context of criminal law,[31] but it does not fit well with the subject at hand. Within our context—efficiency theories of remedies— punishing of innocents is not only permitted but it is even commendable, *according to the standards of the theory itself*. Unlike the criminal, the person who has performed an efficient breach has performed a *good* action. Nonetheless, being ordered pay damages penalizes that person.

A more promising response to the charge that efficiency theories of contract support the infringement of individual rights (as they are traditionally understood) is to argue that contract law does not foist obligations on citizens in the same way that say, tort, or criminal law does. Contracting parties *choose* to be bound by this area of the law; they should, therefore, be regarded as having consented to any consequences that flow from it. This response is essentially an elaboration of the idea (noted above) that contract remedies may be regarded in efficiency theories as, essentially, another kind of implied (in-fact) term. By ordering remedies, courts are doing no more than giving effect to the terms of a contract that the parties have agreed to. The parties have consented to the content of those remedies, and so to their imposition by a court.

The consent argument provides the strongest defence against the charge that efficiency theories allow for the violation of individual rights. But while no airtight refutations of it appear readily available, three brief comments show why it is not entirely unproblematic. First, the arguments

---

[31] But note that critics of utilitarianism are rarely persuaded by this response, either because they disagree on the facts or because they consider it a sufficient objection that in principle the theory allows individuals to be sacrificed for the general good.

the law because they rely on concepts, language, and reasoning that are radically different from those employed by legal actors themselves.

The idea behind the transparency objection is not merely that judges do not write like economists or that the economic reasoning judges use is less sophisticated than that used by professional economists. The objection, rather, is that legal arguments are essentially about individual rights and individual responsibility rather than about efficiency or any related concept. To be sure, judges sometimes explicitly consider the effects that their rulings will have on commercial activities, social welfare, and contracting activity generally. But in the main this is not the way judges reason. The difference, moreover, is one of kind, not of degree or depth of reasoning. The legal explanation for why breach of contract attracts damages is not that damages are necessary in order to deter future breaching parties, but that the defendant has caused harm to the plaintiff that, as a matter of justice, he ought to try and make good. The defendant has a duty in justice to make good *to the plaintiff* the harm she caused the plaintiff. From the legal perspective, remedies are viewed as just that— remedies, and they are presented as the means by which a wrong is remedied. From the efficiency perspective, by contrast, a remedial order is regarded as a signal to future contracting parties to behave appropriately. In principle, it does not even matter in this view that the defendant pays the damages to the plaintiff. The efficient incentives could be produced by requiring the defendant to pay a fine to the state, and for the state to offer compensation to plaintiffs.[36] There is virtually no point of contact, then, between the legal explanation and the efficiency-based explanation. The same point can be made in respect of nearly every efficiency-based explanation of contract rules.

That there is a difference in kind between efficiency-based explanations and legal explanations of the law seems indisputable. But does this matter? The relatively little attention devoted to this question in efficiency theories suggests that at least some efficiency theorists think all that matters is whether their theory fits the legal rules and decisions, and that it does not matter whether those explanations are consistent with how the law explains itself. Indeed, it is often presented as a virtue of efficiency theories that they cut through the allegedly obfuscating rhetoric of traditional legal argument. In this respect, defenders of efficiency

---

[36] From an efficiency perspective, the reason the law requires defendants to pay plaintiffs rather than requiring all payments to be made to and from a central account is, essentially, administrative convenience. This scheme avoids the use of a middleman—the state.

theories follow in the tradition of Bentham and, more recently, the American legal realists, in holding that the 'law in the books' is a poor guide to why cases are decided as they are.

But even if it is agreed (for the sake of argument) that legal explanations of the law are unhelpful, an alternate explanation that disregards the former altogether is clearly incomplete. As I explained in the discussion of the transparency criterion (1.6), to successfully explain a self-reflective human practice, such as the law, one of the things that must be explained—that must be made intelligible—is how that practice understands itself. Law is comprised not just of rules and results in cases, but also reflects a characteristic form of reasoning, all of which must be accounted for by a complete theory. A theory that reveals legal reasoning as nothing more than meaningless rhetoric fails in this task. Instead of making legal reasoning intelligible, the theory leaves us with a mystery: why do judges and lawyers explain the law as they do if the real explanation is entirely different? Indeed, it is this discontinuity between legal and efficiency-based explanations that explains the hostility many practicing lawyers and judges express towards efficiency theories of law. Legal actors are understandably uncomfortable with an explanation of the law that is so at odds with how they understand what they are doing.

If they wish to rebut the transparency objection, therefore, defenders of efficiency must offer an explanation as to why legal reasoning appears largely unconcerned with efficiency. One possibility that can be rejected is that legal actors are involved in a conscious conspiracy, a kind of massive fraud, to misrepresent what they are doing. Given the nature and number of legal actors that must be supposed to be taking part in the alleged conspiracy, this explanation is prima facie implausible.

A more promising explanation is that legal rules and decisions are the product of hidden-hand evolutionary processes that lead inevitably, and without conscious design or even awareness, to efficient law. One version of this kind of explanation is a variant of the Darwinian idea of the 'survival of the fittest'. It supposes that societies in legal systems with inefficient laws are less successful than societies with efficient laws, with the consequence that, over time, the inefficient societies will either be taken over by the efficient societies or fade away.[37] A second version holds that inefficient laws are more likely to be overturned by appeal courts than efficient laws because they are more likely to be litigated.[38] Plaintiffs have an incentive to appeal inefficient laws because the expected net gain

---

[37] Hayek (1982).   [38] Rubin (1977); Priest (1977); Goodman (1978).

is greater. By definition, an inefficient law precludes the exploitation of certain economic benefits.

Evolutionary hidden-hand accounts of this sort have focused on explaining why legal rules are efficient. But to rebut the transparency objection, evolutionary accounts of the efficiency of law must also explain why legal actors *explain* the law using different concepts; why, in Bentham's words, 'law shews itself in a mask'.[39] I am unaware of any evolutionary account that has attempted to provide such an explanation, yet we might suppose as to its general form.[40] Such an evolutionary account might claim that efficiency is better promoted if the true meaning of rules and decisions are not made explicit. The process of bringing efficiency issues to the surface might result in judges behaving inefficiently — say, by engaging in wasteful or inaccurate attempts to assess the efficiency of rules directly. Alternately, the prospect of citizens becoming disenchanted with the legal system might serve as an explanation for why efficiency arguments do not come to the fore in legal reasoning. Such a view, of course, is paternalistic and somewhat conspiratorial — it supposes that the entire citizenry is a collection of ingénues who must be shielded from the harsher facts of the world.

It is not easy to assess arguments made along the foregoing lines. They rely on difficult-to-prove — or disprove — empirical assumptions. For this reason, their attractiveness turns, to a large degree, on whether there exist other plausible explanations of the legal phenomena in issue — a question we cannot answer until the end of this chapter. But as I argued in 1.6, evolutionary and other hidden-hand accounts of law and legal reasoning are prima facie vulnerable to certain objections. The main objection is that in light of the sophistication and number of legal actors involved in legal reasoning it seems implausible to suppose that they are collectively in the grip of an unseen irresistible force. The proposition seems especially implausible when it is remembered that it is not merely judicial decision-making that is supposed to be externally controlled, but also judicial explanations of that decision-making. In other words, even when judges and other legal actors are consciously trying to explain what they are doing they are deluded.

Moreover, the concept that legal actors are meant to be unaware of — efficiency — is not an unfamiliar one. As I have noted, efficiency is little

---

[39] Bentham (1977) Chapter II, s.1.
[40] Using utilitarian explanations of concepts like 'rights' as a model: Sidgwick (1874) Book 4, Chapter 3; Hare (1982).

more than a contemporary term for utilitarianism or general welfare — concepts that legal actors and others have been aware of for millennia. In short, the hidden-hand that is meant to explain judicial reasoning must both be powerful and well-hidden to work as well as such arguments suppose. The only limitation on its scope is that it is not so powerful and well-hidden as to prevent proponents of this explanation from discovering it.

For these reasons, while the attempts that have been made to rebut the transparency objection cannot be discarded out of hand, such explanations face serious obstacles. Unless these obstacles can be overcome, efficiency theories will remain incomplete. The 'externality' of efficiency theories of contract law thus poses a significant drawback to such theories.

4.1.7. SUMMARY OF CRITICISMS OF EFFICIENCY THEORIES

This completes my discussion of the most important general objections to efficiency theories of contract law. Perhaps the first conclusion to be drawn from this discussion is that these objections operate at different levels. The most straightforward objection, the fit objection, cannot be evaluated without undertaking a detailed study of the economic effects of particular rules. This objection is assessed using economic arguments, often of great complexity. The morality and transparency objections, on the other hand, can be assessed only by taking a position on certain fundamental issues in general legal theory. These objections are assessed using philosophical, moral, and sociological arguments. Readers who wish to know more about those arguments are directed to Chapter 1 and to the sources cited therein. Readers who wish to look more closely at the fit question will find further examples of economic explanations in the chapters that follow. The other main lesson of the preceding discussion is that the most important objection to efficiency theories is the transparency objection. Prima facie, the externality of efficiency-based explanations of contract law leaves a large gap in their explanatory power.

4.2. OTHER UTILITARIAN THEORIES

My discussion of utilitarian theories of contract law concentrates on efficiency-based utilitarian theories because they are the most important and most developed examples of utilitarian theories. But other utilitarian theories exist. Like efficiency theories, they suppose that contract law is an institution designed to promote a particular conception of, or aspect of, human well-being, which it does by setting incentives. They differ from efficiency theories, and from each other, primarily in terms of what each regards as the valuable behaviour that contract law promotes. The most important of these alternative theories are described below. The discussion is brief because these theories share the same general strengths and weaknesses of efficiency theories.

4.2.1. PROMOTING DISTRIBUTIVE JUSTICE

In a well-known article, Anthony Kronman argued that at least some contract laws should be understood as designed to promote a particular conception of distributive justice.[41] More specifically, he argued that various rules could and should be understood as designed to promote the long-term welfare of the least well off in society. There are strong similarities between Kronman's theory and efficiency theories. Both assess legal rules in terms of their consequences on individuals' welfare. The main difference is that rather than asking whether contract law maximizes overall welfare, Kronman asks whether contract law promotes a particular distribution of welfare.

Kronman's article is sometimes thought to provide an answer to the normative question about contract law that is the focus of this chapter. But it is not clear that Kronman's aim was to provide a general justification for contractual obligations (as opposed merely to explaining certain limits on such obligations). In any event, the value of distributive justice —the focus of the article—is a weak basis on which to justify, or even to criticize, contract law generally. As I have already noted, contract law is a poor tool for altering existing distributions of wealth. Contract law rules can affect the distribution of wealth only insofar as people agree to make contracts. Furthermore, redistributive contract law rules can often be avoided by the parties changing other terms of a contract (e.g., changing the price of goods in response to the legal imposition of warranties), and insofar as they cannot be avoided in this way (e.g., if they are part of the rules on duress or mistake), their effects can be negated by parties choosing not to make contracts. To the extent that contract law rules are strongly redistributive, better-off parties have an incentive not to make contracts—or at least not to make them with those who are worse off. But the most fundamental objection to regarding distributive justice as an answer to the normative question is that it is difficult to explain on this

[41] (1980).

basis why a law of contract is necessary at all. If no contracts were ever made, the distributive issues that Kronman's article focuses upon would simply not arise.

4.2.2. PROMOTING VALUABLE RELATIONSHIPS

Some scholars have suggested that the justification for contract law is that it promotes close or special relationships between people.[42] In this view, the self-imposed obligations that contract law facilitates are valuable not because of their material consequences, but because they place those subject to them in special—and valuable—relationships with each other.

The moral ideas on which 'special relationship' theories are based were discussed in 3.1.4. Briefly, the idea is that promises, agreements, and other self-imposed obligations place individuals in special relationships because they require those subject to them to treat the interests of the beneficiaries as special and distinct. Making and keeping agreements brings people closer together. I further explained that special relationships are appropriately regarded as valuable, indeed as intrinsically valuable, because their existence is one element in a good life. The theory now being considered uses these conclusions as the basis for arguing that the justificatory aim of contract law is to promote special relationships by promoting the practice of making self-imposed obligations.

Defenders of this view have not articulated the details of how contract law promotes the practice of making self-imposed obligations, but in general terms, that explanation will be the same as the explanation offered by efficiency theories. Both efficiency theories and 'special relationship' theories value self-imposed obligations, and both regard contract law as a tool for facilitating the making and performing of such obligations. Thus, just as efficiency theories argue that the law provides incentives to facilitate the practice of entering (prima facie efficient) contracts, a special relationship theory would argue that the law provides incentives to facilitate the practice of entering (prima facie relationship-building) contracts. In both, remedies are awarded not in order to do justice between the parties, but to induce others to enter contracts in the future.

For those attracted by the structure and general approach of utilitarian theories, but uncomfortable with regarding efficiency or any close substitute as a worthy moral goal of the law, special relationship theories of

---

[42] Raz (1982); De Moor (1987); Smith (1996).

contract are appealing. It is important to stress, however, that because the basic structure and approach of special relationship theories is the same as that of efficiency theories, the main objections to efficiency theories apply equally to special relationship theories. More specifically, the objections that efficiency theories wrongly subvert individual interests to broader social goals, and that they are improperly 'external' to legal reasoning, apply equally to special relationship theories.

4.2.3. PROMOTING AUTONOMY

A third non-efficiency-based utilitarian approach justifies contract law on the basis that it promotes the valuable good of autonomy. More specifically, contract law promotes autonomy by expanding the range of options available to individuals. Contract law increases choice, and choice is good because autonomy is good.

In this view, autonomy is not the same thing as freedom of contract, at least in the sense that the latter notion is normally understood. Freedom of contract is an aspect of negative liberty, of freedom from coercion and other infringements of liberty. In a contractual setting, it exists insofar as individuals are left free to make or not to make contracts. Autonomy, in the sense intended here, requires not merely the absence of coercion (though that is important), but also certain positive conditions, in particular an adequate range of options. A person who has only one choice of how to live may not be subject to coercion, but she will be unable to exercise meaningful autonomy and hence unable to achieve an autonomous life. The importance of autonomy, in this view, is that it allows a person to be, in Joseph Raz's words, 'the (part) author of his own life' — and to achieve this it is necessary to have a choice as to how to lead one's life.[43]

The value of autonomy is also distinct from the value that efficiency theories ascribe to individuals being able to satisfy their desires. Both autonomy theories and efficiency theories regard the basic function of contract law as that of making available options that might not otherwise be available. But each offers a different moral justification for this function. Efficiency theories value increased options because they increase the possibilities for individuals to obtain the material benefits and hence the welfare associated with those options. Autonomy theories value increased options because this increases the possibility of autonomous action — regardless of the material or utilitarian consequences of taking up those options.

[43] (1986) 369.

Exactly what constitutes an 'adequate range of options' is a difficult question, but for the purposes of defending autonomy theories of contract it is not necessary to provide a definite answer. It is sufficient to agree that the range of options that exist in a society without contract law will sometimes be inadequate. If this is conceded, the argument can then be made that contract law is justified because it increases individual choice. The explanation of how this happens is essentially the same as the efficiency theories' explanation of how contract law facilitates (mutually beneficial) agreements, namely, that contract law makes available options that would otherwise be unavailable.

As should be evident, autonomy theories, like special relationship theories, are similar in structure and approach to efficiency theories. Each regards voluntary agreements as good things—albeit for different reasons (efficiency, special relationships, autonomy)—and each regards contract law as providing a set of incentives to, essentially, make it easier for individuals to make such agreements. It further follows that for those attracted by the structure and approach of efficiency theories, but uncomfortable with such theories' foundations, autonomy theories of contract are, again, appealing. But as was true of special relationship theories, the main objections to efficiency theories apply equally to autonomy theories.[44]

4.3. RIGHTS-BASED THEORIES

The second, and arguably still the orthodox category of answers to the normative question of what justification, if any, exists for contract law is provided by rights-based theories of contract.[45] Rights-based theories regard contractual obligations as obligations not to infringe individual rights, and regard contract law as giving legal force to such obligations. In this view, contract law is concerned with duties that contracting parties

---

[44] In *Risks and Wrongs*, Jules Coleman (1992) defends a non-efficiency based utilitarian justification for contract law. At first reading, his position seems to be that contract law's distinct virtue is that it promotes, via the promotion of market arrangements, political and social stability in heterogeneous societies. Stability, however, seems an unappealing moral foundation—repressive regimes can be stable. A close reading suggests that, for Coleman, another (and probably prior) distinct virtue of market economies is the more straightforward one of helping individuals to achieve their goals. This reading suggests Coleman is defending an efficiency theory. But an alternative interpretation, supported by certain passages (e.g. at 192), is that markets are also valuable because they expand our options and hence make an autonomous life more possible. If this is the correct interpretation, then Coleman's view fits into my last category of alternative utilitarian justifications.

[45] e.g. Fried (1981); Barnett (1986); Benson (2001); Weinrib (1995).

owe to each other rather than any broader social goal, be it the promotion of efficiency, social wealth, or whatever.

My explanation of rights-based theories begins with a general discussion of three issues: (1) the meaning of rights in rights-based theories, (2) the understanding of *contractual* rights in rights-based theories, and (3) the role of remedies in rights-based theories. Following this general discussion, I consider how the core features of contract law are explained in rights-based theories. The section concludes with an examination of the main objections to such theories.

4.3.1. THE MEANING OF 'RIGHTS' IN RIGHTS-BASED THEORIES

Rights-based theories of contract typically understand rights in the traditional or 'Kantian' sense.[46] Rights, in this view, reflect classically individualist values. This individualist perspective is expressed in four main ways in rights-based theories.

First, it is expressed in the idea that the *foundations* of rights are individualist. These foundations are typically regarded as either the protection of specifically individual interests (say an interest in owning property or achieving personal autonomy) or, following Kant again, as flowing from a particular conception of human agency. It would be inappropriate, in this view, to explain our rights as grounded in, say, utilitarian considerations of general welfare.

Second, the individualist conception of rights adopted in rights-based theories is expressed in the related idea that rights-based *duties* have priority over considerations of general welfare and utility, however defined.[47] To say that Jane has a duty to do X and that John has a right that X be done is to say that, exceptional circumstances aside, Jane ought to do X even if Jane could, say, improve the general welfare of society more by not doing X. John's right that Jane do X is not merely *a* reason that Jane should do X, to be added to and weighed against all the other reasons for and against Jane doing X, but is instead a reason that excludes the ordinary reasons for doing or not doing X.

Third, the individualist conception of rights is expressed in the idea that the *content* of rights-based duties is essentially negative duties. In particular, the basic legal rights in the area of private law are the familiar rights to non-interference with one's person, property, or liberty. In the strict version of this view, no one has a positive right *to* anything—

---

[46] Kant (1797).   [47] Dworkin (1978) 90–96; see also Nozick (1974) 30.

whether that thing is an object, food, a certain level of welfare, education, or whatever. Insofar as such claims are valid, they are valid on the basis of different considerations (and as such are not relevant to contract law according to the view discussed here). One way of expressing this point is to say that private law draws a strict line between misfeasance (harming another) and nonfeasance (failing to benefit another). An act of nonfeasance, such as failing to give to charity, may reveal the actor as lacking in virtue (the virtue of charity), but it raises no question of rights, and hence is not a proper subject for legal regulation in this view. Only misfeasance attracts liability.

A fourth feature of rights, as they are understood in rights-based theories, follows from the above. Because rights are essentially negative, they must be understood as correlative to duties: my right to non-interference with my property is correlative to your duty not to interfere with my property. If one person's rights have been infringed, then another person has breached a duty.

4.3.2. THE NATURE OF CONTRACTUAL RIGHTS IN RIGHTS-BASED THEORIES

Up to this point, I have said nothing about how rights-based theories regard the formation and content of a contractual obligation. This is because different rights-based theories regard the formation and content of contractual obligations differently depending on the answer they give to the analytic question about the nature of contractual obligations that I discussed in the previous chapter. Thus, theories that adopt promissory answers regard contractual rights as rights to the performance of a promise (3.1). Alternately, theories that adopt reliance-based answers regard contractual rights as rights to compensation for losses suffered as a result of induced reliance (3.2). Finally, theories that adopt the answer provided by the transfer model regard contractual rights as ordinary property rights (3.3).

In this section, I focus on the explanation provided by rights-based *promissory* theories. Rights-based versions of reliance and transfer theories exist,[48] but in view of the previous chapter's conclusion that promissory theories provide the best answer to the analytic question, such versions will be put to the side for the moment. It is worth mentioning, however, that aside from the discussion in this section, most of what I say

---

[48] Transfer theories, in particular, are nearly always associated with a rights-based normative approach: e.g. Barnett (1986); Benson (2001); Weinrib (1995) 50–53.

about rights-based approaches could be adopted by advocates of reliance or transfer theories.

Promissory theories, recall, understand contracts as self-imposed, promissory obligations. In my earlier discussion of such theories, I noted that the most important objection to them is an essentially moral objection (3.1.4). Stated in rights-based terms, the objection is that promissory obligations are essentially obligations to benefit others rather than obligations not to harm others. If this objection is accepted, then the legal enforcement of promises (and agreements) conflicts with the fundamental distinction in rights-based theories between misfeasance and nonfeasance.

While recognizing the significance of this objection, I argued in the previous chapter that it is not, in the end, sustainable (3.1.4). As a brief summary, recall first, that promissory theories, properly understood, are similar to transfer theories in regarding contractual rights as property-like rights. The difference is that transfer theories regard these rights as having been *transferred* by contracts, whereas promissory theories regard them as having been *created* by contracts. Drawing on an analogy to property law rules that specify how property rights are created (e.g., intellectual property); I then suggested that the best explanation of how promises create rights is a two-part story. The first part explains why allowing individuals to create promissory rights is a good thing generally. The second part, explains why promissory rights have to be in the form of rights; in other words, why they are promissory *rights* (and not merely ordinary reasons to act one way or another). I further explained that, for the theory to be convincing, promising would have to be a 'good thing' because it is intrinsically valuable, and not merely instrumentally valuable (valuable because of its consequences). An example of how promising can be intrinsically valuable was then provided by the 'relationship' theory of promising. According to this theory, promises both create and are constitutive of a valuable relationship between promisors and promisees. Promises do this because they oblige promisors to treat promisees differently from everyone else; in effect, the promisee's interests must be treated as superior to everyone else's interests. Crucially, making a promise in this view is not merely an (instrumental) tool for achieving a closer relationship (though it may also be that); it is a constitutive part of the relationship. Take away the promise and the relationship is not the same.

An explanation of promising along the lines of the relationship theory is not vulnerable, as are utilitarian explanations, to the objection that it cannot explain why promissory rights are *rights*. Promises have the value that they have only when they are treated as creating rights. If it were understood that promises could be broken sometimes (in order to do 'more good' than through performance), then they would never—and not just in a particular case—create the sorts of relationships that make them valuable. It is precisely because promises create duties to perform that they have intrinsic value—hence to deny that they create such duties would eliminate this intrinsic value. It follows that, although the above account of promising starts with the 'good' of promising, what is produced by a promise in the end is a *right* in the classical sense described above.

If such an explanation is correct, rights-based theories are consistent with regarding contractual rights as essentially promissory rights. In the remainder of my discussion of rights-based theories, I shall assume then, that contracts are promises or something closely analogous.

4.3.3. THE ROLE OF REMEDIES IN RIGHTS-BASED THEORIES[49]

The primary concerns of a rights-based theory of contract are to explain how contracts create rights and to define the content of these rights. But before we can consider whether the law is consistent with this account, we need to understand how the rights that it regards contracts as creating might be given effect in a legal system. In other words, we need to understand how rights-based theories understand remedies.

A preliminary observation is that rights-based theories cannot use the same concepts that they use to explain the creation and content of contractual rights to explain remedies. The idea that contracts create duties to perform does not imply a particular view about how courts should respond to claims that such duties have been breached. Of course, the courts should respect the same rights that citizens should respect. They should not break contracts or induce others to do this. But it is consistent with such duties for courts to refuse to do anything in the face of an actual or threatened breach of contract. The vendor who fails to deliver promised goods infringes the purchaser's rights, but a third party who fails to prevent the vendor from breaching or who fails to sanction the vendor does not infringe those rights.

It follows that to explain the kinds of orders that courts make in contract cases, rights-based theories must be supplemented by other justifications. The arguments discussed below are intended to provide such

---

[49] I discuss this issue in more detail in 11.1.1.

justifications with respect to two ways that a legal system might give force to a concern for rights-based contractual obligations: (1) by directly enforcing contractual obligations, and (2) by attaching consequences to the breach of such obligations.

Directly enforcing contractual obligations: The role of specific performance

One way that a legal system might give legal effect to contractual obligations is by directly enforcing these obligations. That is, a court might order contracting parties (on pain of punishment) to do the very thing they promised to do in their contracts. An order of specific performance is usually regarded in this way in rights-based theories—it is regarded as the direct enforcement of a primary contractual right. Rather than attempting to remedy the harm that a breach has caused, such an order is regarded (in such theories) as an attempt to ensure that the contract is performed.

Of course, an explanation of direct enforcement orders cannot merely state that contracting parties ought to fulfill their contractual duties. The explanation must further show how the law is justified in stepping in and *ordering* a person to do this on pain of criminal sanctions. Consistent with the harm principle (3.1.4), the law does and should generally leave people free to act as they please until and unless they harm others. A pre-emptive strike—in the form of the court *anticipating* the violation of a contractual right and then acting to prevent that violation—requires special justification.

A complete explanation of why and when the state (through the courts) is justified in ordering individuals to act in certain ways is one part of a general theory of the state. But for present purposes, it is sufficient to make the (uncontroversial) point that direct enforcement orders are justified when, and because, the defendant has shown herself unwilling to perform her legal obligations. The defendant is ordered to perform for the simple reason that she has shown herself unwilling to do so. The order is therefore justified on the basis that it is the only way to prevent a wrong from happening or continuing to happen. In practice, unwillingness to perform is likely to be established by the fact that the defendant is in court and has thus far failed to perform. But the reason for the order is not, fundamentally, that there was a breach, but rather that the breach (together with the fact that dispute is now in court) establishes the defendant's unwillingness to perform. In principle, therefore, direct enforcement might be justified in a case in which a defendant made clear prior to the date of performance that he was unwilling to perform. The last point underscores the fact that, understood in this way, a direct enforcement order is in design a pre-emptive interference with individual liberty. It is, in principle, justified because the court is convinced of the certain wrong that will occur (or continue to occur) unless it acts. But like other pre-emptive actions by the state (e.g., prohibitions against publishing defamatory material), it might legitimately be subject to further conditions. As we shall see, this qualification is important when explaining the actual rules on specific performance.

Attaching consequences to breach of contract: The role of compensatory damages

A second way that a legal system might give force to rights-based contractual obligations is to attach consequences to their breach. Examples of this approach are requiring wrongdoers to pay compensation or ordering them to be punished. An order of damages is therefore typically regarded in this way in rights-based theories—as an order that the defendant compensate the plaintiff for the harm caused by infringing the defendant's contractual rights.

The explanation of why and when consequences may legitimately be attached to the breach of a contractual right is grounded in the concept of justice (11.1.1). This is particularly the case when those consequences take the form of compensatory damages. Non-justice-based explanations of damages do indeed exist—recall the utilitarian explanation—but they are not useful for our present purposes. To incorporate them would amount to coupling a rights-based account of contractual obligations with a utilitarian account of remedies; this sort of approach is examined and rejected when I discuss 'mixed theories' later in this chapter.

Justice takes various forms (e.g., distributive, retributive, corrective). The form of justice appropriate to explaining judicial orders depends on the nature of the orders. In respect of contract law, and focusing on the usual remedy of compensatory damages, the obvious candidate for a justificatory explanation is *corrective* justice. Corrective justice is concerned with the justice of duties to repair or to rectify harms, and in particular with duties to repair harms caused by one's wrongful actions. Corrective justice might thus be described as individual or personal justice.[50] The

---

[50] Corrective justice can be contrasted with both distributive justice—the justice of schemes for distributing goods, income, and other resources—and retributive justice—the justice of punishment: Aristotle (1962) Book V; Finnis (1980) Chapter VII; Miller (1987) 260–63; Perry (2000).

general idea underlying corrective justice is that individuals have a duty to repair or 'correct' wrongful losses they have caused. What counts as 'wrongful' is not specified by the concept of corrective justice. Corrective justice is meant to explain (secondary) duties to repair rather than (primary) duties not to cause wrongful losses. Primary duties must be explained on other grounds. In a rights-based theory, those grounds are individual rights: a wrongful loss is a loss that arises from rights-infringing behaviour. Such behaviour includes, as we have seen, breach of contract.

I explore the meaning and value of corrective justice in more detail in 11.1.1. For present purposes, it is sufficient to note that, assuming corrective justice is indeed valuable, it provides a justification consistent with rights-based theories for a court to order a contract breaker to pay compensatory damages.

With these general observations in place, I turn now to examine the rules that make up the law of contract. For the most part, this examination is a summary of points explored in more detail in Part III.

4.3.4. RIGHTS-BASED EXPLANATIONS OF THE MAIN FEATURES OF CONTRACT LAW

A compelling argument can be made that the basic rules of contract law are consistent with the rights-based model described above. Stripped to its essentials, a contractual action involves the plaintiff either asking the court to order a recalcitrant defendant to do what he promised to do or alleging that she suffered a wrongful loss for which the defendant is responsible and ought to pay compensation. If successful, the defendant is ordered either to perform the contract or to remedy the wrongful loss, which in contract cases typically means paying the plaintiff a sum of damages equal to the value of the promised performance ('expectation damages'). Orders of specific performance appear, on the surface at any rate, to be exactly what rights-based theorists say they are: orders to defendants to fulfill their contractual duties. As for damages, both the foundation of the claim (the plea that the defendant caused the plaintiff's wrongful loss) and the nature of the remedy (an order that the defendant pay a sum of money to the plaintiff equal to the value of performance) appear consistent with the nature and correlativity of contractual rights and duties, and with the principle of corrective justice that is understood as giving them force.

Consistent with a rights-based account, the only interests represented before the court in a contract case are those of the parties; the court does not hear from representatives of the public or other persons whose future behaviour is, according to utilitarian theories, the law's real concern. Furthermore, the law is, in principle, interested exclusively in the history of the parties' relationship and in whether *that history* justifies the order sought. Thus, in contract cases, the courts' concern, broadly stated, is to determine whether a promise was made, what the promise said, and whether it was performed. Assuming that (as I argued above) the enforcement of promises is generally consistent with rights-based moralities, this focus is appropriate from a rights-based perspective. Significantly, the question of whether the order sought will induce contracting parties to behave differently in the future is, in principle, not relevant.

A court's inquiry in a contract case is also limited in other ways that are consistent with a rights-based account. In determining whether a contract has been formed, for example, a court does not ask whether the plaintiff was a good or bad person or, with rare exceptions, whether the purported contract contemplated a particularly valuable or worthwhile endeavour. No action lies for failing to enter a contract that would have been of great benefit to the plaintiff or even for failing to enter a contract that would have greatly benefited both parties. As one rights-based theorist notes, '[t]he focus is solely on whether two acts of will of the requisite kind—offer and acceptance—have occurred, not on the substantive satisfactions which the parties may have sought to procure committing themselves to these terms.'[51] The courts' concern, in short, appears focused on the rights possessed by the plaintiff, and whether those rights were infringed by the defendant.

Finally, but arguably of greatest importance, the requirement that the plaintiff prove that it was *the defendant* who caused the injury is consistent with both the rights-based view that rights are correlative to duties in private law and the corrective justice notion that a wrongdoer has a duty, owed to the injured party, to repair the losses he has caused. The law's response to breach of contract is conceptually consistent with this idea; courts respond to breach either by directly enforcing rights or by providing corrective justice. A defendant who has breached a contract is required either to do directly that which she was under a duty to do (to perform the contract) or to pay damages *to the plaintiff* in a sum equal to the value of the promised performance. That damages are paid to the plaintiff is emphasized because rights-based theories can explain why, from the legal perspective anyway, this rule is a fundamental feature of

---

[51] Benson (1995) 308.

contract law and of private law generally. In rights-based theories, unlike utilitarian theories, it a requirement of principle that damages be paid to plaintiffs. Ernest Weinrib summarizes the foregoing conception of private law as follows:

'Accordingly, the intrinsic unity of the private law relationship can be seen in private law's embodying in its structure, procedure, and remedy the correlativity of right and duty. The plaintiff's right to be free of wrongful interferences with his or her entitlements is correlative to the defendant's duty to abstain from such interferences. The plaintiff's suffering of an unjust loss is the foundation of his or her claim against the person who has inflicted that loss. The transference from the defendant to the plaintiff of a single sum undoes the injustice done by the former to the latter. Whether the issue is the ground of the claim or the mechanics of processing it, each litigant's position is the mirror image of the other's. Conceived in this way, private law makes a coherent juridical reality out of the relationship of doer and sufferer.'[52]

The basic structure of contract law then, seems consistent with rights-based theories. Whether the detailed rules that govern the day-to-day operation of contract law are also consistent is a different question, but it is one that is most conveniently addressed by considering the various 'fit' objections that have been directed at rights-based theories. But before turning to consider these and other objections that have been made against rights-based theories, it is appropriate to mention here that one objection to which rights-based theories are not vulnerable is a transparency objection (1.6). Unlike utilitarian theories, rights-based theories are internal to the law; the language, concepts, and reasoning used to explain contract law are, in broad terms, similar to that used by legal actors. Courts regularly declare that there is a duty to perform a contract, that this duty is owed to the other contracting party, and that a breach of the duty supports a secondary obligation to compensate the victim. Most strikingly, compensatory remedies for breach are regarded in legal terms as just that—*remedies*. From the legal perspective, they are awarded for the essentially retrospective reason that the defendant wrongfully injured the plaintiff and not, as the utilitarian explains, for the prospective reason of influencing future contracting behaviour.

Fit objections

The rights-based explanation just described is compelling, but it is not, of course, universally accepted. Of the various objections that have been

[52] (1995) 144.

directed at rights-based explanations, the most common and important is that (notwithstanding what was said above) such explanations do not fit the rules and decisions that make up contract law. This objection is often articulated as a criticism of the 'textbook' account of contract in which contracts are described as rights-based.

Two kinds of fit objections can be distinguished. The first objection is that rights-based accounts are too vague to explain much of anything. In determining, for example, what distinguishes an offer from a mere invitation to treat, or an unlawful threat from mere commercial pressure, concepts like 'rights' and 'duties' are said to be insufficiently fine-grained to explain what the law is doing in any but the easiest cases.[53] The imprecision of rights-based moralities is then usually contrasted with the alleged specificity of efficiency and other utilitarian moralities.

There is undoubtedly some truth to this objection. The building blocks of rights-based theories do not typically support mechanical formulae capable of producing uniquely specified answers to difficult issues. Weinrib's account of private law, for example, rarely descends below the level of general principles. It does not include a scheme of legal rights that even a very sophisticated judge could use to resolve hard cases, and it is difficult to imagine that such a scheme could be produced on the basis of their or any other rights-based theory.

But granting that rights have this feature, it is not clear this shows a weakness of rights-based theories. The indeterminacy objection typically focuses on the explanation of rules dealing with the formation and content of a contract (the rights-based explanation of remedial rules, as I explain in a moment, is relatively determinate.) Yet from a rights-based perspective, the rules dealing with the formation and content of a contract are essentially about identifying the existence and content of a promise. Assuming that (as I have argued) there are good rights-based reasons for enforcing promises, the questions that courts must address when using these rules concern the nature of promises, not the nature of rights. Various arguments deployed in the previous chapter, and in Chapters 5–7, show that the concept of a promise is instrumental in explaining formation and content rules, and rights-based theorists may therefore adopt these arguments.

Moreover, the alleged imprecision of rights-based theories counts against such theories only to the extent that alternative theories are able to explain the law in greater detail. Admittedly, efficiency and other

---

[53] Trebilcock (1993) 78–84; Shavell and Kaplow (2001) 1005–1006.

utilitarian theories appear, at first instance, to be capable of providing a fine-grained analysis of legal rules. The factors relevant to assessing efficiency can in principle be weighed by a mechanical, even mathematical, test for determining liability. But as I explained earlier in this chapter, *in practice* efficiency standards do not give determinate answers to difficult legal questions. In respect of nearly every such question, the empirical data needed is unavailable. Ultimately, then, competing theories of contract cannot claim to be any more precise than rights-based ones.

The more important version of the fit objection to rights-based theories is a straightforward charge of inconsistency. The charge is that various features of contract law are inconsistent with the idea that contract law rests on a foundation of individual rights. Four features of contract law merit special attention in this regard: (1) the existence of content-based limits on contractual freedom, (2) the existence of fairness-based excuses for non-performance, (3) the strictness of contractual liability, and (4) the weakness of contract remedies.

Content-based limits on contractual freedom

By content-based limits on contractual freedom, I refer primarily to the rules on consideration and 'unenforceable contracts' (understood here to mean contracts that are contrary to public policy, such as immoral contracts and contracts in restraint of trade, rather than merely contracts to do acts that are illegal *per se*). In broad terms, the difficulty with these rules from a rights-based perspective is that they appear more concerned with the object or purpose of an agreement than with its existence, the way it was formed, or any other rights-related concern. On the assumption that there are good rights-based reasons for enforcing agreements generally, it would seem to follow that all agreements that are made freely and that do not involve illegal acts or purposes ought to be enforced.

Starting with the consideration doctrine, an initial response is that the doctrine is difficult to explain on the basis of *any* general theory of contract, including utilitarian theories (6.3). The most plausible explanation of consideration, however, regards it as akin to a formality, such as a seal (6.3.1). Understood in this way, the doctrine is consistent with rights-based theories, even if they do not require it. According to this formal justification for consideration, the basic purpose of the rule is not to classify contracts according to their objects or purpose, but merely to assist courts in identifying promises that are seriously and carefully made. Assuming that there are rights-based reasons for enforcing promises, this purpose is broadly consistent with such reasons.

The rules on unenforceable contracts are more difficult to explain using a rights-based model. Such rules seem based not so much on a concern for the rights of the parties or of third parties as on a concern for the *value* of the activities required or promoted by the relevant agreements (7.3.2). More specifically, the relevant contracts are set aside not because someone's rights will be infringed, but instead, because the activities they promote are thought to be degrading, immoral, or otherwise not valuable. Thus, the rules regarding prostitution contracts, surrogacy agreements, and other so-called 'immoral' agreements seem plainly to be animated by concerns about the value of the relevant activity. These concerns may well be justified (in at least some cases), but they cannot easily be explained using the traditional notion of rights adopted in rights-based contract theories.

Fairness-based excuses for non-performance

'Fairness-based excuses' represent a second piece of evidence for those who claim that rights-based theories of contract do not fit the law. By this term, I mean essentially those rules that provide relief in cases of so-called unconscionable or exploitative bargains. In broad terms, such rules provide relief in cases in which one contracting party has taken advantage of the other's vulnerability, where vulnerability is understood as a 'state of necessity' (e.g., where the crew of an endangered ship agrees to a rescue by the sole available rescuer), or as reduced cognitive abilities (e.g., contracts made by minors, 'poor and ignorant persons', consumers). Such rules appear inconsistent with a pure rights-based model of contract because, on the one hand, neither wrongdoing nor lack of consent is established (if either were proven, then the terms of the agreement would not matter) and on the other hand, because they make the validity of a contract turn, at least in part, on the substantive fairness of its terms.[54]

One response to this objection is to point out that while that English law contains various rules of the sort just described, unconscionability is not a general excuse for non-performance (though it is in certain common law regimes, notably the United States). Thus, it is exceptional that exploitation *per se* is a sufficient reason to have a contract set aside.

A second, more important response is that many unconscionability cases are explicable on grounds that are consistent with a rights-based

---

[54] Broadly similar issues are raised by rules stipulating that one contracting party must assist or look after the interests of another, for example the duty of disclosure in insurance contracts or a bank's duty to ensure that sureties who are in a close relationship with the principal debtor obtain independent legal advice.

approach. Thus, in 9.2.4, I suggest (albeit tentatively) that cases involving cognitive defects are often explicable as cases of, essentially, 'presumed' duress, undue influence, or simple lack of agreement. In these cases, the substantive unfairness of the bargain functions basically as evidence of a presumed (but not yet proven) procedural defect. On the other hand, cases involving states of necessity are explicable on the basis that the disadvantaged party did not consent. In these cases, the function of the substantive unfairness requirement, I suggest, is to show that the lack of consent led to an unjust enrichment (9.2.6).

The above suggestions are controversial; they also fail to account for the widespread view that unconscionability is a distinct kind of defect. But even if they are accepted, they cannot account for all the cases in which 'fairness' excuses are successful. In particular, they have difficulty accounting for cases in which parties rely on statutory excuses (e.g., those found in the *Unfair Terms in Consumer Contracts Regulations, 1994*).

The strictness of contractual liability

A third feature of contract law that might be thought inconsistent with a rights-based account of contract law is that contractual liability is strict. It is no defence to argue that a breach was 'not my fault', and the narrowness of the frustration doctrine means that a plea of changed circumstances is rarely successful. These rules raise difficulties for rights-based models because, as I noted when discussing corrective justice, while rights-based defences of strict-liability exist,[55] the usual view of rights-based theorists (as exemplified in Weinrib's work)[56] is that liability for damages requires wrongdoing and that wrongdoing means fault. The corrective-justice based duty to repair is a duty to repair *wrongfully* caused losses, and it is not clear how someone can act wrongly (in the moral sense) without also being at fault. Admittedly, strict liability also poses problems for most utilitarian theories. Indeed, any theory that can explain why fault is normally a necessary ingredient of liability in tort law (as efficiency theories do) will have difficulty then explaining why fault is apparently not required in contract law. But this difficulty is acute for rights-based theorists, since for them wrongdoing is a basic requirement for civil liability.

To my knowledge, no rights-based theorist has addressed this objection squarely. In Chapter 10, however, I suggest that strict liability in contract may be explained on the basis that promissory obligations are in fact (and

---

[55] Epstein (1973).   [56] (1995) 147–52.

not just in law) conjunctive obligations. Specifically, promissory obligations are understood by those undertaking them to be obligations to use best efforts and reasonable care to perform the primary promissory obligation (e.g., to deliver goods) *and* obligations to compensate the promisee in the case of innocent non-performance (e.g., to compensate in the case of innocent non-delivery). If this is correct, then what appears to be a regime of strict liability is actually fault-based. In an ordinary breach of contract case, wrongdoing is established either because the promisor's failure to perform the primary obligation was blameworthy *or* because, although the original breach was not blameworthy, the promisor was at fault in failing to fulfill his secondary promissory obligation to compensate. According to this explanation, the reason promissory obligations *appear* to be strict is because fault in the second case goes without saying, insolvency being the only excuse recognized in law for failing to pay a monetary sum.

This explanation therefore reconciles the practice of the courts with the idea that fault should be a prerequisite to an order to pay damages. But the explanation is admittedly quite different from the one traditionally given by the courts.

The weakness of contract remedies

The fourth and probably most significant way in which rights-based theories of contract have been accused of providing a poor explanation of the existing law is with regard to remedies for breach of contract. The rights-based idea that there is a duty to perform a contract, critics claim, is inconsistent with the common law's permissive attitude towards contract breakers. Evidence for this position is said to be provided by the rule that an order of damages (not specific performance) is the presumptive remedy for breach, and by the rule that an intentional breach does not incur punitive sanctions.

Looking first at specific performance, I suggested above that, from a rights-based perspective, the direct enforcement of a contractual right is prima facie appropriate in cases in which an individual has demonstrated that she will not otherwise respect that right—which is normally proven by the fact of breach together with the fact that the parties are in court. On this basis, it would seem that specific performance should be more widely available. Of course, specific performance is not always possible or desired by victims of breach. But this does not explain why it is not granted whenever it is possible and desired.

One response to this objection is to argue that direct enforcement of the original contractual duty is, strictly speaking, impossible once breach has happened (11.2.1). By definition, what was promised to be done by a particular time can no longer be done by that time. According to this response, the most the defendant can do is to perform an action that is similar to the original duty.

The more promising response, however, states that specific performance is not a primary remedy because it poses a special risk to personal liberty. Consider that nearly all contractual obligations are, at least in theory, a personal service obligation; they are obligations *to do* something. Direct enforcement of such obligations has acquired a special symbolic meaning in post-feudal societies. In particular, they are experienced as akin to a kind of servitude. On this basis, it is arguably appropriate to require special justification before ordering specific performance. Such justification would be present where, say, the contractual obligation is an obligation to not do something (e.g., a restrictive covenant) or where damages cannot adequately compensate for the harm that will be suffered (e.g., unique goods) or where the obligation is entirely impersonal (e.g., paying a sum of money). It may well be questioned whether the current law evaluates claims for specific performance correctly, particularly in cases involving corporate defendants (11.2.1). But in broad outline, the above reasons for ordering specific performance are consistent with the cases in which specific performance is available in the common law. The more important point, however, is that the limits on specific performance can be explained as arising not because of the nature of rights, but because of general considerations relating to the appropriateness of pre-emptive judicial enforcement of rights.

Though less studied, the objection that rights-based theories are inconsistent with the law's refusal to punish deliberate breach is arguably more significant.[57] The law, like morality, normally treats intentional and unintentional wrongdoing differently. Intentional wrongdoing is normally punished—either through the criminal law or by punitive damages. Damaging another's property through lack of care is a tort, but damaging the same property deliberately is a crime. Thus, if breach of contract is a wrong—as rights-based theories assert—it would seem to follow that deliberate breach ought to be punished. Explanations of the law's refusal to punish breach that are consistent with rights-based theories can be constructed—for example, the idea that breach of contract is not a serious a wrong or that it is too difficult to distinguish intentional from non-intentional breach—but they seem too thin to support such a

---

[57] See Smith (1997).

clear and basic rule of contract law. In the end, the law's refusal to punish deliberate breach of contract remains a puzzle for rights-based theories of contract.

In conclusion, the above survey of fit objections to rights-based theory presents a mixed picture. On the one hand, a number of the better known fit objections turn out to have little force. On the other hand, significant areas of the common law of contract cannot be explained using rights-based criteria and in some cases are inconsistent with such criteria. So far as fit is concerned, the overall conclusion to be drawn, and bearing in mind what was said earlier about the 'structural fit' between rights-based notions and contract law, is that while rights-based notions seem able to account for much of contract law, they cannot account for all of it.

4.3.5. THE BEHAVIOURAL OBJECTION TO RIGHTS-BASED THEORIES

Rights-based theories do not rely on particular assumptions about human behaviour, and so there is nothing directly equivalent to the 'unrealistic assumptions' objection to efficiency theories (4.1.4). Nonetheless, there exists a close cousin to this objection. Though rarely articulated explicitly, this objection seems to underlie, at least in part, the hostility that certain scholars exhibit towards rights-based theories of contract law. I refer here to the idea that notions such as 'rights', 'duties', and 'justice' are too far removed from the world of commercial contracting to ground a realistic explanation of contract law. The decision whether to enter a contract and then whether to perform that contract is based, it is said, on financial considerations rather than notions of individual rights and duties. It follows, according to this view that the rules governing contracting behaviour are, and should be, governed by similar commercial considerations.

This objection is not a significant one. Although it is clear that most contracting parties *enter* contracts for commercial reasons, it does not follow that the parties always regard the obligations thus created in a self-interested commercial light. But even if they adopt this view, it does not follow that the rules governing such activities are, or should be, based on commercial norms. Should a murderer who murders for profit or to get rid of a business competitor be treated differently than any other murderer? To be sure, the setting in which a particular activity—be it making contracts, manufacturing products, or trying to destroy rivals— takes place may help in defining what counts as wrongdoing. But if the idea that courts should uphold individual rights and duties is valid, there is no reason to suppose it does not have a place in every sphere of human activity. If breaking a promise is breaking a moral duty, this is the case regardless of the promise's complexity or the particular motives of the promisor and promisee.

4.3.6. THE MORAL OBJECTION

In Chapter 1, I argued that it counts in favour of a theory of contract law that it reveals the law as based on foundations that are recognizably moral in kind or character (1.5). Judged against this standard, rights-based theories pass without difficulty. The idea that contract law vindicates individual rights is clearly recognizable as a *moral* justification for the law.

I also noted in Chapter 1 that some scholars go further, arguing that it counts in favour of a theory of law if it shows the law as based not just on recognizably moral foundations, but as based on the best (or at least 'good') moral foundations. Although I did not endorse this position, it is worth noting here that those who do rarely attack rights-based theories on this basis (rather, it is a criterion more often used against non-rights-based theories). That said, it seems likely that for at least some scholars the popularity of utilitarian theories arises from a deep scepticism about the coherence of notions like 'individual rights' and 'individual duties', at least when applied to the contractual sphere. In discussing the moral objection to efficiency theories (4.1.5), I observed that that there is a well-established view, encapsulated in Bentham's famous description of rights as 'nonsense upon stilts', that regards 'rights talk' as at best mere rhetoric and at worst a deliberate attempt to hide the utilitarian basis of morality. To say 'there is a right to do X' is, on this view, to say no more than that for good utilitarian reasons X ought to be permitted. This is not the place to debate the merits of this view, but I note that those who accept it *and* who think a good theory should rest on compelling moral foundations will conclude that rights-based theories are seriously flawed.

There is also a second, quite different, moral objection that might be directed against rights-based theories of contract law. This objection holds that an institution that is clearly and widely recognized as being of great social benefit cannot be explained exclusively through a rights-based theory. More specifically, when we think of contract law, we think first of what it helps us to do—not of what it stops us from doing. Unlike tort or criminal law, the bulk of contract law is presented not as prohibitions on behaviour, but as criteria for exercising legal powers; contract law rules are power-conferring rules. This perspective is not merely commercial actors' view of a contract; it is legal actors' view of contract law. It is reflected, for example, in the organization of contract law courses in law schools. Rather than teaching offer and acceptance, consideration, and so forth as elements that (like the torts concepts of duty of care, causation, and standard of care) establish responsibility for another's loss, teachers present these concepts as conditions to be fulfilled in order to create contracts.

It seems clear that, as this objection supposes, an account of contract law that entirely ignores the benefits that contracts help us to achieve is missing something. But the rights-based promissory theory defended above is not open to this criticism. As I have explained, that theory regards the good that promises (and hence contracts) help to achieve as crucial in explaining the force of promissory obligations (3.1.4). The only qualification, an important one, is that the good of promising remains in the background at the level at which contract law itself operates. Those adopting this view can therefore agree that contract law does much good, and that this good is part of the reason the law exists, but then maintain that at the level of explaining specific rules, the good of contracting is not a relevant consideration.

4.4. MIXED THEORIES

Not surprisingly, many scholars regard the choice between purely utilitarian theories and purely rights-based theories of contract as too limited. One response to this view is to point out (as I have done above) that rights-based promissory theories give a role to the kinds of values highlighted by utilitarian theories of contract, albeit not at the level of justifying individual rules. Similarly, it might be noted that utilitarian theories give a role to concepts of rights, albeit not at the level of justifying first principles. A second response, which I have also endorsed, is to acknowledge that no single theory can explain all of the law. In this section, I focus on a third response, which is the development of theories that fully integrate utilitarian and rights-based considerations.

The 'ad hoc mixture' version

What I shall call 'mixed' justifications for contract law are of two kinds. Probably the more common kind holds that the justifying mixture is an ad hoc and essentially unstable compromise. In this view, some parts of contract reveal utilitarian foundations, other parts reveal rights-based foundations, and yet other parts are a compromise between both foundations—but there is no overarching explanation for why contract law is divided up in this way. The explanation lies in the vagaries of litigation, judicial history, and other contingent factors.

There can be no question that this view of contract is at least partly accurate. It is highly unlikely that a rigidly monolithic theory could account for each detail of a human institution that has been created by thousands of people acting over hundreds of years. Moreover, the popularity of both rights-based and utilitarian reasoning generally makes it unlikely that either could be excluded entirely from such an institution. As such, the 'ad hoc mixture' theory is not really a theory, but rather a conclusion that no single 'theory' of contract law can explain everything.

The 'two questions' version

A philosophically more interesting version of the mixed approach to contract law argues that the mixture is not an unstable compromise, but instead a rational recognition of the fact that different answers should be given to different types of questions. This variant of a mixed theory has been little developed in contract scholarship, but well-known examples of the genre are found elsewhere in law, particularly in the literature on theories of punishment. Thus, in response to the unresolved impasse between deterrence (utilitarian) and retributive (rights-based) theories of punishment, H.L.A. Hart and others suggested that these alternative theories of punishment be regarded not so much as competing but as providing answers to different questions.[58] In particular, the retributivist theory, Hart argued, answers the question 'who should be punished?' (answer: offenders), while the utilitarian theory answers the question 'why punish?' (answer: to deter crime). Applied to private law, this sort of reasoning would suggest that different answers be given to questions regarding 'rights' and 'remedies' respectively. More specifically, the suggestion is that questions regarding the formation and content of a contract be determined on rights-based grounds, while questions regarding the remedies for the breach of 'rights' be determined on utilitarian grounds.[59]

Theories of this kind deserve serious consideration, but prima facie they appear vulnerable to an objection that is also made against mixed theories of punishment. The objection is that despite appearances, the mixture remains ad hoc. Even accepting that the questions 'what rights

---

[58] (1968).

[59] Theories along these general lines (though not focused on contract law and not limited to utilitarian justifications for remedies) are found in Birks (2000) and Honore (1988).

do we have?' and 'what should be done when our rights are infringed?' are different, it is not clear why the answers to these questions should be grounded in different, and even conflicting, moral considerations. It is not clear, in other words, why these questions are *morally* different. If we care about rights when determining our primary obligations, why stop caring about them when determining secondary obligations? This is true even if (as I argued above) rights-based theories must be supplemented by the concept of corrective justice in order to explain compensatory orders. As we saw, both the identification of the wrong to which corrective justice responds and the measure of compensation for that wrong can be determined, in this approach, by rights-based reasoning. Corrective justice responds to wrongs, and an explanation of those wrongs cannot be divorced from an explanation of rights.

One suggestion might be that a wrongdoer has by his wrongdoing forfeited his right to liberty, and is thus available to be used as a tool for utilitarian purposes. But if this were true it would be acceptable to order a defendant's legs to be cut off for a minor breach of contract. Whatever we might think of this possibility in the criminal law context, it seems wrong in principle in the context of contract law. Disproportionate punishment, like punishing the innocent, infringes the defendant's rights. The defendant is being used a tool.

4.5. FAIRNESS-BASED THEORIES

Another alternative to utilitarian and rights-based approaches is found in theories that regard contract law as founded, at least in part, on values that do not fit easily under either the utilitarian or rights-based labels. It is difficult to generalize about the theories that might fall into this group, but a significant number regard contract law as founded, at least in part, on values of 'fairness', broadly defined. In this category are found arguments to the effect that contract law reveals a concern that contracting parties not exploit or take advantage of each other or that contracting parties treat each other fairly, or in good faith, or even altruistically. Some of these arguments might be couched in utilitarian or rights-based terms, but the fit is not natural. Although behaviour that is unfair may be inefficient or infringe another's rights, a concern for 'fairness', properly understood, cannot be reduced to a concern for either efficiency or rights. Fairness is a distinct good.[60]

---

[60] Finnis (1984).

How much of contract law is explicable on such grounds is a difficult question. But it is not necessary to answer this question here because even the most ambitious 'fairness' theories do not purport to be *general* theories of contract in the sense that is the focus of this chapter. Rather than explaining why contract law is needed or justified, they instead explain why contractual obligations that are (presumably) justified on other grounds should be either limited or expanded by notions of fairness. For example, the idea that the rules on mistake and frustration excuse parties from performing when doing so would be unfair to them (8.3.2) does not tell us why contracts should ever be enforced. The conclusion that it is not unfair to enforce a particular contract is not a reason *for* enforcing that contract. Such reasons are only found in 'positive' theories of the sort provided by utilitarian and rights-based accounts of contract law.

4.6. CONCLUSION

The main conclusion to be drawn from this chapter is that while both efficiency-based utilitarian theories and rights-based theories offer prima facie plausible justificatory accounts of contract law—they are the leading accounts—neither category offers a perfect justification. This too should not be surprising—contract law is, after all, a human institution.

In respect of efficiency theories, I argued that while there may be few features of contract for which a prima facie plausible efficiency-based justification cannot be offered, there are also few features of which it can be said with certainty that they are efficient. The data needed to draw firm conclusions about the efficiency effects of the relevant rules does not exist (and probably never will exist). The more serious objection to efficiency theories, however, is not that they fail to fit the rules that make up contract, but that their explanation of the law is radically different from the way that the law explains itself—and, furthermore, this is an inconsistency for which these theories cannot easily account. Bluntly, efficiency theories fail what I call the transparency criterion because they cannot satisfactorily explain why the law presents and explains itself in terms that, from an efficiency perspective, are either meaningless or misleading. Viewed from the inside, contract law is not driven by efficiency concerns.

Rights-based theories have little difficulty explaining why the law explains itself as it does. For the most part, the legal explanation is recognizable as a less theorized version of the explanation offered by rights-based theories. The main challenge for rights-based theories is to account for a number of rules that, on the surface anyway, appear inconsistent with—do not 'fit'—the idea that contractual obligations are based on a concept of individual rights. I suggested that some of these apparent inconsistencies can be explained away or are equally problematic for efficiency theories, but others—for example, the law's refusal to punish deliberate breach of contract—cannot be easily explained.

As for the *morality* of these theories, while neither the concept of efficiency nor rights is immune from possible moral criticism, each of these concepts, at a minimum, satisfies the criteria of being a recognizable moral concept. Theories based on these notions can therefore account for law's claim to be morally justified. This is sufficient ground, I argued, for these theories to satisfy the 'morality criterion' for a good theory of contract law.

The second, and arguably more fundamental, conclusion to be drawn from this chapter is that rights-based theories are, on balance, more persuasive than efficiency theories or any other version of utilitarian theories. The basis for this conclusion is that the 'transparency' objection to efficiency theories is more serious than the 'fit' objection to rights-based theories. The former is a general objection, the latter is localized to certain parts of contract law.

This conclusion—that rights-based theories best answer the justificatory question about contract law—fits neatly with the previous chapter's conclusion that promissory theories best answer the analytic question about the nature of contract law. Let me explain. In my discussion of promissory theories in Chapter 3, I noted that the main objection to such theories is essentially moral—enforcing a promise seems to be enforcing a duty to benefit another, and so appears inconsistent with the harm principle. The response to this objection was that promises can properly be regarded as a means of *creating* property-like rights (to performance) where none existed before. I further argued that the rights created by promises are best understood as based not on utilitarian considerations of general welfare, but on the intrinsic value of promises to those who make and perform them. Only a non-utilitarian explanation is able to explain satisfactorily why promises are understood to displace ordinary considerations about whether or not a promised act should be done. Only a non-utilitarian can explain, in other words, why promises create promissory *rights*. The argument of the last chapter, therefore, was that both in terms of their creation and their content, promissory rights are the kind of rights that rights-based theories of contract see contract law protecting. The idea that contracts are promises is not only consistent with regarding contractual obligations as rights-based, it supports this conclusion.

Viewed from the perspective of the normative concerns raised in this chapter, a similar conclusion is reached. The rights-based account of contract defended in this chapter is consistent with those rights being promissory rights. Indeed, most of the discussion of rights-based theories assumed for the sake of argument that contractual rights were promissory rights. By contrast, efficiency theories (and other utilitarian theories) cannot easily be reconciled with the idea that contracts are promises. As I have noted at various points, it is of the essence of a promissory obligation that, exceptional circumstances aside, a promise should be kept even if it turns out to be inconvenient, inefficient, or otherwise undesirable to perform it. A promise displaces the ordinary reasons, including utilitarian reasons, which a promisor would normally take into account in deciding whether or not to do the promised act. This conception is at odds with the idea, basic to efficiency theories, that in some circumstances it is permissible, indeed desirable, to break a contract. In efficiency theories, contractual obligations are meant to be treated precisely as if the relevant parties are not under promissory obligations, but instead are simply under an obligation to do whatever is right 'all things considered'. Indeed, regarding contracts as promises is inconsistent not just with the idea of efficient breach, but also with the more basic idea that the intentions of contracting parties should be respected. If the law treats a promise to deliver a car as giving the promisor the choice to perform or not, then the law is not respecting the promisor's intentions. The promisor promised to deliver the car; the law has, apparently, changed the terms of the contract. Of course, if when we enter a contract we can be understood as *in fact* (and not merely in law) making a disjunctive promise to perform *or* to pay damages, then efficiency theories can be reconciled with promissory theories. But aside from the difficulty of explaining specific performance on this basis (is the promise 'to perform or pay or perform late if so ordered by court'), the suggestion is empirically implausible. In theory, contracting parties might understand contractual promises in this way, but it is difficult to believe that more than a minority of contracting parties actually understand themselves to have made disjunctive promises. To conclude, supporting an efficiency theory appears inconsistent with regarding promises *qua* promises as the focus of contract law.

PART III

Contract Law Doctrines

Part III examines the main substantive doctrines of the common law of contract from a theoretical perspective—offer and acceptance, consideration, mistake, frustration, and so on. The order of the chapters follows the sequence of issues potentially raised by any contract law claim. Thus, we begin with formation issues (Chapters 5 and 6), followed by content issues (Chapter 7 and 8) and performance issues (Chapters 9 and 10). The final chapter (Chapter 11) examines remedies for breach.

The issues examined in Part III sometimes overlap with those discussed in Part II. To avoid excessive cross-referencing, I have tried, wherever possible, to summarize the relevant points from Part II. The cross-references that remain will assist readers seeking a fuller explanation.

A final point is that it should not be assumed that just because a particular legal doctrine is examined in Part III that this doctrine is a part of *contract* law, properly understood. The doctrines discussed in Part III are included here because they are generally thought to be a part of the law of contract; they are found, for example, in nearly all contract textbooks. But whether these doctrines are all properly regarded as part of the law of contract is one of the main questions that I address in this part.

5

Establishing Agreement: The Law of Offer and Acceptance

This chapter examines the rules on offer and acceptance from a theoretical perspective. For many law students, the rules on offer and acceptance are presented as a largely mechanical affair, serving to describe the positive procedural requirements for a valid contract. Their often technical application should not, though, obscure the theoretical importance of the offer and acceptance rules. These rules provide the baselines for what is, and what is not, a contract. They form the core of contract law, and as such they are crucial in understanding contract law's theoretical foundations.[1]

This chapter follows most theoretical discussions of offer and acceptance in that it focuses upon *analytic* questions regarding the rules of offer and acceptance. Analytic questions, in this context, are questions about what (if anything) is distinctive about contractual obligations. This has been a recurring question throughout this book as I have explored which rules and doctrines properly attach to contract law, and which should more properly belong to tort law, unjust enrichment, or other areas of private law. In the case of offer and acceptance, I have already stated that this is a foundational part of contract law. But it remains to determine whether the offer and acceptance rules are consistent with the orthodox theory of contract which views contracts as self-imposed obligations (i.e., promises). If offer and acceptance rules could be explained using only a justification other than the upholding of promises—say, the goal of protecting reliance—promissory theories of contract would collapse.

The chapter itself proceeds as follows. First, the 'core offer and acceptance rule' is considered in light of how the leading theoretical views about contract account for it. Second, I examine the most important

---

[1] It is arguable that nearly everything else that is commonly thought to be a part of contract law is either only contingently important, not a part of contract law, or a part of offer and acceptance law. This argument is examined throughout Part III and it is, therefore, premature to assess it here.

qualifications to that core rule (i.e., the objective test and unilateral contracts), again from a theoretical perspective. Following that, I turn to consider specific rules regarding invitations to treat, postal communications, certainty, and completeness; all of these are rules that courts use to determine whether an agreement has been reached. Finally, in the fourth section, I discuss the common law rules on revocation and breaking off negotiations. This last discussion focuses on the implications of these rules; in particular, it focuses on whether critics of the common law are correct in claiming that these rules produce harsh or inequitable results.

5.1. THE CORE OFFER AND ACCEPTANCE RULE

Stripped to its essentials, the doctrine of 'offer and acceptance' provides that to form a valid contract an 'offeror' must make an offer to do or not do something (normally in exchange for something else being done or not done) to an 'offeree', and the offeree must accept (by agreeing to) that offer. This core rule is subject to important qualifications, and these will be addressed shortly. First, though, it is important to consider this core rule from the perspective of the leading answers to the analytic question about the nature of contractual obligations that were discussed in previous chapters (especially Chapter 3). More specifically, how do these leading answers explain the core offer and acceptance rule?

5.1.1. PROMISSORY THEORIES

The orthodox answer to the analytic question about the nature of contractual obligations is that contracts are self-imposed obligations; more specifically, contracts are promises or, if not promises, then agreements or something similar (3.1). There is a difference between a promise (or a pair of promises) and an agreement, and that difference may be relevant in understanding certain aspects of offer and acceptance law, but for the moment we shall ignore the distinction (using 'promise' and 'agreement' interchangeably, and adopting the label 'promissory theories') in order to focus instead on the link between offer and acceptance law and the general idea of a self-imposed obligation.

There is an evident connection between the core offer-acceptance rule and the idea of contracts as self-imposed obligations. The core rule regards an offer as an expression of willingness to undertake an obligation (typically made conditional on the offeree agreeing to do something in return). An acceptance, in turn, is regarded as expressing agreement to the terms of the offer (and thus typically is an agreement to do the requested act in return for the offeror's undertaking). The core offer-acceptance rule thus provides, in principle anyway, that contracting parties control the contract-making process: both the existence and the content of contractual duties are up to the parties. Contractual obligations are obligations that persons impose upon themselves.

This basic, but fundamental, point can be illustrated by contrasting the above view of contractual obligations with the standard view of tort and unjust enrichment obligations. My (tort) obligation to drive carefully and my (unjust enrichment) obligation to return money mistakenly paid into my bank account exist regardless of whether I wanted to incur these obligations. These obligations are imposed by law. In contrast, a contractual obligation to deliver a passenger to a destination or to pay money in advance for promised goods will not arise (according to the core rule) unless at some earlier point the person obliged expressed an intention to undertake such an obligation.

5.1.2. RELIANCE THEORIES

The leading group of alternatives to promissory theories about the nature of contractual obligations is 'reliance' theories. These theories claim that contractual liability is not grounded in promises or agreements, but rather that it is grounded in inducing another to rely upon you. For example, imagine I promise a factory owner that I will deliver a new machine to him but then fail to do so. Imagine further that in the meantime the factory owner has incurred expenses to prepare for the arrival of the machine and, in addition, refused an alternative offer to supply the machine—he has *relied* on my representation. It is because of such reliance, these theories claim, that courts award damages; the existence of a promise or agreement may very well have been what induced the reliance, but they are not essential in grounding contractual liability.

If such a reliance account is correct, the core offer and acceptance rule raises an obvious question. Specifically, why do courts look for offers and acceptances—and not 'reliance-inducing statements'—when they seek to determine whether contractual obligations have been created? The fact that courts use the offer and acceptance rule will necessarily result in some instances in which induced reliance will trigger no contractual obligations. Imagine a scenario in which a local authority announces that it will build a swimming pool in a certain location. Relying on the statement, a family of avid swimmers purchases a house near the proposed site. Should the authority fail to construct the pool, the family will have relied to its detriment, but, nevertheless, it will have no contractual action because no offer and acceptance has occurred. At the same time, there will be instances in which contractual obligations will be created despite no reliance having occurred. This is what occurs in many sale contracts —an offer and acceptance is made, but neither party exhibits any reliance until some time after the deal has been made.

In response to these points, defenders of reliance theories suggest that *in practice* the core offer and acceptance rule serves as a good proxy for what the law really cares about—reliance. Consider, first, that reliance is difficult to prove, especially when it consists of a lost opportunity to take up alternate contractual arrangements. In such cases, the offer-acceptance rule may stand as a practical way of identifying reliance inducing statements. In response to the fact that the rule allows liability to be created before reliance has occurred, theorists might respond that such reliance will usually occur shortly after the offer and acceptance.

As for situations where the rule *does not* protect reliance (recall the swimming pool example), consider that reliance based liability is usually conditional on establishing proximity or a 'special relationship' between the parties.[2] Just as a degree of proximity is required in the tort of negligent misrepresentation, the same must be true in contract if contract aims to protect reliance (3.2.2).[3] As such, the process of looking for offer and acceptance can be regarded as a means to ensure that an action to protect one's contractual reliance includes the requisite degree of proximity among the parties (a proximity that does not exist between the swimmers and the local authority). Parties who have gone through this process are, by definition, in a close relationship. According to reliance theories, the core offer and acceptance rule, therefore, provides the appropriate circumscription in which contractual actions should take place.

Readers familiar with Fuller and Purdue's explanation of expectation damages as a proxy for reliance damages (3.2.2, 11.3.2)[4] will recognize a similar line of reasoning in the above explanation of offer and acceptance. And like their theory, the 'proxy' explanation for offer and acceptance merits serious consideration. Nevertheless, it is not the most straightforward way to explain the core rule. In particular, if reliance-inducing statements are the law's primary concern, why do judges and others not make this concern more transparent? It is also puzzling why so little has been written about the somewhat arbitrary treatment of reliance-inducing statements: statements that satisfy the offer-acceptance rule will

---

[2] e.g. *Caparo Industries plc v Dickman* [1990] 2 AC 605.   [3] Spence (1999) 25–59.
[4] Fuller and Purdue (1936).

attract liability, but others that are quite similar will not. A large body of law has developed about precisely this issue when it arises in the context of an action for negligent misrepresentation. Yet in contract law, this issue is ignored.

5.1.3. TRANSFER THEORIES

The second alternative to the orthodox promissory view of contracts is found in what I described in Chapter 3 as *transfer theories* of contract. According to 'transfer theories', a contract does not so much *create* a right to performance as *transfer*, at the moment of formation, an already existing property-like right to performance (3.3). Contracts are thus analogized to acts that transfer ownership in physical objects—for example the handing over of a watch—with the proviso that what is handed over is an abstract right, not a corporeal thing. It further follows that transfer theories regard offers and acceptances as analogous to those physical acts that effectively transfer ownership in objects. Physical transfers of ownership normally require an intention to transfer and an acceptance of the transferred object. The process of offer and acceptance is regarded, in transfer theories, as satisfying these same requirements. The only proviso, again, is that what is offered, and then accepted, is a right to performance rather than a physical object.

Transfer theories of contract seem able to account for the basic legal requirement that contracting parties must, through the voluntary process of offer and acceptance, reach an agreement. If a contract is a transfer of rights, then, just as in the transfer of physical objects, the transferor and transferee must at some point agree to the transfer. The transferor must agree to relinquish the relevant right and the transferee must agree to accept it—and there must be a single point in time when these two acts can be regarded as coinciding. In a transfer theory, this point in time is when a valid acceptance is made. In addition, transfer theories are consistent with the law's disregard for reliance, benefit, or anything else that is external to the offer and acceptance process. In a transfer theory, all that matters is whether the parties agreed to transfer the relevant rights.

The main difficulty for the above explanation of offer and acceptance concerns *what* contracting parties are understood to be offering and accepting. When contracting parties make offers and acceptances they do not purport to offer to *transfer* a right (however described). What they do offer is to undertake an obligation. Contracting parties do not say 'I hereby transfer to you a right to the performance of such and such act done by me' (or anything similar), but rather say 'I promise (or agree, undertake, covenant, or will) to do such and such act'. The language of offer and acceptance is the language of promising, broadly understood, rather than the language of transfer. Moreover, such language is not merely a matter of convenience or style. A statement such as 'I hereby transfer the right to the performance of such and such future act done by me' is arguably not even coherent. As I argued in Chapter 3 (3.3.3), 'performance rights' are not normally regarded as things that can be owned—or that even exist prior to the making of a contract. Having the liberty to deliver my bicycle to you next week is not the same as *owning a right* to deliver the bicycle, which right can then be transferred like an ordinary property right.

5.1.4. CONCLUSION

The conclusion suggested by these observations is that of the three leading views on the nature of contractual obligations, the orthodox view—which states that contracts are promises or some other kind of self-imposed obligation—remains the most natural account of the *core* offer and acceptance rule. The next question is whether that account remains as compelling once we look beyond the core offer and acceptance rule. The short answer, which will not surprise anyone with more than a passing knowledge of contract law, is that it does not. The longer (and more controversial) answer is that, despite difficulties in explaining certain aspects of offer and acceptance law, the orthodox view still provides the best overall account of the offer and acceptance rules.

The remainder of this chapter is devoted primarily to defending the above proposition. I do so by examining the most important alleged inconsistencies between promissory theories and the (remaining) rules on offer and acceptance. A preliminary observation is that scholarly responses to these alleged inconsistencies generally fall into three main categories. The traditional response is to interpret the law and the model in a way that makes the law fit the model. The second response, seen in the work of Atiyah and Fuller and others, is to conclude that the orthodox promissory view of contracts is wrong, and to argue instead for an alternative view (typically either a 'reliance' or 'transfer' theory). The third response claims that the orthodox model of contract is correct, but does not attempt to explain the apparent anomalies within that model. Instead, this response argues that lawyers need to rethink what counts as 'contract' law. In this view, allegedly inconsistent rules find a home in tort, unjust enrichment, or another body of law. Insofar as there is a theme to the discussion below, it is that while each of these responses has its place,

the third response — reclassifying inconsistent rules as non-contractual —
deserves more attention than it has received.

5.2. BEYOND THE CORE OFFER AND ACCEPTANCE RULE

On the surface, promissory theories mesh well with the core offer and
acceptance rule. But a closer analysis of offer and acceptance reveals
certain features of the rule, as well as certain contractual situations, for
which promissory theories prima facie cannot offer a straightforward
account. Critics of promissory theories have drawn attention to these
alleged inconsistencies. This section will focus on these objections to the
promissory account of the offer and acceptance rule. At the same time,
the section will also consider other leading answers to the analytic question of contract theory vis a vis these features of offer and acceptance, so
as to determine whether they can offer better explanations.

5.2.1. THE OBJECTIVE APPROACH

A common objection to the idea that contracts are promises or another
type of self-imposed obligation is that such an idea is inconsistent with
the *objective* approach to contractual interpretation.[5] The fact that judges
interpret contracts by 'external', objective standards seems inconsistent
with an account of contract that declares obligations to arise from promising — an act that is said to be inherently subjective. If contracts truly are
based on promises, judges should look at parties' subjective or 'inner'
intentions. That they do not do this shows that promises cannot be the
source of contractual obligations as claimed by the orthodox accounts.

Scholars who draw attention to this apparent shortcoming of the
orthodox account of contract typically continue by noting that the objective approach is entirely consistent with the leading alternative to promissory theories — reliance theories. Indeed, these scholars (quite rightly)
say that an objective approach is required if reliance is to be protected. If
the aim of contract law is to protect persons who rely on representations
(as reliance theories claim), judges should focus on objective, external
appearances — because it is upon those same external appearances that
the parties themselves rely.

But while the objective approach is consistent with the core idea of reliance theories, these theories cannot claim to provide the only satisfactory

---

[5] Atiyah (1981) 21.

explanation for this feature of the offer and acceptance rule. More specifically, I suggest that, upon closer examination, the 'objective approach objection' is, at most, only weakly damaging for promissory theories.

The primary (but not exclusive) response of promissory theories to the objective approach objection is to point out that its force is greatly weakened once it is acknowledged that there exists a difference, both in law and in promissory theories, between the process for determining *the meaning* of a contract and the process for determining *the existence* of a contract. That the legal test for discovering a contract's meaning is an objective one is not disputed by promissory theories. But as I make clear in Chapter 8 (8.1.1), this feature of contract law is not problematic for promissory theories—the *meaning* of a promise *is* established by external evidence. The question at hand, though, concerns the judges' approach to establishing the very existence of a contract. So far as this question is concerned, the objection is correct to assume that judges should be required to determine whether each of the parties had formed the requisite subjective intent to make a promise. A subjective approach to this question is appropriate because (though the matter is not beyond controversy) promises can only be *made* intentionally—and a search for intent is necessarily subjective (3.1.1).[6] If I sign a paper that I think is a birthday greeting, but actually is a 'promise' to donate money, I have not made a promise, regardless of external appearances; we cannot promise by mistake or inadvertently. But the objection is incorrect so far as it assumes without question that the courts actually apply an objective approach to *this* question. It is not in fact clear whether the courts approach questions regarding the very intention to make a contract from an objective or a subjective approach. There is little jurisprudence addressed specifically to this question, and such that exists is inconclusive.[7]

---

[6] See Rawls (1971) 344–48, Finnis (1980) 308, Endicott (2000b) 162. For a contrary view see Goddard (1987) 269–70.

[7] Most discussions of the objective approach do not distinguish between the creation and the meaning of a contract. But the cases cited in support of the basic rule invariably focus on questions of meaning: e.g. *Smith v Hughes* (1871) LR 6 QB 597, *Centrovincial Estates plc v Merchant Investors Assurance Company Ltd* [1983] Com LR 158. Examples of a subjective approach to the creation question can be found in the cases of '*non est factum*', where the rule is that parties are not liable for signing documents if they did not understand their basic import: *Howatson v Webb* [1907] 1 Ch 537. Other examples can be found in cases that consider whether a party had the necessary 'intent to create legal relations', and with whether or not certain terms should be considered incorporated into a contract. The only study to have focused directly on the courts' approach to creation issues concluded that the courts often apply a subjective approach: De Moor (1990). A contrary view is expressed in Chitty (1999) 2–148 (but with no cases cited).

In the event that I am mistaken—in other words, that it can be proven that the legal test for determining the existence of a contract is objective— one can still imagine other responses that promissory theories might offer to the objective approach objection. One of these responses might be that courts adopt an objective approach for evidentiary reasons.[8] The idea here is that objective appearances provide the best, or at least the most trust- worthy, evidence of the internal (subjective) intentions that courts really care about. The objective approach, in this view, functions like the *Statute of Frauds'* requirement that certain contracts be in writing. The main limitation on this explanation is that it cannot easily explain why courts would ignore reliable evidence of subjective intentions in those cases when it is available (although a similar objection could be directed at the *Statute of Frauds*—since it directs courts to ignore reliable oral evidence of the existence of an agreement).

A second possible response to the objective approach objection is that that the test is not actually a part of the law of contract.[9] According to this response, in those cases in which an offeror's subjective intentions and objective expressions overlap (as they normally do), it is appropriate to conclude that that the offeror has undertaken a contractual obligation. But in those rare cases in which the intentions diverge, then insofar as the law holds a person liable for 'breach of contract', this liability is not actually founded on contractual principles. Rather, the liability is essen- tially reliance-based, and as such is either a part of tort law or closely related to tort liability. The 'offeror' is liable because he made a neg- ligent misstatement or, more broadly, because he induced the offeree to rely.

This explanation supposes that the legal description of the objective approach as a contract law rule is mistaken. But it is understandable that courts might make such a mistake. There is no obvious extra–contractual home for reliance-based liability that is founded on the objective approach. It is not equivalent merely to liability for a negligent misstate- ment, since it does not require a false statement of facts—and even if did the tort of negligent misstatement was not itself recognized until 1964.[10] The other reliance-based duties that the common law (arguably) recog- nizes have been shoe-horned into existing categories, in particular con- tract.[11] Of course, the current classification of the objective approach as contractual also has substantive consequences. Breach of a contract

---

[8] Treitel (1995) 1.   [9] e.g. Fried (1981) 62–63.
[10] *Hedley Byrne v Heller* [1964] AC 465.   [11] McBride (1994); Spence (1999).

established on the basis of this approach gives rise to contractual remedies (expectation damages and specific performance). To this extent, an objective approach is inconsistent with promissory theories, because if the aim of the objective approach, in this view, is to protect reliance, then liability grounded on it should similarly be reliance-based (i.e., reliance damages).[12]

Overall, it may be concluded that while the objective approach does not fit perfectly with promissory theories, it is a less serious objection to such theories than is often assumed.

5.2.2. SIMULTANEOUS EXCHANGES

A second possible objection to the orthodox view that contractual obligations are self-imposed is that it cannot account for contracts involving simultaneous exchanges. In many such exchanges—for example, buying from a vending or ticket machine, making a purchase in a store, or taking a bus—it is difficult to find an offer or an acceptance, and hence difficult to find a promise or an agreement. Putting money into a machine, handing over goods, getting on a bus, etc., are all intentional acts, but in most such cases the parties do not *agree or promise or undertake* to do anything. Rather they simply do something (e.g., hand over money, get on the bus, etc.).

Of course, judges purport to find an offer and an acceptance in these kinds of transactions. They say, for example, that stepping on a bus is an offer to purchase a ride, which offer is then accepted when the bus pulls away. They also often conclude that one of the parties has impliedly undertaken certain obligations—for example vending machine owners are liable for the obligations concerning quality, title, etc., implied by the *Sale of Goods Act* 1979. But, in most such cases at any rate, such instances seem clear examples of courts 'reasoning backwards'. In other words, the courts declare that a contract exists and *then* seek to find something resembling an offer and acceptance.

But what conclusion should be drawn from these observations about simultaneous transactions? The conclusion that is drawn most often is that the orthodox promissory view of contracts should be replaced by an

---

[12] A third possible response is that one of the things that people subjectively intend is that their words should be understood objectively. This response fails to address the underlying objection because the intentions that matter when determining if a promise has been made are not intentions about the meaning, but intentions about undertaking obligations. A person who intends his words to be understood in the ordinary way, but then mistakenly says 'I promise' has not made a promise because he did not intend to make a promise.

alternative conception that can account for simultaneous transactions. Thus, it is sometimes suggested that contract law should be defined as the body of law that deals with all 'juridical acts' by which a person is able to intentionally change his or her legal relations with other persons. Thus defined, contract law includes both executory agreements and simultaneous exchanges. Both involve juridical acts: in the former, the parties intentionally agree to undertake obligations, while in the latter the parties intentionally agree to give up ownership to certain things.[13]

The objection to this conception of contract law is that it would also bring within the category of contract various acts that arguably should be kept outside. Wills, ordinary gifts, acts constituting the abandonment of property, adoption, and changing one's name are just a few of the many examples of juridical acts that have never been considered contractual. To be sure (and consistent with civilian thinking in this area), there are links between the rules that apply to all of the above acts. The main link is a concern for individual autonomy; more specifically, it is a concern to give individuals the means to control their legal relations with others. This common concern is reflected in, *inter alia*, broadly similar rules regarding 'capacity' that are applied to all juridical acts. But at the same time, there are important differences between juridical acts; in particular, there are important differences between the justifications for legally recognizing such acts. There exist a variety of unproblematic explanations for why individuals are allowed to give away their property. The ability to do this is rightly regarded as a standard implication of ownership. But as I explained at some length in Chapter 3, the situation is quite different as regards the enforcement of self-imposed obligations. The power to put oneself under an *obligation* to give something away in the future cannot sensibly be described as an implication of ownership. A different justification is required. On the not unreasonable assumption that the categories of basic obligations—tort, contract, and unjust enrichment—should reflect the reasons for holding persons to be under these obligations, it follows that it is appropriate to differentiate between categories of juridical acts.

A second suggestion for re-conceptualizing contract law so that it can accommodate simultaneous transactions draws on the view, championed by Atiyah and others, that contractual liabilities are significantly (or even

[13] This view can also explain why unilateral contracts are regarded as contractual despite the fact that (as I explain below at 5.2.4) there is nothing resembling acceptance in such transactions. A person who makes an offer to enter a unilateral contract intends to change her legal relations with others.

exclusively) reliance-based or enrichment-based (3.2). Contracts of simultaneous exchange fit neatly into this view. When I give money to a
merchant at a market, I do so in reliance on the merchant's representation
that he will sell me goods. In addition (and arguably more importantly),
by accepting my money, the merchant has received a benefit. If the
merchant simply keeps this benefit, he will therefore be unjustly enriched.

This explanation of the source(s) of liability in contracts of simultaneous exchange is persuasive. But given the objections regarding ordinary contractual obligations as reliance-based or benefit-based (3.2.2), it
may be asked whether the explanation argues not so much for rethinking
the orthodox theory of contract law, but instead for rethinking the orthodox view that such transactions are contractual. Why not admit that
simultaneous transactions are not contracts at all because they do not
contain a genuine offer and acceptance? More specifically, why not classify them as what they appear to be on their face—conditional transfers
of property?[14] The party who initiates the exchange (e.g., by putting
money in a vending machine) is making a conditional transfer: she is
inserting the money 'on the condition that she gets her chosen item in
return'. Like other conditional transfers, this transfer can give rise to
legal consequences if the conditions are not met. But those consequences,
which Atiyah correctly identifies as reliance or enrichment-based, find
their home not in contract law, but in tort law (e.g., negligent misstatement) and unjust enrichment law. Indeed, the law of unjust enrichment
already gives relief in just such cases. If I give a merchant money *on the
condition* that he gives me certain goods at that moment, and if he then
fails to do so, he is regarded, on the standard view of unjust enrichment
law,[15] as unjustly enriched—and so liable to return the money if I so
demand.

If simultaneous exchanges were understood in this way, a large number
of transactions that lawyers have long regarded as contractual would no
longer be so classified. Conceptually, however, the change to contract law
would be small. Lawyers and judges are used to thinking of contracts as
formed by parties *undertaking* mutual obligations (this is why judges try
to force simultaneous exchanges into the traditional offer and acceptance
mould). In addition, the practical reasons for classifying such exchanges as
contractual have less force today than previously. Until recently, the consequence of classifying such transactions as non-contractual would be to
significantly reduce the rights of the parties to the exchange. The law on

---

[14] As suggested in Corbin (1952) s.4.   [15] Burrows (1993) 250–322.

unjust enrichment is only now emerging from a long period of neglect in the common law diminishing the need to keep these situations within the law of contract. More significantly, until *Donaghue v Stevenson*[16] was decided in 1932, purchasers of goods had no recourse against manufacturers unless they had a direct contractual link with such manufacturers. And until *Hedley Byrne v Heller*[17] was decided in 1964, purchasers similarly had no recourse in respect of negligent misstatements concerning goods except insofar as those representations were part of a contract. Under the old law, therefore, a benefit of classifying simultaneous transactions as contractual is that doing so provided purchasers with better protection against faulty goods, false representations, or simply not getting goods at all. Under current law, purchasers still have fewer rights under tort law and unjust enrichment law than under contract law,[18] but the difference is relatively small. More importantly, while such policy-based concerns will understandably influence judicial decisions, they do not support classifying as contractual those transactions that appear fundamentally non-contractual.

A final observation is that this view of simultaneous exchanges regards such exchanges, once complete, in the same way that transfer theories of contract regard contracts generally. Recall that transfer theories view contracts as instantaneous exchanges of already existing property-like rights (3.3). Thus, all contracts are regarded, in effect, as simultaneous exchanges—albeit the exchange contemplated is not, in the standard case at least, an exchange of tangible objects, but of incorporeal rights. For reasons explained earlier, transfer theories are unpersuasive when offered as general theories of contract (3.3.3, 5.1). But these theories do fit neatly with simultaneous exchanges. A simultaneous exchange genuinely is an instantaneous exchange of already existing property.

I conclude, then, that while non-orthodox theories of contract (reliance theories, transfer theories) can explain why simultaneous exchanges are thought to be contractual, the more persuasive view is that simultaneous transactions should not be regarded as contractual exchanges at all. This view is consistent with the orthodox understanding of contracts as self-imposed, promissory obligations.

---

[16] [1932] AC 632.   [17] [1964] AC 465.

[18] Contractual remedies are more generous than awards of restitution under unjust enrichment law; there are limits on the recovery of pure economic loss in tort, and the *Sale of Goods Act* 1979 implies warranties of quality, etc. into sales contracts.

5.2.3. THE KIND OF SELF-IMPOSED OBLIGATION: THE BILATERALITY OF CONTRACTS

Throughout the preceding discussion, I have used the terms 'promise', 'agreement', and 'undertaking' interchangeably when describing contracts as self-imposed obligations. And, for many purposes, these terms are indeed interchangeable. But it is important to recognize that these terms are not identical—and the distinction between them becomes significant in resolving another source of tension between promissory theories and the rules on offer and acceptance.[19] This tension stems from that fact that promises are essentially unilateral acts while contracts, by their nature, are bilateral.

The orthodox view holds that contracts are promises or, more accurately, pairs of promises. Promises, as explained earlier, are essentially unilateral acts. Ordinary language demonstrates the unilateral nature of a promise: We say, '*Jane* made a promise'. The language of contract, on the other hand, is prima facie bilateral: '*Jane and Tom* made a contract'. Of course, both a promisor and a promisee are necessary to make a promise because, unlike an oath, a promise cannot be made 'in the air'.[20] The promisee, though, is only a passive recipient in the process; ordinary language is again instructive: We say *Jane makes* a promise to John to do X, and not *Jane and Tom make* a promise to Tom that Jane will do X.

An immediate difficulty therefore arises when we try to use promises to explain the offer and acceptance process: the act of accepting an *offer* in a common law contract does not look anything like the act of 'accepting' a *promise*. What the offeree accepts (in the legal sense) is a proposal by the offeror, the terms of which proposal bind the offeror *and* the offeree to do something for one another. In a contract for the sale of goods, for example, the purchaser does not merely accept the vendor's offer to deliver goods on a certain date. Rather, she will only be able to accept this proposal by agreeing *in return* to pay for those goods. A single promise cannot give life to the contract, but instead *both* parties must agree to do something. Admittedly, the requirement that each party to a contract must agree to something for the other is explained not as an aspect of the offer and acceptance rules, but rather as a consequence of the consideration rule. But even without the consideration rule, the overwhelming majority of contracts are bilateral by their very nature. So the question remains as to how promissory models can account for bilateral contracts.

---

[19] See generally, De Moor (1987); Penner (1996).
[20] Fried (1981) 40–41; Stoljar (1988); Atiyah (1981) 157–60.

The usual explanation given by those who defend the promissory model is that a contract in which each party agrees to do something for the other party is a pair of conditional promises. Each party has made a promise, conditional on the other party's promise. The difficulty with this suggestion is that if each promise is conditional on the other, neither party is under an obligation to do anything.[21] The purchaser's promise to pay £50 for goods is conditional on the vendor delivering the goods. But the vendor's promise to deliver the goods is conditional on the purchaser's promise to pay £50. Explained in this way, contracts create endless loops of obligations.

For scholars who believe that contracts are self-imposed obligations, the obvious response to this point is to conclude that contracts are agreements rather than promises. An agreement is best understood as a joint undertaking or mutual project to bring about a future state of affairs.[22] The terms of the agreement specify what each party to the agreement will do. When you agree, you agree *to do something;* and when you have an agreement *each party agrees to do something.* Because each party to the agreement is bound, it takes two active participants to make an agreement. Moreover, just as the outcome of the process of offer and acceptance is a single thing—a contract—the process of coming to agreement creates a single thing—an agreement. As described by James Penner,

'An agreement contemplates a future state of affairs both parties to which are bound to bring into existence, though their actions in doing so are differently defined and set out. The obligations of the parties to bring this state of affairs are not *conditional* but *defeasible.*'[23]

The concept of agreement thus fits the standard model of the bilateral contract better than does the concept of a promise. But—and this is the other main point I wish to make in this section—this conclusion does not seem particularly significant for understanding the nature of contract law. The existence of various exceptions to the consideration rule—notably contracts under seal and unilateral contracts (6.3)—suggests that not all contracts are agreements. Equally, it is clear that not all agreements are contracts. An agreement whereby X and Y agree to donate money or services to A will only satisfy the consideration requirement if

---

[21] Penner (1996) 6.
[22] A second meaning of 'agreement' is to 'agree in judgment' (e.g. 'I agree that Renoir is an overrated artist'). This meaning does not concern us.
[23] (1996) 333–34.

X and Y each agree to make the donation *in return* for the other party's undertaking—which need not be the case. Thus, while it is seems clear that most contracts are agreements rather than mere promises, there does not seem to be anything in the rules of offer and acceptance or consideration that preclude the enforcement of promises *per se*. Most contracts are agreements, but in principle promises seem also to be enforceable. More to the point, in a legal system without the consideration rule (such as civil law systems) mere promises would be enforceable.[24]

That a legal system that enforces agreements would also enforce promises (or vice versa) makes sense. The arguments canvassed in Chapter 3 for enforcing promises apply to agreements, and the reverse is also true. Promises and agreements are created in similar ways. Promises are created by intentionally communicating an intention to undertake an obligation. Agreements are created by two parties intentionally communicating an intention to undertake obligations. It might be argued that agreements are more valuable than promises because they involve co-operative activity between two persons. But this difference is a matter of degree, not kind. The essential element of both promises and agreements from the point of view of the person to whom the relevant obligation is owed is that the person owing the obligation has undertaken it voluntarily. Whatever value agreements are thought to possess (e.g., creating special relationships, facilitating efficient transfers of property) promises also possess (3.1.4, 6.3.2). In short, while there may be reasons to sometimes draw a distinction between agreements and (mere) promises (which reasons I consider when I discuss the consideration doctrine in 6.3), there does not seem to be anything in the nature of promises or agreements *per se* that argues for enforcing one but not the other.

Finally, the relative unimportance, from a theoretical perspective, of the distinction between promises and agreements is consistent with the tendency of judges to use the language of both promises and agreements

---

[24] An interesting question is whether it follows from the above that eliminating the consideration rule would make the acceptance requirement redundant in the case of (mere) promises. There would appear to be at least two reasons for maintaining the requirement (as is done in civil law systems). First, while the role of the promisee in the creation of promissory obligations is essentially passive, it is arguable that at a minimum the promisee should be given an opportunity to reject an unwanted promise. An acceptance requirement ensures this opportunity is given. Second, an acceptance requirement could fulfil a formal function (6.1), by making clear that the promisee has received ('heard') the promise, as well as by helping to impress on the promisor the significance of the promise. This is an important function in the case of (mere) promises, since they are, by definition, gratuitous, and so not usually made in commercial settings.

when describing contracts. When judges refer to a standard bilateral contract they typically describe it as an agreement. Offers to make a unilateral contract, on the other hand, are usually described as promises. This change in terminology usually goes unnoticed. Moreover, when judges refer to the individual parties who have formed a contractual *agreement* they often describe them as promisors and promisees. The explanation for this apparent inconsistency would appear to be simply that the English language does not contain the words 'agreeor' or 'agreee' or anything similar. The consequent mixing of terminology is confusing,[25] but it is consistent with the idea that promises and agreements are similar kinds of things.

I conclude, then, that while many contracts cannot be explained using a promissory model, strictly defined, such contracts are explicable if such models are understood to refer to the broader category of self-imposed obligations—within which category is included agreements. This is the sense in which the term 'promissory' is used generally in this book.

5.2.4. 'ACCEPTANCE' BY CONDUCT: THE STATUS OF UNILATERAL CONTRACTS

A 'unilateral contract' arises when one party makes an offer to pay or benefit another party in the event that the other party performs a particular act. For example, a unilateral contract is formed when a person returns property in response to an offer of reward, or when a buyer sends an order in response to a 'standing offer' to sell goods, or when a real estate agent sells a house on the promise of a commission. The distinctive feature of unilateral contracts—and the reason they are important from a theoretical perspective—is that 'acceptance' takes the form not of *agreeing* to do an act, but rather of *actually doing* an act requested by the offeror.

The first theoretical point to be made about unilateral contracts is that their legal recognition supports the argument made in the last section that not all contracts are agreements. A unilateral contract is not an agreement for the simple reason that the 'offeree' at no point agrees to do the requested act.[26] Rather, the offeree simply performs the act. Consistent with this conclusion, the offer in such cases is not accepted in the usual meaning of this requirement. To be sure, judges say that performance is

---

[25] An alternative would be to adopt the practice found in many civil law regimes of referring to contracting parties as 'creditors' and 'debtors' (the distinction turning on whether the party owes or is owed the obligation in question).

[26] See generally Tiersma (1992).

acceptance. But this seems an evident fiction. I do not look for a lost dog in order to *accept* the owner's promise to pay a reward for finding the dog; I look for the dog to satisfy the conditions of the reward. Moreover, it is a strange 'offer' that cannot be accepted by saying 'I accept' or something similar—yet the 'offeree' of an offer of a unilateral contract cannot 'accept' other than by performing an act.

The communication made by the offeror in a unilateral contract is thus best described as a conditional promise (of the kind that is sometimes wrongly assumed to represent all contracts): X promises to pay Y £100 *if* Y does such and such an act. From the perspective of promissory models, such promises are, in principle, unproblematic. They should be enforced for the usual reasons that promises (and agreements) should be enforced. That said, there are two aspects of the courts' approach to such promises that raise difficult questions: (1) the rule that such promises may be revoked prior to performance, and (2) the rule that the 'offeree' must have knowledge of the offer when performing.

Revoking offers to enter unilateral contracts

The first puzzle posed by unilateral contracts is why offers to make such contracts may be revoked at any point prior to performance. Performance, as I said, cannot plausibly be described as acceptance. On the other hand, a clear oral or written acceptance of such an offer does not qualify as acceptance. More generally, it is not clear why acceptance in any form is required to make such offers enforceable. Given that these offers are conditional promises, there is nothing for promisees to actually *accept*. At most, promisees might communicate that they have heard the promise and intend to act upon it.

It might be thought that the explanation of the performance requirement lies not in the logic of offer and acceptance, but rather in the consideration rule. The requirement of mutual consideration is said to be satisfied in a unilateral contract by the performance of the requested act— and not before. Thus, it might be argued that the reason the offer is not binding until performance is because the consideration requirement is not satisfied until performance. But this way of characterizing perform-ance also seems based on a fiction (6.3.3). Performance does not satisfy the standard test for consideration because, by definition, it is not done *in exchange* for the promise. The performance happens *after* the promise. It is a consequence of the promise, not a *quid pro quo* for it.

I suggest that this rule cannot, in the end, be explained using a promis-sory model. Even it is agreed that a promise requires both acceptance and consideration to bind, performance does not satisfy either of these requirements. Instead, and for reasons that I discuss when examining the consideration rule (6.3.3), this rule seems best explained on the basis of a concern for protecting induced reliance. The significance of performance is that it constitutes clear reliance on the promise. In view of the general objections to reliance-based liability (3.2.1), it may be queried whether the current rule is justified. In this regard, it is interesting to note that some legal systems stipulate that offers to enter unilateral contracts can be binding from the moment they are made.[27] Be that as it may, the current English rule is evidence that promissory theories cannot explain all features of offer and acceptance.

A final observation before leaving this feature of unilateral contracts is that even reliance theories have difficulty explaining the rule that acceptance does not occur *until performance is complete.* Strictly applied, this rule permits offers to enter unilateral contracts to be revoked after they have relied upon. An offer of £1,000 to anyone who swims across the English Channel may be revoked when a potential 'offeree' is nine tenths of the way across. This rule seems best explained as an attempt by the courts to carry through the idea that performance is a form of acceptance. Acceptance, by definition, is all or nothing. In this light, it is not surprising that courts have tried hard to avoid this rule in cases in which there has been significant reliance on the promise.[28] Nor is it surprising that they have strained to find a legal basis for such decisions.

The knowledge requirement

A second question raised by unilateral contracts is whether a person who performs a requested act must be aware of the offer at the time of performance. Should I be able to collect a reward for finding a lost dog if I am unaware of the reward? The predominant view in the courts is that knowledge is necessary, but the cases are not consistent, and the knowledge requirement is often criticized.[29] Thinking about the nature of promises helps to explain why this issue is contentious. On the one hand, the orthodox rule is consistent with the conclusion that unilateral contracts involve conditional promises. Promises, conditional or not, are

---

[27] German law, for example, provides that promises of rewards need not be accepted to be valid: S 257 BGB. The *Principles of European Contract Law* state simply that '[a] promise which is intended to be legally binding without acceptance is binding': Art 2:107, Ole Lando, Hugh Beale (eds.) *Principles of European Contract Law* (2000, pp 1578).

[28] *Errington v Errington* [1952] 1 KB 290.

[29] Mckendrick (1997) 381.

made by *communicating* an intention to undertake an obligation (3.1). Such communication implies that the promisee has knowledge of the promise. It follows that a promissory obligation does not exist in cases in which the conditions stipulated in a conditional promise are satisfied without knowledge of the promise. Of course, the performing party may subsequently learn of the promise (certainly this will happen in all the cases that get to court). But at that point it is too late. The promise is conditional on performance of a *future* act. If Jane says to Ann, 'I promise to give you £100 if you cut my lawn', but Ann has *already* cut Jane's lawn, then Jane cannot be under a *promissory* obligation to give Ann the £100. The 'if' in the promise clearly refers to a future event. It might be possible, if odd, to make a promise of reward conditional on a past event having happened ('I promise to give you £100 if you cut my lawn yesterday'), but in the normal case anyway, a conditional promise does not carry this meaning.

On the other hand, the specific kind of unilateral contract case in which the knowledge requirement is most controversial—those involving offers of rewards or prizes—arguably fall into a special category in this regard. The distinguishing feature of offers or rewards or prizes is that, by definition, they are offers 'to the world' (or at least to an indeterminate and unknown class of persons). This is significant because, as we have seen (3.1.1), it is of the essence of a promise that it is meant to place the promisor under an obligation to treat a particular person(s)—the promisee(s)—differently from everyone else. The promisor is meant to regard the promisee's interests, at least so far as the subject matter of the promise is concerned, as excluded from—and superior in kind to—the ordinary run of reasons for and against doing certain actions. But once the class of 'promisees' becomes 'the world', this essential feature of promising makes little sense. It is not possible to treat everyone's interests as superior to everyone else's interests. This suggests that an offer of a reward may not actually be a promise, at least in the ordinary sense. Our language suggests as much: we (normally) describe such communications as 'offers' of a reward rather than 'promises'. If this is correct, the confusion over the need for knowledge when 'accepting' offers of rewards is understandable. The conditions for a valid offer of a reward will be different from those normally applied to contracts. Offers of a reward are more like oaths than promises; more specifically, they appear to be a kind of unilateral and conditional 'juridical act'. In this respect, they are similar to a will, which is also unilateral and conditional (on the death of the testator). Interestingly, the beneficiary of a will can, of course, enforce the will without knowing of its existence at the time the relevant condition was satisfied. It is arguable that the same rule should be applied to rewards. The main point I wish to make, however, is that the special 'quasi-promissory' nature of rewards helps to explain why judges have difficulties establishing the preconditions for their validity. And these difficulties are shared, of course, by those who wish to make sense of contract law. The answer then, for contract theorists, may be to acknowledge that such 'contracts' do not belong on the map of contract law at all—rather, they belong in some other area of private law.

5.3. DETERMINING IF AN AGREEMENT HAS BEEN REACHED

To this point, my discussion of the offer and acceptance rules has focused primarily on how to classify the sorts of arrangements that satisfy these rules. I have been asking, in other words, what the offer and acceptance test is a test for. Judges and lawyers, however, are more concerned with the question of whether particular arrangements satisfy the offer and acceptance rules. What they typically want to know is whether an agreement—in the form of an offer matched by an acceptance—was actually made. This question raises at least three issues I have not yet examined: (1) What is the distinction between an offer and an invitation to make an offer (an 'invitation to treat')? (2) Where and when is a contract formed? And (3) How complete, certain, and matched by an acceptance must an offer be in order to be binding?

5.3.1. INVITATIONS TO TREAT

This question at issue here is whether a particular communication—say an advertisement in a newspaper—should be regarded as an actual offer that gives rise to a contract or as merely an invitation for the recipient to make an offer of her own. If the communication is the latter, it is merely an 'invitation to treat', and carries no legal significance.

The issues raised by this question are largely factual. To determine if a communication is an offer, the court must determine if the communication, properly interpreted, reveals an intent to be bound by an acceptance of that communication. The common law, like other legal systems, has established factual presumptions for addressing this question. For example, there is a rebuttable presumption that advertisements are invitations to treat. Such presumptions are in part merely generalizations; in the common law world, most advertisements do not, as a matter of fact, indicate an intention to be bound and so courts will make a prima facie assumption that any particular advertisement reveals a similar intention. But it is important to stress that presumptions also help to solve what is effectively a co-ordination problem. A co-ordination problem arises, broadly speaking, in situations where it is important for the purposes of co-ordinating behaviour that *a* rule be established, but where it does not matter which of a number of possible rules is adopted. For example: which side of the road—the left or the right—should cars travel upon? The status of advertisements arguably raises a similar issue. The presumption that they are offers and the contrary presumption both seem prima facie reasonable. If a judge were confronted with this question for the first time, it would not be clear which presumption was the more reasonable as a matter of fact. In most civil law systems, for example, it is presumed that advertisements *are* offers. What is clear, however, is that it is important to have *a* presumption. The existence of a presumption lets informed parties know their rights and duties; and it puts parties who wish a contrary rule to govern their situation on notice that they must indicate such an intention.

5.3.2. THE TIME AND PLACE OF FORMATION

The question of where and when a contract is concluded raises complex issues, but it is arguably as amenable to a similar analysis as the previous question. The general rule in the common law is that a contract is formed where and when the acceptance is received by the offeror. This 'rule of reception' (to use a civil law term) fits neatly with the idea that contracts are agreements; an agreement is formed only when the fact of agreement is communicated between both parties. The last step in this process is communication of the acceptance to the offeror, thus a contract is formed where and when this happens.

The complexities arise when we try to explain the exception to the rule of reception known as the 'postal' or 'mailbox' rule. According to the postal rule, an acceptance by post is effective where and when it is *posted* (unless the offeror has stipulated otherwise or the use of the post is unreasonable).[30] The postal rule thus appears prima facie inconsistent with the idea of contracts as agreements, since it contemplates an 'agreement' being formed prior to one of the parties to it having communicated to the other his willingness to enter the agreement. In such a case, the parties might well be 'in agreement' in their minds, that is, each party

---

[30] *Adams v Lindsell* (1818) 1 B & B Ald 681.

might at the moment of posting be willing to enter an agreement. But to *make* an agreement, both parties must communicate their willingness to enter the agreement. If mere agreement 'in one's mind' were sufficient, the entirety of an agreement could be constructed in silence.

The postal rule may be nothing more than a historical anachronism, but it is worth spending a few moments considering whether a plausible explanation can be given for the rule. Three possibilities present themselves: (1) the agency explanation, (2) the implied consent explanation, and (3) the efficiency/fairness explanation.

The agency explanation

One explanation sometimes advanced for the postal rule is that the post office is an agent of the offeror.[31] The acts of an agent are treated as if they were the acts of the principal; thus, if the post office is the agent of the offeror, the contract with the offeror is formed at the moment the post office receives it. The short answer to this suggestion is that, whatever its historical basis, in contemporary society it clearly is a fiction to regard the post office as an agent of an offeror. None of the ordinary requirements of agency are satisfied; in particular, the post office has not agreed to act as the offeror's agent.

The implied consent explanation

A second possible explanation of the postal rule is that the offeror has impliedly consented to acceptance taking place upon posting. Two questions are raised by this explanation. The first is conceptual: is it actually possible to change the rules—by consent or otherwise—that govern when an acceptance takes place? This question is raised because, as I noted a moment ago, it is a necessary feature of agreements that each party must learn of the other's desire to enter the agreement. Although it is possible to be *in agreement* about some matter without knowing of this fact, it is not possible, by definition, to *make* an agreement about which one of the parties is unaware. Like promises, agreements are communicative acts. But unlike promises, they are fundamentally bilateral: both parties to the agreement must communicate the relevant intention to undertake the obligation. This (conceptual) feature of agreements cannot be altered by consent or otherwise.

---

[31] Discussed in Gardner 1992 'Trashing With Trollope: A Deconstruction of the Postal Rules in Contract' 12 OJLS 170.

But while it is not possible to consent to acceptance happening at the time of posting, it would be possible for consent to be treated *as if* acceptance took place at this time. That is, the offeror could consent to be governed by those rules that would apply if acceptance actually happened on posting (e.g., no revocation after posting, the governing law is the offeree's jurisdiction, etc.). Described in this way, this second explanation of the postal rule is complex, but it is conceptually coherent. The postal rule, in this view, amounts to a rule that offerors are bound by implied promises in their offers not to revoke such offers after an acceptance has been posted and in other respects to treat any contract eventually concluded as if it had been made on posting of the acceptance. This promise is binding despite not being accepted or given in exchange for consideration. As such, it is an exception to the normal rules of contract law, but is not, I suggest, theoretically problematic. As we have seen, there is nothing in the nature of promises that demands either acceptance, nor (as I argue in the next chapter) that they be made in exchange for consideration.

The second question raised by the implied consent is empirical: is it true, as a matter of fact, that offers to which the postal rule apply contain implied promises (or 'implied consents') of the kind just described? This is a difficult question. Even if it is assumed that most offers contain implied-in-fact terms regarding the method of acceptance, it is not clear whether such terms support the postal rule as opposed to a rule of reception. Offerors who are aware of the postal rule can be assumed to have consented to the former, but the rule itself cannot be explained on this basis. My impression—though I know of no way of proving this—is that offerors are as likely to have impliedly consented to a rule of reception as to a postal rule. For reasons that I discuss in the next section, there is nothing in the substantive merits of either rule to suggest that the postal rule is superior to the rule of reception—or vice versa. If anything, a rule of reception might be thought the more natural rule, as it replicates the ordinary understanding of agreement. That the civil law generally adopts a rule of reception shows, at a minimum, that the postal rule is not self-evidently the rule that contracting parties would adopt.

The efficiency/fairness explanation

A third explanation of the postal rule supposes that the rule has nothing to do with the nature of agreements, promises, or contracting parties' intentions generally, but is based instead on external values. According to this explanation, the postal rule is *imposed* by the law on contracting parties in order to achieve a desirable result. In the efficiency based version of the explanation, the desirable result is an efficient result. Specifically, it is argued that the postal rule is efficient because it encourages offerees to engage in (efficient) reliance on offers earlier than would be the case under a rule of reception.[32] The postal rule is said to encourage such reliance because the offeror is precluded from revoking at an earlier point than under a rule of reception. In the fairness-based version of this explanation, the desirable result is a fair result. Specifically, it is argued that the postal rule is fair because allowing offerees to revoke their offers after an acceptance is posted (as happens under a rule of reception) would be unfair, since the offeree may have assumed that a valid contract was formed, and then relied on that assumption.

Each of these suggestions is vulnerable to the objection that it ignores the negative effects of the postal rule on the relevant value (efficiency, fairness). Consider the efficiency based explanation. It is, of course, efficient to facilitate reliance on an efficient contract. But if an offeror regrets his offer, say because circumstances change or because he learns of a more desirable offeree, then any contract that results from such an offer is unlikely to be efficient. This is the reason (from an efficiency perspective) that offerors are generally allowed to revoke prior to acceptance. The general rule gives offerors the opportunity to revoke offers that could lead to inefficient contracts up to the time at which they know that an offeree has accepted (and so is likely to begin relying). The postal rule, by shortening the period allowed for revocations, will therefore result in more inefficient contracts being formed. It follows that, from an efficiency perspective, each rule has advantages and disadvantages. A rule of reception discourages reliance (prior to receipt) and encourages revocations. The postal rule sets up the opposite incentives—it encourages reliance (after posting), and discourages revocations. Given that both revoking and relying can be prima facie efficient actions, it cannot be said in general that one rule is more efficient than the others.[33]

A similar point can be made with respect to the fairness explanation. Prima facie, a rule of reception appears unfair since one effect of this rule is that offerees who rely after posting their acceptances will sometimes

---

[32] Posner (1995) 113–14.

[33] It might be argued that the postal rule is efficient because under a rule of reception the offeree cannot safely rely until she *knows* that her acceptance has been received. To obtain this knowledge will require further communication (e.g. a telephone call to the offeror), thus increasing 'transaction' costs. But, again, this argument ignores the potential value of revocation. Offerors wishing to revoke safely in a system applying the postal rule must either wait until the offer has expired or ensure, *by a further communication*, that the offeree has not accepted.

find that such reliance is wasted. But equally, the postal rule can be described as unfair since one effect of this rule is that offerors who revoke their offers before receiving an acceptance, and who then rely on that revocation (say by making a contract with a third party), will sometimes find that they are bound by their original offer. Of course, if offerors know that they may be bound by an offer despite not having received an acceptance, then they act at their own risk. But absent a legal rule to that effect, there is no reason for offerors to make this assumption.

In the end, none of the above explanations of the postal rule are convincing. Whether one focuses on the intentions of the parties, efficiency, or fairness, the relevant arguments offer equal support for both a rule of reception and a postal rule. The conclusion to be drawn, I suggest, is that like the rule about advertisements, the postal rule is best understood as one of two possible solutions to what is essentially a co-ordination problem. As I noted above, co-ordination problems arise in situations where it is important that *a* rule be established, but where it does not matter which of a number of possible rules is adopted. Postal communications give rise to this kind of problem. Whether one approaches the issue from the perspective of efficiency, fairness, or offeror intention, it is useful to have a presumptive rule one way or the other. Either a rule of reception or the postal rule can fulfill this need. Neither seems more advantageous on the merits. What is important, however, is to have *a* rule. When the problem of postal communication is characterized in this way, it is no surprise that common law and civil law systems solve the problem in different (but equally defensible) ways.

5.3.3. CERTAINTY, COMPLETENESS, AND MATCHING ACCEPTANCE

A third question that arises when determining if an agreement has been reached is whether the offer was certain, complete, and matched by the acceptance. Here again, the issues facing a court are largely factual.

The courts' understanding of 'agreement' is similar to the everyday definition in that a reasonable degree of completeness, certainty, and consistency is what is required. But how much? Obviously, neither law nor ordinary reasoning can provide a neat rule. For example: is a summary 'heads of agreement' written in advance of a more detailed final agreement binding? Is an oral agreement that contemplates the parties signing a written agreement binding if the written agreement is not signed? The answer in each case will depend on the facts in question: how complete is the head of agreements summary, etc.? There is little that legal theory can add to our understanding of such questions, aside from counselling courts to rely on the good sense of experienced judges. The appropriate rule or decision should, of course, take into account the reasonable expectations of the parties; such expectations are critical in determining what 'goes without saying' in the parties' transactions (8.1.2). These reasonable expectations, in turn, are drawn from the context in which the parties negotiate—the industry practices, the past dealings of the parties, ordinary expectations of fairness, etc. In addition, as is true in other areas of factual dispute, the courts can and do lay down factual presumptions to promote certainty and avoid co-ordination problems. For example, in the common law it is held that the price in a sale of goods contract normally does not need to be specified: a reasonable price will be assumed.[34] The contrary presumption is made in many civil law jurisdictions.

It is sometimes said that common law courts, in particular English common law courts, apply the rules regarding certainty, etc. too rigidly, refusing to enforce what reasonable parties would regard as a binding agreement.[35] There is no doubt some truth to this claim, but it should be remembered that the context in which many commercial parties are dealing is one that assumes each party can look after itself and that no agreement is final until 'signed on the dotted line'. This context is the background or the implicit understanding against which many (if not most) commercial agreements are negotiated in common law countries, particularly in the United Kingdom. Some scholars might prefer that contracting parties conducted themselves with a view to co-operation rather than competition. But until contracting parties *themselves* hold such a view, it is improper for courts to ascribe it to them. It is true, of course, that commercial parties often commence performance before they have what the law would recognize as a binding agreement. And there is nothing wrong with such behaviour. The law, though, should not treat such arrangements as if they were contractual if the ordinary requirements for a contract are not satisfied. Contractual duties, as I have emphasized elsewhere (3.1.4), are in principle quite onerous. Unlike duties in tort law, contractual duties require parties to positively benefit others—and simply because they have said or written something. It is appropriate that courts proceed carefully before concluding that such duties have been created.

---

[34] *Sale of Goods Act* 1979, ss 8 (2).
[35] Lord Denning famously held this view: e.g. *Gibson v Manchester City Council* [1978] 1 WLR 520.

Non-contractual protection

In considering the above issue, the possibility that disappointed parties may have recourse to non-contractual protection must also be kept in mind. If the full range of such protection is not recognized by courts, a neutral application of the offer and acceptance rules may indeed lead to harsh results. Equally, a failure by critics to appreciate such protection may lead to unfair criticism of the offer and acceptance rules. Three sources of non-contractual protection are particularly important.

The first is unjust enrichment law, which supports claims to recover the value of benefits conveyed in anticipation of a contract that did not materialize.[36] A claim for what is sometimes called *quantum valebut* (for goods) and *quantum meruit* (for services) is reasonably well-established in common law, although the late recognition that such claims are part of a general duty to reverse unjust enrichments[37] has meant this source of liability has not always been foremost in the minds of contract scholars.

A second source of non-contractual protection is a duty to pay for requested services.[38] A party that has provided services requested in anticipation of a contract may be able to recover on this basis if he has not been paid. There is debate amongst scholars as to whether such an action is part of unjust enrichment law or part of a distinct species of obligation,[39] but for our purposes it is sufficient to acknowledge that plaintiffs normally can recover the value of services provided in anticipation of a contract.

Finally, a disappointed plaintiff may try to recover on the basis not that he conveyed a benefit to the defendant, but that he incurred expenses in justifiable reliance on the defendant's representations that he would be paid. In other words, the plaintiff may seek protection on the basis of a claim in estoppel (6.3.5). This is potentially the widest basis for relief, since the plaintiff has the possibility of claiming for all reliance-induced losses, regardless of whether those losses transmit to a benefit for the defendant. The main hurdle to making such a claim, at least in England, is the rule that estoppel may not be used to found a cause of action. In a contractual setting, estoppel is generally available only to prevent plaintiffs from insisting on their already-existing contractual rights. Some common law jurisdictions have abandoned this controversial limitation,[40] and even in England there are exceptions to the rule, but for now this limitation means that estoppel is of little use to a party seeking to recover

---

[36] See Burrows (1993) 250–321.   [37] *Lipkin Gorman v Karpnale Ltd* [1991] 2 AC 548.
[38] McBride (1994).   [39] McBride (1994); Penner (1997); Beatson (1991) 21.
[40] e.g. Australia, the United States.

for losses incurred in anticipation of a contract. I discuss the substantive merits of expanding the relief available for reliance-based liability in the next section (as part of a discussion of 'bad faith') and in the next chapter (in the discussion of estoppel).

The above survey of non-contractual protection available to plaintiffs demonstrates that, barring those cases in which the defendant accrues no benefit, this protection is adequate. The case of pure reliance aside, it is difficult to think of a situation where a less rigidly applied law of offer and acceptance would support contractual liability, yet where the above sources of non-contractual liabilities would not offer protection. To be sure, the remedy for breaching a contractual obligation is contractual (expectation damages or specific performance), while the remedy in the case of non-contractual liability is either restitution of benefits, reimbursement for the fair value of services, or reliance-based damages. The difference can be significant (though in practice these measures often overlap: 11.3.2), but insofar as it is the only difference between contractual and non-contractual protection, the law cannot be accused of acting harshly by requiring that the conditions for contractual liability be strictly satisfied. Contractual remedies, like contractual duties, impose onerous burdens.

5.4. PRE-CONTRACTUAL LIABILITY: REVOCATION, BREAKING OFF NEGOTIATIONS, AND BAD FAITH

In the common law, an offer may in principle be withdrawn or 'revoked' without incurring liability at any time prior to acceptance. This rule is consistent with the basic idea of contracts as agreements: until acceptance, there is no agreement, and thus there is no possibility of liability in contract. A revocation may, of course, lead to liability in tort—but only if the offeror negligently or fraudulently represented that he would not revoke. Merely changing one's mind does not turn a prior offer into a misstatement.

Civil law systems, by contrast, typically impose two limits on an offeror's ability to revoke an offer; each of these limits has conceptual implications for the common law.

5.4.1. FIRM OFFERS

The first limit found in most civil law systems is that an offer may not be revoked if the offeror stipulated that it would remain open for period of time (a 'firm offer').[41] The common law's approach to firm offers, by contrast, is that they are enforceable *only* if they are given in exchange for an undertaking by the offeree. A 'gratuitous' firm offer is not enforceable.[42] This approach is explained not on the basis of the offer and acceptance rule, but rather as a consequence of the consideration rule. It is regarded as one implication of the general rule that a promise is not binding unless made in exchange for consideration.

The invalidity of gratuitous firm offers is often cited by those who object to the consideration rule. Such objectors point to the harm that may befall offerees who rely on such offers as evidence of the rule's unfairness. This and other criticisms of the consideration rule are discussed in the next chapter. The point I wish to make now is that gratuitous firm offers also raise an interesting offer and acceptance issue. The issue arises from the fact most such offers are not 'accepted', or at least they are not accepted in the usual way. A person who reads an advertisement stating that an offer will remain open for seven days does not normally say anything to the offeror in reply. And even when the offer is made to a particular person, there is nothing to which the offeree can actually 'accept' or even 'agree'. The offeree is not required to do anything or even (as in the case of donative or gift promises) to receive something. The most that offerees can do in such cases is to acknowledge that they heard the offer.

Described in this way, it seems clear that, unlike ordinary offers, a gratuitous stipulation that an offer will remain open for a period is a (mere) promise rather than an offer to enter an agreement. The offer itself may contemplate an agreement, but the time stipulation is a unilateral undertaking. The significance of this for understanding the law of offer and acceptance is that *if* gratuitous firm offers were enforceable, this would count as another example of the law enforcing promises rather than agreements. Given that it is widely assumed that the only barrier to enforcement of gratuitous firm offers is the consideration rule, this conclusion therefore supports the point made earlier that, from the perspective of offer and acceptance principles, both agreements and mere promises are and should be enforceable. Stated differently, such limitations as exist on the enforceability of mere promises are not grounded in

---

[41] The rule is clear in civil law, but both its justification and legal classification (i.e. contractual or extra-contractual) are controversial. While I do not discuss the civil law perspective, my comments below help to explain why these issues are controversial.

[42] *Hyde v Wrench* (1840) 3 Beav 334.

the law of offer and acceptance (but instead are grounded in rules that I examine in the next chapter — in particular, the consideration rule).

5.4.2. REVOKING IN BAD FAITH

A second situation in which civil law systems typically limit an offeror's ability to revoke an offer (and to withdraw from negotiations generally) is when the revocation is made in 'bad faith'. In most civil law systems, a bad faith revocation will leave the offeror liable for reasonable expenses incurred by the offeree.[43] English law, by contrast, is said not to concern itself with the reasons for revocation. If the revocation does not constitute a breach of contract, a tort such as negligent misstatement, or give rise to an unjust enrichment, it attracts no liability. This approach to bad faith revocations is usually explained on the basis that there is no 'duty to negotiate in good faith'[44] and, more generally, that there is no 'general principle of good faith'[45] in English law.[46]

From a theoretical perspective, the primary questions raised by the English approach are whether it is accurate to say that English law provides no protection against bad faith revocations and, assuming an affirmative answer is given, whether English law *should* provide such protection. A subsidiary question is whether introducing a good faith principle would lead to the creation of new substantive obligations or whether, instead, it would merely involve the re-classification of existing rules under a new heading. In the first case, it would be accurate to speak of the *introduction* of a duty of good faith, but the second case is better described as the *recognition* of such a duty. These two approaches are theoretically distinct, though in practice they often run together. For if it is true that there is a sufficient unity among the existing rules (of tort,

---

[43] Zimmerman and Whittaker (2000) 236–57; Kessler and Fine (1964).

[44] e.g. *Walford v Miles* [1992] 2 AC 128, 138

[45] *Interfoto Picture Library Ltd v Stiletto Programmes Ltd* [1989] QB 433, 439.

[46] The qualifier 'English' law is necessary because some common law jurisdictions have adopted, to a limited extent, the principle that contracting parties must act in good faith during negotiations: see e.g. *Hoffman v Red Owl Stores* 133 NW 2d 267 (United States), *Walton Stores (Interstate) Ltd v Maher* (1988) 164 CLR 387 (Australia). It should also be kept in mind that, while England does not enforce general duties of good faith, there exist a number of specific rules that are explicitly based on good faith concepts (e.g. the requirement that parties to an insurance contract must act in 'utmost good faith': *Banque Keyser v Skandia (UK) Insurance Co Ltd* [1990] 1 QB). Finally, but potentially of greatest significance, good faith standards are making a noisy arrival into some areas of English contract law via European Community Law (notably consumer contracts: see s.3.1 of the *Unfair Terms in Consumer Contracts Regulations*, 1994). I discuss these aspects of good faith in Chapters 8 and 9.

estoppel, and unjust enrichment) that deal with revocations to justify grouping them under a separate category of good faith, this will no doubt result in further developments. A final subsidiary question will be discussed towards the end of the chapter: is 'bad faith' deserving of its own legal category? Or is it merely a label for a specific type of reliance-based duty?

Defining bad faith

Before any of these questions can be addressed, it is necessary first to provide a definition of 'bad faith revocation'. This is a notoriously difficult task, but it cannot be avoided. Debates about bad faith revocation (and about the concept of bad faith generally) are frequently conducted at cross-purposes. What one lawyer calls a bad faith revocation, another may call fraud or negligent misstatement or even breach of contract. This definitional task is important, moreover, even if it turns out to be the case that (as is often asserted) the common law reaches the same results in 'bad faith cases' as does the civil law, albeit through different mechanisms.[47] If we are trying to *understand* the law, and not merely obtain relief for a client, the way that sources of liability are classified is important. To understand contract law, and private law generally, it is necessary to establish whether liability in 'bad faith' situations is properly understood as based on contract, tort, unjust enrichment, or on a distinct ground. The answer tells us something fundamental about the nature of private law. It also tells us something about what the appropriate remedy ought to be.

It is perhaps easiest to begin the definitional inquiry by establishing what a bad faith revocation is not. A bad faith revocation is not, or is at least not merely, a breach of contract, a tortious wrong, or an event giving rise to an unjust enrichment, as these categories of liability are *properly* understood. The point here is not that, as a matter of ordinary usage, the phrase 'bad faith' could not be used in describing breaches of contract or misrepresentations or even, with some ingenuity, unjust enrichments. In ordinary usage, even ordinary legal usage, the label is used in a myriad of ways. Rather, the point is that defining bad faith this broadly renders the phrase useless. Unless 'bad faith revocation' means something that 'breach of contract', 'tortious wrongdoing', or 'unjust enrichment' does not, it is redundant. There already exist more precise ways of describing these kinds of liability. For 'bad faith revocation' to be a meaningful

---

[47] e.g. Zimmerman and Whittaker (2000) 653.

concept—something worth arguing about—it must identify a source of liability different from contract, tort, and unjust enrichment.

When asking if liability for a bad faith revocation can be distinguished from liability in contract, tort, or unjust enrichment it is important, of course, that these categories themselves be defined properly. A conclusion to the effect that English law achieves the same results through contract, tort, and unjust enrichment law that the civil law achieves through the concept of bad faith does not show that bad faith is an unnecessary concept. If English law subverts the proper scope of contract, tort, or unjust enrichment to achieve such results, then English law may indeed need a bad faith concept in order to explain its own rules.[48] That said, I will not make this argument. The common law rules that currently support such liability as exists for revocations—which are found primarily in the law regarding negligent misstatement and claims for the return of benefits transferred on a failed condition—are uncontroversially a part of tort law or of unjust enrichment law.[49]

In light of these observations, it is tempting to define a bad faith revocation as a revocation that is objectionable for a reason *other* than a reason that would make the revocation a breach of contract, a tort, or an event that gives rise to an unjust enrichment. But such a definition would not be very helpful: it merely replaces the adjective 'bad faith' with 'objectionable', and limits slightly its range of possible meanings. A useful definition will tell us what makes a revocation objectionable *aside* from something that could give rise to an action in contract, tort, or unjust enrichment.

The literature on bad faith provides limited help in this regard; it rarely goes much beyond stating that 'bad faith' is acting in bad faith. A recent comprehensive survey of the topic (by two authors *favourable* towards good faith standards) is not atypical in concluding that, so far as

---

[48] If this were the case, then the current status of bad faith would be similar to the status of unjust enrichment before its recent recognition in English law as a distinct cause of action. During that period, the *results* reached in particular cases were consistent with the idea that unjust enrichment was a distinct source of liability. But lacking the conceptual apparatus to explain these results, the common law shoe-horned them into other categories, such as contract or tort.

[49] This is not quite right. Some instances of liability for pre-contractual negligent misstatements are undoubtedly better described as simple promissory liability. The reason they are not so described is not because English law lacks a doctrine of good faith, but because of the common law consideration rule. I note also that at least part of the explanation for why some civil law systems, in particular the German system, resort to good faith concepts to explain pre-contractual liability is that their tort law precludes recovery for pure economic loss for negligence, including negligent misstatement.

'what good faith actually means . . . not much can be said; and what can be said is not very helpful for deciding concrete cases'.[50] Rather than providing a *definition* of good faith, scholars working in this area typically provide illustrations or examples of bad faith.[51]

I will consider some such examples, but first it should be asked whether any conclusions should be drawn from the fact that it is not possible (it appears) to offer anything resembling a precise definition of bad faith—indeed any definition at all. One conclusion that is commonly drawn by English lawyers is that rules invoking the concept of 'bad faith' (or the converse—'good faith') give too much discretion to the judiciary. This view is sometimes assumed to reflect outdated ideas about the proper role of judicial law-making. The point, however, is deeper; indeed, it goes to the very nature and purpose of law. Whatever else the law is meant to do, it is meant to give people (including judges) guidance as to how they should lead their lives. A rule specifying that people must act 'in good faith', like a rule specifying that people should 'act morally', does not, *if nothing more is said*, fulfil this function. We already know that we should act 'properly'; we do not need the law to tell us that. If the law is to fulfil its function of guiding behaviour, it must specify what acting 'properly', 'morally', or in 'good faith' means in relatively concrete terms. Many scholars regard laws that fail to do this as not really laws at all.[52] But even without adopting this view, the basic objection to such laws is clear: they conflict with the ideal of the rule of law. The rule of law requires that legal officials be constrained by publicly announced rules, such that individuals are able to know in advance their legal duties.[53] A rule that simply directed citizens to act properly would fail in this respect.

One response to this charge is to say that while it may be difficult to give a general definition of 'bad faith revocation', courts using this concept can, and have, developed reasonably clear rules for dealing with particular sorts of situations. For example, German law contains a large number of rules proscribing situations that a German scholar would explain as illustrations of 'bad faith revocations' behaviour—but that do this without using the words bad faith or anything similar.[54] The difficulty with this response, at least for a common law lawyer, is that it is

---

[50] Zimmerman and Whittaker (2000) 30. Kessler and Fine (1964) reach a similar conclusion.

[51] e.g. Zimmerman and Whittaker (2000); Kessler and Fine (1964).

[52] e.g. Raz (1994) 210–38.   [53] e.g. Fuller (1969) 33–91.

[54] e.g. Zimmerman and Whittaker (2000) 18–32.

precisely the rules that can be explained without using the term 'bad faith' that are also most easily explained using the classical private law concepts. As I will explain in a moment, it is the results that *cannot* easily be accommodated within a tort, contract, or unjust enrichment analysis that are difficult to explain without using a term such as bad faith.

Another response to the 'definitional' objection to rules employing standards of good or bad faith is to say that while these standards cannot be reduced to concrete guidelines, in practice judges, lawyers, *and citizens* 'know bad faith when they see it'. That is, the standards are in practice predictable, even if they cannot be described in advance. On this view, concepts of good and bad faith belong to the category of things that we 'know and recognize' even though we cannot define them. They are 'basic concepts' that cannot be reduced to, or explained in terms of, other concepts. It seems reasonable to assume that such concepts exist (e.g., consent: 9.1.2). Aside from taking a broad detour into linguistic theory, the only way to determine if this is true of bad faith is to consider some examples and then to ask if we do indeed 'know bad faith' when we see it. My view, which I defend below, is that insofar as the examples do not raise clear claims in contract, tort, or unjust enrichment, it is far from self-evident that the behaviour they describe amounts to acting in bad faith.

5.4.3. DEFINING BAD FAITH BY EXAMPLE

Examples of bad faith revocation invariably involve induced reliance in some form.[55] A typical example might involve a vendor who enters lengthy negotiations with a buyer for the sale of certain property. At the last moment, and after the buyer incurs various expenses in anticipation of the sale, the vendor sells the property to a friend. Unknown to the buyer, the vendor had from the beginning planned to sell to the friend: the negotiations with the buyer were begun merely as a fallback position in the event that the deal with the friend fell through.

It seems clear that the actions of the vendor in this example are open to criticism. The question is whether we need the concept of bad faith to make such criticisms—and if we do, whether those criticisms should support liability in law.

To begin, there is a strong likelihood that the buyer in this example will have an action against the vendor in unjust enrichment, contract, or tort. If the buyer conferred a benefit on the vendor, then in principle, an action

---

[55] e.g. Zimmerman and Whittaker (2000) 236, 532.

in unjust enrichment should be (and in English law would be) available to the buyer to recover the benefit of those expenses. Furthermore, if the vendor's representations to the buyer amounted to an implicit or explicit promise not to deal with another buyer—as is often the case—then the vendor should in principle be liable for breach of promise in contract. As we have seen, English law does not currently support this possibility because promises that are not given in exchange for something of value— consideration—are not enforceable as contracts. On the facts of my example, it is unlikely that the buyer promised to do anything in exchange. This result—no liability for a gratuitous promise—may be criticized, but it is not a reason for introducing a concept of bad faith revocation into English law. The source of the problem—assuming for the moment that there is a problem—is the doctrine of consideration. Finally, but most importantly, the vendor may be liable in tort for a misrepresentation. If at the time of making the representations that induced the buyer to incur expenses the vendor negligently or fraudulently misrepresented his intentions to the buyer, then the vendor should— and would—be liable for misrepresentation. On the facts of the example, it is likely that the vendor did falsely represent an intention to deal exclusively with the buyer, and thus the vendor would likely be liable in misrepresentation.

Many cases of 'induced reliance revocations' will thus properly lead to liability in the common law without it being necessary—or appropriate— to invoke a concept of bad faith revocation. The concept of a 'bad faith revocation' adds nothing to the above bases of liability. Of course, not all induced reliance revocations ground liability in contract, tort or unjust enrichment. Consider the following scenario. A vendor knows that a particular buyer is interested in acquiring her property. The vendor further knows the buyer cannot conclude a deal without an expensive inspection of the property. The vendor informs the buyer—truthfully—that she intends to sell the property to the buyer assuming the buyer is interested and that reasonable terms can be agreed upon. She says these things to the buyer because she wants to encourage the buyer to do an inspection (the vendor knows that an inspection is a necessary prelude to any sale). Suppose, further, that the buyer and vendor have completed numerous sales in the past. The buyer performs the inspection and various negotiations are undertaken, but then the vendor revokes the offer at the last minute. In this example, the vendor has not broken a promise (the vendor was careful to say 'I intend to sell' rather than 'I promise' or 'I agree' or 'I undertake' to sell), nor was the vendor unjustly enriched (the inspection was of no benefit to the vendor), nor, finally, did the vendor misrepresent her intention (she simply changed her mind). If the buyer were to recover the cost of expenses from the vendor in such a case, it would seem necessary to invoke a concept of 'bad faith revocation' or something similar.

But the question is whether the vendor, who (we will now assume) did not break a promise, tell a falsehood, or become enriched, has done something that should count, legally, as acting in bad faith. Two approaches to addressing this question need to be distinguished: (1) bad faith as bad motive, and (2) bad faith as unreasonable behaviour.[56]

Bad faith as bad *motive*

The first, which follows the core or traditional understanding of bad faith, focuses on the vendor's motives for revoking. According to this approach, the vendor acted in bad faith if she revoked for 'bad' reasons. This approach is consistent with regarding bad faith as a distinct reason for legal liability; rare exceptions aside, liability in contract, tort, or unjust enrichment is not dependent on the defendant's motives.

But what sorts of reasons for changing one's mind might qualify as bad faith reasons? Some answers to this question merely replace the term 'bad faith' with a synonym. For example, it is sometimes said that a revocation is in bad faith if, having encouraged the other party to incur expenses in the expectation that a contract would be completed, the party revokes for an 'unreasonable', or 'illegitimate' reason, or for a reason outside the 'reasonable expectations' of the relying party. None of these terms add anything to 'bad faith'. That they are frequently invoked in discussions of bad faith merely illustrates the difficulty of formulating a rule based on bad faith that does not itself refer to bad faith.

One possible answer that does not beg the question is that a bad reason is a reason unrelated to the merits of the proposed contract. In a standard commercial contract, these merits would be the contract's commercial merits (e.g., the price, and other terms). But the definition suggested by this answer is too broad. According to this answer, a vendor would be considered in bad faith if she withdrew after learning that the other party supported a fascist movement or had had an affair with her husband. Views might differ regarding the validity of the vendor's value judgments, but assuming that the vendor makes these judgments, it is

---

[56] e.g. Ghestin and Goubeaux (1977) 592–602, Zimmerman and Whittaker (2000) 20; Hesselink (1988).

difficult to regard her decision to revoke as blameworthy. Indeed, refusing to deal with persons that one regards as immoral is usually regarded as a sign of high moral character. Other non-commercial reasons for revoking clearly *are* objectionable, but for reasons that seem better explained on grounds other than bad faith. Consider the anti-Semite who breaks off negotiations on learning that the other party is Jewish, or the racist who revokes on learning that the other party is married to a black person. Such behaviour clearly is objectionable. But the reason it is objectionable is that it is discriminatory, not that it is in bad faith. As such, it should be and, in many legal systems, is dealt with by anti-discrimination law, rather than by a duty to act in good faith. Of course, in a system that lacked anti-discrimination law, judges might search for another principle —such as good faith—that they could use to give effect to such concerns. But whatever the practical merits of using good faith in this way, it provides no basis for defining the *meaning* of good faith. Understood in this way, good faith is reduced to nothing more than a catch-all residual category.[57]

Another occasion that might give rise to a charge that a revocation was in bad faith is where the actor's behaviour is irrational. Suppose that the vendor in my example revoked the offer because a black cat walked in front of her on her way to signing the contract. Such a reason may be ridiculed, but it lacks the moral element necessary to label it a bad reason. It is a silly or stupid reason. Moreover, if bad faith were equated with irrational reasoning, it would follow that offerors should be liable for irrationally refusing to go ahead with agreements because of their genuine, but misguided, belief that they would lose money in the deal.

What is left? The answer, once the class of reasons comprised of commercial reasons, non-commercial rational reasons, discriminatory reasons, and irrational reasons is placed to the side, is—not much. The only possibility would seem to be the case where the sole reason for revoking is a desire to harm the other party *and* where there is no underlying reason for this desire aside from enjoyment of the other's discomfort. Such cases, which must be rare indeed, seem evidence more of mental incapacity than of bad faith—especially when it is remembered that the revoking party must have formed her bad desire *after* commencing negotiations. If the desire to harm existed from the start of negotiations, relief would almost certainly be available under the heading of misrepresentation.

---

[57] The merits of residual categories are discussed briefly in the next chapter's examination of possible justifications for consideration: 6.3.3

For these reasons, establishing liability for bad faith revocation on the basis of the motives of the defendant seems unlikely to be of much value in identifying a distinct and valid category of bad faith revocations. Offerors often act carelessly, thoughtlessly, stupidly or without adequate regard for the other party's interests, but they rarely act for a motive that is itself morally blameworthy (and when they do, they usually fall afoul of anti-discrimination legislation). Their intent is typically to look after their own interests, rather than to harm those of the other party. It might well be argued that a particular revoking party should have taken the other party's interests into consideration more fully (see below). But a failure to do this is not to act with a bad motive. Looking out for one's own interests may not be the highest of motives, but it is not a bad motive—if it were, the overwhelming majority of contracts would be made in bad faith.

Bad faith as unreasonable *behaviour*

The second approach for evaluating whether a revocation was in bad faith focuses not on the morality of the revoking party's motives, but rather on the reasonableness of her actual behaviour. According to this view, bad faith consists in not giving reasonable weight to the interests of the person with whom you are negotiating. One way of interpreting this standard is to say that a duty of good faith obliges offerors to look after the interests of offerees, even going so far as to give them the same weight as the offerors' interests. The relationship between contracting parties could then be analogized with fiduciary relationships, or even family relationships. In this view, contracting is more a co-operative enterprise than a competitive or adversarial exercise.

Adopting this approach to all contracts would have serious consequences. Aside from the question of whether it is workable to expect contracting parties in a competitive economy to look out for one another's interests to this extent, introducing such a *generalized* duty would be a significant violation of the harm principle (3.1.4). It would subject offerors to a positive duty to benefit others—a duty that would encompass not only those with whom an offeror was in a contract, but also those with whom an offeror *might* be in a contract.

A more limited—and therefore more plausible—interpretation is that a bad faith revocation occurs when, having *induced another to incur expenses* in anticipation of a contract, the offeror then revokes, and does so without offering to compensate the offeree for her expenses. In this view, the duty to look after the offeree's interests arises from the fact that the offeror has induced the offeree to rely.

If this interpretation is correct, two consequences follow. First, liability for a bad-faith revocation should be regarded as one aspect of the broader idea of reliance-based liability. The arguments for reliance-based liability that I considered in Chapter 3's discussion of reliance theories of contract (3.2) apply directly to reliance that is induced in anticipation of signing a contract. Indeed, the standard example of 'pure' reliance-based liability is liability that is said to arise in certain cases of revoked offers. Thus understood, bad faith (at least so far as revocations are concerned) is not actually a distinct category of legal liability — it is just another name for what is (more properly) called reliance-based liability.

The second consequence of accepting the above definition of bad faith revocation is that it may be objected to on the same moral grounds as reliance-based liability generally. Briefly, this objection is that it is difficult to find a moral space for a liability that is based neither on the (contractual) duty to keep your promises nor on the (tort law) duty to tell the truth — as the notion of reliance based liability asserts (3.2.1). In my example, if the vendor has made a promise, then her liability is explicable on ordinary promissory grounds. Reliance does not matter. But if she has not made a promise, then it would seem she ought to be free to change her mind — and free to do so without having to offer compensation. The point — and effect — of saying 'I promise' is to bind the speaker to doing the promised action. To promise is not merely to state an intention to do something, but to exclude the possibility of changing one's mind about doing that thing. By contrast, the point of saying 'I intend to do X' rather than 'I promise to do X' is precisely to retain the liberty to change one's mind. Stated differently, while it may not be particularly nice or virtuous to let others down when they have relied upon you, those persons should have a weak claim in law against you because it is part of the very meaning of a statement of mere intention that the speaker reserves the right to change his or her mind. If potential relying parties want protection against the risk that the other party will change her mind, they should ask for it (which is what negotiating parties often do in pre-contractual negotiations: they ask for exclusivity agreements and for compensation for expenses in the case of revocation).

Consider again my example of the vendor who backs out at the last moment after having encouraged the buyer to incur expenses in anticipation of a contract. Suppose that she does so because an unexpected business opportunity presented itself in respect of the land in question. It is difficult to describe her reasons as 'bad'. She is not trying to harm the buyer; she simply wants to look after her own interests. But has she acted unreasonably by revoking or at least by failing to offer the buyer compensation for his expenses? Normally, if we make no promises and tell no falsehoods we incur no liability for what we say. The counter-argument here is that the vendor actually encouraged the expenses. But we encourage others in this way all the time. Imagine that I set up a fruit stand on a remote road. Suppose that my hope that the quality of my fruit will encourage motorists to make a detour to my stands proves correct. Suppose, further, that I tell everyone who stops that I plan—but do not promise—to be open every day. Then, one day, I decide to take a day off. Ought I to be liable, even in principle, to those motorists who incurred wasted expenses in the anticipation of making a contract for fruit with me? That the answer is negative seems clear. I may have encouraged others to rely, but not having made a promise to them (or a false representation), they rely upon me at their own risk.

In the end, the arguments for including a general principle of good faith in contract negotiations are less convincing than they may initially appear. The question is not whether there should be some form of pre-contractual liability—there already is in the areas of tort, unjust enrichment, and to a lesser extent, estoppel (6.3.5). Instead, proponents of introducing a duty to negotiate in good faith must first identify situations that should ground liability, but are not covered by existing law, and then demonstrate why a general duty of good faith is the best solution to these cases, rather than, for instance, expanding tort liability.

5.5. CONCLUSION

I began this chapter by stating that the rules of offer and acceptance are at the core of contract law and that they form the basis for the legal recognition of self-imposed obligations. We have now seen that this core is itself tied up with several basic features of the common law of contract, such as the consideration rule and the principle of the objective standard. The interaction between these features generates exceptions and puzzles that are not easily explained away—for instance offers of reward and the postal rule. Also, we run into difficulty in matters where the law of contract intersects with other areas of the law: tort, unjust enrichment, and estoppel. This should not be surprising, since it is precisely in such places that we should expect analytic questions about the nature of the law to be the hardest. Though I have not given any hard and fast answers in many of these areas (indeed, I think I have made it clear that there are none) I hope to have clarified some of the questions. This clarification shows that the promissory approach to the rules of offer and acceptance continues to provide the most fruitful framework within which to search for answers.

6

The Kinds of Agreements that are Enforced: Formalities, Intention to Create Legal Relations, Consideration, and Estoppel

Offer and acceptance are an essential part of any agreement. But that is not the end of the matter. In the common law, there are three additional positive requirements that must be fulfilled for an agreement to be valid: (1) contracting parties must intend to create legal relations, (2) each party to a contract must provide consideration, and (3) certain contracts must be in writing, or satisfy some other form requirement. These requirements are well-known and simple to identify in case law. A more challenging task is to explain *why* these additional requirements exist. In other words, why are only *some* types of agreements enforced?

The leading explanations for the offer and acceptance rules, as we have seen, are each consistent with valuing freedom of contract (5.1). Insofar as the law imposes additional requirements beyond offer and acceptance, that freedom to contract is impinged upon. More specifically, individuals' intentions may be frustrated if what they perceive to be a legally binding agreement turns out not to be legally binding because of the absence of consideration, a formality, or an intent to create legal relations.

Because of the restrictions they impose, many scholars are sceptical as to whether the requirements examined in this chapter are justified. They offer their own explanations for these requirements—explanations that are often very different from the law's 'internal' justifications. The consideration rule has been especially contentious. My own conclusion is that these requirements are related to a prima facie valid concern; however, whatever concern is at stake may not fully justify the requirements themselves.

I begin by examining form requirements, then turn to intent to create legal relations and finally, consideration (and estoppel). The form requirements and the intent requirements are examined first because understanding them helps greatly in understanding the consideration requirement—or so I shall argue.

6.1. FORM REQUIREMENTS

Certain categories of contract must not only satisfy the offer and acceptance rule, but must also conform to certain forms or procedures if they
are to be legally binding. Typical form requirements include requirements that contracts be made in writing,[1] under seal, or that they be made
before witnesses. Some scholars have also suggested that the common law
requirement of consideration is essentially a form requirement. This
suggestion is examined in the (separate) discussion of consideration later
in this chapter.

By definition, the reason for having what I will call a form requirement
will not be apparent on the face of the requirement. A writing requirement, for example, cannot be justified on the ground that written agreements are different in kind from oral agreements. Both speaking and
writing are means of communication; in principle, either can be used to
make an agreement, and thus to make a contract. The explanations for
why form requirements exist are therefore derivative explanations. Formalities are justified on the basis that they protect or promote values that
are related only indirectly to the particular actions that the formality
requires.

In his article 'Consideration and Form,'[2] Lon Fuller identified three
such values or (as he called them) 'functions' that form requirements may
serve: (1) the evidentiary function, (2) the cautionary function, and (3)
the channelling function. The *evidentiary* function is served when the
formality provides evidence of the agreement's existence or content (e.g.,
if the formality requires that the agreement be witnessed or in writing).
The *cautionary* function is served when the formality ensures that parties
have time to reflect on what they are doing (e.g., if the formality requires
that a contract be signed before a lawyer or notary). Finally, the *channelling* function is served when the formality ensures that the parties' actions
have legal consequences only insofar as they intend them to do so. A
requirement that a particular kind of agreement must be made under seal
could serve this function: it is reasonable to assume that parties who
comply with this agreement want their arrangement to be legally binding.
Their compliance with the form requirement signals this intention.

It is easy to discern the usefulness of the three functions that
Fuller identified. It is also clear that the standard examples of form

---

[1] e.g. contracts for the sale of land: *Law of Property (Miscellaneous Provisions) Act* 1989, s.2.
[2] (1940).

requirements — writing, seals, witnessing — fulfill one or more of these functions at least to some degree. So why are formalities required only for certain categories of contracts? The answer, of course, is that there are also costs attached to form requirements. The main cost is that insofar as parties are unaware of the relevant requirements, they may discover that they have not made a contract when they thought they had. Parties who clearly, freely, and consciously attempt to create a binding agreement may fail to do so merely because they fail to satisfy a form requirement. This can have serious consequences if (as is typically the case) one or both of them relied on the agreement being binding. A related point is that form requirements increase the costs of contracting. They require potential contracting parties to do something in addition to making an offer and matching acceptance. Sometimes these extra steps are relatively minor (e.g., reducing an oral agreement to writing), but in other cases they are significant (e.g., visiting a lawyer).

These observations suggest that the arguments for and against form requirements must be made on a case by case basis. The advantages and disadvantages described above vary in intensity depending on the nature of both the contract in question and the formality in question. More specifically, and drawing again on Fuller's article, two factors are particularly important when deciding whether any particular form requirement is justified. The first is the extent to which the 'natural features' of the arrangement in question satisfy the three functions just described. For example, if the agreement is between commercial parties, it is usually clear that the parties have reflected on what they were doing and about whether they intended their agreement to be legally binding. By contrast, this cannot be assumed in the case of door to door sales. The second factor that must be considered in determining whether a particular form requirement is justified is the *extent* of the burden the requirement imposes. Requiring that contracts be signed before lawyers is more burdensome than requiring that they be in writing. Burdens are also relative to the value of the contract: a form requirement is more burdensome when it is applied to contracts of small value. Finally, a form requirement can be more or less burdensome depending on how easily the relevant parties can learn about it. Thus, it may be significant, for example, that the parties entering the relevant category of transaction are usually advised by lawyers.

Viewed from this perspective, the evaluation of form requirements raises what are primarily practical questions. Form requirements can assist courts in identifying (genuine, serious) agreements. But on the other hand, form requirements may force courts *not to enforce* certain agreements which arguably should be enforced. Provided that there are good reasons generally for courts to enforce agreements, form requirements appear a mixed blessing in that they have both good and harmful effects. Whether the benefits of any particular form requirement outweigh its cost is largely a technical question.

Finally, I note that before evaluating a particular requirement on the above grounds it must first be determined that the requirement in question is actually a form requirement. As regards the standard examples of writing, seals, witnessing, etc., this is not an issue. But in some cases it is difficult to determine if a rule is meant to serve one or more of the formal functions identified above as opposed to a substantive function. In the common law, the most important example of such a rule is the consideration rule. I return to this interesting, and difficult, aspect of formal requirements later in this chapter (6.3.1).

6.2. INTENT TO CREATE LEGAL RELATIONS

It is orthodox law that, to create a valid contract, the parties must 'intend to create legal relations'.[3] The theoretical question raised by the intent requirement is the same general question mentioned in the introduction to this chapter: Why is such a requirement needed?, What role does it play? Of course, courts should not enforce agreements that the parties did not wish to have enforced. But why must contracting parties also express a *positive* intent to be legally bound? Why is it not sufficient that the parties made a serious agreement? As we shall see, there is no obvious answer to this question.

In thinking about the role of the intent requirement, three situations in which courts have applied the requirement need to be distinguished. The first situation is the one noted above—where contracting parties have expressly or by implication stated that they do not want their agreement to be enforceable. A 'letter of intent', for example, might state that 'the obligations contained in this agreement are not legally binding'. Such statements should, of course, be respected. At the same time, however, they do not require the protection of a distinct 'intent to create legal relations' form requirement. Ordinary rules of contract interpretation will suffice to protect parties who do not wish to be bound. In other words, when parties say 'we don't want to be bound', the principle that

---

[3] *Balfour v Balfour* [1919] 2 KB 571.

courts should give effect to the intention of the parties will serve to respect their wishes;[4] the courts are respecting, not ignoring, the parties' agreement.

The second situation in which the intent requirement has been given as a reason for refusing to enforce an agreement is where the parties did not intend their statements to be taken seriously. This was the reason given by the defendants in the case of *Carlill v Carbolic Smoke Ball Co.*[5] for why their offer to pay £100 to anyone who became sick after using their smoke ball should not be enforced (the argument was rejected). Again, it is uncontroversial that if parties do not intend their words to be taken seriously, the courts should not enforce any agreement they may have appeared to reach. But here too, a separate intent requirement is not needed to reach such a result. A non-serious 'offer' is simply not an offer at all. The reason is not that the offeree did not intend to be *legally* bound, but that he did not intend to be bound, period. The joker does not intend to enter any sort of agreement, legal or otherwise. The result in such cases is therefore explicable on the basis of the ordinary offer and acceptance principles.

The third situation in which courts have used the intent requirement as a reason for refusing to enforce an agreement is where the agreement was made in a 'domestic or social' setting (hereafter 'domestic agreements').[6] There is a rebuttable presumption that agreements made in such settings are not binding, and this presumption is normally explained on the basis that the parties did not intend their agreement to be legally binding. It is this third category that raises interesting theoretical issues. To be sure, many of these cases can be explained on the same foundation as cases in the first two categories—that the agreements were not meant seriously or that the parties did not intend them to be legally binding. But it seems unlikely that all cases in this third category can be explained on these grounds. Domestic agreements are often extremely serious, and the

---

[4] One difficult question raised by such cases (and also by cases falling into the second category, discussed below) is whether such expressions of intention should be interpreted objectively or subjectively. The previous chapter's discussion of the objective approach to contract interpretation suggests that insofar as the meaning of a *term* in an agreement is in issue (which is what is happening in this first category), then an objective approach is appropriate. On the other hand, insofar as the question is whether the parties intended to make an agreement at all (which is the question raised by the second category of cases), a subjective approach is appropriate. That the law is not entirely clear on this question (e.g. De Moor (1990)), may be a result of courts failing to distinguish between that different categories of intent to create legal relations cases.

[5] [1893] 1 QB 256.   [6] *Balfour v Balfour* [1919] 2 KB 571.

parties making them are often unaware, even in the vaguest way, of the possible legal implications of these agreements.

Unlike in the first two situations, then, cases in which the intent requirement is used to refuse to enforce domestic agreements cannot be explained on the basis of other, ordinary contract law rules. The question thus arises: what is the justification, then, for the presumption that domestic agreements are not intended to be legally binding? The most compelling justification, I suggest, is that the special value associated with such agreements would be diminished if they were legally enforceable. Let me explain. Domestic agreements are different from ordinary commercial agreements. Specifically, they are not bargains in the ordinary sense of the term; the parties do not enter them to gain personal advantages. Rather, domestic agreements are made in order to promote the parties' *shared* interests. This shared interest lies both in the subject matter of the agreement (children, housework, etc.) and in the goal of strengthening the relationship itself. Domestic agreements are therefore both expressive of, and a constitutive feature of, the parties' relationship.[7] Making (and performing) such agreements is an integral part of what it means to be in relationship, and part of the reason they are valuable.

The significance of this for the law is that legally enforcing domestic agreements will arguably diminish this aspect of their value. This is not because litigation would eliminate any hope of reconciliation between the parties; once the dispute has reached litigation, the parties' relationship is no longer domestic in the sense described above. The reason is rather that the mere threat of legal enforcement can change the character, and hence the value, of domestic agreements. Part of the value of domestic agreements is that they are meant to be performed because of a shared interest, rather than self-interest. To the extent that the law provides an external reason, grounded in self-interest, for complying with the terms of a domestic agreement, such agreements may come to be viewed in a different way. It will become less clear that they are performed because this is part of what the relationship entails as opposed to reasons of self-interest. The argument concludes that to ensure that the character—and thus the special value—of domestic agreements remains intact, the law should normally refuse to give them legal backing. The only exception would be cases in which apparently domestic agreements are not actually regarded by the parties in this way. In such cases, enforcement is appropriate

---

[7] Though not focusing on the intent requirement, a useful general discussion of this topic is Penner (1996).

because the value of this kind of (not truly domestic) agreement is not diminished by enforcement.

I conclude that a concern for the special value of domestic agreements provides a compelling explanation for why courts normally refuse to enforce such agreements. It also explains why a distinct 'intent' requirement exists at all (though it does not explain why the requirement is described as an *intent* requirement).[8] Unlike the explanations offered for the first two categories of intent cases, this explanation cannot be expressed in terms of some other (ordinary) contract law rule.[9]

6.3. CONSIDERATION

It is a fundamental rule of the common law of contract (though not of the civil law) that, with the exception of contracts under seal, each party to a valid contract must do or agree to do something in exchange for the undertaking of the other party. Common law lawyers call the thing that is done or agreed to be done 'consideration'; and the rule itself is called the consideration rule. The most obvious consequence of this rule is that a promise to make a gift—a 'donative' promise—is in principle unenforceable, no matter how seriously the promise is made. Another example of what I shall call a 'gratuitous' promise is a promise to compensate another for past services. Many promises to guarantee debts, as well as 'firm' offers (promises to keep an offer open for a set period), are also gratuitous.

There is probably no rule in the common law of contract that has been subject to more criticism than the consideration rule. The reasons for this criticism are not difficult to identify. First, the rule appears to give rise to clear injustices. Parties who reasonably rely on serious promises may find themselves with no recourse against a failure to perform if they did not

---

[8] But what courts say when they actually apply the requirement is often consistent with this explanation. Thus, in the leading case of *Balfour v Balfour* [1919] 2 KB 571, Atkin LJ described domestic agreements as follows: 'The consideration that [one] really obtains for them is that natural love and affection which counts for so little in these cold courts. The terms may be repudiated, varied or renewed as performance proceeds or as disagreements develop, and the principles of the common law as to exoneration and discharge and accord and satisfaction are such as to find no place in the domestic code.'

[9] A final point is that this explanation does not employ the kind of rights-based reasoning that, I have argued, generally underlies contract law (see especially 4.3). The explanation for why domestic agreements are not enforced is based not on the parties' rights, but rather on broader social values. Thus explained, the intent requirement provides evidence against supporters of exclusively rights-based accounts of contract law.

provide consideration for the promise.[10] Second, there is no obvious explanation for the rule. As I noted above, there is nothing in the concept of promise or agreement that suggests a transaction is any less a promise or an agreement if it lacks consideration. Nor does the suggestion that contractual obligations are best understood as essentially reliance-based obligations (3.2) explain the consideration requirement. Consideration is normally established not by actually doing something (i.e., by relying), but rather by merely promising to do something. Nor, finally, can the consideration rule be explained on the grounds of fairness.[11] The rule is satisfied regardless of the values of what is exchanged—the promise of a mere peppercorn is sufficient.[12] Furthermore, assuming that a gratuitous promise is freely and seriously made, there is nothing unfair in permitting a promisee to sue upon such a promise.[13] The promisor is being asked to do no more than what she promised to do.

Observations such as these, together with the fact that civil law systems appear to function perfectly well without a consideration requirement, have led some contract theorists to conclude that the consideration rule is best regarded as an indefensible historical anachronism.[14] But a number of justifications for the rule have also been defended. The main task of the remainder of this chapter is to explore three such justifications: the formal justification, the substantive justification, and the realist justification.[15] For ease of exposition, each justification is examined separately, but they can be, and often are, combined.

6.3.1. THE FORMAL JUSTIFICATION FOR CONSIDERATION

The best known justification for the consideration rule supposes that the rule has an essentially formal function.[16] In this view, the rule is justified on similar grounds to those that justify writing requirements and other

---

[10] In certain common law jurisdictions, the doctrine of estoppel (which I examine near the end of this chapter) will sometimes provide relief in these instances; but in the United Kingdom, which permits estoppel to be raised only as a defence, it is of little help.

[11] But see Gordley (1981).

[12] *Chappell & Co v Nestle* [1960] AC 87.

[13] e.g. Crompton J in *Tweddle v Atkinson* 1 B. & S. 393.   [14] e.g. Fried (1981).

[15] Justifications *not* examined include those found in Gordley (1995), Brudner (1993), and Benson (2001).

[16] The seminal statement is Fuller (1941). Consistent with my explanation of formalities, this justification can be, and has been, adopted by contract theorists who in other respects have little in common; see e.g. Eisenberg (1979;1982); Posner (1977); Gordley (1997); Goetz and Scott (1980); Barnett (1991).

form requirements. Specifically, the consideration rule serves the same cautionary and channelling functions that (as we saw above) formalities often serve.

The explanation of how the consideration rule serves these functions rests on two propositions (each of which incorporates ideas from my earlier discussion of formal requirements: 6.1). The first is that gratuitous promises are a clear example of the kind of promise for which formal requirements of validity are prima facie justified. More specifically, the core case of a gratuitous promise—a donative promise—raises clear concerns about whether the promisor reflected carefully on his promise (the cautionary function) and about whether the promisor intended the promise to be legally binding (the channelling function). The second proposition is that one consequence of the consideration rule is that promisors who wish to make a gratuitous promise binding can do this *if* they satisfy a form requirement. A gratuitous promise becomes legally binding if it is made under seal or if it is made in exchange for 'nominal' consideration, such as a peppercorn or £1. A seal is a clear formality, and nominal consideration appears to play the same role. Neither has any apparent substantive function. Each fulfills two of the functions that formalities typically fulfill: the cautionary function (in that each requires the promisor to take an additional step), and the channelling function (in that promisors who take such steps clearly signal their desire to be bound).

Thus understood, the common law consideration rule appears strikingly similar to the requirement found in civil law regimes that donative promises are not binding unless they satisfy a formality (e.g., a writing or notarization requirement). Indeed, according to this explanation, the civil law account of what kinds of promises are binding provides a more illuminating description of what actually happens in the common law than that provided by common law description. If the formal justification is correct, then rather than describing the rule as (roughly) 'only promises made in exchange for consideration are binding', the rule should be described as (roughly) 'promises are generally binding, although some promises, such as gratuitous promises and promises for the sale of land, also require the presence of a formality such as a seal or nominal consideration'.

The formal justification thus appears to provide a prima facie plausible explanation—and justification—for the consideration rule. Before this conclusion may be affirmed, however, three potential objections need to be addressed.

Inconsistency with invalidity of certain categories of gratuitous promises

The first, and least serious, objection is that formal requirements of validity appear unnecessary for certain kinds of gratuitous promises. Until recently, the most important such promise would have been one promising an 'upward variation' of an existing contract—say where an employer promises to pay a contractor extra to complete work that the contractor was already contractually obliged to do. Traditionally, such promises were unenforceable on the basis that the promisees had not promised to do anything in exchange other than what they were already contractually obliged to do. Promising to perform a 'pre-existing duty', it was said, was not good consideration.[17] Though there are concerns related to promises to perform a pre-existing duty,[18] such concerns are not related to cautionary or chanelling issues. This is because such promises are made between parties who *already have* legal relations with one another—and we can assume that those relations were created with serious reflection and with intent to create legal relations. Therefore, in the context of promises to perform a pre-existing duty, consideration is not necessary as a form requirement.

But whatever its historical significance, an objection based on the pre-existing duty rule carries little weight (in the United Kingdom at any rate) since the decision in *Williams v Roffey Bros*.[19] In that case, the court effectively overturned the traditional rule, holding that promises to perform a pre-existing duty provide good consideration so long as the promisee receives a 'practical benefit' in return. Given that a practical benefit may consist in avoiding the cost of finding someone else to do the relevant work, it would appear that consideration will be found in all variations, save those in which the promisor was effectively promising a gift. This result is consistent with the formal justification, since it is precisely donative promises that, in this view, are the main focus of the consideration rule.

A second example of a gratuitous promise for which formal requirements might seem unnecessary is a gratuitous promise to keep an offer open for a set period. Such promises are typically made in a commercial setting, and often between parties who have discussed the length of the term (the period for which it will be open). For this reason, it might be concluded that they also do not raise the same cautionary or channelling

---

[17] *Stilck v Myrick* (1809) 2 Camp 317, 6 Esp 129.
[18] Notably a concern for whether they have been made under duress: 9.1.1.
[19] [1991] 1 QB 1.

issues raised by donative promises—and so should be enforced despite the lack of consideration. But the legal invalidity of such promises seems only weakly inconsistent with the notion that consideration is justified by form requirements. Consider that, although promises to keep an offer open are not donative promises, they are also not standard, bargained-for promises. Furthermore, they can be, and often are, made between parties who have had no prior contract. For these reasons, it may be reasonable to suppose that promises to keep an offer open are more likely to be made incautiously than ordinary promises. If this is correct, treating consideration as a formal requirement in these situations makes good sense.

Inconsistency with validity of unilateral contracts

A second possible objection to the formal justification is that it fits poorly with so-called 'unilateral contracts'. More specifically, an offer to enter such a contract, though gratuitous, may bind the offeror even though no formality has been complied with. Let me explain. A unilateral contract is a contract in which the offeree is said to 'accept' the offer not by agreeing to do a requested act, but rather by simply doing the act. An example is a reward for finding a lost cat. From the perspective of the formal justification, the difficulty raised by unilateral contracts is that the consideration for the relevant promise (e.g., the offer of reward) is said also to consist not in agreeing to do the requested act, but, again, simply in doing the act. It may be questioned whether such performance is properly described as consideration (given that it is not done *in exchange* for the promise: see below at 6.3.3). But for present purposes, the important point is that, however it is described, performance in unilateral contracts does not fulfill the formal function that, according to the explanation now being examined, consideration normally fulfills. Performance happens too late to serve a formal function. Performance in a unilateral contract happens *after* the relevant promise has been made. The formal justification suggests, therefore, that promises to enter such contracts should not be enforceable unless a seal or other formality is used.

But the significance of this objection depends on whether promises to enter unilateral contracts are the kinds of promises for which formalities ought to be required. On the one hand, promises to enter unilateral contracts are properly characterized as *gratuitous* promises. To be sure, the promise does not bind until the requested act is performed. But the promise itself is not made *in exchange* for anything; by definition, no one is obliged to perform the requested act. On the other hand, a promise to enter a unilateral contract clearly is not a donative promise—an offer of reward is not an offer to make a gift—and so it cannot be assumed that it raises the same cautionary and channelling concerns that donative promises raise.

In considering the above question, it is important to distinguish between two kinds of promises to enter unilateral contracts: promises made to specific individuals, and promises 'to the world' (i.e., to the general population). As an example of the first kind of promise, consider a promise made by a scrap metal dealer to a contractor to pay so much per ton for scrap metal. Promises of this kind seem closer to ordinary bargain promises than to donative promises in terms of the need for a formality. They are typically made in a commercial setting, and often are preceded by negotiations or at least discussion of terms. More importantly, there is usually a reasonable opportunity to withdraw the promise if it is later regretted. Of course, a normal offer can also be withdrawn prior to acceptance—but the period in which this can be done is often very brief (in oral contracts it can be a matter of seconds). In a unilateral contract, in which acceptance is by performance, this period is normally longer. Enforcing such promises therefore appears consistent with the formal justification for consideration.

As an example of the second kind of promise to enter a unilateral contract—a promise 'to the world'—consider a newspaper notice promising a reward for finding a lost dog. Promises of this kind raise a variety of special concerns (basically because it is not clear they are actually promises: 5.2.4). But for present purposes, the main point is that such promises seem, again, closer to ordinary bargain promises than to donative promises in terms of the need for a formality. Admittedly, a promise to the world is not preceded by negotiations or indeed by any communication with the potential beneficiaries. But the steps required to make such a promise (e.g., placing an advertisement) typically satisfy the cautionary and channelling concerns that formalities are meant to address. The promisor will have time to reflect.[20] In addition, as with the first category of promises to enter unilateral contracts, there is usually a period of time in which such promises can be withdrawn.

I conclude, then, that the second objection—which states that the

---

[20] This is not true, of course, for *all* 'promises to the world'. Consider a person who discovers that her car has been vandalized and then makes the following statement to a crowd of bystanders: 'a thousand dollars to anyone who tells me who did this'. Such a promise raises clear cautionary and channelling concerns. And it is no answer to say that such a promise could be refused enforcement for the lack of an intent to create relations: the very point of using a formality is to avoid having to rely on this doctrine.

alleged consideration in unilateral contracts (i.e., performance) cannot fulfill a formal function—is also not a serious one. With respect to the two types of unilateral contracts I described above, it is not clear whether a formality ought to be required at all. The 'natural features' of these contracts are such that a 'cautionary-based' formality (in the form of consideration) appears unnecessary.[21]

Inconsistency with legal explanation of the doctrine

Finally, the third, and most significant, objection to the formal justification for consideration is that it is inconsistent with how the rule is described and understood by common law judges and lawyers. Common law judges and treatises do not explain the consideration rule by saying that 'all agreements are in principle enforceable though gratuitous agreements require formalities such as nominal consideration or a seal'. What judges say is that *all* contracts require consideration. Furthermore, consideration is not described or explained as a formality, or analogized to a writing or sealing requirement. It is presented as a substantive requirement of validity. In addition, the significance attached to the rule (as evidenced by the space devoted to it in textbooks) seems inconsistent with regarding the rule as a mere form requirement.

The significance of this objection depends on whether, and to what extent, it counts in favour of a theoretical explanation of the law that it supports the legal or internal explanation. As we saw in Chapter 1 (1.6), views differ on this essentially methodological question. For the moment, it is sufficient to make two points. First, the 'consideration as formal requirement' explanation should not be regarded as an entirely external justification. Formal requirements are both common and widely accepted; it follows that the formal justification is the kind of justification that judges *could* accept, even if they have not done so yet (for an example of a justification that does not meet this test, see the realist justification examined in 6.3.3). Second, it is understandable that judges might describe the rule as serving a substantive purpose (even if this is not the case), because at one time the rule did arguably serve such a purpose. The historical evidence in support of this second point will be found in the discussion below of the realist justification for consideration (6.3.3).

This discussion has shown that the formal justification for consideration offers a plausible explanation for the consideration rule. But before

---

[21] Admittedly, this explanation does not explain why judges nevertheless purport to find consideration in unilateral contracts. For a fuller treatment of this issue, see 5.2.4.

concluding that it also offers the best explanation of the rule, two alternative explanations must be examined.

6.3.2. SUBSTANTIVE JUSTIFICATIONS FOR CONSIDERATION

As I just noted, judges typically present consideration as a *substantive* requirement of validity. This leads naturally to asking whether there exists a substantive justification for the rule. Is there a justification that can explain why consideration should be required, in and of itself, and not merely as a proxy for something else that the law cares about? Two such justifications are examined below: the economic value (of donative promises) justification, and the intangible value (of donative promises) justification.

The economic value justification

One substantive justification sometimes put forward for the consideration rule is that gratuitous agreements have no economic value.[22] More specifically, the suggestion is that the core example of a gratuitous agreement— a donative promise—is in economic terms a 'sterile' or zero-sum transaction. Gifts, it is said, merely redistribute, rather than increase, the wealth of a society.

This suggestion is unpersuasive. From an economic perspective, donative promises are valuable for the same reason that ordinary promises are valuable—they facilitate beneficial reliance (4.1.1). Specifically, the promise of a gift (like any other promise[23]) increases 'the present value of an uncertain future stream of transfer payments'.[24] That is, it allows the promisee to rely (to her benefit) on the promise. A promise to give a movie ticket for a show that takes place the following day, for example, makes the actual giving of the ticket more valuable than if it was simply handed over unannounced an hour prior to the show. Similarly, an enforceable promise to make a gift of money increases the value of the actual gift; the promisee can use the money in advance of actually receiving it (say, by using it as collateral for a loan).

Of course, this explanation of the value of donative promises assumes that the actual giving of gifts is itself (economically) valuable. But, again, donations are, in this respect, similar to ordinary exchanges. A donation is a voluntary transfer, and voluntary transfers are assumed to be mutually

---

[22] Bufnoir (1924) 487; Fuller (1941) 815.   [23] Goetz and Scott (1980).
[24] Posner (1977) 412.

beneficial (4.1). Why else would the parties agree to the transfer? From this perspective, the only difference between gifts and bargain exchanges is that part of the value of a gift lies in the fact that it is given *as a gift*. The donee and (especially) the donor typically value the donative intent that accompanies a gift. This difference is not significant from an economic perspective: both non-pecuniary benefits and pecuniary benefits are economically valuable (4.1). Indeed, pecuniary benefits are themselves valuable only because of the non-pecuniary satisfaction of preferences that they facilitate.

From the perspective of the economic value that they create, then, donative promises are no different in principle from ordinary bargained-for promises. This is not to deny that in practice there is one significant economic difference between donative promises and ordinary promises. There is a greater risk that promisors who make donative promises will make mistakes (because of the non-commercial nature of the promise). Specifically, the promisor may make a mistake either about the value that she will obtain from the gift or (more commonly) about the value that the other party will obtain. If such a mistake is made, the assumption of mutual benefit does not apply. For this reason, there is a plausible economic argument for treating donative promises as special. But it is an argument that supports a formal rather than a substantive justification for consideration. If the economic objection to donative promises is that they may be made incautiously, then the solution is to impose a formal requirement of validity on such promises—which is precisely the basis on which the formal justification (discussed above) explains the consideration rule.

The intangible value justification

The other main substantive justification offered for the consideration rule is that legally enforcing donative promises would make them less valuable.[25] More specifically, the justification is that legally enforcing the core category of such promises—donative promises—would make these promises less valuable.

This justification is similar to the justification, discussed earlier, for the rule that domestic agreements are presumed not to be intended to be legally binding (6.2). It rests on two related propositions. The first (which I have already discussed) is that donative promises have a special 'intangible' value. This intangible value is the value that is associated with

---

[25] Eisenberg (2001) 229–30; Penner (1996); Radin (1987).

the donative intent that, by definition, accompanies any true gift. As I noted a moment ago, both donors and donees value gifts not just for their practical consequences, but for the donative intent with which they are made. The expression of this intent is considered valuable in and of itself. Moreover, such expressions of donative intent are regarded (rightly in my view) as valuable not just by the relevant donors and donees, but by other people as well. Most people attach a value to living in a society in which gift-giving happens.[26]

The second proposition is that the legal enforcement of donative promises would detract from their special value. This is said to be the case because gifts possess a special value only insofar as they are made with a donative intent. A gift made because of the threat of legal sanction ceases to be a gift—and so loses the special value associated with gifts. Of course, it is not supposed that donative promisors who face a threat of enforcement would always perform for this reason. But the mere possibility of enforcement, it is said, will change the character of the performance. Once it is known that a donor *could* be forced to make the transfer, and thus that the donee *might* be acting out of non-donative motives, the intangible value of all gifts will be lessened. It is not enough, in other words, that donors actually act for donative motives; they must also be *seen to be acting* for such motives. This can only be achieved, the explanation concludes, if courts refuse to enforce donative promises—as stipulated by the consideration rule.

This is an interesting justification for consideration, but it is vulnerable to a number of objections. First, the justification appears inconsistent with the rule that donative promises are enforceable if they made under seal or for nominal consideration.[27] A donative promise made under seal or for nominal consideration remains in substance a donative promise. So why are such promises enforceable? Second, it may be queried, on purely empirical grounds, whether enforcing donative promises would actually cause people to devalue their performance. I know of no way to test the asserted link, but my impression is that it is a weak one. The law does not play a large role in how most people think about gifts. As well, the message conveyed by a decision to enforce donative promises might well be interpreted as *affirming* the intangible value of gift-giving. Third, and

---

[26] e.g. Titmuss (1970).

[27] In this regard, it is interesting that some American jurisdictions refuse to accept either a seal or nominal consideration as an alternative to consideration. But on the other hand, in a number of American jurisdictions gratuitous promises are enforceable if in writing: Farnsworth (1999) 86–87, 90.

most importantly, insofar as the enforcement of donative promises makes gift-*giving* less valuable, that value would necessarily be transferred to the act of making donative *promise*s. It would be transferred because if donative promises are enforceable, then the act of making such promises resembles the act of physically making a gift. The promise itself would become the gift; thus, the intangible value of gift-giving would not be lost, but would instead attach to *that* act.[28]

6.3.3. THE REALIST JUSTIFICATION: CONSIDERATION AS A GOOD REASON FOR ENFORCEMENT

The formal and substantive justifications just discussed have a common feature. Both assume that the rule for which they offer a justification is correctly described by the orthodox account of consideration. These justifications therefore assume they are trying to justify a rule to the effect that (roughly) gratuitous promises are not enforceable. The essential feature of the justification now being considered—the 'realist' justification—is that it rejects this initial assumption. According to the realist justification, the orthodox description does not accurately convey how the rule actually operates. According to defenders of this view, *in practice* the consideration rule functions like an umbrella or catch-all concept. Specifically, courts use (or manipulate) the rule in order to take into account a wide variety of factors for and against enforcing agreements, few of which have much to do with 'consideration' in its technical sense. These factors include concerns for issues such as good faith, duress, and the protection of reliance. In the realist view, the rule's justification is that it provides an umbrella concept that courts can use to give effect to these and other concerns.

As developed by Patrick Atiyah—the leading defender of this approach—the realist justification is, in part, an historical explanation of the law.[29] Atiyah argues that courts in the 17th and 18th centuries understood the consideration rule very broadly; to say there was 'good consideration' simply meant that there was a 'good reason' to enforce the contract.[30] This reason might be, for example, that the promisor had a

---

[28] Of course, not everyone is aware of the law, and so not everyone would regard donative promises in this way. But the justification under consideration applies only to the extent that people are aware of the law.

[29] Atiyah (1986) 179–243. For an earlier argument along similar lines, see Corbin (1917–18).

[30] 'It seems highly probable that when the courts first used the word "consideration" they meant no more than that there was a "reason" for the enforcement of a promise. If the consideration was "good", this meant that the court found sufficient reason for enforcing the promise.' Atiyah (1986) 182.

prior moral obligation to do what he promised to do or that the promisee had relied on the promise. Conversely, to say that an agreement lacked good consideration meant that there was a good reason *not* to enforce the promise—for example, that it was not intended to be binding, that is was made under duress, that it was to do something illegal, or that it was part of an unconscionable bargain. Atiyah then explains that, in the late 19th and early 20th centuries, this broad understanding of consideration underwent a transformation. Under the influence of formalist theories of law, lawyers began to describe consideration using the technical language of reciprocal benefits or burdens familiar to lawyers today. But this new way of explaining the rule, Atiyah concludes, did not accurately describe what courts were doing then—or now. With the exception of a few courts misled by the modern rhetoric, what courts were, and still are, actually doing is what they have always been doing—asking if there are good reasons to enforce (or not) the agreement. Of course, courts do not do this openly; instead, they pay lip-service to the orthodox (modern) rule. The reality, however, is that they manipulate the rule or the facts so that they can 'find' or 'invent' consideration—and vice versa. It is for this reason that Atiyah's theory is 'realist'; he asserts that the law in the books is different from the law in practice (1.7).

Like much realist scholarship, this explanation of the consideration rule cannot be evaluated properly without a detailed analysis of a large body of case law. But even a brief survey suggests that many well-known 18th and 19th century cases support the interpretation. One example is the 1853 decision of *White v Bluett*,[31] in which Pollock CB suggested that a father's promise to pay his son's debt if the son ceased complaining was unenforceable for absence of consideration, because the son had 'no right to complain'. This suggestion is perplexing when viewed from the perspective of the orthodox rule. In legal terms, the son had a clear 'right' to complain (complaining is legal). A more plausible explanation—and one consistent with the realist thesis—is that the father did not intend his promise to be legally binding or that it was given under duress or undue influence. A second example is *Hamer v Sidway*,[32] an American case from 1891 that is often contrasted with *White*. In *Hamer*, an uncle's promise to give his nephew $5,000 if the nephew refrained from 'drinking, using tobacco, swearing and playing cards until age 21' was enforced. From the perspective of the orthodox consideration rule, the facts of *Hamer* are similar to *White*: in each, the plaintiff agreed to refrain from exercising

---

[31] (1853) 23 LJ Ex 36.   [32] 27 NR 256 (1891)

his liberty. But from the perspective of the realist interpretation, there is a clear difference. The agreement in *Hamer* helps to promote a moral lifestyle. As such, there would have been a 'good reason', in Atiyah's language, to enforce the agreement. A third, and final example is the 19th century case of *Stilck v Myrick*,[33] in which a ship's captain reneged on a promise, made during the course of a voyage, to pay his crew higher wages. Lord Ellenborough stated that the agreement was unenforceable for lack of consideration, on the basis that the crew had merely agreed to do what they were already legally bound to do. Again, the stated explanation is unconvincing. Regardless of their prior obligations, the crew had agreed to do something of value in exchange for the captain's promise (a point explicitly acknowledged in the recent case of *Williams v Roffey Bros*).[34] A more convincing explanation—and, again, one that is consistent with the realist interpretation—is that enforcing such bargains encourages extortion. If such bargains were enforced, sailors might be encouraged to exploit their 'monopoly' with respect to the supply of sailors at sea. Significantly—and also consistent with the realist interpretation—just such an explanation was stated explicitly by a court in the 18th century case of *Harris v Watson*.[35]

In historical terms, then, the realist interpretation fits well with a number of well-known decisions. Whether its broader historical claims are sustainable is more debatable,[36] but for present purposes it is not necessary to enter this debate. This is because even if Atiyah's interpretation of what courts in the 18th, 19th, and early 20th centuries were doing is accepted, it does not follow that courts *today* are doing the same thing. Indeed, the analysis of cases such as *White v Bluett, Hamer v Sidway*, and *Stilck v Merrit* might be thought to argue *against* the claim that contemporary courts treat consideration as an umbrella concept, since today these cases would almost certainly be decided using other legal doctrines. *White v Bluett* would be decided on the basis that the parties lacked intent to create legal relations or that the agreement was made under duress (doctrines little developed at the time of these cases).[37] The result in *Hamer v Sidway* could be reached simply by applying the contemporary

---

[33] (1809) 2 Camp 317 & 6 esp 129.   [34] [1991] 1 QB 1.
[35] (1791) Peake 102; 170 ER 94.   [36] e.g. Ibbetson (1999) 141–45, 204–208, 236–41.
[37] Intent to create legal relations cases illustrate this point nicely. In *Shadwell v Shadwell* (1860) 9 CBNS 159 absence of consideration was the reason given for refusing to enforce an agreement between family members, while in the more recent case of *Jones v Padavatton* [1969] 1 WLR 328 a court refused on similar facts to enforce the agreement on the basis of a lack of intent to create legal relations.

(technical) consideration rule, since agreeing not to drink, etc. actually satisfies that rule (because agreeing to restrict one's liberty is a burden). Finally, the decision in a case like *Stilck v Myrick* would (after *Williams v Roffey Bros*)[38] focus directly on questions of economic duress (a doctrine that, again, was undeveloped at the time of *Stilck*).

This observation—that contemporary courts would not need to express their concerns for issues like duress, illegality, or intent to create legal relations under the heading of consideration—thus limits the scope of the realist claim. But even accepting that the range of 'reasons' a contemporary court would take into account when applying the consideration rule is narrower than it would have been in the past, it can be argued (as Atiyah does) that courts are still engaged in fundamentally the same exercise. In this view, contemporary courts use consideration to give effect to a variety of factors that cannot be given effect even under the present doctrines of duress, illegality, intent, etc. In particular, it is said that courts use the rule to give effect to concerns for things such as detrimental reliance (on which Atiyah places special importance),[39] unconscionability,[40] substantive fairness,[41] and good faith generally.[42] None of these factors is explicitly relevant to determining the validity of a contract on the orthodox common law view. But as I have discussed elsewhere, many lawyers and scholars think that courts should take such concerns (or at least some of them) into account.[43] According to the realist interpretation, this is exactly what the courts do under the name of applying the consideration rule.

As I mentioned above, assessing this essentially empirical argument is difficult within the scope of this book. Nonetheless, four observations may be offered. First, given that (as I just said) many judges believe

---

[38] [1991] 1 QB 1. *Roffey Bros* is an interesting case because it both supports Atiyah's historical explanation and puts into question his account of contemporary law. At issue was the validity of a head contractor's promise to pay over the contractually agreed rate to a subcontractor (who had run into financial difficulties). The court held that the consideration rule was satisfied because the head contractor received a 'practical benefit' in return for his promise (namely that the work would be done without the head contractor having to find another subcontractor), and it further held that any concerns about exploitation should be dealt with directly by the doctrine of duress. The decision thus supports Atiyah's historical account because the court said reasonably clearly that the real issue in earlier pre-existing duty cases was duress. But at the same time the court affirmed that the consideration rule should be applied *now* in a narrow technical sense.

[39] See Atiyah (1979; 1981), Fuller and Purdue (1936).

[40] Waddams (1976); Gordley (1981).

[41] Gordley (1981); Atiyah (1986) 329–54; Smith (1996b).

[42] Beatson and Friedmann (1995) 3–24, 153–70, 399–426.

[43] Reliance: 3.2; unconscionability: 9.2; substantive fairness: 9.2.5; good faith: 5.4.

factors such as reliance, unconscionability, substantive fairness, and good faith should matter—and given that many also think consideration in its technical sense should *not* matter—it is prima facie unlikely that the doctrine is *never* used in the way that the realist interpretation suggests. Second, there is one application of the consideration rule that fits neatly with the realist thesis. This is the long-standing rule that in unilateral contracts consideration is supplied by the performance of the requested act.[44] This seems a clear example of invented consideration. To be sure, in the orthodox definition, consideration is said to be satisfied by 'a *performance* or a return promise'.[45] But it is also a fundamental tenet of the orthodox definition that the performance or return promise 'must be bargained for'—meaning that it must be 'sought by the promisor in *exchange* for his promise'.[46] By definition, performance in a unilateral contract does not satisfy this condition because it does not happen until *after* the relevant promise has been made. The finding of a lost dog, for example, is not done in exchange for an earlier promise of reward because the promise was already made by the time the alleged exchange took place. Of course, the definition of consideration could be amended to state that it is satisfied by either promising to do something in exchange for a promise *or* by doing something in order to fulfill a condition of a promise. But when defined in this way the rule loses whatever semblance of coherence it ever possessed. There is no theory of consideration that regards making a promise and performing a requested act as equivalent acts.[47] But enforcing such contracts is, of course, consistent with the realist thesis. Performance in a unilateral contract is a clear example of (legitimate) detrimental reliance; as such, it amounts to what Atiyah would describe as a good reason for enforcement.

The third observation is that, aside from unilateral contracts, it seems clear that courts do not regularly, or even frequently, 'ignore' and 'invent' consideration in the way that this interpretation suggests they do. In an ordinary contract of sale case, for example, contemporary judges would not use the consideration rule to invalidate an agreement in which the

---

[44] Other agreements in respect of which the consideration rules are explicitly not applied include certain categories of bailment agreements: see Treitel (1995) 143–44.

[45] Pollock (1950)133, approved by Lord Dunedin in *Dunlop v Selfridge* (1915).

[46] See previous footnote.

[47] That some courts have not permitted promisors to withdraw promises to make a unilateral contract once the requested performance has begun lends further support to the realist explanation: *Daulia Ltd v Four Millbank Nominees Ltd* [1978] Ch 231. It is difficult to see how *beginning* to do a requested act could count as consideration or indeed as anything else that courts should care about—beyond being clear evidence of reliance on a promise.

real reason for invalidity is that the agreement was not relied upon or was substantively unfair or was made in bad faith. Judges might try to manipulate other rules in order to set the agreement aside, but they will not conclude that consideration is missing in a case in which the orthodox test is so plainly satisfied. More generally, it is difficult to think of a contemporary case in which an agreement was not enforced on the basis of the consideration rule when the real reason for this finding was not that consideration (in the technical sense) was missing, but that there existed a different 'good' reason not to enforce the agreement.[48] Similarly, it is difficult to find contemporary cases in which courts have invented consideration in order to enforce an agreement that clearly did not satisfy the technical test.[49] Even if courts wanted to do this, the occasions on which it would be necessary to do so would be very rare; aside from pure gifts, the technical rule of consideration is, as a matter of strict law, easy to satisfy. Thus, while the agreement between the nephew and uncle in *Hamer v Sidway* may have been the sort of valuable arrangement that courts have 'good reason' to enforce, it also satisfied the orthodox understanding of the consideration rule. It might be thought that *Williams v Roffey Bros* is itself a case of invented consideration, in that the court found consideration in circumstances in which previous courts had refused to do. But as I have argued above, the idea that consideration may consist of a 'practical benefit' is better understood as reinforcing the contemporary technical understanding of consideration. The sub-contractor's promise to do the work was a promise to do something of real benefit to the contractor because, regardless of the subcontractor's legal

---

[48] Admittedly, prior to the decision in *Williams v Roffey Bros* [1991] 1 QB 1, cases in which the performance of pre-existing duty was held not to be consideration could be explained in this way. It might be thought that the sub-category of such cases dealing with promises to release a debt in exchange for part payment can still be explained in this way, since the traditional rule still applies in such cases: *Re Selectmove Ltd* [1995] 2 All ER 531. This rule seems unlikely to survive, but even if it does it provides little support for the realist interpretation. The part-payment rule does not show courts manipulating the technical rule for other good reasons. Instead, the rule is a good example of courts mechanically *following* (the traditional understanding of) the technical rule despite the unfairness that might arise.

[49] A possible counter-example is *Chappell & Co v Nestle* [1960] AC 87, in which the court held that sending in chocolate wrappers amounted to consideration. The case should be used carefully, however, as the consideration question was raised as part of an infringement of copyright claim, and then only in the context of determining whether the wrappers could form *part* of the consideration (a concept that, strictly speaking, has no real meaning in contract law). For an argument that American courts enforce commercial promises regardless of the existence of consideration, see Farber and Matheson (1985).

obligations (to do the work), there was a strong likelihood that, without the new agreement, the work would not be done.[50]

The fourth and final observation—which supports the previous one—is that it may be questioned whether it makes normative sense to suppose that courts are acting in the way the realist explanation assumes they are acting. The point here is not a simple objection to courts employing fictions and manipulating facts when applying the consideration rule. Those defending the realist interpretation (such as Atiyah) argue that courts should be explicit about the rule's function as an umbrella concept. Nor is the objection that factors such as reliance and good faith simply should not matter in the law. This claim is, of course, often made (3.2.1; 5.4), but it is not my present concern. Rather, the objection is that for courts to do what the realists suppose they do is inconsistent with the rule of law. Let me explain. It is basic requirement of the rule of law that the law be clear and predictable.[51] But if the realist understanding of the consideration rule were adopted explicitly, the effects of the rule would always be unclear and unpredictable—and this would be true even if courts were explicit about what they were trying to do. This is the case because, as Atiyah states explicitly,[52] it is a fundamental assumption of the realist interpretation that the list of 'good reasons' that may be introduced under the heading consideration is never closed. Even if reliance, good faith, and unconscionability were given separate and full recognition in the law, it would still be necessary, in this view, to keep the doctrine of consideration. The rule's ultimate purpose, in the realist view, is to function as a residual category; it allows judges to rely on reasons that have not been, and in some cases arguably cannot be, incorporated explicitly into the law. Presented in this way, the basic normative argument for adopting the 'good reason' interpretation of consideration is that contract law requires at least one openly discretionary test for validity. To the extent that this argument is accepted, the law of contract will conflict with the rule of law.

---

[50] Other cases which, arguably, can be explained in this way include: *Williams v Williams* [1957] 1 All ER 305; *Ward v Byham* [1956] 2 All ER 318; *New Zealand Shipping Co Ltd v A. M. Satterthwaite, The Eurymedon* [1975] AC 154; *North Island Shipping Co Ltd v Hyundai Construction Co Ltd, The Atlantic Baron* [1979] QB 705.

[51] Fuller (1969) 33–49.

[52] 'To talk of abolition of the doctrine of consideration is nonsensical. Consideration means a reason for the enforcement of a promise. Nobody can seriously propose that all promises should become enforceable; to abolish the doctrine of consideration, therefore, is simply to require the courts to begin all over again the task of deciding what promises are to be enforceable': (1986) 241.

Of course, the rule of law is not the only criteria for good law. The law must also be substantively just; and to become substantively just it must be allowed to evolve. Thus, there clearly must be avenues by which judges can introduce previously unrecognized arguments for or against legal liability. In Atiyah's view, consideration plays this role. But there clearly is a limit, though it is difficult to define, as to how far judges should be invited to use their discretion in this way. I suggest that the realist interpretation goes too far; it does not merely permit, but positively invites courts to make new law, and it places no restrictions on this invitation. I conclude, then, that rule of law concerns provide a further reason for rejecting the realist interpretation, at least in its stronger versions.

6.3.4. CONCLUSION TO CONSIDERATION

Our examination of the consideration rule suggests that no explanation can account for all of its various features. But the examination also suggests that it would be wrong to conclude (as some have concluded) that the rule is entirely without rationale. Viewed historically, the consideration rule can arguably be described as representing little more than a requirement that there be a 'good reason' to enforce an agreement. Today, some cases and rules (in particular, the rule that performance is consideration in unilateral contracts) can also be explained in this way. But, overall, the formal justification for consideration (first elaborated by Fuller) provides the most plausible explanation for the modern consideration rule. This is particularly true insofar as the rule is applied to the core case of a gratuitious promise—a donative promise. Although this explanation is inconsistent with how courts typically explain the rule, it is consistent in broad terms with the substance of the rule.

A final point to keep in mind is that this conclusion is consistent with believing that the consideration rule should be reformed. Indeed, it helps to explain why calls for reform are commonly made. The consideration rule may play a formal role, but nothing I have said suggests that it is the only or the best way to fulfill that role—or even that the role needs to be fulfilled at all. Concluding that the *Statute of Frauds* plays a formal role (which it clearly does), does not commit one to supporting the statute. By their nature, formalities are justified by fact-specific, contingent arguments. A sophisticated legal system might function perfectly well without the *Statute of Frauds*. Similarly, it might function perfectly well without a consideration rule. The requirement of intent to create legal relations could be expanded to fulfill the (small) role that, according to the formal justification, consideration now fulfills. Alternately, the above conclusion is consistent, at a minimum, with the belief that the legislature ought to follow the civil law lead and replace the consideration rule with a more transparent formality (e.g., a notarization or writing requirement). Indeed, any other belief seems inconsistent with that conclusion.

6.3.5. PROMISSORY ESTOPPEL

The doctrine of promissory estoppel (hereafter 'estoppel') is usually taught as an ancillary topic to the consideration rule. But from a theoretical perspective, the issues raised by estoppel are arguably more important—and certainly more difficult—that those raised by the consideration rule. In particular, estoppel raises fundamental questions about the role of reliance-based liability in the law of contract (on which generally, see 3.2).

According to the orthodox (though not universal) view, an estoppel arises as follows: one person ('the speaker') makes a representation of intent or a promise of such a nature that it is intended to affect legal relations and to be relied upon—and then is, indeed, relied upon.[53] The effect of an estoppel, in broad terms, is that the speaker is prevented ('estopped') in law from retracting or denying his statement—*regardless of whether consideration was provided in exchange* by the relying person ('the listener'). For example, imagine that we have a valid agreement whereby I am to rent your cottage in France for two weeks. As part of the agreement, I am required to cut the lawn. Suppose further that, before I go to France, you tell me it is not necessary that I cut the lawn. Assuming that I do not cut the lawn, then notwithstanding our rental agreement, and notwithstanding that I offered no consideration in return for your releasing me from my obligation, you will have no recourse against me—you will be estopped from claiming that I breached that agreement.

In the United Kingdom, estoppel is limited by the rule that (with certain exceptions) it can be used only as a *defence* to the speaker's attempt to assert otherwise valid contractual rights.[54] Estoppel cannot be used to found a cause of action—it is a 'shield not a sword'. In a variation of the example above, imagine that, shortly after our agreement is concluded, you tell me that I will be free to use the car you have left at the cottage (this was not part of the original agreement). Believing you, I leave my car at home—only to find on arrival that you changed your mind and lent the car to a friend. Since estoppel can only be used as a

---

[53] Treitel (1995) 102, McKendrick (1997) 104.
[54] *Hughes v Metropolitan Rly* (1877) 2 App Cas 439, 448.

defence (a shield), I cannot sue you for use of your car. Mere donative promises, no matter how much reliance they induce, cannot be enforced. In some common law jurisdictions, though, notably the United States[55] and (more recently) Australia,[56] the sword/shield rule has been relaxed.

Three views of estoppel

The main theoretical issue raised by estoppel is simply stated: why does the doctrine exist?; what role or function does it play? The answers that have been given to this question reveal three different views about estoppel. According to the first view, the purpose of the doctrine is to protect detrimental reliance. More specifically, its purpose is to protect persons who reasonably and detrimentally rely on the representations of others, promissory or otherwise.[57] For those who take this 'reliance' view, estoppel is distinct from promissory liability (at least as promissory liability is normally understood). As we have seen, the obligation to keep a promise is created simply by communicating an intention to undertake an obligation (3.1). Of course, promisees often rely on promises made to them, but this is not an essential feature of promising. It further follows that in this view estoppel is not, ultimately, a contract law doctrine. According to the traditional view of contract law (which view I defended in Chapter 3), contractual obligations are essentially promissory obligations. Assuming this view is accepted, estoppel is either a part of the law of tort or part of another non-contractual species of liability (and as such is usually described by advocates of this view as 'equitable' estoppel rather than 'promissory' estoppel).

According to the second view, the purpose of estoppel is the same as the purpose of contract law generally—to enforce promises.[58] In this 'promissory' view, the only difference between a standard contract claim and a claim based on estoppel, is that the latter does not require consideration. The estoppel doctrine is thus portrayed as a means by which courts can avoid at least some of the limitations on promissory liability imposed by the consideration rule. This view implies two additional conclusions. The first is that the requirement that the listener rely on the communication is either a fiction or unimportant. Second, this view regards estoppel as firmly a part of contract law.

---

[55] s. 90 Restatement 2d *Contracts*.
[56] *Walton Stores (Interstate) Ltd v Maher* (1988) 164 CLR 387.
[57] Spence (1990); *Walton Stores (Interstate) Ltd v Maher* (1988) 164 CLR 387.
[58] Yorio and Thel (1991); Farber and Matheson (1985).

Finally, according to the third or 'mixed' view of estoppel, the purpose of estoppel is to enforce relied-upon promises.[59] This view regards both the existence of a promise *and* reliance on that promise as important in principle. Both are required. It follows, in this view, that while estoppel is essentially contractual—it focuses on promissory communications—it is distinct from the ordinary (purely promissory) case of contractual liability. Unlike in the ordinary case, the courts dispense with the need for consideration, and substitute, as an alternative requirement, reliance on the promise.

At first instance, the first of these three views—the reliance view— appears to fit best with the law. In my initial description of the doctrine, I said that it focused on representations (and not just promises) and, further, that it was triggered by induced reliance. What seems important, in other words, is that a person was induced to rely—not that a promise was made.

On closer inspection, however, the picture is less clear. Defenders of the mixed view and, in particular, the promissory view, argue that the actual operation of the doctrine fits their views better than the reliance view. To assess these arguments, four features of the doctrine will be examined: (1) the requirement that a statement of intention *or* a promise be made, (2) the requirement that the relevant communication be relied upon, (3) the 'remedies' for estoppel, and (4) the sword/shield rule. To simplify the discussion, these features will be examined from the perspective of only two of the three views described above—the promissory and reliance views. For the purposes of 'fit' issues now under consideration, the mixed view is (as I have suggested) a simple mixture of the other two views. The mixed view will be reintroduced as a distinct category only at the end of the inquiry.

The requirement of a statement of intention *or* a promise

In comparing the promissory and reliance views, the first question that needs to be addressed is whether it is indeed the case that estoppel can be triggered by a mere representation of intention (promissory or otherwise) or whether, instead, only a promise counts.[60] An initial observation is that notwithstanding my above description of the orthodox account (in which I referred to both promises *and* representations), many textbooks describe

---

[59] Burrows (1983) 244; Seavey (1951); Fuller and Purdue (1936).

[60] Admittedly, there are clear instances of 'estoppels' that can arise without a promise— notably estoppel by representation and estoppel by convention. Our focus, however, is on the core category of promissory estoppel.

the doctrine using exclusively promissory language. Thus, in Cheshire, Fifoot and Furmston it is stated that in order to establish estoppel 'there must be a promise, either by words or by conduct'.[61] Significantly, the authors do not go on to suggest that (mere) representations of intention are given legal force in other ways. Promissory language is particularly evident in American descriptions of the doctrine. The Restatement of Contracts (2d) discusses estoppel under a section (s.90) entitled 'Promise Reasonably Inducing Action or Forbearance', the substantive terms of which refer exclusively to promises.[62] American textbooks similarly refer to 'promises' rather than 'representations' when discussing estoppel.[63]

In theory, the case law should provide a clear answer to this question, but in practice it does not. This is because while (mere) statements of intention are distinct in principle from promises, in practice they are not easy to distinguish—especially when, as is usually the case (because of the sword/shield rule)—the relevant communication is made in a contractual setting. In such settings, to be certain that a particular communication is only a representation of intention and not a promise, explicit language to this effect is usually required. Thus a speaker might say 'It is my intention/plan/hope to do X', but then add the disclaimer 'but I am not promising to do X'. None of the best known estoppel cases deal with communications that contain explicit language of this kind. Rather, the communications in these cases are expressed in language that is either clearly or arguably promissory. For example, in the leading case of *Central London Property Trust v High Trees House Ltd*,[64] the landlord's communication to his tenant 'confirm[ing] . . . the ground rent should be reduced' was described repeatedly as a promise, and appears clearly to have been a promise. As for what courts *say* they are doing, the picture is again unclear. Some cases refer to representations, but others refer to promises. A notable example of the latter is, again, Lord Denning's decision in the *High Trees* case. After discussing the older view that estoppel was limited to statements of existing fact, Lord Denning listed a number of cases and then concluded: 'As I have said they are not cases of estoppel in the strict sense [i.e., involving statements of fact]. They are really promises.'[65]

---

[61] Cheshire, Fifoot and Furmston (2001) 111. See also Burrows (1983) 239–44.

[62] Section 90 reads: 'A promise which the promisor should reasonably expect to induce action or forbearance on the part of the promisee or a third person and which does induce such action or forbearance is binding if injustice can be avoided only by enforcement of the promise . . . '

[63] Farnsworth (1999) 95.   [64] [1947] 1 KB 130.

[65] *Central London Property Trust v High Trees House Ltd* [1947] 1 KB 130, 131.

I conclude, then, that with respect to this first feature of the doctrine the promissory view appears to fit what courts actually do as well as the reliance view.

The requirement of reliance

Turning to the second feature of the doctrine, the reliance requirement, we have seen that the orthodox account clearly supports this requirement —and so supports the reliance view of estoppel. If the purpose of estoppel is to protect reliance, then it makes sense, of course, for courts to make reliance a condition of liability. But again, the accuracy of the orthodox account may be questioned. To be sure, judges usually mention reliance when describing the doctrine. But when judges actually apply the doctrine, reliance seems to play little role. The *High Trees* decision is again illustrative: Lord Denning stated that for the doctrine to come into play, the promise must be 'intended to be acted upon and in fact acted upon'— but he then said nothing with regard to whether the defendant invoking estoppel actually met this requirement. Admittedly, it is almost certain that the defendant did rely—for example by not seeking alternative accommodation, or simply by the fact of not paying the full original rent. But this was not mentioned. Moreover, the fact that we can be confident that reliance occurred in this case (despite the lack of evidence) illustrates the difficulty of finding examples to prove or disprove this feature of the orthodox account. In practice, it is rare that promises (or mere statements of intention for that matter) do not induce reliance, especially when they are made seriously and in the context of existing legal relations (as required by the doctrine). What is needed, in order to prove the reliance view, is evidence of contract cases in which courts denied estoppel arguments on the basis of the reliance requirement. But it is not clear that any such cases exist.[66] In jurisdictions, like England, in which estoppel can be used only as a defence, such a case would be one in which estoppel was denied because, although the plaintiff had waived the relevant obligation, and although the defendant had not performed that obligation, it was proven that the defendant would not have performed regardless of the plaintiff's waiver—in other words, that the plaintiff did not rely on the waiver. There do not appear to be any such cases. In jurisdictions in which estoppel can be used as a cause of action, it should, in theory, be easier to find cases in which estoppel claims are denied because the plaintiff

---

[66] As I discuss below, reliance clearly does matter, however, in determining if, and when, a speaker who has waived contractual rights may re-assert her original contractual rights.

who should rely, did not (if the orthodox account is correct). Yet two surveys of American case law on estoppel concluded that the reliance requirement existed in name only.[67] Finally, it should be noted that, while the matter is not beyond controversy, the prevailing view is that ordinary reliance as opposed to *detrimental* reliance is sufficient to establish an estoppel.[68] The reliance explanation of estoppel, however, supposes that the kind of reliance that matters is detrimental reliance (on the basis that non-detrimental reliance, by definition, does not cause harm, and so is not suitable for 'protection'). The promissory view, of course, does not require reliance to be exhibited.

The 'remedies' for estoppel

A third feature of the estoppel doctrine that needs to be examined when comparing the reliance and promissory views is the remedies (to use the term broadly) to which it gives rise. Do these remedies protect the complainant's 'promissory' interest in having a promise performed (as the promissory view asserts) or do they protect the complainant's 'reliance' interest in not suffering a reliance-based loss (as the reliance view asserts)? Here again, the evidence does not give a clear answer. In English law, which generally does not permit estoppel to be used as a cause of action, the issue of the appropriate measure of damages for an estoppel does not arise. Insofar as there is a 'remedy' for estoppel, it is to 'enforce' the relevant communication by denying legal effect to any contractual terms that are inconsistent with that communication. For example, if a purchaser informs a manufacturer that an ordered product need not conform to a particular specification in their contract, the effect of that communication (if estoppel is established) is that the purchaser cannot enforce the contractual specification. In one respect, this rule supports the promissory view of estoppel. Rather than precluding the speaker from enforcing his contractual rights, *to the extent that the listener relied*, the courts simply give the communications full effect—as if they were ordinary contractual statements. Thus, the purchaser in our example will be estopped from reasserting the original specification even if the manufacturer's reliance is trivial in comparison to the purchaser's savings *and* the purchaser offers to compensate the manufacturer for his reliance. Significantly, this same approach—treating the communication as an ordinary contractual statement—is adopted in those (exceptional) cases in which estoppel is permitted as a cause of action. Under the doctrine of

---

[67] Yorio and Thel (1991); Farber and Matheson (1985).   [68] Treitel (1995) 105.

proprietary estoppel, for example, a landowner who represents to another that the owner's land will be conveyed to him will be required to do so if the other relies on that representation — even if the value of the reliance is less than the value of the land.[69] The remedy in such cases is always specific performance — which, of course, is entirely consistent with promissory conceptions of remedies.

But in another respect, the courts' approach to 'enforcing' estoppels supports the reliance view. According to the orthodox understanding, an estoppel 'suspends' rather than 'extinguishes' contractual rights.[70] Thus, a speaker who is estopped from asserting contractual rights is allowed to reassert those rights if he gives reasonable notice and the listener is no longer prejudiced by the reassertion. From the promissory view of estoppel, this rule is difficult to explain: promises do not have a time limit. But if the purpose of the estoppel is to protect reliance, the rule makes sense: reliance is temporal.

As I noted above, the (English) rule that estoppel cannot be used as a cause of action makes it more difficult to determine whether the remedies for estoppel support the promissory view or the reliance view. A consequence of the rule is that English courts are not required to determine the measure of damages for 'breach' of an estoppel. Thus, they are not required to determine, for example, whether a promisee who relies to the extent of £500 on the promise of a gift of £1,000 should be awarded £500 or £1,000 in the event the gift is not made. On the other hand, jurisdictions that *do* allow estoppel as a cause of action, such as the United States and Australia, should, in theory, prove more useful for comparing the reliance and the promissory views. Unfortunately, the evidence from such regimes also fails to give a clear answer. In the United States, the question of the appropriate measure of damages for estoppel was hotly debated during the preparation of the second Restatement of Contracts.[71] The end result, however, was a famous — and famously vague — compromise. Section 90 states that the remedy 'may be limited as justice requires'. Today, the proper interpretation of s. 90 remains a matter of controversy. Most textbooks suggest that reliance damages are the presumptive remedy under s.90,[72] but a number of surveys of the case law have concluded that standard contractual remedies (expectation damages or specific

---

[69] *Pascoe v Turner* [1979] 1 WLR 431; Burrows (1983) 242.
[70] *Tool Metal Manufacturing Co Ltd v Tungsten Electric Co Ltd* [1955] 1 WLR 761.
[71] American Law Institute Proceedings (1926) Vol IV, Appendix 98–99, 103–104.
[72] e.g. Farnsworth (1999) 98–100.

performance) are actually the norm.[73] The Australian position is normally described in terms similar to those of s.90[74] (though not always),[75] but again, in most of the cases in which estoppel has been used successfully as a cause of action, the courts have awarded either expectation damages or specific performance.[76]

The sword/shield rule

Finally, a fourth feature of estoppel that needs to be examined is the rule (in England) that estoppel can be used only as a defence (a shield) and not as a cause of action (a sword). Is this rule (and the exceptions to it) better explained by the promissory or the reliance view? Consistent with my previous observations, I will suggest that each view explains this rule equally well.

The promissory view provides a satisfactory, though complex, explanation for the sword/shield rule. This view states, in effect, that the sword/shield distinction must be understood in conjunction with the consideration rule. Let me explain. Recall that the consideration rule is best understood (I argued) as providing form requirements for contracting parties (6.3.1); the form requirements serve to ensure that the parties have reflected seriously (the cautionary function) and that they have clearly intended to create legal relations (the channelling function). With gratuitous promises, these functions of the consideration rule are especially important. This is because the very nature of such promises makes it more likely that persons will make them hastily or without intent to create legal relations. In response to such concerns, the consideration rule requires, in effect, that certain formal requirements be obeyed, such as nominal consideration or a seal. But this is not always the case. Recall that there are certain types of unilateral contracts which, though gratuitous, by their nature, *do not* raise channelling or cautionary concerns— and that the courts do not require consideration (properly understood)[77] for them to be enforced. According to the promissory explanation, estoppel claims are akin to these type of contracts: they represent an example of a gratuitous promise that does not raise the type of concerns associated with the core case of a gratuitous promise—a donative

---

[73] Yorio and Thel (1991); Farber and Matheson (1985); Wangerin (1986); Becker (1987).
[74] *Walton Stores (Interstate) Ltd v Maher* (1988) 164 CLR 387, esp. 423–24.
[75] e.g. Gummow J, in *Esanda Finance v Peat Marwick* (1997) 188 CLR 241, 299.
[76] Spence (1999) 69.
[77] The qualifier is necessary because, as we have seen, though courts claim to find consideration in such cases, what they find is not *really* consideration: 6.3.3.

promise. As such, courts do not require consideration to enforce estoppel claims.

More specifically, the reason courts do not require consideration in estoppel claims, in this view, is that such cases do not raise cautionary or channelling concerns. But this is the case *only* when estoppel is used as a shield. This is because, in such cases, the parties are (nearly always) already in a valid contract—and, thus, they have *already* taken the proper steps to establish legal relations. In these instances, the form requirements provided by consideration are unnecessary.

The situation is not the same, though, when estoppel is used as a cause of action. In this instance, the parties typically do not have pre-existing legal relations. Therefore, the form requirements provided by consideration remain necessary to ensure that the parties indeed wished to enter legal relations after appropriate reflection. If courts were to permit estoppel as a cause of action, consideration's formal function vis a vis gratuitous promises would be almost entirely negated. All gratuitous promises would be enforceable in principle (or at least all relied-upon gratuitous promises).[78]

A final point is that the promissory explanation of the sword/shield rule fits well with the many exceptions to this rule in the United Kingdom and other common law jurisdictions. As we have seen, formal requirements are by their nature controversial (6.1). Moreover, the extent to which such requirements are needed depends on changing features of the legal system and of society generally. In this light, it is not surprising that the sword/shield rule is not applied in all cases or in all jurisdictions.

The reliance view's explanation of the sword/shield rule is grounded in quite different moral values, but in functional terms it is similar to the promissory explanation. In this view, the rule is presented as a response to the difficulty courts face when trying to distinguish legally relevant reliance from legally irrelevant reliance. Assuming for the sake of argument that the law should protect the reliance interest, it is clear that only certain instances of induced reliance should give rise to obligations (3.2).

---

[78] But this explanation does not explain why estoppel cannot be used as a cause of action in cases in which the parties *already have* legal relations and the relevant communication relates to those relations (i.e. in cases involving claims to enforce *upward* variations of existing contracts). But this feature of the rule, which also presents difficulties for the reliance view, can be explained on different grounds. Like the traditional 'pre-existing duty' rule, it functioned as a (blunt) device to protect against duress. This feature of the rule is now relatively unimportant following the decision in *Williams v Roffey Bros & Nicholls (Contractors) Ltd* [1991] 1 QB 1 that the consideration requirement may be satisfied in such cases by a practical benefit.

People who rely on weather forecasters or on the campaign promises of political parties do so at their own risk. It follows that a test must be developed for determining what sorts of reliance are legally relevant. For reasons discussed in 3.2, such a test will focus on identifying statements that, broadly speaking, are made in the context of a 'close relationship'. In other words, the test will be similar to the tests currently used to determine what sorts of reliance-inducing statements might give rise to liability for negligent misstatement.[79]

The obvious difficulty with this or any similar test is that it is extremely vague. What counts as a close relationship? When faced with questions of this sort, a common response of the English common law (and of legal systems generally) is to impose 'bright-line' or 'blanket' exclusionary rules. An example is the rule that a person below the age of 18 lacks the legal capacity to establish a contract.[80] From the perspective of the reliance view of estoppel, the sword/shield distinction performs a similar function. Cases in which estoppel is used as a defence as opposed to a cause of action are more likely, *as a class*, to satisfy the test that the relevant statements were made in the context of a close relationship. This is because one situation in which it is clear that parties (normally) have a close relationship is when they are already in an existing legal relationship; the parties' relationship is, by definition, 'close to contract'. The sword/shield distinction limits the scope of estoppel to just such relationships. The rule can be explained, therefore, on the basis that it is an easily applied test by which to distinguish, in a rough way, between legitimate reliance-based claims and ones that are not legitimate.

Like the formal explanation provided by the promissory view, this justification is also able to explain why exceptions are made to the sword/shield rule. Clarity and predictability are important, but it is also important that plaintiffs receive compensation for real harms. It is for this reason that blanket exclusions typically give way, over time, to more finely grained rules—witness the history of the rules governing recovery for negligent misstatement or for nervous shock. The same process is arguably happening with the blanket rule against using estoppel as a cause of action.

The above survey of the main features of the law on estoppel suggests that it is difficult to choose between the promissory view and the reliance

---

[79] On which, see *Caparo Industries plc v Dickman* [1990] 2 AC 605.

[80] Other examples that are closer to our concerns include the blanket restriction on liability for negligent misstatement prior to *Hedley Byrne v Heller* [1964] AC 465 and the restrictions that still exist on recovery in tort for nervous shock: *McLoughlin v O'Brian* [1982] 2 All ER 298.

view on the basis how each fits the law. Though neither fits the law perfectly, each offers a prima facie plausible account. The third of the three views of estoppel that I mentioned at the outset — the mixed view — was not directly examined in our survey, but we can conclude that it too offers a plausible, but not perfect, fit with the law. Recall that the mixed view supposes that both the fact of a promise *and* the fact of reliance are important in principle to support a plea of estoppel. As we have seen, though each of these claims is plausible, neither is uncontroversial.

The moral foundations of estoppel

Given this conclusion, a further question that must be addressed is this: how well do these different views of estoppel succeed in the basic task (for interpretive theories) of revealing an intelligible order in the law? In the case of the law, such an order will be a morally intelligible order (1.5). The question may therefore be rephrased in this way: to what extent is the understanding of estoppel presented by these theories consistent with the law's other moral commitments, and with the nature of morality generally? Are the ideas that estoppel protects reliance, or promises, or both *normatively* coherent?

Considered from this perspective, the mixed view presents the least compelling explanation of estoppel. The normative objection to this view is that it presents estoppel as an ad hoc mixture of incompatible elements. According to the mixed view, the doctrine of estoppel is concerned with promises, but it is concerned with them only insofar as they induce others to rely. From a normative perspective, such a doctrine appears incoherent for the simple reason that the moral significance of promises and the moral significance of reliance are different. A promise is a promise regardless of whether it has been relied upon (3.1). A rule that promises are enforceable only if they have been relied upon thus appears to be an arbitrary limitation on the scope of promissory liability. Reliance, for its part, may be induced by non-promissory statements. A rule that reliance matters only when it is induced by a promise thus appears to be an arbitrary limitation on the scope of reliance-based liability. It is no response to these objections to say that reliance is an alternative to consideration. This begs the question: in what sense is reliance an alternative? None of the possible justifications for consideration support the idea that reliance could fulfill the same formal or substantive function as consideration. In short, while there may be good reasons for caring about promises and good reasons for caring about reliance, it is difficult to think of a good reason for caring *only* about relied-upon promises.

Contract Theory

By contrast, the reliance and promissory view each suppose that estoppel aims to protect a single interest—the reliance interest or the promissory interest. From a normative perspective, the main question raised by these views is thus the basic one of whether it is morally justified for the law to protect the relevant interest (reliance, promises). I addressed this difficult question in Chapter 3;[81] my conclusion was that only one of these two interests—the promissory interest—should be protected by the law. If this (admittedly controversial) conclusion is accepted, it follows that the promissory view of estoppel scores better on this final criterion. Alone of the three views examined, the promissory view makes moral sense of the law of estoppel.

Conclusion

Two conclusions may be drawn from this discussion of estoppel. The first is that estoppel remains somewhat of a puzzle. Each of the leading explanations is vulnerable to certain fairly obvious objections. The second conclusion, which relies in part on moral arguments developed in Chapter 3, is that the best overall explanation of estoppel is provided by the promissory view—a view that regards the doctrine basically as a means of avoiding the consideration rule in situations in which its formal function is not needed. Estoppels, in this view, are just ordinary promises.

[81] For promises at 3.1.4 and for reliance at 3.2.1.

7

The Kinds of Agreements not Enforced: Substantive Limitations on Enforceability[1]

In this chapter, I examine substantive limitations on the enforceability of agreements. 'Substantive limitations' here refers to rules which declare certain agreements, or clauses within agreements (hereafter 'agreements'), to be unenforceable on the basis of the *kind of activity or action* that is required by, or closely linked to, those agreements. Examples include the rules dealing with: agreements to sell human organs, prostitution agreements, gambling agreements, unduly restrictive covenants, agreements that require or result in criminal or tortious conduct, and agreements to oust the jurisdiction of the courts.

Agreements featuring the types of activities described above are subject to rules that preclude courts from enforcing them. Because these rules focus on the *nature of the activity* associated with a contract, they can be distinguished from rules which focus on procedural defects (duress, capacity, etc.) and from rules which focus on substantive fairness (unconscionability). As such, this chapter uses the label 'substantive limitations on enforceability' to indicate invalidity rules that focus on the content of contractual obligations rather than on their mode of creation.[2]

This label, 'substantive limitations on enforceability', requires a preliminary observation concerning terminology. Note that I do not use the terms 'illegal' or 'contrary to public policy', both of which are sometimes invoked to describe the kinds of agreements discussed in this chapter. The reason is that both terms may be misleading. The description 'illegal contracts' is not accurate in that there are many substantive limitations which have nothing to do with illegal activities insofar as illegal is understood in its usual, criminal law sense. It is not a crime to agree to an invalid restrictive covenant. Moreover, even where the activity in question

---

[1] This chapter draws on Smith (1995; 1996).

[2] This distinction is not meant to deny that certain 'substantive limitations' might be explicable using notions of procedural defects or unconscionability—though in my view this is rarely the case (see discussion of unconscionability in 9.2).

is illegal in the strict sense, it is typically the activity, not the contract itself, that is illegal. And, finally, even in those rare cases in which the very act of making the contract is illegal, the relevant question for contract law is not whether the contract is illegal, but whether it is enforceable. Illegality is a matter for criminal law.

As for 'contrary to public policy', that description may also be misleading. 'Public policy' is often understood as referring to contracts that are objectionable because of their effect on the general public as opposed to the agreeing parties. For reasons explained below, this is not true of all contracts that are subject to substantive limitations. Furthermore, the phrase is often used to identify just one subclass of substantive limitations, namely those in which the relevant activity is objectionable, but not illegal. It is therefore under-inclusive in that some substantive limitations focus on activities that are indeed illegal.

Questions of terminology aside, the chapter examines four possible justifications for the existence of substantive limitations on the enforceability of agreements. These are: (1) the punishment justification, (2) the dignity of the courts justification, (3) the no obligation justification, and (4) the wrongdoing principle justification. A fifth possible justification— the unconscionability justification—is left for Chapter 9 (9.2). For present purposes, it is sufficient to mention that this additional explanation can account, at most, for only a small number of decisions in this area.[3]

In evaluating the above justifications, I will consider how they answer three closely related questions about the contract law rules on unenforceable agreements.[4] First, and most important, what justification is there for courts to disregard the principle of freedom of contract so as to refuse to enforce agreements that are prima facie valid? And furthermore, is that justification always the same, or does it vary according to the substantive limitation in question?

The second question raised by substantive limitations on enforceability can be seen, roughly, as a proximity question: what sort of connection is required between an 'objectionable' activity and an agreement so that courts will refuse to enforce the agreement? A contract to commit murder will certainly be invalid—the connection between the activity and the

---

[3] I discuss—and reject—such explanations in the case of restraint of trade law in Smith (1995).
[4] The qualification 'contract law' is necessary because many of the most challenging theoretical questions relating to unenforceable agreements concern claims to recover a benefit transferred under an invalid agreement—which claims are governed by the law of unjust enrichment.

agreement is obvious enough. But what about a contract between an aspiring murderer and a gun merchant?

The third question regarding substantive limitations concerns which kinds of activities qualify as undesirable, immoral, or objectionable (hereafter 'objectionable'). The answer to this question will often be supplied by criminal or regulatory law. But these sources of law do not provide a complete answer to this question. There are interesting theoretical questions regarding how and why contract law can deem certain activities to be objectionable even when they are not wrongful on other legal grounds.

I have just identified three questions that arise when considering substantive limitations on agreements; a complete account of this area of law must address each of these questions. But in evaluating the four justifications mentioned above, only those that can plausibly answer the first question—what is the basic rationale for substantive limitations— require a deeper inquiry into the theoretical issues represented by the second and third theoretical questions. As I will show, only two of the four justifications that I list (the no obligation and wrongdoing principle justifications) merit this more detailed examination.

A final preliminary comment is that the positive law in this area is both highly complex and subject to wide disagreement regarding its actual content. Even more than usual, therefore, I focus in this chapter on the general theoretical issues raised by substantive limitations rather than on details of legal doctrine.

7.1. THE PUNISHMENT JUSTIFICATION

One possible justification for substantive limitations on enforceability is that they punish wrongdoers. The person who has committed murder in order to obtain a promised payment should not only go to jail for his crime, but if he has not been paid, he should be punished further by denying his contractual claim to payment.

Judges have undoubtedly been influenced by this aim in some cases. But the 'punishment principle' is a weak justification for a finding of contractual invalidity. As a form of punishment, a finding of contractual invalidity is ineffective and, more importantly, frequently unjust. Non-enforcement is an ineffective punishment because it has neither the symbolic nor material consequences normally associated with punishment. Non-enforcement of a contract is hardly regarded as a 'mark of wrongdoing'; the failure to obtain an expected benefit is not comparable to a fine or imprisonment or even, for that matter, to liability in tort law. Indeed, the absence of a fine, imprisonment, or other sanctions directed at the wrongdoer, means that non-enforcement does not satisfy the normal definition of punishment.[5] In addition, non-enforcement actually benefits some wrongdoers. In my example of a contract to commit a murder, to the extent that non-enforceability punishes the murderer it will, at the same time, benefit the payer (who is also guilty of a crime). As for the justice of punishing by non-enforcement, the obvious difficulty here is that non-enforcement is a punishment that is added to some, but not all, crimes. Moreover, the material effects of non-enforcement can be disproportionate to the gravity of the crime. Non-enforcement is thus arbitrary punishment.

For the above reasons, punishment cannot stand as a plausible justification for substantive limitations. A court's refusal to enforce an agreement may resemble a weak form of punishment in some instances (see the 'wrongdoing' principle below at 7.4), but punishment can hardly be accepted as the *primary* justification for substantive limitations.

7.2. THE 'DIGNITY OF THE COURTS' JUSTIFICATION

A second possible justification for substantive limitations on enforceability is that they are necessary in order to uphold the 'dignity of the courts'.[6] To enforce contracts in which the parties are engaged in objectionable behaviour, it is sometimes said, would taint the courts' dignity.

It seems likely that the 'dignity principle' has influenced certain courts, but again, it is a weak justification for the law. One of the great virtues of our legal system is precisely that it will protect the rights of bad people. The murderer has a right not be tortured by the state or by other prisoners, and the courts will uphold this right. What the courts will not do is to help a person, bad or good, *to do* something bad. But that is a different issue. If the wrongdoer, or anyone else, is asking the courts to do something wrong—for example to give him money that is not his or to enforce a contract he obtained by duress—then the courts should, of course, refuse. But the courts do not need to rely on a principle of upholding their dignity to reach this result. They simply need to apply the law properly.

Insofar as it is possible to find a distinct idea underlying the dignity principle, it would seem to be the idea that the courts should not do

---

[5] Hart (1968) 4–5.   [6] Wright (1939) 90; Devlin (1959) 59.

something which, though not actually wrong according to usual legal principles, is nevertheless *thought to be wrong* by a significant portion of the population. If most people think that courts should not enforce the contracts of wrongdoers, then the courts should act on this sentiment, regardless of the justice of doing so. Simply stating this principle reveals its weakness: the courts' refusal to do something merely because most people *think* it is unacceptable would reduce judicial decision making to popular referenda. The dignity of the courts is preserved by fairly applying the law regardless of public opinion. Indeed, few things are more likely, in the long run, to bring the courts into disrepute than a policy of favouring popular opinion over the demands of justice. As such, the dignity explanation for substantive limitations is unconvincing.

7.3. THE 'NO OBLIGATION' JUSTIFICATION

A third possible justification for substantive limitations on enforceability is found in the idea that a promise or an agreement to do an objectionable activity lacks the obligatory force normally associated with agreements; there is no moral obligation, and hence no legal obligation, to do an objectionable activity. This justification has received little treatment in the literature on substantive limitations. In my view, though, it provides the broadest, and most convincing, explanation for the core categories of substantive limitations on enforcement.

The no obligation principle is different in kind from the preceding two principles and from the 'wrongdoing' principle that I examine next. Each of these other explanations justifies substantive limitations on the basis of a concept that is external to the law of contract (e.g., punishment, the dignity of the courts, etc.). Each assumes that, insofar as ordinary contract law principles are concerned, a valid contract has been formed. By contrast, the no obligation principle is internal to contract law. It supposes that the reason the contract is unenforceable is that no valid contract was created—just as if, say, the contract lacked consideration or a necessary formality.

An example may help in understanding the no obligation principle. Suppose that an agreement is made between two parties to murder a third party. Suppose further that neither party has yet acted on the agreement, nor brought the matter before the courts. Consider now the following questions: are the parties to this agreement under a moral obligation to carry out the murder? If one of the parties refuses to go along with the agreement, does the other have a justified complaint against him? The answer to each of these questions is a clear 'no'. What is equally clear, from this example, is that this conclusion—which states that the parties are under no obligation to carry out the contract—does *not* arise from one of the other explanations for substantive limitations. That is, this conclusion has not been arrived at so as to punish the parties or to uphold the dignity of the courts or to ensure that the wrongdoers do not profit from their crime. Each of those explanations assumes what the example denies: that the agreement was binding between the parties in the first place. Non-enforcement is a punishment, for example, only if the plaintiff had a prima facie valid contractual right. But it is clear that the parties in my example are not under an obligation to perform their agreement, and the reason, in general terms, is that an obligation to do an activity of this sort is not morally binding in the first place. The agreement to murder has not been morally binding between the parties from the moment it was made. Considerations relating to punishment, the dignity of the courts, or plaintiffs profiting from their wrongs do not even enter the question.

Explaining *why* a promise or agreement to do an objectionable activity is not morally binding raises complex issues, some of which I touch upon below. But it seems uncontroversial that the proposition itself is true. As the example illustrates, it is part of the common understanding of promises, agreements, and other voluntary obligations that they are not binding if their object is an objectionable activity. 'But I promised' is regarded neither as an excuse nor a justification for doing an objectionable activity. Moreover, this is true even if the objectionable nature of the activity is not immediately apparent. A promise to give a ride to a friend ceases to bind when it is learned that the friend needs the ride in order to steal another's property.

Why are immoral promises not binding?

I stated above that it is part of the conventional understanding of promises that promises to do objectionable activities are not binding. Utilitarian and rights-based theories of promising offer different explanations for that understanding. In utilitarian theories of promising, which value promises for their instrumental value in facilitating beneficial activities, the explanation is simple: promises to do objectionable activities are not binding because performing the activity would harm utility or social welfare. Thus, a promise to murder is not binding from an efficiency-based utilitarian theory because murder itself is inefficient.

Rights-based theories of promising sometimes try to explain this feature of promising on the basis that the object of the agreement is inalienable.[7] But while this approach might fit certain categories of objectionable activities (e.g., baby-selling, prostitution), it seems too narrow to explain all such activities. The rules dealing with restrictive covenants, gambling, or minor criminal offences, for example, do not appear to deal with the exchange of anything that could be described as inalienable. A more promising approach, I suggest, builds on the idea (explained earlier: 3.1.4) that, while promissory obligations are essentially individualistic, rights-based obligations not to harm others, *part* of the story for why such obligations exist is that they are intrinsically valuable elements of a close or special relationship between persons. On the basis of this view of promising, it can be argued that promises to do wrongs are not binding because the good that is normally associated with close relationships is not realized in a case in which the promise is to do an objectionable activity. In the same way that autonomy has no value when exercised in pursuit of non-valuable ends (*choosing* to murder is no more valuable than murdering in an unthinking rage),[8] close relationships have no value when they are formed in order to pursue non-valuable ends. The relationship that is formed between persons who make an agreement to murder a third person has no value.

The discussion that follows will not concern itself further with these different views of the underlying moral foundations of promissory obligations. In principle, utilitarians and rights-based theorists have different views about what sorts of activities are objectionable, and why they are objectionable. But in practice their judgments about particular activities usually coincide. In any event, from the perspective of trying to understand how *contract law* operates, such distinctions as exist turn out to be relatively insignificant.

Having established that the no obligation principle offers a prima facie plausible justification for at least certain substantive limitations, I turn now to consider the other two issues raised by such limitations

7.3.1. THE SCOPE OF THE NO OBLIGATION PRINCIPLE: (A) CONNECTING THE ACTIVITY TO THE CONTRACT

In considering the scope of the no obligation principle, the first question that needs to be addressed is this: what connection is needed between a contract and an objectionable activity for the no obligation principle to apply? As we have seen, substantive limitations can apply not only to contracts that *require* an objectionable activity, but also to those that

---

[7] Barnett (1986b).   [8] Raz (1986) 298–305, 380–81.

facilitate such an activity. Furthermore, certain other contracts may be declared invalid merely because they are 'closely connected' to an objectionable activity (perhaps because they have been performed using objectionable means). A successful explanation of substantive limitations should, therefore, be able to account for all three of these situations in which a court can declare a contract to be invalid because of its association with objectionable activities.

The no obligation principle clearly applies in the first case, in which the explicit or implicit terms of a contract require that an objectionable act be done. A contract to murder a third person is unenforceable because one of the acts that is required by the contract—to murder—is objectionable. Of course, the payer's obligation to pay is not, considered in isolation, objectionable, but its validity rests of the validity of the obligation to murder.

Second, and for similar reasons, a promise to do an act that will assist or facilitate an objectionable act is also not binding on the basis of the no obligation principle. It is not binding because it is wrong—objectionable —to assist another in doing an objectionable act. A promise to sell a gun to a person intending to use the gun to murder another is not binding because the vendor would be assisting in the commission of an objectionable act. The main difficulty raised by such cases is the practical one of distinguishing acts that are properly regarded as assisting an objectionable activity from acts that are related only tangentially to objectionable activities. A thief needs to be healthy, and thus to eat, in order to continue stealing; but does this mean that a person who provides a meal to a thief is assisting in the thief's wrongdoing? There is no simple answer to such questions, but contract law courts can, at least, turn to criminal law jurisprudence for instruction. The criminal law is regularly asked to determine what counts as assisting in the commission of an objectionable act.

We have just seen that that the no obligation principle covers two situations where the common law may connect an agreement to an objectionable activity: when a contract *requires* an objectionable act or when it *facilitates* such an act. A more difficult challenge for the principle is to explain those rules that provide for the invalidity of a contract that, although innocent on its face, is 'closely connected' to an objectionable activity.

For example, suppose that we have a contract whereby I am to sell you eggs for six months. Suppose further that, when I arrive to make the first delivery, you refuse to accept the eggs because you learn that I am stealing the eggs from Farmer Brown. In the event that I sue you for breach of contract, a court may refuse to grant my demand because of my 'connection' to an objectionable activity—theft.[9] The no obligation principle has difficulty explaining just such a situation. Recall that the principle is founded on the proposition that a promise to do an objectionable activity creates no obligation. But, in this case, there is nothing objectionable about our agreement—the activity of buying and selling eggs is beyond reproach.

As we shall see, the wrongdoing principle that I discuss next applies neatly to cases such as the egg example. But is also seems possible that the difficulty such cases pose for the no obligation principle can be resolved, in many scenarios anyway, by using traditional tools of contract law interpretation. I refer to the traditional willingness of common law courts to discover implied terms in contractual agreements (8.2). With regard to the topic at hand, it is reasonable to believe that 'no objectionable means are to be used' is an implied term of most agreements. In our example, therefore, my act of using stolen eggs would constitute an initial breach of our agreement obligation, leaving you under no contractual obligation to me. I did not provide you with what you asked for—rightfully procured eggs— so I therefore have no right to ask for payment. This explanation does, of course, raise interesting issues regarding unjust enrichment. But from the perspective of contract law, it offers a plausible account of how 'close connection' situations can be explained using the no obligation principle.

The above explanation describes how the no obligation principle might account for courts' refusal to enforce contracts that are merely connected to objectionable activities. But the idea that contracts contain an implied term to the effect that no objectionable means will be used to fulfill the terms of the contract cannot explain all such cases. More specifically, it cannot account for an agreement in which you agree to pay me for some eggs and you *are aware* that I am are likely to fulfill the contract using stolen eggs. Perhaps you even told me that you did not care how I obtained the eggs. Such an agreement clearly does not contain an implied 'no objectionable means' term; we have explicitly agreed that objectionable means *are* acceptable.

But although the agreement just described could not be invalidated using implied terms, it would be still invalid on the basis of the no obligation principle—regardless of how the eggs in question were

---

[9] *Ashmore, Benson, Pease & Co Ltd v AV Dawson Ltd* [1973] 1 WLR 828. But note that mere illegality in performance does not always preclude a contractual claim: Chitty (1999) 841–42.

ultimately procured. It would be invalid because agreements of this sort clearly *facilitate* objectionable activities. And, as I explained above, agreements that facilitate objectionable activities are covered by the no obligation principle.

7.3.2. THE SCOPE OF THE NO OBLIGATION PRINCIPLE: (B) DEFINING 'OBJECTIONABLE'

The third, major question related to substantive limitations that the no obligation principle must address is also scope-related. This question asks: what *sorts of activities* should be classified as objectionable? In addressing this question, my aim is not to produce an exhaustive list of objectionable activities. Such a list would number in the thousands, if not millions. Instead, I will concentrate on identifying the general considerations that courts do, or should, take into account in determining if a contract is associated with an objectionable activity.

From the perspective of a court deciding a contract law case, perhaps the most fundamental question raised by this issue is whether an activity ought to be regarded as objectionable if, and only if, it is labelled as such by other parts of the legal system. Is the list of objectionable activities identical to the list of activities labelled wrongs by private law (torts, breach of contract, breach of trust, etc.), criminal law, and regulatory law? This basic question subdivides into two questions, which I consider in turn: (1) Are all legal wrongs objectionable activities? (2) Are all objectionable activities legal wrongs?

Are all legal wrongs objectionable activities?

A declaration, by a different part of the legal system, that a certain activity is wrongful should, in theory, be adequate proof that the same activity is objectionable (and therefore unenforceable) from the perspective of contract law. In most cases, this principle is indeed a good guide. A contract law court should not attempt to come up with different definitions of murder or theft than those developed by criminal law courts. But the fit is not perfect. As we have seen, the no obligation principle is grounded in a pre-legal moral principle that applies only when the activity in question is one that, *for moral reasons*, should not be done. It does not apply, in principle anyway, to activities that, though contrary to positive law, are not objectionable in the ordinary moral meaning of objectionable. The modern state, however, prohibits a variety of activities that are not immoral or wrongful in this sense. For example, it is a common requirement that a person must have a licence or obtain permission from a regulatory body in order to carry out a certain kind of work. Failure to obtain a licence is often punishable by a fine, regardless of the actor's knowledge. Yet a person who unknowingly fails to obtain a licence is hardly a wrongdoer in the moral sense. It follows that in cases such as these the no obligation principle does not apply.

Of course, a person's *knowledge* that an otherwise unobjectionable activity is prohibited by positive law can make doing that activity wrongful. Morally, we ought to obey the law (or at least, this is the only conclusion that judges can reach consistent with their positions). A failure to obtain a licence despite knowing that one is required is thus wrongful; and a contract that requires or facilitates this result is therefore covered by the no obligation principle.

Admittedly, refusing to obtain a licence is not as serious a wrong as, say, theft. And theft is not as serious a wrong as murder. But the no obligation principle does not distinguish between degrees of wrongdoing: the principle that an obligation to do an objectionable activity is not binding applies regardless of how objectionable the activity is. This may seem harsh, but it should be kept in mind that different considerations apply when courts turn to consider whether a party to an unenforceable contract ought to be awarded restitution of any benefits conferred under the contract. The no obligation principle is based on contractual principles, whereas the availability of restitution in respect of benefits transferred under an unenforceable contract is (or at least should be) determined by non-contractual principles of unjust enrichment law.

Moralistic restrictions on enforceability

The flip side of the previous question is the question of whether it is appropriate for a court to classify an activity as objectionable for the purposes of assessing contractual validity even though the activity is not otherwise regarded as wrongful by the legal system. To answer this question it is necessary to explore in some detail the meaning of 'objectionable'.

Broadly speaking, an activity might be regarded as objectionable for one of two reasons: either because it is harmful to others, or because it is for some other reason worthless, immoral, or degrading (hereafter 'non-valuable'). Understandably, most objectionable activities that are harmful to others are also legal wrongs.[10] Thus, here we are in essence

---

[10] Of course, criminal and tort law, etc. do not sanction all possible wrongs. It follows that, in theory, a court might find that a particular activity wrongly harms others, and thus is objectionable, even though it is not a legal wrong. In practice, however, courts in contract cases are (rightfully) hesitant to second guess criminal law or tort law.

asking whether activities of the second sort—non-valuable activities—
ought to be viewed as objectionable for the purposes of the no obligation
principle.[11] As a matter of positive law, it seems fairly clear that there are
activities that are regarded in this way. Examples of substantive limitations that focus on activities that, at first blush anyway, do not harm
others (and are lawful) include gambling agreements, commercial surrogacy agreements, prostitution agreements, agreements contrary to marriage, and (some) restrictive covenants. The exact number of what I shall
call 'moralistic' limitations is a matter for debate, but that the category
exists seems clear. From a normative perspective, however, it might well
be asked whether a category of moralistic limitations should exist. If the
relevant activity is consensual, why should the law care whether or not the
activity is not valuable according to another criterion? Moralistic limitations appear to be simple instances of legal paternalism—of the courts
deciding for individuals what is and is not in their best interests.

One way of evaluating this normative objection to moralistic limitations is to ask whether such limitations are contrary to the limits on state
action imposed by the 'harm principle' (3.1.4). According to the harm
principle, individuals should be left free to live their lives as they choose
except insofar as they harm others, where harm is understood in the
ordinary sense of non-consensual interference with person, property, or
liberty. The mere fact that a person is involved in an activity that is
considered worthless or even degrading does not justify limiting that
individual's liberty: the state may interfere only if the activity harms
others. Though not immune from criticism, the harm principle is supported, in broad terms, by most moral theories, especially in discussions
of the proper scope of criminal law and private law.[12] The principle is also
expressed, despite certain clear exceptions,[13] in the practice of our criminal and private law courts. Thus, while few people would think it valuable to spend all of one's waking hours drinking alcohol, or watching
game shows, or reading pornographic magazines, it is neither a tort nor a
crime to live in this way.

Respect for the harm principle, then, argues against legal *prohibitions*
on visiting prostitutes, reading pornography, or doing other activites that,
though worthless or degrading, do not harm others. But it is far from

---

[11] Some (merely) non-valuable activities are illegal, for example the possession of
restricted drugs.
[12] e.g. Feinberg (1986).   [13] e.g. *R v Brown* [1992] 2 WLR 441.

clear that the harm principle enjoins courts from refusing to enforce contracts to do such activities. The harm principle is grounded in a concern for the state interfering with individual liberty. Refusing to enforce a contract is not an interference with freedom. A refusal to enforce a prostitution contract does not deny or limit a person's freedom to engage in prostitution; the court is merely refusing to assist persons who wish to engage in prostitution. No sanction is attached to a court's decision not to enforce the agreement.[14]

The conclusion that refusing to enforce a contract is not a limitation on freedom in the way that criminal or tortious liability is a limitation on freedom does not mean that courts should act on whatever reasons they please when deciding whether or not to apply moralistic restrictions on enforceability. If there are good reasons to enforce contracts in general, then good reasons are required before refusing to enforce particular kinds of contract. The presumption should be in favour of enforceability. The point of the foregoing discussion is simply that a good reason need not be the kind of reason that would be needed in order to justify criminal or tortious liability. In principle, it is enough that the activity is not one that the state should assist or promote.[15]

Assuming, then, that it is permissible, in principle, for courts to apply moralistic restrictions, the next question is what sorts of restrictions are appropriate. In other words, what kinds of (non-harmful-to-others) activities are properly regarded as immoral or degrading or worthless? Clearly, this is a difficult question. Moreover, common law judges, who deal primarily with claims of alleged harm, are not especially well-trained to make such decisions. They have no more expertise in what makes an activity non-valuable than do the parties that appear before them. Courts may also be swayed by improper considerations, such as pandering to

---

[14] Hart (1994) 33–38. This distinction does not deny that the material consequences of refusing to enforce a contract can be serious (even taking into account possible claims in unjust enrichment); the difference between a sanction and a refusal to assist is a difference in kind, not amount. For a contrary view (based on the idea that contract law validity rules are fragments of larger sanction-based rules), see Kelsen (1979) 63.

[15] One possible objection to moralistic restrictions is, of course, that there are simply no such things as non-valuable, non-wrongful activities. In this view, comparing the value of reading pornography with the value of, say, reading Plato is like comparing the value of eating pistachio ice-cream with the value of eating strawberry ice-cream. Addressing this (in my view) implausible claim is outside the scope of this book, but it is worth noting that claims of this sort often turn out, on closer inspection, to be claims about the proper scope of criminal law or claims about the practical difficulty of determining what activities are immoral or worthless or degrading. Pure 'value sceptics' are relatively rare.

public sentiment. In principle, legislatures are better suited to addressing questions of value, but they rarely take an interest in rules that pertain only to contractual validity.

There is a risk, therefore, that judges may not correctly identify objectionable activities—that they will substitute prejudice for sound reasoning. Because of this risk, the normal presumption should be that individuals know best what is or is not valuable behaviour. Courts should use their authority to apply moralistic restrictions sparingly.

The kinds of agreements that the courts actually subject to moralistic restrictions can be grouped into two broad categories: (1) autonomy-restricting agreements, and (2) market-expanding agreements. These categories provide a rough guide—but no more—for when such restrictions may be appropriate, thereby reducing the likelihood that legal actors will regard moralistic restrictions as an area of the law that is determined only by the predilections of individual judges. In addition, most of the agreements in those categories possess features that, as we shall see, weaken the normal presumption that individuals are better able than judges to determine what is valuable.

Autonomy-restricting agreements

Autonomy-restricting agreements are agreements (or clauses in agreements) that are invalidated because they allegedly attempt to unduly limit the liberty of one or both parties to the agreement. The most prominent examples of such agreements are unreasonable restraints on trade; other examples include restraints on personal liberty, contracts of self-enslavement, and contracts in restraint of marriage.

From a contract theory perspective, autonomy-restricting agreements are interesting in that the alleged reason that they are not enforced—that they restrict autonomy—is a general feature of contractual obligations. By their very nature, contractual obligations restrict individual autonomy. Indeed, they represent one of the few ways by which a private individual may legally restrict the future freedom of another. Of course, the law generally permits and even encourages such restrictions. From the standpoint of a concern for autonomy, this can be justified on the ground that enforcing contracts generally increases our options (contracts permit us to do things we could not do otherwise). But the examples of contractual obligations listed above are thought to be different from standard contractual obligations in this regard. Autonomy-restricting agreements are thought to *unduly* restrain future freedom. They impose restrictions that are regarded as unnecessary from the standpoint of autonomy (in that they are not necessary in order to make otherwise valuable options available) or any other legitimate purpose.[16]

Given that all agreements restrict autonomy, the idea that certain agreements should be invalidated on the ground that they *unduly* restrict autonomy is a controversial one. And as I will suggest below, there is good reason to think that judges are sometimes too ready to conclude that agreements unduly restrict autonomy. But at the same time, there are two reasons for thinking that the long-standing rules that provide for the invalidity of such agreements are, in principle at any rate, justified. The first is that unnecessary restrictions on liberty are regarded as undesirable in nearly all moral theories, whether those theories are rights-based or non rights-based. Such restrictions are undesirable both from the perspective of the individual (restraints make it more difficult for individuals to live an autonomous—and hence valuable—life)[17] and from the perspective of society (restraints on liberty impede the flow of goods and labour in the market).

The second reason is that the kinds of agreements to which the rules on autonomy-restricting agreements apply (e.g., restraints on trade, restraints on marriage, and self-enslavement clauses—hereafter 'restrictive covenants') differ from ordinary contracts in that the parties' self-interest provides a relatively weak guarantee that the agreement will not unduly restrain autonomy. In an ordinary contract, contracting parties' perceptions of their interests line up with what is actually in their interest, and at the same time, they also line up with society's interests. This is why freedom of contract remains the general principle in this area of the law. But with respect to restrictive covenants, there is greater than usual risk that these different interests may not converge. Contracting parties often make mistakes when assessing the nature and significance of restrictive covenants. Because such covenants typically deal with low-probability, distant possibilities—for example, that an employee will quit his employment, or that the vendor of a business will want to re-enter the field—there is a higher than usual risk that individuals entering such agreements will make cognitive errors. Individuals frequently discount the significance of low-probability events happening, and even when they do not do this, they often have difficulty forecasting the kind and degree of restraint that is appropriate.[18] This means that mistakes happen, and the result of these mistakes can be detrimental to the value of freedom. In

---

[16] Smith (1995).   [17] Raz (1985) Chapters 14 and 15.
[18] Trebilcock (1993) 120–29, 153–54; Kreps (1990) 116–18.

addition, from a broader perspective, there is a clear risk that individuals may enter autonomy-restricting agreements that, though attractive to those individuals, conflict with society's interest in maintaining a free flow of goods and labour.

In theory, then, it seems appropriate for courts to apply substantive limitations in respect of autonomy-restricting agreements. In practice, though, it is questionable if courts have done a good job in so doing. Studies of trade law suggest that courts are sometimes too quick to substitute their own judgment for that of the parties as to the reasonableness of a restraint.[19] Indeed, a strong case can be made that protecting the autonomy of the market (as opposed to the autonomy of the individual) is best handled by competition law.[20] Courts, therefore, should proceed cautiously; in particular, they should be cautious when they seek to invalidate agreements in order to protect the freedom of the market, as opposed to that of the individual.

Market-expanding agreements: the problem of commodification

A second category of moralistic restrictions focuses on agreements for the sale of things that, in the law's view, should not be sold. I will call such agreements 'market-expanding agreements', and the substantive limitations that invalidate them 'market-limiting restrictions'. Examples of market-expanding agreements include surrogacy contracts, contracts to sell human organs, and prostitution contracts. In each case, the act, service, or thing sold—child bearing, the transfer of a human organ, sexual relations—is unobjectionable in itself. The transaction is considered objectionable only when it is made as part of a sale or exchange. It is the 'commodification' of child bearing, sex, or giving organs that raises a problem.[21]

Market-limiting restrictions on enforceability are controversial.[22] One possible justification for them is that market-limiting restrictions protect individuals from engaging in activities that are not conducive to a good or

---

[19] Trebilcock (1986); Smith (1995).

[20] Consistent with this conclusion, the most serious kind of market restraints—horizontal restraints on liberty (e.g. cartels)—are now governed largely by competition law rather than the common law of restraint of trade: Whish (2001).

[21] Thus in a 1905 case dealing with a contract entered into by a marriage bureau (an early form of dating agency), the court invalidated the contract on the ground that it involved 'the introduction of the consideration of a money payment into that which should be free from any such taint': *Herman v Charlesworth* [1905] 2 KB 123, 130 (this particular rule has since been overturned).

[22] See generally Trebilcock (1993) 23–57.

valuable life. The idea here is that being a prostitute, for example, is not a good way to live (nor, for that matter, is going to a prostitute), and thus, out of a concern for prostitutes' own well being, courts should refuse to enforce agreements that promote this lifestyle. Of course, not everyone will agree that being a prostitute (or a surrogate or paid organ donor, etc.) is a bad way to live, but it is widely recognized that commodifying the body is, in general, objectionable.

This first justification is essentially paternalistic; the courts are saying that they know better than prostitutes, etc. what is in the prostitutes' own best interests. As I noted above, the standard objections to paternalism have less force when paternalism is expressed through a decision not to enforce a contract as opposed to, say, a decision to impose criminal liability. It might also be added that paternalism is less objectionable when the individuals concerned are in a poor position to recognize what is in their best interests. This will often be true of persons who enter market-expanding agreements. Sometimes, as in the case of surrogacy agreements and some donor agreements, the problem is the same risk of cognitive error that arose with respect to restrictive covenants. This risk exists because the long term consequences of the kinds of actions that surrogate mothers and organ donors agree to perform can be difficult to predict. But a more general problem is that market-expanding agreements are often entered into by people who are in financial difficulty and have few available options.

But this last point also puts into question the substantive grounds for concluding that market-expanding agreements are not valuable. The consequence of refusing to enforce prostitution contracts or surrogacy contracts, etc. is often to remove one of the few options available to those offering such services. To be sure, this first justification for market-limiting restrictions is not grounded in a concern for the *financial* interests of contracting parties. It is grounded in a view of their interests in not commodifying their bodies. Still, we should be sceptical about grounding legal rules in 'higher' interests of this kind when the effect of the rules is to make those whose higher interests are at stake worse off in a very real sense. Significantly, market-limiting restrictions differ in this respect from restrictions on autonomy-restricting agreements, in that the latter are meant to apply only to *unnecessary* restraints on liberty. Thus, if a particular post-employment restraint is necessary in order that, say, a particular job be offered, it will be permitted. The rules providing for the invalidity of market-expanding agreements, by contrast, operate in an all or nothing fashion. The rules do not assess whether the particular

used to explain other moral notions, it cannot itself be explained using such notions. There is little that can be said about this first possibility. The idea that the wrongdoing principle is a foundational moral concept is plausible. At the same time, it is not self-evident that the principle is actually regarded in this way by most people—and the existence of these common perceptions is the only test for such principles.

A second possibility is that the wrongdoing principle is grounded in the idea that unjust enrichments should be reversed. More specifically, the wrongdoer has been unjustly enriched as a result of his wrongdoing. There are two difficulties with this explanation. The first is that the wrongdoer is not enriched as a result of his wrongdoing until he has actually performed the relevant wrongful act. Yet to explain substantive limitations on enforceability, this explanation must account for the *invalidity* of an executory contract (as opposed to explaining why property transferred under a contract should be returned). For this explanation to convince, therefore, invalidity must be regarded as a kind of prophylactic designed to *prevent* unjust enrichment. The second, more serious difficulty is that the basic requirement of unjust enrichment law that the relevant enrichment was obtained *at the expense of* the other party[24] is not fulfilled in such cases. Although the plaintiff who murdered in order to receive a promised payment will benefit from his wrongdoing if he is paid, his benefit is not received at the expense of the defendant—it was at the victim's expense. Stated differently, the defendant, who wanted the murder committed, would not be unjustly deprived by having to pay the promised money.

This leads me to the third, and arguably most persuasive, explanation of the wrongdoing principle, which supposes that the principle is not rooted in legal foundations at all. Rather, courts' decisions not to enforce objectionable agreements are explained as an echo of a larger political decision—a political decision to deny the tools of contract law to wrongdoers.

According to this third explanation, to make sense of the wrongdoing principle, the larger institution of private law dispute resolution must be considered from a political or scarce resources perspective. More specifically, the state's practice of providing enforcement to private contracts should be seen as a service. With regard to contract resolution, the state is providing a legal and enforcement service to citizens—in much the same way that the state provides educational, recreational, or police services.

---

[24] Birks (1985) 132.

And, significantly, none of these services are fundamental or inalienable rights in the manner of the right to speech or the right to dignity of the person. Such services are, to be sure, integral to what we consider 'society'. But the allotment of them is subject to political choices regarding the allocation of resources—not everyone is entitled to have every service all the time.

Returning to the matter at hand—the wrongdoing principle—the above account of political choice seems to explain it best. From this perspective, when a court refuses to enforce a contract that is associated with an objectionable activity, the court is reflecting the political will of the state. The state has chosen, in other words, to deny the service of contract enforcement to wrongdoers.

The state's decision to refuse to provide enforcement of contracts in certain instances is hardly radical; nor does it amount to a punishment explanation (considered and rejected above). An analogy may be made to a state's decision not to renew the driver's licence of a recalcitrant speeder. The action is not so much an act of punishment (that is handled by other means), but rather it is the state announcing that it no longer wishes to provide the service at a road system to that person. The state has decided that the resources spent on providing roads to speeders are better spent in other ways. And, in a similar way, the state may withdraw the service of enforcing private contracts from those who are engaged in objectionable activities.

Of course, the state still needs to explain why it has decided to refuse to provide legal services with respect only to certain kinds of agreements. But this is not difficult to do. In broad terms, the reason is to encourage good behaviour. The state has an obvious interest in encouraging its citizens to obey the law and more generally to act properly. Among the various ways the state can pursue this end, one is by refusing a plaintiff's request to enforce a contract if the plaintiff has engaged in objectionable behaviour that is closely connected to the contract. A refusal both declares publicly that the activity is objectionable and makes such activities less lucrative than they would be if the state helped the parties.

7.4.1. THE SCOPE OF THE WRONGDOING PRINCIPLE: (A) CONNECTING THE ACTIVITY TO THE CONTRACT

The wrongdoing principle provides a justification for why courts might impose substantive limitations on contracts. For the reasons just explained, that justification is plausible enough to proceed to the second question relating to substantive limitations—the proximity question.

Recall that the no obligation principle explains the invalidity of contracts that require objectionable activities as well as contracts that facilitate or assist such activities. And the principle arguably also explains why contracts that are merely connected to objectionable activities may be invalid.

The wrongdoing principle can account for all three levels of proximity without difficulty, largely because, unlike the no obligation principle, it is an explanation that is external to contract law. The no obligation principle refers to the moral obligations that are (or are not) created by promises so as to explain substantive limitations. In contrast, the wrongdoing principle, I have argued, views these imposed limitations as a political choice, a choice wherein the state decides that those associated with objectionable activities shall not have access to contractual enforcement. If substantive limitations represent a political choice aimed at targeting those who enter agreements associated with objectionable activities, there is, therefore, no reason to differentiate between agreements that explicitly require objectionable acts and agreements that are just connected to them. As such, the proximity question associated with substantive limitations is less problematic for the no profit principle than it is for the no obligation principle.

7.4.2. THE SCOPE OF THE WRONGDOING PRINCIPLE: (B) DEFINING 'OBJECTIONABLE'

It is left to determine *which* activities the wrongdoing explanation of substantive limitations can justifiably include as objectionable. Recall that the 'no obligation' explanation can legitimately classify as objectionable both illegal activities and certain activities that are morally objectionable but not illegal (7.3.2). This is not the case with the wrongdoing principle.

The essence of the wrongdoing principle is that it represents an external, political choice whereby the state chooses to deny the service of contractual enforcement to certain individuals. In principle, it would seem possible for the state to justify such a decision on the grounds that the individual was involved in, or contemplated becoming involved in, an activity that was non-valuable or immoral, even though it was not actually wrongful (in the sense of harming another person). But in practice, the traditional understanding that the wrongdoing principle applies only to wrongdoers seems appropriate. Although individuals do not have a right to have their contracts enforced, a decision to deny such a service to particular persons should not be made lightly. It sends a strong message that the activity done or contemplated by that individual was wrongful. As such, it is appropriate to limit the wrongdoing principle to cases in which the relevant activity is actually wrongful, in the sense of harming another. Prostitution agreements, surrogacy agreements, and other such contracts that do not obviously harm another are, therefore, beyond the reach of the wrongdoing principle.

A final important point is that while it is possible, of course, to support both the no obligation principle and the wrongdoing principle, it is not strictly possible to apply both principles to the same agreement. The reason is that insofar as the no obligation principle applies, there is no agreement—and thus no contract—to which the wrongdoing principle could apply. If the defendant has no obligation in the first place, the courts do not need to use the idea of refusing to provide legal services to explain why the plaintiff loses; the plaintiff loses because the defendant had no obligation to perform. Given that I concluded that the no obligation principle potentially covers all, or nearly all, substantive limitations, this suggests that the wrongdoing principle has a small role to play in this area of contract law. (But as we shall see in the next chapter, it plays a significant role in explaining the law of duress and misrepresentation.)

7.5. CONCLUSION

This chapter has explored theoretical issues that surround substantive limitations on contractual enforceability. Such limitations represent instances where courts declare an agreement to be invalid because of the *content* of the agreement; contracts to commit crimes, surrogacy contracts, and restrictive covenants are prominent examples. The chapter examined four possible explanations for why a court may be justified in imposing substantive limitations on agreements that are otherwise valid. The most convincing and most broadly applicable explanation, described as the no obligation principle, holds that a promise to do something immoral has no obligatory force, and therefore agreements founded on such promises are invalid. The appeal of this explanation is that is internally consistent with other aspects of contract law, and that it offers the closest fit to the law itself. Another promising explanation for substantive limitations is the wrongdoing principle, which states that such limitations can be explained as instances in which the state has made a political choice to withdraw enforcement services from wrongdoers. The wrongdoing explanation is weaker in that it is girded by principles that are external to contract law. In addition, it is more limited insofar as it does not apply to those substantive limitation situations wherein an activity is described as objectionable even though the activity in question does not

classifying rules as content rules cannot be undertaken separately from that of investigating their theoretical foundations. It is not possible, in other words, to answer the definitional question without also addressing substantive questions, such as the two mentioned at the outset. At this point, therefore, I limit myself merely to noting that the primary focus of this chapter is on the rules that deal with the interpretation and implication of terms in a validly formed contract. It follows (for reasons I discuss below or in separate chapters)[2] that I will not say anything about the rules for determining the existence of offers, acceptances, and contractual terms generally; nor will I say anything about unenforceable ('illegal', etc.) agreements. Remedial rules are also not discussed. On the other hand, the rules dealing with mistake, frustration, and discharge for breach will be examined as part of the discussion of implied terms (though I also consider these rules, albeit more briefly, from a different perspective in 9.3). Finally, the varieties of statutorily implied terms that appear to be grounded in a concept of unconscionability (e.g., the *Unfair Contract Terms Act* 1977 or the *Unfair Terms in Consumer Contracts Regulations* 1994) are left to Chapter 9. What remains is still a large category, though one linked by common themes—or so I hope to show.

The discussion begins by examining the interpretation of express contractual terms, focusing in particular on three aspects of this process: (1) the 'objective approach', (2) the importance of context, and (3) the rules of interpretation. The conclusions of this discussion provide the background for the subsequent examination of implied terms, under which heading are discussed: (1) excuse rules (especially the rules on mistake, but also frustration and discharge for breach), (2) 'individualized' implied terms (e.g., terms implied under the 'business efficacy' test), and (3) 'standardized' implied terms (e.g., terms implied into sales contracts by virtue of the *Sale of Goods Act* 1979).

Finally, it may be useful to mention at this point that the substantive arguments of the chapter fall into two general themes. The first is that the classical view of contracts fits better with the common law's content rules, including the rules pertaining to mistake and to standardized implied terms, than is often supposed. The second—which is arguably a theme for the entire book—is that it is difficult to say when interpretation ends and creation begins.

---

[2] See in particular 5.2.1 (offers, acceptances) and 11.1 (remedial rules).

8.1. THE INTERPRETATION OF EXPRESS CONTRACTUAL TERMS

'Interpretation' here refers to the process of determining the meaning of a contractual agreement—of determining, that is, what it is that contracting parties have in fact agreed or promised to do.[3] It follows that, insofar as courts rely on values such as fairness or efficiency in fixing the content of a contract, the courts are engaged in a process of *addition*— of imposing terms—rather than interpretation (except if the agreement explicitly or implicitly incorporates such values—see below). To what degree, then, do courts engage in the process of interpretation versus that of addition? This question is a central concern of the chapter. I address it first from the perspective of the courts' approach to express terms.

8.1.1. THE OBJECTIVE APPROACH

It is orthodox law that courts interpret contractual terms not by seeking the subjective or 'inner' intentions of contracting parties, but rather by asking how the terms would have been reasonably or 'objectively' understood.[4] Contractual terms mean what the person to whom they were communicated—the 'listener'—reasonably understood them to mean.[5]

The objective approach is often used as evidence in support of the view that contractual obligations are imposed by the law and not by the parties (as classical theory would have it).[6] More specifically, the rule allegedly supports the view that the law imposes contractual obligations in order to protect induced reliance.[7] Reliance is induced on the basis of appearances, thus it makes perfect sense—if the law is indeed

---

[3] The interpretation of contracts is related to the concept of 'interpretive theories of law' discussed in Chapter 1. But the particular issues examined in this chapter (e.g. the distinction between objective/subjective meaning and the need for 'gap-filling') are different from those discussed in Chapter 1.

[4] *Deutsche Genossenschaftsbank v Burnhope* [1995] 1 WLR 1580, 1587.

[5] *Investors Compensation Scheme v West Bromwich Building Society* [1998] 1 All ER 98, 114. The apparent exception—a word or phrase will not be given its usual or objective meaning if the listener knew the speaker did not intend to convey that meaning: *Hartog v Colin and Shields* [1939] 3 All ER 566—confirms the rule. Meaning is still determined by what the listener reasonably understood the words to mean; such cases are simply a particular application of the principle (discussed below) that words must be understood in context— which here includes knowledge of the meaning that the speaker intended to convey.

[6] e.g. Collins (1997) 206–207.

[7] Atiyah (1979) 731–33, 742, 744–47.

concerned about such reliance—for it to adopt an objective approach to interpretation.[8]

It seems clear that the objective approach is consistent with a concern for protecting reliance. But it is less clear that the objective approach is, in fact, inconsistent with the classical view's assertion that it is the parties who establish a contract's content. It is true that, insofar as the classical view is understood to mean that contract law gives force to the inner 'will' of the parties, there is an evident inconsistency. But there is no obvious reason why this understanding of the classical view must be adopted. It is not a part of the promissory version of the classical view, as that version is understood in this book. In Chapter 5, I defended the idea that a subjective approach is appropriate in determining if contracting parties intended to *make* an agreement. But I offered no defence there or elsewhere of the idea that the content or *meaning* of an agreement or promise depends on the inner wills of contracting parties. Nor was this idea raised, let alone defended, in the general discussion of promissory theories in Chapter 3. Indeed, it is difficult to identify a contemporary common law scholar who defends this position. And even among the 19th century English lawyers who supposedly championed subjectivist will theories,[9] not to mention the civilian scholars who apparently still do,[10] it is difficult to find anyone who argues that the *meaning* of a contract should be understood in terms of inner wills. Rather, such authors typically argue something different with respect to contract meaning. What they argue is that, in the event of a divergence between the actual meaning of a contract and what one or both parties intended it to mean, the contract might be able to be set aside on the grounds of mistake.[11] Although I do not share this view of mistake (for reasons explained below), the point I wish to make here is that it is consistent with adopting an objective approach to the meaning of a contract's terms. In short, I suggest that insofar as a concern for the inner will has a role to play in contract law, that role is in respect either of the question whether the parties entered a contract at all (discussed in Chapter 5) or the question of whether a prima facie valid contract ought to be set aside for a defect of consent (discussed in the next chapter).

This brings me to the second, more common (and also more defensible) understanding of the classical view. According to this second

---

[8] One way this view is expressed is to say that the law rejects a subjective approach because it would cause too much uncertainty: McKendrick (1997) 15. A concern for uncertainty is a concern for protecting those who rely on appearances.

[9] See discussion in Atiyah (1979) 405–408.   [10] e.g. Ghestin (1988) ss 31ff.

[11] Ghestin (1993) ss 490ff.

understanding, to say that the parties establish the content of a contract, or even to say that the content is established by the parties' 'wills', is to say no more than that contracts are promises or (more commonly) agreements. This version, which I defended in Part II's discussion of general theories, *is* consistent with the objective approach. It is consistent because what contracting parties have agreed to is determined by what their agreement means, and meaning is always objective.[12] A word *means* what it is reasonably understood to mean rather than what the speaker intended (or, confusingly, 'meant') it to mean. This is why Humpty-Dumpty's famous statement—'when I use a word, it means just what I want it to mean, no more and no less'—sounds so peculiar.[13] Imagine that John says to himself, 'whenever I say "dog" from now on, I will mean "cat"', John then says to Ann (who is unaware of John's plan), 'I promise to give you a dog.' The *meaning* of John's statement is just what it appears to mean: 'I promise to give you a dog.' As Wittgenstein observed, a purely private language is an impossibility:[14] words are used for communication, and communication requires shared or public meanings.

The claim that the objective approach to interpretation is inconsistent with the classical view is thus mistaken, unless the (implausible) subjectivist version of the classical view is adopted. But discussing the claim is useful for two reasons. First, it joins the concerns of this chapter to the general discussion of promissory obligations in Chapter 3. Specifically, the idea that promissory (or 'agreement-based') obligations are based on (public) meaning rather than the inner wills of promisors is linked to the idea, defended in 3.1.4, that promissory obligations are grounded in the value of special relationships. These ideas fit together. Part of the reason promissory relationships are valuable is that individuals can choose whether or not to enter them. But in choosing to enter a promissory relationship what a person is choosing to enter is something defined in shared or 'objective terms'. The special nature of a promissory relationship, which requires the promisor to treat the promisee's interests as privileged in certain ways, is created and defined by communicating an intention to undertake an obligation. Communication is built into the idea of a promise (or an agreement), and communication, as I have said, is always an objective or public act. Stated differently, it would be inconsistent with the necessarily public and interpersonal nature of promising (or agreeing) to suppose that promissory obligations are grounded in the inner wills of promisors.

---

[12] Putnam (1973).　　　[13] Davidson (1986).　　　[14] Wittgenstein (1972).

The second reason it is useful to examine the above claim is that it links the objective approach to the rules discussed in the remainder of this chapter. More specifically, the idea that the meaning of a communication is established by uncovering objective meanings, rather than by uncovering a speaker's inner or subjective intentions (what I shall call the 'mental state' view), is fundamental to the arguments that follow.

8.1.2. INTERPRETATIVE SOURCES: THE IMPORTANCE OF CONTEXT

In saying that the objective meaning of an agreement is its *only* meaning, it is not suggested, of course, that particular words or combinations of words always have the *same* meaning. Modifying my previous example slightly, if John and Ann agree that whenever John says 'dog' he means cat, then the next time John says 'dog' *to Ann*, the meaning of what John says will be the thing ordinarily called 'cat'. Although language must be shared, it is possible for there to be only two sharers.

The above observation leads me to the general and familiar point that words must always be understood in their context. To determine the objective or 'publicly shared' meaning of a word, both the relevant 'public' and the content of what that public 'shares' must be identified. In the above example, the most important fact about the context in which John spoke is that John and Ann had agreed that the word 'dog' had a certain meaning between them. In other cases, what matters is how a word is understood within a particular trade or industry: an instructive example is the case in which it was successfully argued that the word 'white' should be interpreted as meaning black, where, by trade usage, 'white selvage' meant a selvage that was relatively dark.[15] Other contextual factors that are relevant in contractual settings include: the parties' negotiations, their past dealings, the purpose of the contract, industry practices, community standards, and even (I shall argue) shared normative understandings.

The plain meaning rule

The importance of context in ascertaining the meaning of words and phrases supports recent judicial pronouncements to the effect that courts should take into account all the background knowledge 'which would reasonably have been available to the parties in the situation in which they

---

[15] *Mitchell v Henry* 15 ChD 181 (1880) reversing Sir George Jessel in the Court of Appeal who declared that 'nobody could convince him that black was white'.

were at the time of the contract'.[16] But what is at first glance puzzling is the traditional (and often still applied) rule that, other than in cases of clear ambiguity, external evidence of meaning is not permitted.[17] According to this rule, courts should normally look no farther than the plain or literal meaning of a word or sentence. Even accepting that 'plain' meaning to a lawyer may differ from plain meaning to others, the traditional exclusion of contextual evidence, of whatever kind, appears difficult to reconcile with my previous comments about the importance of context.

One explanation of narrow interpretation is that it is based on essentially administrative or efficiency concerns.[18] The suggestion here is that it is difficult—and hence costly—for judges to take into account the contexts in which terms are used, especially when they are unfamiliar with those contexts. A narrow approach solves this problem by giving contracting parties incentives to write their contracts using words that a judge can understand with little or no additional information. It is accepted that this approach will inevitably result in some contractual terms being enforced in a way that does not account for the context in which they were used. But the harm caused by occasional misinterpretations are outweighed, according to this explanation, by the benefits that arise from encouraging parties to write contracts that courts can easily understand. In short, courts read contracts narrowly because they want to give contracting parties incentives to write contracts that should be read narrowly.

No doubt judges sometimes refuse to undertake intensive contextual interpretation for this reason. But this efficiency-based explanation cannot completely account for the tradition of narrow interpretation. For one thing, it does not explain why the courts have shifted, in principle anyway, from this narrow approach to a more contextual approach. More importantly, this efficiency-based explanation for the practice of narrow interpretation is in conflict with efficiency theorists' overall account of

---

[16] *Investors Compensation Scheme v West Bromwich Building Society* [1998] 1 All ER 98, 114. American law has adopted this approach even more explicitly: '[t]he overarching principle of contract is that the court is free to look to all the relevant circumstances surrounding the transaction. This includes all writings, oral statements, and other conduct by which the parties manifested their assent, together with any prior negotiations between them and any applicable course of dealings. . . . The entire agreement, including all writings, should be read together in the light of all circumstances.' Farnsworth (1998) 276–77.

[17] *Jacobs v. Batavia & General Plantations Trust Ltd* [1924] 1 Ch 287, 295; A more recent example is *The Nile Rhapsody* [1992] 2 Lloyd's Rep. 349, 407.

[18] This explanation is similar to the efficiency-based 'penalty explanation' of implied terms that I discuss below at 8.3.4.

implied terms. As I will explain below, it is a central assumption of efficiency explanations of implied terms that it is inefficient for contracting parties to try to write 'complete' contracts (contracts that specify what should happen in every possible contingency, no matter how unlikely). The costs entailed in writing such a contract (assuming this is even possible) outweigh its benefits. It is more efficient, therefore, for the law to complete contracts when the extra detail is needed. The significance of this conclusion for the present issue is that it applies with equal force to attempts to write contracts using only 'plain' terminology. In the same way that adding detail is costly, it is costly to translate idiosyncratic terminology into non-idiosyncratic terminology. Instead, courts could make such translations as needed. Moreover, just as extra detail is rarely needed, 'plain' language is rarely needed. Except in the rare cases in which a contract is litigated, it is the parties rather than the courts that interpret the contract—and contracting parties presumably understand the context in which their contracts are written. Efficiency reasons do not, therefore, provide a convincing explanation for courts' preference for narrow interpretation.

I suggest that the best explanation for the narrow interpretation tradition is the one that equates narrow interpretation with fully contextual interpretation. More specifically, the context in which most common law contracts were (and still are) written was a context in which it was understood that contract terms were meant to be read narrowly. The judge-made common law of contract developed in response to claims brought by commercial litigants, and in respect of contracts that, for the most part, were drafted by sophisticated lawyers. It was understood by those drafting and reading such contracts that the words within them should be read narrowly and literally. The context of commercial drafting, in other words, is one that asks the reader to ignore the context outside of the physical document. *Why* this is the context is not strictly relevant, but the reason is undoubtedly found in the importance that commercial lawyers place on reducing opportunities for misunderstandings.

In this light, the recent acknowledgement by English courts of the importance of contextual interpretation should be understood not so much as a change in how courts interpret contracts in practice, but as a recognition that narrow interpretation is not in every case the best way to give effect to the principle that interpretation is *always* contextual. The advantage of relegating narrow interpretation to a rule of practice rather than of principle is that it makes it easier for courts to look beyond narrow meaning in those cases—often, but not always, non-commercial—in which a broader approach is appropriate. Notwithstanding what I said above, in *certain* contracting contexts external evidence should be taken into account.

Vagueness and indeterminate terms

Taking context into account does not, of course, eliminate entirely problems of vagueness and ambiguity. No matter how much context is taken into account, all contracts are indeterminate in some respects. Indeterminacy is a general feature of communication.[19] How many hairs must a man lose before he is 'bald'? The answer is not clear, and it will normally remain unclear even if we know everything there is to know about the context in which the word 'bald' is being used. Many contracts contain similarly vague terms (e.g., 'reasonable', 'timely', 'in good faith', and so on). Even apparently precise terms can give rise to similar questions. The context of a contract of sale may make clear that 'delivery on Friday' means delivery at the purchaser's residence, in a box, and during working hours—yet leave unclear whether the vendor must bring the goods inside or, if inside, to the room the goods are ultimately destined for. Does delivery of a freezer mean delivery to the purchaser's difficult-to-reach basement or loft? The famous case of *Raffles v Wichelhaus*[20] appeared to involve indeterminacy of this kind: even after the context was taken into account, it was not clear which 'Peerless' ship the contract referred to.

Courts faced with contract claims that are based on ambiguous or vague terms must address a number of questions. To begin, courts must determine if the uncertainty is such that the parties should be regarded as having failed to reach an agreement at all (as appeared to be the ruling in *Raffles*). This is an issue of offer and acceptance law. If it is decided that the requisite agreement was reached, the court must next stipulate a meaning for the term. I will say something about how this is done when I discuss 'gap-filling' below (the process is the same). For the moment, I offer three general observations with regard to courts stipulating the meaning of a term.

First, it is difficult to determine when a judge is stipulating or creating a meaning for a particular term as opposed to simply interpreting its meaning. Interpretation is not a mechanical process; it requires difficult judgments and evaluations. But, equally, creation of contractual meaning is not done on a blank slate; the interpretative sources always have some

---

[19] Endicott (2000; 2000b).   [20] (1864) 2 H & C 906.

between losses and gains, and by fault-based criteria. The resulting conception of fairness might be summarized in the familiar idea that it would be unfair to hold persons to contractual obligations that, through no fault of their own, are significantly more onerous than they had anticipated.[37] This conception is not easily expressed in a formula (as we shall see), nor can it be slotted neatly into a broader moral theory. But given the primary role that fairness plays in much moral reasoning, this is arguably a virtue rather than a defect of the account. It is unlikely that a basic normative concept such as fairness could be reduced to a mechanical formula.

Whether this or any such conception of substantive fairness *should* play a role in regulating contracts in a market economy is a difficult question, but one that I will leave to the general discussion of substantive fairness in Chapter 9 (9.2.5). The present discussion focuses exclusively on the question of whether, assuming substantive fairness is a legitimate concern, this notion is useful in understanding mistake cases.

That a contract entered into on the basis of a mistaken assumption may sometimes be unfair (in the sense just described) seems difficult to deny. To be obliged to pay a million pounds for, say, a fake Rembrandt is a rather bad deal. Admittedly, the risk that the painting was a fake might well have been factored into the sale price, such that the price was discounted by a factor equal to the likelihood that the painting was a fake. But it would be implausible to assume that contracting parties always factor such risks into the price—and to assume that they do so accurately. Contracting parties may make a mistake about the *likelihood* that they will be mistaken in believing a painting is by Rembrandt. In such a case, the result may be a substantively unfair contract.

The basic test for mistake—the 'fundamental' mistake test—can plausibly be explained on this basis. More specifically, the (rare) cases in which courts have set aside contracts for mistake appear to be cases in which the relevant parties were not just mistaken about an important factual assumption, but in which they were also mistaken about the likelihood that they would be mistaken.

Fairness explanations and the 'mutual mistake' rule

But while the need for a fundamental mistake seems consistent with a concern for fairness, one feature of the law relating to mistake that is

[37] This concept of fairness might also be described using the notion of unconscionability (9.2), the idea being that it would be unconscionable to insist on performance of an obligation that, through no fault of the obliged party, is radically more burdensome than was assumed when the obligation was undertaken.

more difficult to explain on this basis is the common law rule that an operative mistake must be *shared*. From a fairness perspective this rule is puzzling. An unfair contract is unfair to just one of the contracting parties—so why is it not sufficient to show that this party was in error?

A partial (though only partial) answer to this objection is that few cases involving unilateral mistakes are actually unfair. Let me explain. Unilateral mistake cases can be divided into two categories: (1) cases in which the vendor made the mistake (by charging too little or by selling something that she still needed), (2) cases in which the purchaser made the mistake (by paying too much or by buying something he did not really need). In most vendor mistake cases, the purchaser's superior information was acquired as a result of previous efforts. A geologist who purchases mineral-rich land from an unknowing farmer typically learned the true value of the land because of his training and research. Likewise, the art expert who recognizes a previously unrecognized old master in a junk shop is able to do so because of her training and because of the time she spends trawling through junk shops. In cases of this sort, enforcing the contract is consistent with a concern for fairness.[38] Permitting purchasers in such cases to profit from their knowledge does no more than reward them for their past efforts.

Of course, some vendor mistake cases cannot be explained in this way. A purchaser's superior information is sometimes acquired casually, say at a party or on a crowded bus. This is what occurred in the famous American case of *Laidlaw v Organ*, where the purchaser by chance acquired information that a British naval blockade was about to be lifted. He immediately bought tobacco at a price far less than that at which tobacco was sold just a few hours later, when the information became public. As such, the purchaser profited from a mistake on the vendor's part, despite expending little or no effort. But enforcing such contracts may still be fair, or at least not significantly unfair. This is because of a second feature of vendor mistake cases: the consequence of the vendor's mistake is (merely) that the vendor foregoes a benefit or profit that she *might have* made. The vendor is not made worse off, at least not in the ordinary sense of 'worse off'. Admittedly, from a purely financial perspective it might be said that there is no difference between a loss incurred and a gain not realized. But from the perspective of the (common sense) notion of fairness employed here, there is a clear difference. We experience disappointment and often

---

[38] The concept of fairness employed here is not, however, the basic 'substantive fairness' concept of equality in exchange. Rather, it is the very different notion of 'just desserts'.

regret when we learn that we missed out on opportunities for gain. But diminutions in present assets are regarded much more seriously. The reason is not mysterious: we plan our lives using assumptions about our assets. Overestimates cause havoc to those plans. Underestimates do not.[39] From a fairness perspective, a mistake that causes a person to lose or accidentally give away a thousand pounds is more serious or 'fundamental' than a mistake that causes a person to, say, not win a thousand pounds in a lottery — or through a contract.

For these reasons, it may be concluded that contracts involving *vendor mistakes* are rarely unfair, or at least rarely significantly unfair. The rule that such contracts are enforceable is therefore consistent with a fairness explanation. But cases involving *purchaser mistakes* are different. Neither of the considerations just discussed apply to such cases. The 'past efforts' justification does not apply because enforcement does not reward the vendor for his past efforts. The vendor is simply benefiting from the purchaser's mistake. To be sure, the vendor may argue that the reason he knows the true value of the thing sold is that he was an expert or that he undertook research. But the vendor would have acquired this information in any event. Moreover, this is not information that the purchaser is then able to appropriate for her benefit. As for the second justification — the 'lost opportunity' idea — it does not apply because a purchaser who enters a contract on the basis of a mistaken assumption ends up with something that she does not want (or at least does not want at the price that was paid). For example, a purchaser who buys land for commercial development only to discover that the land had been zoned parkland does not merely fail to obtain a benefit (the profit she would have made on the development); she also experiences a real diminution in her present assets. She is in a worse position than she was in prior to entering the contract.

The common law's approach to *purchaser* mistake cases, therefore, is difficult to explain from a fairness perspective. But the significance of this inconsistency is liable to be overemphasized. Cases involving purchaser mistakes are fairly rare — probably because purchasers typically ask vendors about the relevant facts. As well, insofar as purchasers fail to ask vendors about these facts, they are often at least partially at fault for this failure. In a land sale, for example, the vendor may not be aware that the purchaser wants the land for commercial development. Finally, it is worth noting that common law courts outside of the United Kingdom have

---

[39] Smith (1996b).

sometimes given relief for unilateral mistakes; and when they have done this, the cases have usually involved purchaser mistakes.[40]

Fairness explanations of the 'loss lies' rule

Another feature of the law relating to mistake cases that is difficult to explain from a fairness perspective is the rule that, with rare exceptions,[41] the losses that arise from a mistake are borne entirely by one or the other party. The contract is either enforced or not enforced. This is puzzling because if the relevant mistake was neither party's fault (as this explanation assumes), then a concern for fairness would appear to demand that its costs be shared by both parties.[42]

This objection is well-founded, but, again, its significance is easy to overstate. A distinction must be drawn between three kinds of losses that might arise on the setting aside of a contract. The first is the loss of the benefit or profit that the parties might have realized had the contract been enforced. Consistent with the distinction drawn a moment ago between gains foregone and losses incurred, a concern for fairness does not entail that 'losses' of this kind be shared. It is not clear that foregone profits truly represent a loss, but, if they do, losses of this kind are relatively insignificant. The second kind of loss is that which arises when either or both contracting parties have transferred benefits to the other on the assumption that the contract was valid. This is a genuine loss, but it can be and is reparable by a (non-contractual) claim in unjust enrichment for restitution.[43] This leaves only the third kind of loss, which is loss in the form of wasted reliance on an anticipated contract. This is again a genuine loss, and it is not reparable by an order of restitution (because restitution is available in such cases only with respect to transferred benefits). In such cases, then, the rule that losses must lie where they fall is difficult to defend from a fairness perspective. But it is difficult to think of a case in which a contract has been set aside for mistake that involved this third kind of loss.[44]

---

[40] *Obde v Schlemeyer* 353 P.2d 672 (1960); Farnsworth (1999) 248–50.

[41] The 'equitable' doctrine of mistake enunciated by Lord Denning in *Solle v Butcher* [1950] 1 KB 671 provides that a contract may be set aside 'on terms'. This doctrine, which was rarely followed, seems to have finally been laid to rest by the decision in *Great Peace Shipping Ltd v Tsavliris Salvage (International) Ltd.* [2002] 4 All ER 689.

[42] Fried (1985) 72.

[43] *Strickland v Turner* (1852) 7 Exch 208; Burrows (1993) 126–30.

[44] A possible counter example is *Associated Japanese Bank v Credit du Nord SA* [1988] 3 All ER 902, in which the court held that a contract to guarantee a loan to purchase non-existent machines could be set aside for mistake. The courts also held, however, that properly interpreted the contract contained an implied term that the machines existed.

Conclusion to fairness explanations of implied terms

Overall, there is a reasonable (but not perfect) degree of fit between the fairness explanation and the main features of the law relating to mistake. Admittedly, the fairness explanation does not provide a fine-grained explanation that explains why this or that difficult case was decided precisely in the way it was decided. Aside from the vagueness of the general notion of fairness, most mistake cases raise a number of conflicting fairness-based considerations. The relevant factors—implied allocations of risk, fault, past efforts and investments, foreseeability, and reliance—rarely all point in the same direction. As we shall see, though, the same is true of alternate implied-term explanations of 'excuse' rules.

8.3.4. THE EFFICIENCY EXPLANATION OF MISTAKE CASES

There is a well-developed theoretical literature on efficiency explanations of implied-in-law or 'default' terms.[45] Most of that literature applies to implied-in-law terms generally, but in this section my focus remains on mistake cases.

Like the fairness explanation, the efficiency explanation supposes that when courts set aside contracts in mistake cases they do so in order to promote a value external to the contract. That value is efficiency or, more broadly, 'social welfare' or 'utility' (on the utilitarian conception of 'efficiency' adopted here, see 4.1). More specifically, efficiency is promoted, in this view, by rules that provide incentives for contracting parties to act efficiently. The explanations for how the mistake rules encourage efficiency differ according to whether it is a unilateral or a mutual mistake that is at issue.

Shared mistakes

As regards shared mistakes, the basic explanation is that the rules are efficient because they reduce the costs of making contracts. The starting assumption in this explanation is the idea that it is inefficient for contracting parties to try to write 'complete' contracts—defined here as contracts that specify what the parties should do in all circumstances. This is inefficient because certain contingencies are so unlikely to arise that the benefit attendant to stipulating what should happen if they do arise is not worth the cost. Rather, in such cases, it is the law that should provide the relevant terms if and when they are needed. In short, the law can facilitate

---

[45] e.g. Ayres and Gertner (1989); Craswell (1989); Johnston (1990).

contracting by providing a set of default terms that apply automatically unless the parties specify otherwise. In this sense, the rules relating to mistake can be regarded as providing default terms.

As for the content of such default terms, the basic idea is that the terms should approximate the content that the parties would have chosen themselves. In the words of Richard Posner, '[t]he task for a court asked to interpret a contract to cover a contingency that the parties did not provide for is to imagine how the parties would have provided for the contingency had they decided to do so.'[46] One caveat is that, in view of the costs of establishing one-off or party-specific terms, it may be more efficient in practice for courts to pick the default terms that the *majority* of similarly situated contracting parties would choose. The basic idea, however, is clear enough: if potential contracting parties know that courts will allocate low probability risks in the same way that they would have done themselves, they can confidently enter contracts without specifying how those risks should actually be allocated.

The few cases in which relief has been given for mistake fit broadly with the above analysis. In most such cases, the consequence of the mistake is that the contract is particularly onerous or costly for one of the parties (as opposed to merely leading to a windfall profit for one of the parties).[47] For example, in *Magee v Pennine Insurance Co*,[48] the effect of an insurance company's mistaken belief that the plaintiff had a valid insurance contract with them was that they agreed to pay out a sum of money that they did not owe. If the purpose of mistake rules is to facilitate contracting, providing relief in such cases makes sense because people are generally risk-averse. People worry more about entering a contract that might turn out badly for them than they do about entering a contract in which they might not make a windfall profit. The fact that courts will relieve onerous obligations incurred through mistake serves, therefore, as an incentive for risk-averse people to enter contracts.

This 'basic' efficiency-based explanation fits well with certain features of the law, but it is clearly incomplete. If minimizing risk were the only factor for courts to consider, far more contracts would be set aside for mistake (and frustration). Contracts frequently turn out to be

---

[46] (1998) 105. See also Kronman (1978b); Posner (1998) 105; Goetz and Scott (1983) 971.

[47] The American case of *Sherwood v Walker* 33 NW 919 (1887), in which a contract for the sale of a supposedly barren cow was set aside on proof that the cow was capable of breeding, and so more valuable, is the exception. But one reason the case is famous is that is highly unusual for a court to give relief on facts of this kind. The decision is also widely regarded as wrongly decided.

[48] [1969] 2 KB 507.

unexpectedly onerous. A more detailed explanation is therefore required. More specifically, a number of other efficiency factors need to be considered. Three such factors are discussed briefly below.

One factor that needs to be taken into account in attempting to mimic the terms the parties would have chosen is which of the parties is better able to insure against the costs associated with the relevant risk. In general, contracting parties would choose to allocate a risk to the party best able to insure against that risk. Typically, though not invariably, this will be the purchaser, because the purchaser will better know the costs to his business of the risk materializing. A purchaser of land, for example, knows better than the vendor whether it is important that the purchased land be suitable for the proposed construction.

Setting aside contracts for mistake will likely have an effect on the way in which parties write contracts in the future. This effect represents a second consideration for the efficiency perspective. To the extent that courts are willing to imply excusing terms into contracts, contracting parties have less incentive to write complete contracts. Given what I said above, it might be thought that this is always a good thing. But it is, of course, a basic assumption of efficiency theories that individuals are generally in a better position than courts to create efficient contracts (4.1). This is the efficiency-based justification for freedom of contract. There is a tension, therefore, between the idea that parties should write their own contracts and the idea that it is efficient for courts to provide default terms. Broadly speaking, this tension is thought to be resolved, in the efficiency explanation, by courts implying terms only in respect of low probability events or in respect of events the significance or likelihood of which are difficult for contracting parties to assess in advance. The difficulty, of course, is specifying precisely which events fall into this category for the parties in question. A further complication is introduced by the fact that one way of encouraging parties to write more complete contracts is to imply terms into their contracts *that they would not have wanted*. According to some theorists, the courts imply so-called 'penalty terms' in cases in which the parties should have dealt with the relevant issue.[49] The unattractiveness of these terms is intended to give contracting parties incentives to fill the relevant gaps. For example, a rule that contracts will be interpreted narrowly and strictly (such that excuse claims rarely, if ever, succeed) will induce contracting parties who are

---

[49] Ayres and Gertner (1989).

unhappy with such a rule to bargain for terms that provide different results.[50]

A third factor that must be accounted for in evaluating the efficiency of the mistake rules is the effect of these rules on contracting parties' incentives to gather information prior to entering a contract. Everything else being equal, this factor argues for allocating the risk of the mistake to the party best able to have discovered the truth prior to the contract. From an efficiency perspective, the person best able to prevent the mistake (the 'accident') should be given incentives to do so. An enforcement rule which works against this person will have this effect.[51] In sale contracts, for example, the person best placed to learn the truth about the object being sold is usually the vendor (who is in possession of the goods)—a fact which favours enforcement. But exceptions exist, such as cases in which the vendor is a middleman and the purchaser an expert, or cases in which the factual assumption might relate to an external characteristic, such as the existence of a patent or other legal restriction on the use of the good.

So far as shared mistakes are concerned, the end result of taking into account these factors (and others that I have not mentioned)[52] is that, as was true of the fairness explanation, it is difficult to say for certain whether particular decisions are consistent with the efficiency explanation. A prima facie plausible efficiency-based explanation can probably be offered for most cases involving shared mistakes. But to confirm this explanation, a variety of factors that are difficult (if not impossible) to quantify must be taken into account.

Efficiency-based explanations of the 'mutual mistake' rule

A unilateral mistake, recall, cannot ground a defence of mistake. The mistake must be shared. The efficiency explanation of this rule focuses on the incentives the rule creates for the efficient production, utilization, and dissemination of information. As was true of the fairness explanation, the

---

[50] This idea of a court imposing penalty terms is therefore similar to the idea, defended in certain efficiency-based explanations of criminal law, that individuals should be penalized (by the criminal law) when they fail to make a bargain in a situation in which it was possible to make a bargain (e.g. the thief who takes without asking): Posner (1998) 238–42.

[51] The underlying idea is therefore similar to the standard efficiency-based explanation of tort law, according to which the costs of an accident should be placed on the least-cost avoider or preventer of that accident: Calabresi (1970) 135–73.

[52] For example, a broad doctrine of mistake will make contracting generally more attractive to parties who are more likely, in general, to make mistakes—and vice versa: see generally Craswell (1988; 2001).

efficiency explanation applies differently to cases involving vendor mistakes and those involving purchaser mistakes.

The efficiency explanation for refusing relief in vendor mistake cases is reasonably straightforward. Recall that in such cases the purchaser's superior information is usually the result of training or research. The prospector knows the farmer's land contains oil because of his investment in research. From an efficiency perspective, such investments are valuable —they produce useful information—and so they should be encouraged. This is achieved by enforcing the relevant contract. The prospector reaps the reward for his investment. As for those cases in which the purchaser's information was obtained without an investment ('by chance'), the enforcement rule is efficient because it gives the purchasers an incentive to *use* the relevant information.[53] The prospector who casually learns that a parcel of land is rich in minerals has an incentive, under the current rule, to act on this information by buying the land and then mining it. By contrast, under a no-enforcement rule, the prospector might simply ignore the information—with the result that the land might remain undeveloped. This argument applies, note, even if the relevant information will become public knowledge. It is efficient for the information to be used sooner rather than later. More specifically, by acting on the information they possess, purchasers send signals about future demand earlier than might otherwise be the case—allowing the market to react accordingly. In *Laidlaw v Organ*,[54] for example, one effect of the purchaser going to the market and buying tobacco was that the demand for tobacco—and thus the price of tobacco—increased incrementally. This sent a signal to vendors to buy more tobacco and to growers to grow more tobacco—an efficient outcome given that the demand for tobacco would increase when the blockade was lifted. Admittedly, in *Laidlaw* itself, these signals had only a marginal effect in that the information about the blockade became public a few hours later. But from an efficiency perspective, this is irrelevant; a marginal benefit is still a benefit.

The efficiency explanation accounts nicely, then, for the common law's refusal to give relief for unilateral mistakes in cases involving vendor mistakes. But as was true with respect to the fairness explanation, the rule as regards *purchaser mistake* cases is more difficult to explain from this perspective. Enforcing such contracts does not create incentives for vendors to produce or use valuable information. Vendors already have an incentive to learn the true value of their possessions, since they can profit

---

[53] Trebilcock (1993) 113.   [54] 15 US (2 Wheat.) 178 (1817).

from that knowledge. And as for *using* this information, an enforcement rule gives vendors an incentive to keep the information private—a result that is efficient.

From an efficiency perspective, the main benefit of the current rule is that it encourages purchasers to ask questions—which will help prevent mistakes from happening in the first place. But this is a clear benefit only in cases in which the vendor is unaware of the purchaser's mistake. In cases in which the vendor is aware of the mistake, a simpler way of preventing the mistake is to require the vendor to tell the purchaser the relevant information (which outcome can be achieved by not enforcing contracts in which the vendor fails to do this). It is relatively simple for a vendor of land who knows that a potential purchaser is mistaken in believing that the land is zoned commercial, and who knows further that the zoning classification is critical in the purchaser's decision, to inform the purchaser of this fact. Interestingly, it is in cases of exactly this kind that American courts have occasionally given relief for unilateral mistakes.[55]

I conclude that, like the fairness explanation, the efficiency explanation offers a reasonable explanation for *most* of the main features of the law relating to mistake. The explanation fits well with the rules relating to unilateral mistakes; the exception is cases involving purchaser mistakes in which the vendor is aware of the mistake. As regards shared mistake cases, the efficiency based explanation for the basic rule is prima facie reasonable, but it is difficult to tell if particular applications of the rule are efficient. In common with many efficiency explanations, the later task requires taking into account a wide variety of unquantifiable factors. In short, the empirical data needed to confirm the explanation is unavailable.

8.3.5. THE INTERPRETATION EXPLANATION OF MISTAKE CASES

The third and final 'implied-term explanation' of mistake cases is the interpretation explanation. This explanation supposes that when courts set aside a contract for mistake it is because the contract contains an *implied-in-fact* term directing them to do this. The contract is set aside, in other words, because the parties themselves implicitly stipulated such an outcome.

The interpretation explanation is often described as the classical explanation of mistake because it appears to mesh well with the classical view that contractual obligations are strictly binding except insofar as the

---

[55] *Ohde v Schlemeyer* 353 P.2d 672 (1960).

parties provide. This description is broadly correct but it can be misleading for two reasons. First, the interpretation explanation, like the fairness
and efficiency explanations, fits uneasily with the 'classical' idea that
there exists a distinct doctrine, or excuse, of mistake.[56] According to the
interpretation explanation, there is in truth no such doctrine; courts
deciding mistakes cases merely do what they always do when establishing
the content of a contract—interpret the contract. The law relating to
mistake, in other words, belongs alongside the 'business efficacy' test (8.4)
and other tests for implying *in-fact* terms into contracts.

Second, the interpretation explanation also fits uneasily with the classical view that the parties' intentions are to be found in the ordinary
meaning of the express terms that they have used (the 'plain meaning'
rule: 8.1.2). Admittedly, this interpretation does not suppose that the
parties' *actual* intentions should be ignored (as I argued was true of the
fairness and efficiency explanations), but it does suppose that their
expressed intentions should (sometimes) be ignored. This is inconsistent
with the classical belief that the parties' expressed intentions are the best
evidence of their actual intentions.

Two views of implied-in-fact terms

The basic idea underlying the interpretation explanation of mistake cases
is that contracting parties impliedly—but genuinely—stipulate that
their agreement should not be binding in the case that a certain factual
assumption turns out to be false. Thus, if a contract to purchase a painting is set aside because the painting turns out to be a fake, the explanation
is that, on its true construction, the contract reads as if it contained an
explicit term that 'this sale is conditional on the painting being an authen-
tic old master'.

This understanding of mistake is defended in a number of well-known
19th and early 20th century decisions.[57] But in the latter half of the
20th century, this interpretation explanation came under frequent attack
by 'progressive' scholars and judges.[58] This attack was misguided, as I

---

[56] Ibbetson (1999) 225–29; Simpson (1975).

[57] *Krell v Henry* [1903] 2 KB 740, 748; *Taylor v Caldwell* (1863) 122 ER 309, 312; Atiyah
(1979) 436–37.

[58] Atiyah (1986) 244–47; (1995) 254–57; Collins (1997) 276–77; *Davis Contractors Ltd v
Fareham Urban District Council* [1956] AC 696, 728; *The Eugenia* [1964] 2 QB 226, 238.
Compare *McRae v Commonwealth Disposals Commission* (1951) 84 CLR 377. For a general
discussion, see Morris (1997) 149–55.

will explain, but it provides a useful introduction to the main points of contention regarding the interpretation explanation.

The progressives argued that it was an obvious fiction to say that parties had contracted on a certain basis when, by definition, they were not thinking about the relevant event when they signed their contract (if they *had* been thinking of the event, there would be no need to turn to the law of mistake). The progressives' point was not to deny that certain things could 'go without saying'. Rather, it was to insist that a successful plea of mistake required that such 'unspoken things' have at least been before the minds of the contracting parties. Lord Radcliffe neatly expressed the 'mental state' view of a contract's meaning when he stated (albeit in the context of a frustration claim) that there is 'something of a logical difficulty in seeing how the parties could even impliedly have provided for something which *ex hypothesi* they neither expected nor foresaw.'[59] Consistent with this conclusion, judicial and scholarly attention then shifted to thinking about non-contractual bases (i.e., fairness or efficiency) for filling gaps in contracts.[60]

The progressives' objection is unpersuasive. More specifically, the mental state view of meaning on which this objection rests was rejected in our earlier discussion of the objective approach to interpreting express terms (8.1.1). The reasons for that rejection apply equally when the mental state view is applied to establishing the existence and meaning of implied-in-fact terms. In the same way that the meaning of an express term is not established by the speaker's inner intentions, the existence and content of implied-in-fact terms are not established by inner intentions.[61] Both depend on the objective or public meaning of an utterance. The classic illustration is by Wittgenstein:

Someone says to me, 'Show the children a game.' I teach them gaming with dice, and the other says, 'I didn't mean that sort of game'. Must the exclusion of the game with dice have come before his mind when he gave the order?[62]

Wittgenstein's answer is, of course, 'no'. A game with dice was not part of the meaning of the communication, and this is the case even though it

---

[59] *Davis Contractors Ltd v Fareham UDC* [1956] AC 696, 728.

[60] '[T]he movement of the law of contract is away from a rigid theory of autonomy towards the . . . imposition—by the courts of just solutions': *National Carriers Ltd. v. Panalpina (Northern) Ltd* [1981] A.C. 675, 679 (Lord Wilberforce). See also Craswell (1989); Atiyah (1995) 210.

[61] For a clear explanation of this point (on which I draw heavily) see Langille and Ripstein (1996).

[62] Wittgenstein (1972) 33.

is unlikely the speaker was thinking of gambling games, or any other examples of unsuitable games, at the time the instruction was given. If the instructions in Wittgenstein's example were part of a contract, it could properly be held that the contract was breached by teaching the children gaming with dice.

Wittgenstein's example concerns the meaning of an 'express' term— 'game'—but it is just as applicable to the process of establishing implied-in-fact terms in a contract. Indeed (and this point proves significant), the process of interpreting implied-in-fact terms is sometimes difficult to distinguish from that used for determining a contract's express terms. Suppose that a contract requires a bank teller to work from 'Jan 1st to Dec 30th'. The meaning of 'Jan 1st to Dec 30th' will rightly be interpreted as requiring the teller to work on, say, Monday July 10th—even though the parties likely were not thinking of that particular day or any other particular days at the time of signing their agreement. The contract will also rightly be interpreted as not requiring the teller to work on weekends— though again the parties are unlikely to have been thinking about 'weekends' when making the agreement. But it is difficult to say whether the 'no work on weekends' feature of the contract is part of the meaning of the words 'Jan 1st to Dec 30th' or is instead a term that has been implied-in-fact into the contract. Decisions in mistake often raise similar issues. A court's decision that a contract of sale need not be performed because the goods in question never existed might be understood on the basis that the court merely applied the meaning of the vendor's express obligation to deliver. Equally, it might be understood as implying a separate clause to the effect that the vendor's obligation is conditional on the existence of the goods.

The significance of context

Consistent with these observations, the method for determining which terms should be implied-in-fact into an agreement is the same method that I described above when discussing the interpretation of express terms (8.1.1). More specifically, the existence and meaning of implied-in-fact terms are established on the basis of the publicly shared ('objective') assumptions that surround and support the relevant transaction. In respect of mistakes, these assumptions concern the allocation of certain risks in the contract; for example, the risk that particular goods do not exist or are less valuable than the parties assume. Broadly speaking, assumptions about risk are established by uncovering conventional under-standings; more specifically, they are grounded in a range of contextual factors such as past dealings, commercial practices, the purpose of the contract, background legal rules, and shared normative understandings.

In considering the role of context, a recurrent theme is that the context in which many contracts are formed argues *against* implying additional terms. In the same way that commercial contexts often argue for interpreting individual terms narrowly (8.1.2), those same contexts argue for interpreting sentences and entire contracts narrowly (i.e., as they are written).[63] Of particular importance in this regard is that sophisticated contracting parties will factor into their agreements the possibility that they might be mistaken—even if they are not sure at the time exactly which facts they might be mistaken about. An analogy can be drawn to the careful traveller who takes along a sum of money for emergencies.[64] The traveller cannot predict the nature of every emergency that might arises in her travels, but she knows it is possible that an emergency may arise, and she provides for this risk by increasing the travelling money she would otherwise take. Sophisticated contracting parties do the same thing. The contractor who agrees to dig out the foundations for a building knows— or is objectively, and therefore rightly, presumed to know—that the soil condition may be different than he assumes it to be. The sophisticated contractor will provide for this possibility by incorporating explicit excusing clauses or by factoring the risk into the contract price. A court interpreting such a contract should, therefore, hold the contractor strictly to his contractual promise. The literal allocation of the risk—namely that performance is required—is the actual allocation.

Beyond these general observations, there is little that can be said about the process of determining which, if any, terms go without saying in particular contracts. Like the process of interpreting express terms, this is something that occurs all the time as part of ordinary communication. For judges to perform this task properly in contract cases, what is needed is not knowledge of special rules, but knowledge of the relevant context in which the contract was made, including knowledge of the particular ways that contract drafters use words. The common law method of drawing judges from the ranks of experienced lawyers helps to ensure that judges possess this knowledge.

---

[63] With respect to claims of frustration, the conclusion just reached is reinforced by the ready availability of boilerplate force majeure and price-adjustment clauses: McKendrick (1995).

[64] Triantis (1992).

The interpretation explanation and contractual gaps

It is a fundamental assumption of the interpretation explanation that contracts do not contain gaps in respect of particular issues merely because those issues were not before the minds of the contracting parties when they formed the contract. But it does not follow from this assumption that contracts are completely determinate. In the same way that the express terms of a contract can be vague, so too can implied-in-fact understandings.[65] When this happens, it would appear that courts have no choice but to simply *stipulate* a term into a contract. Courts do not, of course, have an absolutely free hand in this regard. The terms of the contract, considerations of fairness or efficiency, or consistency with precedent will limit the range of acceptable options. But within this range, the court is free to choose. This conclusion is consistent with the idea that a basic role of the courts, and of law generally, is to resolve disputes for which the correct answer is not clear.[66]

It is difficult to say how many mistake cases involve vague implied-in-fact terms. On the one hand, we almost never see courts admitting that they have chosen terms for the parties. On the other hand, it is rare that a court's decision, at least in the cases that go to trial, is a self-evident conclusion of the above interpretative process. The line between interpretation and addition is a fine one; the judicial report of a mistake case normally leaves even a close reader unclear on which side of this line the judge ended up. Even the judge may have difficulty knowing when she is merely interpreting, rather than adding, terms.

My own view, which here I can really only report rather than defend, is that cases of true gaps, like cases of true indeterminacy of specific words, are relatively rare.[67] Certainly, the progressives' view that all, or nearly all, claims of mistake require courts to allocate unallocated risks is unwarranted. Indeed, and especially in regard to commercial contracts, the opposite conclusion seems more plausible. Most claims of mistake can be resolved on the basis of ordinary interpretative techniques.

A final point in this regard is that it is unlikely that, in cases in which a true gap exists, the courts can turn to fairness or efficiency norms for the solution to the case. Such norms will not provide an answer because the shared context against which the contract was interpreted is likely to have

---

[65] For an account of how contextual factors such as 'industry norms' or 'conventional understandings' are often indeterminate, see Bernstein (1999).

[66] e.g. Finnis (1984) 281–90.

[67] For an analysis of a number of leading cases that support this conclusion, see Langille and Ripstein (1996).

incorporated those norms itself. A significant part of the shared or 'public' understandings about agreements is comprised of understandings about what should, morally, happen—these understandings, in turn, are to a significant extent grounded in, or influenced by, ideas of fairness and efficiency. In short, one of the things that 'goes without saying' in many contexts is that the arrangement should be fair and efficient. It follows that insofar as it is unclear what the contract means, it will also be unclear what fairness or efficiency (or any other moral value)[68] require.

Does the interpretation explanation fit the law?

The discussion above explains in a general way how the interpretation explanation accounts for the law relating to mistake. Before leaving this topic, however, it will be useful to relate that discussion more closely to the actual rules and decisions in this area of the law.

Perhaps the first point to make is that, as was true of the fairness and efficiency explanations, it will often be difficult in practice to determine if the interpretation explanation is consistent with this or that particular decision. The range and variety of factors that courts should take into account when determining if a contract contains an excusing implied-in-fact term are such that one can rarely be certain if a court has done this properly. These are questions about which reasonable people will disagree (just as they will disagree about the fairness or efficiency of a particular decision).

A second point is that my observations about the nature of the contexts in which most commercial contracts are written are consistent with the rarity of successful pleas of mistake. Given those contexts, it will be rare—as a matter of fact—that the express terms of a contract will be conditional on an unexpressed implied-in-fact term. The requirement that a mistake be 'fundamental' to be operative can be understood as giving effect to this idea.

Third, and finally, the requirement that an operative mistake must be shared fits well with the interpretive explanation. Admittedly, it is possible—since meaning is established on objective grounds—that a contract might contain an implied-in-fact term making the contract conditional on the truth of an assumption that one of the parties knows is false. But this seems highly unlikely (except in certain cases involving purchaser mistakes). As we have seen, the rule regarding unilateral mistakes is both fair and efficient (save in certain cases involving purchaser

---

[68] See generally Raz (1986) Chapters 11, 13.

mistakes). Given that fairness and efficiency norms are themselves
incorporated into the objective or public meaning of a contract, it seems
likely that this objective meaning will also favour enforcement.

8.3.6. CONCLUSION TO THE LAW REGARDING MISTAKE

The conclusion suggested by the above analysis is that each of the three
implied term explanations of the law on mistake—the fairness explanation, the efficiency explanation, and the interpretation explanation—fit
the law equally well. Each explanation is able to account for most—but
not all—of the main features of the law relating to mistake. Moreover,
each explanation runs into difficulties with respect to the same aspects
of the law (the blanket exclusion of a defence of unilateral mistake,
explaining the application of the 'fundamental' mistake requirement to
individual decisions).

This conclusion—that the three explanations fit the law equally well
—is, of course, partly a function of the way in which these explanations
interact with one another. More specifically, each explanation incorporates the other's arguments to a significant extent. As we have seen, the
meaning of a contract is determined at least in part by (publicly shared)
fairness and efficiency norms. But, equally, it is in general both fair and
efficient for courts to interpret contracts and then to uphold that interpretation. Each explanation, then, must accept the other's arguments to
at least some degree.

In light of this conclusion, it is clear that in order to choose between
these three explanations the scope of inquiry must be widened. In particular, it should be asked how well each explanation fits with more general explanations of the law of contract. More specifically, insofar as
fairness or efficiency are important generally in explaining contract law it
is plausible to believe one or the other (or both) are important in explaining the law relating to mistake. But if such values have a limited role in
explaining contract law—as I have suggested in this book—then it is
unlikely they provide the best explanation for the law relating to mistake.
Rather, it is the interpretation explanation that is the most convincing.

8.3.7. A DUTY OF DISCLOSURE?

It is convenient at this point to consider briefly the implications of the
above discussion for the question of whether contracting parties should
be under a duty of disclosure. In broad terms, such a duty would require
that contracting parties disclose, during negotiations, factual information
that they know is important to the other party. The common law, of

course, does not recognize a general duty of disclosure (unlike the civil law), though it does recognize such a duty in a few categories of contractual relationships (e.g., insurance contracts).[69]

None of the explanations discussed above provides arguments for or against a *duty* of disclosure—understood here as a legal obligation that might give rise to damages in the event of its breach. But two of the explanations—the fairness and the efficiency explanations—did suggest that, in certain circumstances, a failure to disclose information should be sufficient reason to refuse to enforce a contract. More specifically, we saw that it is arguably both unfair and inefficient to enforce a contract in which a vendor is aware that the purchaser was entering a contract on the basis of a mistaken assumption. It is but a small step from this conclusion to the conclusion that vendors in such cases should be under a duty (as defined above) to disclose information. This duty is not, of course, equivalent to a general duty of disclosure. Nonetheless, its introduction into the common law would be a significant reform.

8.3.8. FRUSTRATION AND DISCHARGE FOR BREACH: A SHORT NOTE

Insofar as the fairness, efficiency, or interpretation explanation of mistake cases is persuasive, it seems clear that a broadly similar explanation can be given for the rules relating to frustration or discharge for breach. Though differing in certain details, the rules relating to mistake, frustration, and discharge for breach are broadly similar. In each case, the rules provide that, if a significant assumption relating either to the past (mistake) or the future (frustration, discharge for breach) is unfounded, then, barring contractual terms to the contrary, the contract may be set aside.

There is a considerable literature that defends the fairness, efficiency, and interpretation explanations of the law of frustration[70] (though little has been written on discharge for breach from any perspective). Many of the arguments discussed above were drawn from that literature. Rather than repeat those arguments in the context of frustration and discharge for breach, I instead offer three observations. The first is that whichever

---

[69] *Lambert v Co-operative Insurance Society* [1975] 2 Lloyd's Rep 485.

[70] Fairness explanations (which are sometimes described as 'justice' explanations) can be found in *Joseph Constantine Steamship Line Ltd v Imperial Shipping Corp Ltd* [1942] AC 154, 186; Collins (1997) 277–78; Fried (1981) 58–63. Efficiency explanations can be found in Ayres and Gertner (1989); Posner and Rosenfield (1977). Finally, interpretation explanations are defended in *Tamplin SS Co v Anglo-Mexican Petroleum Co* [1916] 2 AC 397, 403; Langille and Ripstein (1996).

of the three explanations is the most persuasive as regards the law on mistake is likely also to be the most persuasive as regards the law on frustration or discharge for breach. As I said, in broad outline, these areas of law are very similar—as least from the perspective of implied term explanations. Second, it may be queried whether it makes sense to recognize a distinct doctrine or excuse relating to frustration or discharge for breach—provided, of course, that one of the three implied-terms explanations discussed in this chapter is accepted. As with the law relating to mistake, the law in these areas becomes just one part of the broader topic of establishing the content of a contract. Third, and finally, in the same way that there exist alternatives to implied-term explanations of mistake, there also exist alternative explanations to implied-term explanations of frustration and discharge for breach. Such explanations are examined (but ultimately rejected) in the next chapter.

8.4. INDIVIDUALIZED IMPLIED TERMS

'Individualized' implied terms are terms implied on a contract-by-contract basis. The example I gave earlier was of an implied promise in a contract for the sale of a car to supply the key for the car. Courts will imply such terms when they are required in order to give the contract 'business efficacy'[71] (or if an 'officious bystander'[72] would have understood them to be part of the contract).

The previous analysis of excuse rules can be applied with little modification to individualized implied terms. Indeed, claims of mistake and the like can plausibly be regarded as claims for the contract to be set aside on the basis of an individualized implied term. The rules on mistake are, of course, applied to all contracts. But to determine if a particular contract ought to be set aside on this basis, courts must apply those (very general) rules to the specific circumstances of the contract. In practice, therefore, mistake rules arguably provide the same kind of individualized terms as does the business efficacy test (which itself is a 'general' rule). Both tests provide general rules that must then be applied to specific facts.

Two prominent questions were raised by the above discussion of implied terms' relation to excuse rules: do courts merely interpret contracts or do they, instead, create new terms? And, if the latter, on what basis do they create those terms? These questions apply equally to the

---

[71] *The Moorcock* (1889) 14 PD 64.
[72] *Shirlaw v Southern Foundries (1926) Ltd* [1939] 2 KB 206, 227.

category of individualized terms. Moreover, the answers should, in principle, be the same for each of these categories of implied term. Those who believe the mistake rules merely direct courts to determine what, if any, implied-in-fact terms are contained in a contract are likely to think the same thing about the business efficacy test. By contrast, those who think that mistake rules require courts to imply-in-law terms based on fairness, efficiency, or some other value, are likely to think that the business efficacy test is similarly explained.

It is worth mentioning that courts and commentators are generally receptive to regarding individualized implied terms as implied-in-fact terms. Indeed, both the business efficacy and officious bystander tests are explicitly presented as tests for determining what 'goes without saying'.[73] The significance of this is that it shows that, in at least some cases, courts and commentators have rejected the mental state view of meaning. In these cases, courts accept that what 'goes without saying' may not have been before the minds of the contracting parties. Admittedly, some individualized implied terms would satisfy the mental state view. But many would not. Consider the example of the promise to supply a key for a car; it is unlikely that the parties were thinking 'key' at the time of signing.

8.5. STANDARDIZED IMPLIED TERMS

The third and final category of implied terms are 'standardized' terms. Such terms are implied by virtue of statute, precedent, or custom on a category-of-contract by category-of-contract basis. For example, s.14 of the *Sale of Goods Act* 1979 implies a term into all sales contracts that goods must be of 'satisfactory quality'. A second example, this time based on precedent, is the term implied into all employment contracts that the employee has an obligation to serve his employer faithfully.[74]

The number and variety of standardized terms make general observations about this category difficult. Certainly, it would be rash to suggest that all such terms can be explained on a single ground. To narrow this discussion, I leave aside for now *mandatory* standardized terms (terms that cannot be waived through a contractual provision). An example is the requirement under s.163 (1) of the *Social Security Contributions and Benefits Act* 1992 that employers must give employees sick pay if certain

---

[73] *The Moorcock* (1889) 14 PD 64; *Shirlaw v Southern Foundries (1926) Ltd* [1939] 2 KB 206.

[74] *Lister v Romford Ice & Cold Storage Co Ltd* [1957] AC 555.

conditions are satisfied. The vast majority of such terms are designed to protect what is perceived to be a vulnerable class of contractors (e.g., employees); for this reason they are discussed in the next chapter's treatment of unconscionability. I also put aside rules that provide for the *invalidity* of certain kinds of contractual terms. Such rules are discussed in the previous chapter (if the prohibition focuses on the allegedly undesirable nature of the activity, e.g., promises to commit a crime) or in the next chapter (if the prohibition fixes on the apparent unfairness of the terms, e.g., the prohibitions found in the *Unfair Contracts Terms Act* 1977).

The usual view of standardized terms is that they are implied-in-law terms, meaning that they are designed to give effect not to the intentions of the parties, but rather to an external value such as fairness or efficiency.[75] In this respect, standardized terms are often contrasted with individualized terms implied in accordance with the business efficacy test. Lord Bridge expressed this view when he said there was 'a clear distinction between the search for an implied term necessary to give business efficacy to a particular contract and the search, *based on wider considerations*, for a term which the law will imply as a necessary incident of a definable category of contractual relationship'.[76]

This view is clearly correct in one respect: a court that implies a standardized term cites as authority a statute, precedent, or custom — not the parties' agreement. But this sense of 'implied-in-law' says nothing about the reason for the statute, precedent, or custom. To determine if a particular standardized term is truly implied-in-fact or implied-in-law we need to know if it is implied in order to give effect to the parties' agreement or, instead, to give effect to external values such as fairness or efficiency. Both views are prima facie plausible in respect of most standardized terms.

Standardized terms as presumptive evidence of implied-in-fact terms

In broad terms, the argument for regarding (non-mandatory) standardized terms as implied-in-fact terms, is that such terms replicate those that

---

[75] e.g. Treitel (1995) 188–94. It is not always clear if terms implied on the basis of custom are included in this view. On the one hand, custom is regarded as something distinct from the parties' agreement. On the other hand, depending on one's view about the nature of law, custom may or may not be regarded as a source of law.

[76] *Scally v Southern Health and Social Services Board* [1992] 1 AC 294, 306. A contrary view was expressed by Lord Scarman in *Tai Hing Cotton Mill Ltd v Liu Chong Hing Bank Ltd* [1986] AC 80.

contracting parties have expressly or tacitly agreed to. More precisely, the argument is that standardized terms are, in effect, presumptions about what the parties to a particular category of contract have, *as a matter of fact*, expressly or tacitly agreed to. They are only presumptions because it is possible that contracting parties did not in fact agree to these terms. But absent evidence to the contrary, it can be assumed, this argument concludes, that the parties have agreed to the relevant standardized term.

This explanation of standardized terms fits most naturally with standardized terms that are implied on the basis of custom. As we have seen, customary understandings are typically incorporated into contracts as part of the background context. Thus, the customary rule that a tenant farmer is entitled to compensation for seed and labour on quitting his tenancy[77] is properly understood as part of the 'objective' or 'public' meaning of tenancy arrangements. Regardless of whether the parties in question were thinking about such compensation at the time of contracting, this custom is part of the public meaning of their agreement.

Standardized terms are created by judicial or legislative action. For this reason, it might be assumed that their origins are quite different from those underlying customary terms. But this is not usually true. Most non-customary standardized terms originated as customary terms; they were first recognized on the basis that they were part of the custom of a trade. Over time, these customary terms, having been recognized in various judgments, attained the status of terms implied based on precedent. These precedents then formed the basis for most statutory implied terms. For example, the customary understanding that a ship must be seaworthy to be insured was eventually enshrined in s.39 of the *Marine Insurance Act* of 1906. The same story can be told of the implied terms in the *Sale of Goods Act* 1979.[78] It goes without saying that in a normal sales contract the goods will be of 'satisfactory' quality. Similarly, it goes without saying that the vendor will 'deliver the goods' (Art. 27), that the purchaser will 'pay for them' (Art. 27), and that the expense of putting the goods in a deliverable state 'must be borne by the vendor' (Art. 29). These terms are necessary to give business efficacy, as it were, to any normal sales contract. Explained in this way, standardized terms are just generalized versions of individualized terms. They represent a decision by law-makers to give legal force to the 'goes without saying' terms that accompany certain kinds of common contracts.

---

[77] *Hutton v Warren* (1836) 1 M & W 466.
[78] Cheshire, Fifoot and Furmston (2001) 149.

The most significant objection to this view of standardized terms is that the law does not actually treat such terms as (mere) 'presumptions'. I discuss this objection in a moment; first I want to consider two false — but popular — objections to this view.

The first objection is a familiar one: standardized terms are not implied-in-fact terms because contracting parties rarely have these terms 'before their minds' when they make their contracts. For example, the parties to an employment contract are unlikely to have had before their minds the large number of terms that the law implies into such contracts — indeed, it is probably impossible to have *all* of these terms before one's mind. This objection may be rejected as it is based on the mistaken idea that the meaning of an agreement is found in the inner wills or intentions of contracting parties (8.1.1).

There is a second objection to the idea that standardized terms are presumptions about what the parties have, in fact, agreed upon. It states that such terms, by definition, are not grounded in the circumstances of the contracting parties; instead, these terms are implied because the contract fits into a particular category. The response to this objection is twofold. First, many of the things that 'go without saying' do this on a category-by-category basis. As we have seen, conventional understandings, trade customs, industry practices, and so on are the main bases for implying terms into contracts. Each of these factors applies on a category-by-category basis. There is no such thing as a conventional understanding of a one-off event; conventional understandings apply to categories of events.

Another response to the 'category' objection is that when courts actually apply standardized terms they typically draw distinctions between different contracts within the general category to which the relevant term applies. Thus, in practice, standardized terms often operate just like individualized terms. For example, a vendor must supply goods that are of 'satisfactory quality'.[79] Similarly, an employee must serve his employer faithfully. To apply these concepts in particular cases, courts need to determine what 'satisfactory' or 'faithfully' means in the particular case. These meanings will differ from the meanings applied to other sale or employment contracts. Admittedly, some standardized terms are framed in language that gives courts little discretion when applying the terms; for example, the *Sale of Goods Act* 1979 requires that the vendor 'deliver the goods' (Art. 27) and that the purchaser 'pay for them' (Art. 27). But in

---

[79] *Sale of Goods Act* 1979, ss 14 (2A).

these cases, the circumstances of the particular contract are unimportant; requirements to pay and deliver are appropriate for all sale contracts.

These two common objections to the idea that standardized terms are evidentiary presumptions are, then, unpersuasive. The more serious objection, as I have already indicated, is that standardized terms are not actually treated by courts as (merely) presumptive evidence of what the parties have agreed to; instead, such terms are binding unless explicitly excluded. They are default terms rather than presumptions. This is inconsistent with the above explanation because, if the purpose of using standardized terms is to assist in uncovering the true meaning of an agreement (as the explanation asserts), then any evidence that proves a particular agreement does not fit the 'standard model' should be sufficient reason not to imply these terms that normally accompany that model. To be sure, there are administrative advantages to regarding such terms as default terms rather than presumptions; courts are not required to engage in complex evidentiary inquiries—they simply ask whether the parties explicitly excluded the relevant term. But while this point blunts the force of the objection, it does not entirely eliminate it. If the underlying rationale for standardized terms is the presumptive evidence rationale, one would expect courts—and legislatures—to at least sometimes describe such terms in this way. This rarely happens.[80]

I conclude that the explanation of standardized terms as presumptive implied-in-fact terms deserves more attention than it usually receives. But certain features of the law remain difficult to explain on this basis, in particular the fact that such terms are treated as defaults rather than presumptions. We need to consider, therefore, whether an alternative explanation might fit the law better.

Contracts as 'things' explanations of standardized terms

One possible explanation of standardized terms is that they are simply the 'legal incidents of those . . . kinds of contractual relationship'.[81] The image underlying this explanation is of contracts as particular kinds of 'things' or 'products', which by their very nature have certain standard

---

[80] An example of how this might be done (albeit in the context of *invalidating* terms) is provided by the *Unfair Terms in Consumer Contracts Regulations* 1994, schedule 3 of which provides an 'indicative and illustrative list of terms which *may* be regarded as unfair' (italics added).

[81] *Mears v Safecar Securities Ltd* [1983] QB 54,78. A similar sentiment is expressed in the idea that a standardized term is one that 'the nature of the contract itself implicitly requires': *Liverpool City Council v Irwin* [1977] AC 239, 254.

features.[82] This is a useful image for appreciating the legal significance of standardized terms. Unlike the civil law, with its concept of 'special' or 'nominate' contracts, the common law does not officially acknowledge that different categories of contracts are treated differently by the law. Given the number of standardized terms in the common law, this picture can be misleading. That said, insofar as this idea is presented as an *explanation* of those terms, it is not very helpful. To say that a term is incidental of a kind of relationship does not tell us *why* it is an incident. It is clearly not the case that contracts are 'things' in the sense that, like cereals for sale at the supermarket, only a limited variety are available and mixing of different types is not permitted. With the exception of the (relatively small) number of mandatory terms, the law allows parties to exclude standardized terms and, more generally, to design contracts that do not fit into any previously recognized category.

Fairness and efficiency explanations

If we ask *why* standardized terms might be classified as the necessary 'incidents' of certain kinds of agreements, the most common answers, not surprisingly, are the same ones that we examined when discussing individualized terms and excuse rules—fairness[83] or efficiency.[84]

In broad terms, each of these answers is prima facie plausible. Most standardized terms are at least arguably 'fair' terms in the sense that, if they were not implied, the contract usually would not be fair. For example, the price charged in most sales contracts would be unfair if the goods were not of satisfactory quality or if the vendor did not guarantee good title. Similarly, the terms of most employment contracts would not be fair if the employee were permitted to use the knowledge gained in her employment to compete with her employer. As for efficiency, most standardized terms are efficient in that they are the terms most contracting parties 'would have wanted' had they bargained about the relevant issue. Few people would agree to buy a product if the vendor explicitly refused to promise its quality—and few vendors would have an interest in refusing such a promise.

Of course, in practice, the law is more complex than I have just suggested. It is clearly not the case that all standardized terms are equally explicable on the grounds of fairness, efficiency, or interpretation. As

---

[82] Leff (1970).
[83] e.g. Treitel (1995) 193; *Re Charge Card Services Ltd* [1989] Ch 497, 513.
[84] Ayres and Gertner (1989).

well, the explanation for why a term is fair or efficient is sometimes much more complex that I have suggested; for example, it is sometimes argued that a term is fair or efficient because it places the burden of initiating negotiations to exclude the term on the stronger or more sophisticated party (in other words, the term is a penalty term).[85] But broadly speaking, and allowing for certain exceptions, most standardized terms are prima facie fair and efficient.

But the critical point when comparing these explanations to the interpretation-based explanation is that standardized terms can, at most, be regarded only as prima facie fair or efficient. More specifically, in the same way that standardized terms cannot serve as more than presumptive evidence of implied-in-fact terms, they cannot be regarded as more than presumptive evidence of what is fair or efficient. It may be fair and efficient to require that goods be of satisfactory quality, or that employees never work for a competitor, in *most* cases, but this is not true in all cases. For example, if goods are advertised as second hand, it may be perfectly fair and efficient to sell them 'as is'. Similarly, if an employer agrees that a prospective employee can work for a competitor, there is nothing unfair or inefficient about a contract that allows for this. In each of these examples, the value of the relevant obligations will be reflected in their price.

According to the fairness and efficiency explanations, then, standardized terms should be treated merely as presumptions as to what is fair or efficient. That these terms are instead treated as defaults means that the fairness and efficiency explanations are vulnerable to the same criticism as the implied-in-fact interpretation. None of the three explanations can satisfactorily explain why standardized terms do not operate as mere presumptions. This apparently central feature of nearly all standardized terms must be explained on grounds of mere administrative convenience.

Conclusion regarding standardized terms

Viewed broadly, and leaving aside mandatory terms, the theoretical issues raised by standardized implied terms turn out to be very similar to those raised by individualized implied terms. Admittedly, the wide variety of standardized terms means it is not difficult to identify specific examples of such terms that seem best explained on just one of three grounds— interpretation, fairness, or efficiency—that I have examined. But in general, the strengths and weaknesses of these different kinds of

---

[85] See above at 8.3.4.

explanations of standardized terms are the same as the strengths and weaknesses in respect of explaining individualized terms or excuse rules.

8.6. CONCLUSION

The arguments in this chapter were meant to answer two related questions about content rules. To what extent are they consistent with the traditional view that the parties, rather than the courts, determine the content of contractual obligations? What is the basis for those rules that do not fit within the traditional view?

The first, and I suggest, most important issue that arises when answering these questions is determining when interpretation ends and creation begins. In defending the objective approach to contractual interpretation, I also defended the idea that a great deal of the content of a contract goes without saying. When context is taken into account, meaning runs out much later than one might initially suppose. We also saw that the alleged counter-examples to the assertion that courts routinely assess context are easily answered when one considers that in some contexts what goes without saying is that the contract will be interpreted narrowly. The implication that I drew from the fact that interpretation does much more work than is initially apparent is that the number of instances where alternative explanations (e.g., fairness or efficiency) are needed in order to make sense of content rules is much smaller than might otherwise be thought. Of course, explaining courts' interpretation of express terms is relatively straightforward. But a broadened view of interpretation can also be used, I argued, to explain standardized terms and excuse rules (though admittedly the story becomes more complex at this point).

Ultimately, I conclude that while privileging the expanded view of interpretation has certain advantages over other approaches—and in particular that it allows us to be clear about what questions to ask, and what kind of answers one might get—no single explanation of content rules is so obviously superior to its alternatives that it should be unequivocally adopted. To assess a particular view of content rules it is necessary, therefore, not just to ask how well it fits the law in this area, but also how well it fits with broader views about the nature of, and justification for, contractual obligations. My ultimate conclusion—that most content rules can be explained on the basis of interpretation without recourse to values external to contract such as fairness or efficiency—should be understood in this light.

9

Excuses for Non-performance: Duress, Unconscionability, Mistake, Misrepresentation, Frustration, and Discharge for Breach

There are certain circumstances in which courts will refuse to enforce an agreement even though it satisfies the requirements examined in the previous chapters, such as offer and acceptance, consideration, intent to create legal relations, and so on. In the common law, these circumstances are described primarily by the doctrines of duress, unconscionability, mistake, misrepresentation, frustration, and discharge for breach. Collectively, these doctrines describe what I shall call the 'excuses for non-performance' recognized in the common law of contract.

The very notion of 'excuses for non-performance' raises an obvious theoretical issue. What, if anything, do these doctrines have in common such that they may be studied together in one chapter? And why consider them after and apart from chapters concerning the formation and content of contracts? The whole of this chapter is basically one (long) answer to these questions. In brief, however, the reason for discussing these doctrines together is based on the belief that insofar as they cannot be reduced to the rules of offer and acceptance or to the rules regarding implied terms, they are not based on contract law principles. This means that (true) excuse rules are not concerned with determining either the existence or the content of a contract. Excuse rules impose external limits on validly created contractual rights. Their origins are therefore found outside the law of contract as strictly defined.

A further theoretical question raised by the above doctrines concerns their normative foundations. What, if anything, is the justification for these doctrines? To foreshadow again, the answer I suggest is that the doctrines of mistake, frustration, discharge for breach and (certain aspects of) unconscionability are best explained on the basis of principles found in the law of offer and acceptance and in the law of implied terms. With respect to these doctrines, therefore, I conclude that while they *might* qualify as true excuse doctrines (which is why I discuss them in this chapter), they are not, in the end, best understood in this way. Rather, the explanations that I gave of these doctrines in Chapters 8 (mistaken assumptions, frustration, discharge for breach) and 5 (mistake as to terms) are more convincing. As for duress, misrepresentation, and (the remaining aspects of) unconscionability, I will suggest that these doctrines are best explained using two principles that are external to contract law. One principle is that courts should not assist wrongdoers. The other is that non-consensual contracts should not be enforced; more specifically, non-consensual contracts that give rise to unjust enrichments should not be enforced. These doctrines, therefore, are *properly* characterized as excuse doctrines.

Throughout this chapter, the party seeking to uphold the validity of the relevant contract will be described as the 'plaintiff', while the party seeking to rely on the relevant excuse (so as to deny the validity of the contract) will be described as the 'defendant'.

9.1. DURESS

The law of duress concerns claims that an otherwise valid contract should not be enforced because it was made under pressure.[1] In broad terms, the common law's response to such claims is that the contract is unenforceable if the pressure arose from a wrongful threat made by the other contracting party.

Two broad categories of theoretical explanations of duress law can be distinguished. The first category includes theories that explain duress in terms of a plaintiff-based wrongdoing principle. Focusing on the *source* of the pressure, this approach views the issue in duress cases as that of whether the plaintiff exerted wrongful or illegitimate pressure. The second category of theories explains the law in terms of a defendant-based consent principle. This approach focuses on the *effects* of the pressure, thereby identifying the issue in duress cases as that of whether the defendant consented to the contract.

In the remainder of this section, the law of duress is examined from each of these perspectives. The assumption underlying this approach is that the two perspectives are distinct. Not all commentators share this assumption; many believe that apparent concerns about consent are really

---

[1] Cases decided under the law of 'undue influence' sometimes raise similar issues: Birks and Yuan (1995b).

concerns about wrongdoing, or vice versa. Even fewer commentators share the section's final conclusion that most (but not all) of the law of duress can be explained and justified on the basis of either perspective.

9.1.1. THE WRONGDOING PRINCIPLE

What I shall call the 'wrongdoing principle' states that a court may refuse to enforce a prima facie valid contractual right if the party seeking enforcement obtained the right through wrongdoing.[2] The wrongdoing principle offers one possible explanation of the law of duress.

The wrongdoing principle can be justified on either of two grounds. The first is that the state may legitimately refuse to provide the services of its courts, including services in the form of court sanctioned orders, to wrongdoers. The details of this ground for non-enforcement were explained in Chapter 7's examination of unenforceable agreements (the 'wrongdoing principle': 7.4). For present purposes, it is sufficient to note that this justification clearly applies to cases in which wrongdoers seek to enforce contracts that were obtained by their own wrongdoing. In these situations, the plaintiff wrongdoer's request for 'enforcement' is a request to use the courts' services, and a successful plea of duress amounts to these services being denied to him.

The second way of justifying the wrongdoing principle is based on the notion that unjust enrichments ought to be reversed. In duress cases, contracting parties who have obtained a contractual right by virtue of their own wrongdoing have, *for that reason*, been unjustly enriched.[3] This enrichment can be reversed by requiring the plaintiff to return to the defendant the

---

[2] The principle is clearly stated in the American case of *Riggs v Palmer* 115 HY 506, 511 22 NE 188, 190 (1889): 'No one shall be permitted to profit by his own fraud, or to take advantage of his own wrong, or to found any claim upon his own iniquity, or to acquire property by his own crime.' See also *St John Shipping Corporation v Joseph Rank Ltd* [1957] 1 QB 267, 292.

[3] So-called 'restitution for wrongs' is well-established in law: Burrows (1993) 376–418. But there is considerable controversy among unjust enrichment scholars as to whether it is based on a principle of reversing unjust enrichments or a policy-based desire to punish or discourage wrongdoing. If the latter view is correct, then the second justification described above is the same as the first one. The details of this debate need not concern us, but I note that contractual duress cases are, in one respect, more amenable to an unjust enrichment explanation than the typical 'restitution for wrongs' case. In such a case (e.g. the trespasser who is ordered to hand over the profits gained by her trespass), the wrongdoer's benefit (her profits) are unlikely to be equivalent to the recipient's loss. Nor is it clear that the wrongdoer's benefit was obtained 'at the expense' of the recipient. But in a duress case, in which the claim is that a benefit in the form of a *contractual right* was wrongfully obtained from the other party, both of these usual requirements for an action in unjust enrichment are satisfied.

relevant contractual right (thus, this idea is often expressed in the phrase 'restitution for wrongs'). In practice, this is achieved by a court refusing to enforce the contract. Non-enforcement thereby achieves restitution.

Nothing in the discussion that follows turns on which of these justifications is thought to be the more compelling. It is sufficient that the wrongdoing principle can be justified on either of these grounds (or on another ground). But it is worth noting that, consistent with my conclusion that duress is a true excuse doctrine, neither of these justifications is based on contract law principles. The first is based on a general policy of encouraging good behaviour. The second is based on a non-contractual principle of reversing unjust enrichments. Indeed, it is because these justifications are non-contractual that the wrongdoing principle also applies to cases in which the relevant wrongdoing does not involve a contract. For example, it applies against the wrongdoer who obtains goods either by physically taking them from the owner or by forcing the owner to hand them over.

From the perspective of contract law theory, the main question raised by the wrongdoing principle concerns what it means to say that a contractual right was 'obtained by wrongdoing'. In addressing this question, I will focus on wrongful threats, as this is the kind of wrongdoing at issue in duress cases. The discussion is structured around three sub-questions. What counts as a threat? What makes a threat wrongful? What does it mean for a right to be obtained by a threat?

What counts as a threat?

The most important distinction when considering what counts as a threat is the distinction between a threat and a warning.[4] A threat is a proposal to bring about an unwelcome event that is made so as to induce the recipient of the proposal to do a requested act (e.g., enter a contract).[5] A warning, by contrast, is a mere prediction that an unwelcome event will happen. In typical cases, warnings can be distinguished from threats by the speaker's lack of control over the unwelcome consequence. Consider the case of a subcontractor whose costs rise dramatically midway through a contract, and who then informs the head contractor that unless he is paid more he will breach. If the subcontractor cannot complete the contract because he

---

[4] Two other kinds of non-wrongful communications that are important to distinguish from threats are requests and offers. The main difference between these communications and threats is that unlike in the case of a threat, a person making a request or an offer does not propose to bring about an unwelcome consequence if the recipient refuses to accede to the request or to accept the offer: see generally Nozick (1969).

[5] Lamond (1996); Raz (1986) 36; Nozick (1969).

is about to go bankrupt, then he is only making a warning (combined with an offer). He is warning the head contractor that he does not have the resources to finish the job. But if the subcontractor is able to complete the contract even with the higher costs, he is making a threat.[6]

The distinction between a threat and a warning is crucial for the wrongdoing principle because while both threats and warnings leave the recipient with the same choice (e.g., enter a contract or suffer harm), only the former can be wrongful. Warning a person that she may be harmed is not wrongful. To the contrary, providing a warning is commendable as it gives the warned person a chance to protect herself. By contrast, a threat to commit a wrong is wrongful by definition (unless it is done in order to avoid a greater wrong).

What makes a threat wrongful?

For the wrongdoing principle to apply, the plaintiff must have acted wrongfully. This requirement is not satisfied merely by showing that the plaintiff made a threat. Although threats always propose unwelcome consequences, they are not always wrongful. Informing a tortfeasor that he will be taken to court unless compensation is paid in respect of a valid claim is a threat, but it is not wrongful.

In the usual case, the reason a threat is wrongful is that the threatened action is wrongful.[7] The gunman's threat is wrongful because it is wrong

---

[6] Contractual modification cases raise a number of interesting issues regarding wrongdoing. Due to space constraints, these will not be discussed here. It is sufficient to note that private law lacks the resources to satisfactorily deal with modification cases in which a carelessly or intentionally low bid (i.e. offer) was made by a financially unstable party. Although the low bid itself counts as a misstatement or a fraud, and thus is wrongful, the wrongdoer's financial situation makes him impervious to the only sanction available in private law—financial penalties. Another way of making this point is to note that any rule that has the effect of forcing such parties into bankruptcy will also remove their incentive to renegotiate—since they will lose any gains made by renegotiating. On the assumption that such parties also lack the assets necessary to complete the contract according to its original terms, a rule that penalizes low bids in such cases will thus be detrimental to both parties. For this reason, non-private law sanctions seem a better response to the problems raised by such cases (e.g. de-certification, or criminal prohibitions on working). For a different view, see: Halston (1991) 662; Farnsworth (1999) 276; Burrows (1993) 179–82; Beatson (1991) 129; Restatement of Contracts (2d) s.89(a); *Uniform Commercial Code* s.2–209(1).

[7] The exception is blackmail. Explaining why blackmail is wrongful is a difficult task: Lamond (1996); Lindgren (1984). But strictly speaking, it is not a question that a theory of duress needs to answer. Blackmail is a crime. From the perspective of contract law, there can be no question of enforcing a contract that is obtained by means that have been declared illegal by the criminal law. For our purposes, the main point to make is that the example of blackmail does not prove, in general, that a threat may be wrongful regardless of the wrongfulness of the threatened action. Blackmail is the *only* case in which this is true.

to injure people. Contract law has little to say about what kinds of action should count as wrongful. This determination is, and should be, made on the basis of general moral and legal considerations. In the common law, those considerations are given expression primarily in criminal law, tort law, and regulatory law. In most cases, therefore, contract law need only look to these other areas of the law for instruction as to what constitutes an illegal threat.

There are, however, two cases in which it is contract law that is relevant for establishing what counts as wrongful for the purposes of duress. The first is breach of contract, which represents a legal wrong that is established (at least in part)[8] by contract law principles. That it is wrong to breach a contract, and thus wrongful to threaten to do so, is true, by definition, on the orthodox view of contract law. This is also true according to most of the theories of contract considered in this book. Admittedly, the 'efficient breach theory' that is supported in some utilitarian theories of contract denies that breach is always wrongful (4.3). In this view, it is efficient (and therefore commendable) to not perform a contract whenever the cost of performance is greater than its value. But even in this view, a *threat to breach* an inefficient contract is necessarily wrongful. The very making of the threat is wrongful (by efficiency standards), because the efficient thing to do in such cases is simply to inform the other party that you will not perform. The making of a threat and any consequences that arise from the threat (including the other party's performance of the contract) are pure waste from an efficiency perspective.

There is a second respect in which the law of contract may be relevant in determining what counts as wrongful. I refer to the fact that courts, in contractual matters, need not be as cautious as they would be when declaring an act to be criminally wrongful. Unlike criminal law and tort law, contract law neither punishes the wrongdoer nor makes him liable for compensatory damages. So far as contract law (and private law generally) is concerned, the only consequence of setting aside a contract for duress is just that–the contract is set aside. It follows that courts do not need to be concerned that declaring certain behaviour wrongful will lead to, say, overextending the criminal courts or the prisons. As well, the material and symbolic consequences of a court mistakenly labelling an action as wrongful in contract are less serious. The result is that, in

---

[8] The qualifier is needed because, strictly speaking, the 'wrong' of breaching a contract (as opposed to the duty to perform) is better described as a tort (3.4; 10; 11.).

principle at any rate, there may be activities that may be regarded as wrongful for the purposes of a finding of duress even though they are not otherwise unlawful. English courts appear to have recognized this possibility.[9]

When is a contractual right 'obtained' by a threat?

The wrongdoing principle, recall, dictates that courts will refuse to assist wrongdoers who wish to obtain the profits of their wrongdoing. The principle, though, is necessarily limited by causation considerations. More specifically, if the principle is to apply in a duress case, it must be shown that it was the plaintiff's threat which induced the defendant to enter the relevant contract. Determining causation in such a case is a difficult theoretical issue; however, the issue of causation itself is a familiar one. Again, tort and criminal law are instructive. Most theoretical work on causation has occurred in these fields.[10] With this in mind, I will limit myself to three observations.

The first and most general observation is that there does not appear to be any reason that a different concept of causation should be applied in duress cases than is used in tort cases. In each, the basic question is the same: did the relevant behaviour cause the relevant event? Courts deciding duress cases appear to share this conclusion. More specifically, such courts have followed the lead of tort cases in rejecting 'but-for' tests in situations in which more than one set of facts is sufficient to produce the relevant event. In both tort and duress cases, courts instead apply what is sometimes called the 'NESS' test. According to the NESS test, an action causes a result if 'it was a necessary element of a set of antecedent actual conditions that was sufficient for the occurrence of the result'.[11] Thus, in *Barton v Armstrong*[12] the contract was set aside for duress even though Armstrong might well have signed the contract notwithstanding Barton's threat to kill him if he did not sign. Given that Barton was a clear wrongdoer, this seems correct.

Second, establishing causation in duress cases often raises difficult empirical issues. In particular, the fact that the duress victim may have had an option of suing the wrongdoer for breach of contract or for a non-contractual wrong, such as wrongfully detaining goods, might lead a court to conclude that the threat was not the reason for entering the

---

[9] *The Universe Sentinel* [1983] AC 366, 401; *The Evia Luck* [1990] 1 Lloyd's Rep 319, 339; *Thorne v Motor Trade Association* [1939] AC 797, 801.

[10] Hart and Honore (1959); Wright (1985); Stapelton (2000).

[11] Wright (1985). [12] [1976] AC 104, 121.

contract.[13] This is because the defendant had a reasonable alternative to agreeing to the threat (i.e., bringing a law suit).

Finally, but most importantly, the requirement that the contract be 'obtained' by a threat is not a test for consent. Admittedly, the requirement does suppose that an operative threat must be capable, in principle, of affecting how the recipient of the threat evaluates her choices. Other than in cases involving multiple causes, the victim must evaluate those choices differently than she would have done had the threat not been made. In the case of an operative threat, the requirement entails that the victim acts differently than she would have done otherwise. But it would be wrong to conclude from this that the victim's consent or 'will' has been overcome. If 'altering reasoning', or even 'altering behaviour', is sufficient to show lack of consent, then no one ever consents to anything. My decision to buy a new car is affected by the fact that my present car is in poor condition. It is also affected by the fact that a car dealer offered to sell me a new car. Whatever consent means, it cannot be the case that facts such as these are sufficient to show that it is lacking. This is not to deny that a threat *may* negate consent. Indeed, I argue for just this conclusion in the next section. The point is simply that the requirement that a threat be operative is not a test for consent.

Conclusion to the wrongdoing principle

The principle that plaintiffs should not be able to enforce contractual obligations obtained by their wrongdoing seems capable of explaining nearly all of the law of duress. As I noted at the outset, what counts as duress in a contractual context invariably amounts to a wrongful threat. The wrongdoing principle can therefore explain the results of such cases.

But two caveats must now be added. First, the wrongdoing principle cannot easily explain why courts set aside contracts in cases in which the plaintiff did not make the threat himself, but merely knew about the threat.[14] To be sure, a person who made a contract with such knowledge would normally be morally censured for doing so. She has taken advantage of another's misfortune. But it is far from clear that mere knowledge of another's misfortune should count as wrongdoing for the purposes of the wrongdoing principle. There is no duty to assist

---

[13] e.g. *Pau On v Lau Yiu Long* [1980] AC 614, 635.

[14] *Kesarmal s/o Letchman Das v Valliappa Chettiar (NKV) s/o Nagappa Chettiar* [1954] 1 WLR 380.

the victim of a threat. So why is it wrong to make such a person an offer?

A second caveat is that the wrongdoing principle cannot explain why courts frequently say that they are concerned not just with wrongdoing but also with consent.[15] The possibility that lack of consent is an element of the wrong in making a wrongful threat has just been rejected. Of course, the explanation may simply be that courts confuse causation with consent. But before adopting this conclusion, the possibility that consent does, or at least should, play a distinct role in the law of duress needs to be examined carefully. After all, the idea that lack of consent is, and should be, a good defence to a contract claim is, in broad terms anyway, a widely shared sentiment.

9.1.2. THE CONSENT PRINCIPLE

What I shall call the 'consent principle' states that a court may refuse to enforce a prima facie valid contractual obligation on the ground that the defendant did not consent to that obligation. The consent principle offers a second possible explanation of the law of duress. More specifically, and like the wrongdoing principle, it can explain most (but not all) of the decisions in this area of the law. But in contrast to the wrongdoing principle, accepting the consent principle, I will argue, commits one to expanding the defence of duress—though perhaps under a different name. As we shall see, such expansion, if taken seriously, would apply to cases not usually thought to fall within even the potential sphere of duress (in particular, 'state of necessity' cases). For this reason, one of the main conclusions of this section is that it would be clearer if the no consent principle were recognized as the basis of a separate doctrine, with 'duress' thus confined to cases in which the wrongdoing principle applies. In short, while I will argue that both the wrongdoing principle and the no consent principle are able, separately, to explain most of the law of duress, I also conclude that it would be simpler, so far as the organization of the law is concerned, if, in future, the term 'duress' was confined to claims of wrongdoing.

To understand the role the consent principle might play in contract law, we first need to consider two questions. Why should consent matter? And, if it does matter, what does consent actually mean? The questions

---

[15] e.g. *Pau On v Lau Yiu Long* [1980] AC 614, 636; *The Siboen* [1967] 1 Lloyd's Rep. 293, 335; *The Atlantic Baron* [1978] 3 All ER 1171, 1183; *The Universe Sentinel* [1983] AC 366, 383; *The Alev* [1989] 1 Lloyd's Rep. 138, 145.

are related in that thinking about why consent matters helps in delimiting the range of its possible meanings. For this reason, I begin the discussion with the initial, normative question.

Throughout the discussion, it will be useful to keep in mind that, assuming that lack of consent is a good reason for refusing to enforce a contract, most successful pleas of duress (as currently defined) will be explicable on the basis of both the wrongdoing principle and the consent principle. A threat of murder, for example, must negate consent if anything does. But it is also useful to keep in mind that the *scope* of any consent principle will almost certainly not be identical to that of the wrongdoing principle. The difference is illustrated in the event that the threat in my murder example is made by a third party (and is not known by the plaintiff). Here, the plaintiff clearly is not a wrongdoer. But from the perspective of a defendant-based concern for consent, this case is indistinguishable from one in which the relevant threat is made by the plaintiff.

The value and role of consent

Many authors regard it as self-evident that consent should matter when determining the validity of a contract.[16] But nothing I have said about either the nature or justification of contractual liability leads to this conclusion. From an analytic ('nature of contractual obligations') perspective, whether contracts are regarded as promises, induced-reliance obligations, or transfers of existing rights, no role is given to the notion of consent (3.1–3.3). A promise, for example, is created by intentionally communicating an intention to undertake an obligation. Intention, not consent, is the required mental state. A promise made in response to a threat (whether by the promisee or a third party) is a true promise. To be sure, there may be a good reason to refuse to enforce this promise. But it will not be because a promise was not made. Our language says as much: we speak of '*promises* made under pressure'. The same is true of induced-reliance obligations and transfers of existing rights. A transfer is made by intentionally transferring the relevant thing; reliance is induced by making the relevant kind of representation.

From a normative perspective, the story is the same. In efficiency-based and other utilitarian theories, the justification for enforcing contracts, broadly speaking, is that enforcement facilitates mutually beneficial transfers of resources (4.1–4.3). From this perspective, a contract that is made

---

[16] e.g. Barnett (1986).

in response to a threat is no different from any other contract. To be sure, the third party's threat is not itself beneficial. Thus, there may be good efficiency-based reasons to discourage such threats. But these reasons will be different from those that justify the enforcement of contracts. From the perspective of the reasons for enforcing contracts, the threat is just part of the background against which contracts are made (such as natural scarcity, natural disasters, and so on). So long as each party *intended* to enter the contract, it is assumed that the contract is mutually beneficial. Why else would the parties enter it? Rights-based theories of contract lead to the same conclusion. This view regards rights to performance as created by promises (or reliance-inducing acts, etc.). And promises (etc.), as I have just noted, are created by an intentional act. Again, there may be good rights-based reasons to refuse to enforce a contract that was signed in response to a threat. But if there are such reasons, they are different from the reasons that rights-based theories give for why contracts are enforced in the first place.

What other reasons, then, might explain why consent should matter in considering whether a contract should be enforced? Two possibilities will be considered: (1) that lack of consent negates responsibility, and (2) that lack of consent gives rise to unjust enrichments.

Lack of consent negates responsibility

The first suggestion supposes consent matters because it is a prerequisite for establishing responsibility and because responsibility is a prerequisite for any finding of legal liability, including contractual liability.[17] It is often said, for example, that if a tortfeasor 'had no choice' but to act as she did (say because subject to a threat of injury) she ought not be liable for the harm caused by her actions. The explanation is not that she did not cause the harm, nor that she lacked the necessary carelessness or intent — the harm itself was intentionally caused. Rather, the explanation is that the conditions for ascribing responsibility were not satisfied. On the same basis, it might be concluded that a defendant should not be held liable on the basis of a contract to which she did not consent.

The idea that consent is a condition of responsibility and responsibility a general condition of liability is appealing. But there is an important difference between how this idea applies to tort cases and how it applies to duress cases. In tort cases, the argument is that non-responsible defendants should not be liable for the harm that they have intentionally

---

[17] e.g. Honore (1988); Perry (1995); Frankfurt (1988) Chapters 1–4, 8.

or carelessly caused. In certain *breach* of contract cases, this same argument might be made. That is, it might be argued that the defendants were not responsible for their misperformance or non-performance, and so should not be liable for the harm caused by it. But in a *duress* case, the equivalent argument makes no sense. The issue when duress is pleaded is whether the contract is enforceable. Liability for harm is not yet an issue. It is only after a court has decided that duress is not an issue that questions of liability for harm can arise. Indeed, insofar as there is an analogy to be made between responsibility arguments in tort cases and responsibility arguments in duress cases, it counts in favour of enforcement. In denying responsibility in a tort case, the court is refusing to change the status quo ante; the loss is left to lie where it fell. The equivalent in a duress case is to *enforce* the contract. So far as contract law is concerned, the requirements for a valid contract are satisfied. The status quo ante is a valid contract.

The analogy to how the concept of responsibility is used in tort cases does not support, therefore, regarding consent as a precondition for a valid contractual obligation. This does not prove that it would be impossible to develop a notion of responsibility that might apply to the formation of contractual obligations. But there are no clear precedents for such a notion. The concept of legal capacity that is used to distinguish between persons who are and are not capable of creating legal rights applies on a person-by-person basis rather than (as in duress) on a situation-by-situation basis.

Lack of consent gives rise to unjust enrichment

I turn now to a second, and more promising suggestion for why consent matters when considering if a contract should be enforced. The suggestion is that consent matters because a non-consensual contract may give rise to an unjust enrichment. Unjust enrichments, in turn, should be reversed. In the case of an executory ('not yet performed') contract, this is achieved by refusing to enforce the contract.

The unjust enrichment explanation of the no consent principle is novel and, at times, complex. But the idea underlying the explanation—that enrichments may be unjust when they are obtained without consent—is simple and familiar.[18] If John delivers money to Jane because of a threat by Bill, then in both law and morality Jane should return the money to John. Significantly, it is John's lack of consent, rather than Bill's

---

[18] Goff and Jones (1998) 307–55; Birks (1985) 173–204.

wrongdoing, that triggers the duty to make restitution in such a case. It is Jane, not Bill, who must make restitution, and she must do so regardless of whether she knew of the threat. That John's consent was impaired is a sufficient reason for restitution. Bill's wrongdoing is significant merely as the explanation for the absence of consent. This is therefore *not* an example of 'restitution for wrongs', and so cannot be explained on the basis of the wrongdoing principle examined in the previous section.

The unjust enrichment explanation of the consent principle does not, of course, suppose that refusing to enforce a contract will result in benefits being returned in the form of money or other tangible property. Insofar as it is valid, the consent principle is first and foremost a defence to a claim for non-performance. It applies, therefore, to executory contracts—contracts in which nothing tangible has yet been conferred.[19] The benefits whose receipt leads to an unjust enrichment must therefore be the contractual *rights* that the plaintiff has obtained under the relevant contract. From the perspective of unjust enrichment law, there is no difficulty in regarding intangibles, including contractual rights, as benefits. Most contractual rights can be bought, sold and transferred like other property. Admittedly, if the orthodox view that contractual obligations are promises (or agreements) is accepted, then the relevant benefits cannot be regarded as having been *transferred* between the parties. It is a basic assumption of the promissory model that contractual rights are *created* rather than transferred by contracts (3.1). Only the transfer model could adopt the latter view (3.3). Yet, notwithstanding that the paradigm example of an unjust enrichment is a mistaken transfer, unjust enrichments can arise without transfers. They arise, for example, if B pays C's debt or if B performs services for C.[20] In these and other cases, the relevant benefit was created rather than transferred. So long as that benefit was created 'at the expense of' B, an action in unjust enrichment is possible. This condition is satisfied with respect to contractual rights.

The idea that a contract, at the moment of formation, confers valuable benefits in the form of rights to performance is, therefore, not problematic.

---

[19] If a non-consensual contract is not enforced, then the plaintiff (who is seeking enforcement) will not receive the money, goods, or services that she would have received had the contract been performed. It might be argued, therefore, that non-enforcement is justified as a prophylactic against unjust enrichment. The objection to this suggestion is that it supposes that, as a matter of principle, the defendant is under a legal obligation to confer the relevant benefit on the plaintiff—and then that the plaintiff is immediately under a legal obligation to return the same benefit.

[20] Burrows (1993) 8–9, 205–30.

But when used to ground an argument in unjust enrichment, it gives rise to two difficult questions. The first is whether, in determining if the plaintiff has been enriched under the relevant contract, the court should focus solely on the rights that the plaintiff obtained or whether, instead, both parties' rights must be taken into account. The former approach is the one that unjust enrichment law takes with respect to benefits conveyed under an *executed* contract. A contracting party is regarded as having been enriched if the money, goods, or services that he received were of value to him. Any money, goods, or services that the other contracting party received are significant only insofar as a separate claim in unjust enrichment is made against that other party ('counter-restitution'[21]). But it is not clear that the same approach is appropriate in the case in which the relevant benefits are contractual rights. Unlike money, goods, or services conferred under a contract, contractual rights cannot be separated from the contract which created them. A contractual right exists only insofar as it is a part of a contract. The process by which one contracting party's right is created *simultaneously* creates the other contracting party's right. As I have already noted (5.2.3), the resulting contractual agreement cannot be reduced to a pair of promises, conditional or otherwise. It is a single thing—an agreement.

The point is a difficult one, but it is suggested that the conclusion to draw from these observations is that to determine what benefit, if any, has been conferred under a non-consensual executory contract, the contract *as a whole* must be evaluated. Specifically, both the burdens *and* the benefits created by the contract must be taken into account to determine if the plaintiff has been enriched. Thus interpreted, the consent principle applies only in cases in which the benefits received by the plaintiff are greater than the burdens he undertook. In short, consent *qua* consent matters only when the contract in question is substantively unfair. The practical implications of this limitation are explored below, in the discussion of the meaning of consent.

The second question raised by the above explanation of the consent principle concerns the way the explanation understands the relationship between unjust enrichment law principles and contract law principles. The explanation assumes that it is appropriate for a court to refuse to enforce a valid contract in order to reverse an unjust enrichment. This assumption is inconsistent with the orthodox view that unjust enrichment principles have no role to play in respect of benefits

---

[21] Birks (1985) 415.

obtained under a valid contract.[22] Contract, it is said, trumps unjust enrichment.

One possible response to this assertion is that it is moot because the same lack of consent that grounds a claim in unjust enrichment also means that the contract is, on contractual grounds, invalid. But this response must be rejected because the very reason the unjust enrichment explanation is now being discussed is that lack of consent is not a pre-requisite to a valid contract (or so I have argued). If the contract was invalid from the start, then no contractual rights—and no benefits— would be created by the transaction and there would be no need to move to unjust enrichment law.

If the orthodox view of the relationship between unjust enrichment principles and contract principles is correct, there is a genuine conflict. But there are good reasons for rejecting the orthodox view. Properly understood, contract principles and unjust enrichment principles do not conflict (here or elsewhere) because these principles address different questions.[23] Contract principles determine if a valid contract has been formed. All that matters from this perspective is whether the require-ments of a valid contract (offer and acceptance, etc.) have been satisfied. Unjust enrichment principles determine if an enrichment should be reversed. All that matters from this perspective is whether the elements of the cause of action in unjust enrichment are established (benefit, deprivation, unjust factor, etc.). In particular, the existence of a contract *qua* contract is, in principle, irrelevant when determining if there has been an unjust enrichment. To conclude otherwise is to conclude that there are unjust enrichments that should not be reversed simply because of the existence of a contract. As a matter of principle, that cannot be right. Exceptional cases aside, the only good reason for denying a claim in unjust enrichment is that there was not actually an unjust enrichment. And the only way to show this is by showing that the ordinary elements of the cause of action in unjust enrichment are not satisfied.

Of course, benefits conferred under a valid contract should normally be immune from a claim in unjust enrichment. But the reason is not that they were conferred under a valid contract. The reason is that the normal elements of the cause of action in unjust enrichment cannot be made out. The transfer was consensual (and was in no other respect defective), and so the necessary 'unjust factor' is missing. That the defendant consented,

---

[22] Goff and Jones (1998) 33–35; Birks (1985) 46–47; Burrows (1993) 251.
[23] Smith (1999).

etc. is a sufficient reason to deny a claim in unjust enrichment. It is the real life fact that most contracts are consensual, in other words, not the legal fact that a contract exists, that explains why claims for the return of benefits transferred under a contract should normally fail. Consistent with this conclusion, common law courts look to the substance of the relevant transaction when assessing claims for the return of benefits conveyed under an unenforceable contract. Such a claim will normally be denied if the agreement was defective merely for want of consideration or because it was not in writing.[24] The courts rightly assume that what matters is not whether the transaction is a valid contract, but whether the relevant transfer of benefits was consensual and not otherwise defective from the perspective of unjust enrichment principles. If it was consensual —which is usually the case when all that is missing is a formality—then there is no unjust enrichment.

In the usual case, then, the facts that give rise to a valid contract mean that any benefits conferred under that contract, whether they be contractual rights or tangible property, do not give rise to an unjust enrichment. But the conclusion is different in the unusual case in which one of the parties did not consent to the contract. Here, the contract is valid so far as contractual principles are concerned (or so I have argued). Nonetheless, the absence of consent may give rise to an unjust enrichment in respect of benefits created or conferred under the contract. If the contract has been performed, the present law requires that the relevant benefits (goods, money, services) be returned in kind or by a monetary equivalent. According to the argument now being considered, the same principle should be applied to the benefits created by an executory contract. The one difference—an important one—is that these benefits (the contractual rights) can be 'returned' merely by a judicial refusal to enforce the contract.

For these reasons, I conclude that, like the wrongdoing principle, the consent principle is not a contract law principle. It is a principle of unjust enrichment law. Thus defined, the consent principle is internally consistent. It does, however, present certain admittedly unorthodox propositions, at least insofar as it is regarded as a complete explanation of the law of duress (e.g., the idea that duress is normatively informed by unjust enrichment law). The full implications of this explanation must wait until we have examined the meaning of consent. But it may be useful to mention here that it is precisely the unorthodox nature of the explanation that

[24] Burrows (1993) 299–304.

will lead me later to conclude that the no consent principle should, ideally, be the basis for a separate legal doctrine, leaving the label 'duress' to cases explained on the basis of the wrongdoing principle.

The meaning of consent

I turn now to examine the meaning of consent. It is this aspect of consent on which discussions of the role of consent in contract law typically focus. More specifically, the point of such discussions is often to reject the consent principle on the basis that implementing it, for whatever reason, would lead to patently absurd results. This conclusion is usually reached by adopting either of two quite different views of consent. As these views form the background for most contemporary discussions of consent, I begin with them.

According to the first view, contracts are nearly always consensual because in every contract, save those where a party acts unintentionally (e.g., in his sleep or where his hand is forced), the contracting parties have the alternative of not entering the contract.[25] The victim of a gunman's threat has a choice between signing the contract or being shot. According to the second, and opposite view, almost no contracts are consensual because parties always contract under pressure, be it pressure for food, clothing, shelter, or whatever. Leaving aside contracts for luxury items and situations in which we might be able to produce the goods or services ourselves, we have no choice but to enter contracts in order to live.[26] The conclusion then drawn from these opposing views is that if a consent principle were taken seriously, the result would be that either no contracts would be set aside for lack of consent (the first view), or (nearly) all contracts would be set aside (the second view).

Those who adopt either of these views typically go on to suggest that the courts' apparent concern for consent really is, and should be, a concern for something else. Many say that courts are concerned with wrongdoing in the sense described earlier.[27] Others say the courts are concerned with behaviour that is inefficient,[28] or with behaviour that leads to an undesirable distribution of resources (although the distinction between such explanations and wrongdoing explanations is not always made clear).[29] Still other commentators suggest that courts in duress cases are not concerned with behaviour at all, but instead with the substantive

---

[25] e.g. Atiyah (1982); Kronman (1980) 478; Trebilcock (1993) 79.

[26] e.g. Hale (1923); Llewellyn (1931) 728; Patterson (1943) 741; Dalzell (1942) 238–39; Dawson (1947) 266–67; Coote (1980) 45.

[27] Fried (1981) 97.   [28] Posner (1998) 126–30.   [29] Kronman (1980) 480.

fairness of contracts.[30] The common thread to these approaches is that the concept of consent is reduced to a concept of something else— wrongdoing, efficiency, distributive justice, etc.

In thinking about this 'sceptical' approach to consent, an initial obser- vation is that people do not ordinarily use the term consent in either of the ways just described. Admittedly, one understands the point being made when someone says that the victim of a gunman's threat had a choice and therefore consented. The speaker is stating that the gunman's victim had *a kind* of choice. But it does not follow that people ordinarily equate consent with merely intentional action. What people actually say is that the gunman's victim did not consent. The same is true of the idea that consent requires a complete absence of any pressure. One under- stands the point being made when it is said that most people have no choice but to enter contracts if they wish to feed themselves. But it is not generally supposed that this fact negates consent. What people actually say is that contracts to buy groceries or to order meals in restaurants are consensual.

Another observation is that it would be a mistake to conclude that because different definitions of consent have different implications for the distribution of wealth, the efficient use of resources, and so on, the meaning of consent must be explained using such concepts. The reasons for adopting a definition are not the same as the consequences of adopting that definition. The laws on theft and murder also have implications for distributive justice and efficiency, but this does not mean they are best explained using such concepts.

Keeping these observations in mind, what might it mean to say that a person's consent to enter a contract was negated by the existence of pressure? Broadly speaking, there are two ways of understanding consent in this context: the 'mental state' view and the 'nature of the pressure' view. The mental state view supposes that consent corresponds to a par- ticular psychological state.[31] In this view, to say that consent was negated by pressure is to say that the pressure prevented a 'consenting' state of mind from arising.

There is one obvious truth in the mental state view. To state that someone did not consent by reason of pressure is to state that at a

---

[30] Dawson (1947) 287.

[31] Judges have occasionally made statements that appear to support this view (e.g. Hobhouse J's reference to the plaintiff's will having been 'overborne': *The Alev* [1989] 1 Lloyd's Rep. 138, 175) but I am not aware of a contract law theorist who has explicitly defended this position.

minimum the person's apparent consent was *induced* by pressure. But this is a statement about causation, not consent. Pressure can negate consent only if it is operative. Causation, however, is not equivalent to lack of consent. The view that they are equivalent is effectively the second of the 'extreme' views of consent noted above, namely the view that consent requires a complete absence of all pressure.

One difficulty with the mental state view is that it is not clear how one might describe the state of mind that is meant to correspond to consent. It is presumably a feeling or sensation that the relevant person is meant to experience. But what sensation? And how can one be certain that the words used to describe it mean the same thing to everyone? A related difficulty is that even if this state of mind could be described, it is not clear how judges (or anyone else) could tell if a person was in that state. Admittedly, criminal law requires courts to assess the defendant's *mens rea*. But even if it is assumed that *mens rea* is defined in terms of a particular mental state (which is debatable), it is a mental state that is relatively concrete in comparison to 'consent'. It is also relatively easy to deduce from external evidence.

But the most serious difficulty with the mental state view is that it does not accurately convey how the term consent is actually used and understood. When we say that a person did not consent to something we do not suppose that we are making a report about that person's state of mind. What we are describing is something that we can actually observe.

This leads me to the second way of understanding consent, which focuses on the nature of the relevant pressure. In this view, to say that consent was negated by pressure is to say not only that the pressure was causally operative, but that the pressure was of a particular kind or quality. Five different approaches to identifying this kind or quality can be distinguished, although three of them can be rejected quickly for reasons already discussed. One approach that can be rejected focuses on the moral quality of the pressure. This approach invariably leads to a version of the wrongdoing principle. It provides definitions of wrongdoing, not consent. A second such approach is one that regards all forms of pressure as equivalent. This approach leads to the 'extreme' views of consent noted above; that is, it leads either to the implausible view that any kind of pressure negates consent or to the equally implausible view that no kind of pressure negates consent. The third approach focuses on the psychological effects of the pressure. This approach leads to a mental state definition of consent.

The fourth approach that focuses on the kind of pressure exerted supposes that pressure negates consent if it detrimentally affects a value other than consent. Common suggestions for this other value include efficiency and distributive justice.[32] In this view, to say that pressure of a certain kind negates consent is to say that enforcing a contract in this situation would lead to a result that is inefficient or that is distributively unjust, etc. What appears to be a concern for consent, in other words, is really a concern for something else.

It is debatable whether this fourth approach actually provides a definition of *consent*. As I noted above, consent is ordinarily understood as a distinct value. But in any event, this approach can be rejected for another reason: it is impossible to tell what is efficient, distributively just, etc., without first knowing what consent means. Efficiency, for example, is promoted by ensuring, broadly speaking, that as many people get as much of what they want as possible (4.2). Yet to determine if people are truly getting what 'they want', it is necessary to establish if those wants are freely—consensually—expressed. The concept of efficiency cannot give a non-circular answer to this question. Voluntary exchanges are assumed to be efficient *because* they are voluntary (4.2). They are not voluntary because they are efficient. A similar point applies to the idea that consent is really about distributive justice. To determine if a particular distribution of resources is just, it is necessary to establish, *inter alia*, whether the distribution is, in part or in whole, the result of consensual exchanges. An apparently unequal distribution may be just if the reason for the inequality is that certain persons consented to giving away some of their wealth. More generally, to assess the justice of a particular distribution of resources one needs to assess the value that members of the society place on those resources. Such assessments cannot be made without stating the conditions under which the valuations are made—one of which will necessarily be that the valuation is made consensually.

By way of introduction to the fifth and final approach to understanding consent, I note that the approaches described above are similar in one important respect. Each attempts to explain consent using ideas that, on the surface anyway, reduce consent to a relatively concrete, if not mechanical, concept. Thus, consent is explained in terms of an undifferentiated notion of 'pressure', a particular 'state of mind', the notion of wrongdoing, or a value such as efficiency or distributive justice. The attraction of such approaches is obvious. They give apparent specificity to what

---

[32] Posner (1998) 126–30; Kronman (1980) 480.

appears, at first instance anyway, to be a radically indefinite concept. But the obvious inadequacies of these definitions suggest that it may not be possible to explain consent in this way. That is, it may be that any plausible account of consent must accept, rather than deny, the imprecision of the notion.

This is the starting assumption of the fifth approach. This approach understands statements about consent as statements about the kinds of pressure that are regarded as ordinary or usual by the members of the relevant society.[33] In this approach, to state that a pressure negates consent is to state nothing more than that it is the kind of pressure that, in this society and at this time, is regarded as one of the ordinary pressures that people are meant to 'put up with'. It is to state that such pressure is regarded as—to borrow a judicial phrase—one of the ordinary vicissitudes of life.

In one respect, the idea that only extraordinary pressure negates consent is an evident truth. If consent is to mean anything useful, it cannot be the case that the ordinary pressures of life are sufficient to negate it. Ordinary pressure is ubiquitous. As well, it is difficult to deny the notion that 'extraordinary' is time and place dependent. As a matter of ordinary language, consent clearly is understood to mean different things in different times and places. What is regarded as ordinary wartime pressure (and thus not negating consent) is quite different from what is regarded as ordinary pressure in peacetime. Consent in a modern liberal democracy is different from consent in a medieval dictatorship.

As such, the objection to the fifth approach is not that it provides a false definition of consent. Rather, the objection is that it provides a meaningless definition. This objection is irrefutable if a 'meaningful' definition is assumed to be one that explains consent in terms of relatively concrete, easily measurable factors. There is no simple test for determining what is regarded as ordinary pressure. But this assumption is questionable. It seems clear that there are certain concepts—let us call them 'basic' concepts—whose meaning cannot be explained in terms of other concepts. Love, friendship, and humour are just a few examples. Such concepts are explained not by applying other concepts, but instead by referring to the kinds of situations that are ordinarily understood to exemplify them. They are explained, in other words, by using examples. What counts as core or paradigmatic examples will change over time and place—but in any given time and place those familiar with the language

---

[33] Birks (1985) 173–74.

will be able to recognize such cases. It is not unreasonable to suppose that such a fundamental concept as consent is of exactly this kind.

Understood in this way, the notion of consent can be given some specificity—though perhaps not the kind that critics are looking for. Broadly speaking, the kinds of pressures that are regarded as extraordinary—and so as negating contractual consent—in contemporary Western market economies are those that leave the recipient with a choice between entering the contract in question or suffering significant harm. Such pressures fall into two main categories. The first is pressure induced by wrongful threats. To be sure, certain kinds of wrongful threats are too trivial or common to be regarded as extraordinary. Furthermore, in certain circumstances (war, famine) even significant wrongdoing is considered normal. But a wrongful threat is not usually regarded as one of the ordinary vicissitudes of life. This is true regardless of the source of the threat (i.e., the plaintiff or a third party).

The second, closely related, kind of pressure regarded as extraordinary is pressure created by a 'state of necessity'. In a contractual setting, a state of necessity arises when, for reasons other than the co-contractor's threat; the only alternative to entering a particular contract is to suffer a serious harm. The classic example is the rescue at sea by a passing ship. The captain of the endangered ship's only alternative to accepting the offer of rescue is to allow his ship to sink. Another example is that of a person needing an antidote to poison in a town with only one pharmacist. The person has little choice but to purchase the antidote from the pharmacist.[34]

The notions of 'wrongful pressure' and 'state of necessity' help to give content to the notion of ordinary pressure. But they do not reduce consent to anything approaching a mechanical standard. There are many forms of wrongdoing that are both trivial and commonplace, and threats to commit such wrongs are not regarded as negating consent. A threat to spit on a person unless that person signs a multi-million dollar contract does not negate consent. Similarly, states of necessity exist to different degrees. To the cook who needs an egg at the last minute for a dinner party, the corner store may have an effective monopoly. The corner store's monopoly is not particularly significant because there are probably other stores not too far away, and because not obtaining an egg is probably

---

[34] A state of necessity is sometimes described as a 'situational monopoly'. In the two examples just given, the party offering the needed service or good effectively has a monopoly with respect to that service or good.

not that serious. But structurally, the situation is identical to the case of the rescue at sea. Indeed, most contracts are formed in situations in which one or both of the parties enjoys at least a small degree of monopoly power. For these reasons, open-textured terms like 'grave' or 'serious' cannot be avoided when trying to describe which wrongful threats and which states of necessity are capable of negating consent.

The charge of vagueness, therefore, cannot be entirely refuted. But what implication should be drawn from this conclusion? The obvious one is that it would be inappropriate for private law to introduce a general defence of 'no consent'. The defence would be too uncertain: it could not be predicted in advance what kinds of pressure courts might declare ordinary as opposed to extraordinary. Asking courts to apply a bare standard of 'ordinary pressure' would therefore almost certainly conflict with the ideal of the rule of law.

The inherent vagueness of the notion of consent does not mean, however, that the consent principle should have no role to play in the law. To the contrary, it is precisely in situations in which ordinary moral reasoning is unlikely to lead to unanimity and, more generally, in which the 'right answer' is not obvious that the law has a clear role to play. By stipulating one solution from among the range of prima facie reasonable solutions, the law can fulfil one of its basic functions of solving co-ordination problems and, more generally, making determinate that which ordinary morality leaves indeterminate.[35] The law has a clear role in making uncertain principles relatively certain. On this basis, it would seem appropriate for law-makers to identify a number of specific and identifiable kinds of pressure that will be deemed prima facie extraordinary. Obvious examples might be 'rescues at sea' or 'threats of bodily injury'.

How well do these observations about the nature of consent and its potential role in the law fit with what common law courts actually do? I will have more to say about this question when I discuss unconscionability in the next section ('state of necessity' cases are typically discussed under this heading), but the short answer is that there is a moderate (though certainly not perfect) degree of fit. Consistent with the above account, the law does not recognize a general defence of state of necessity, but instead offers relief in a few clearly defined categories of states of necessity, such as rescue and salvage at sea. Significantly, such relief, which is given under various headings (not as one part of duress law), is

[35] See in particular Finnis (1980) 231–44.

conditional on the contract in question being substantively unfair.[36] This
condition is consistent with my conclusion above that the consent principle should apply only to substantively unfair contracts (because only
such contracts lead to an unjust enrichment).[37] One might, of course,
expect to see more categories of states of necessity recognized by the
courts if the consent principle was being taken seriously. But the small
number of these categories may simply reflect the kinds of cases that have
come before the courts. Aside from maritime cases, reported decisions
involving substantively unfair contracts that were signed in a serious state
of necessity are rare.[38]

With respect to wrongful threats, the law of duress (as we have seen)
effectively recognizes a general defence of 'wrongful threat'. But because
this defence is also explicable on the basis of the wrongdoing principle (or
so I have argued), its existence does not prove that the law recognizes the
consent principle. On the other hand, the fact that the duress defence is
not limited to substantively unfair contracts, or to serious forms of
wrongdoing, is not evidence against the existence of the consent principle. The wrongdoing principle, which is not limited in these ways, may
be used to explain such cases. The only case in which a wrongful threat
might negate consent yet not raise the wrongdoing principle is where the
threat is made by a third party. Such cases are rare, but the traditional
common law rule is understood to be that such threats invalidate a contract only if they are known by the plaintiff. The consent principle suggests that the rule should state that such threats are a defence only if the
resulting contract is substantively unfair. In principle, this is a significant
difference. But in practice (and keeping in mind the rarity of such cases)

---

[36] 'If the parties have made an agreement, the court will enforce it, unless it be manifestly
unfair and unjust': Brett LJ in *Akerblom v Price* (1885) 7 QBD 129, 132–33.

[37] In most cases, the same result could be reached by holding that the contract is not
enforceable for lack of consent, but then awarding the rescuer the cost of recovery on the
basis of a (non-contractual) action in unjust enrichment. But not always. Consider a case in
which a rescue contract that is made for a fair price is then cancelled before the rescue is
made (say because the endangered ship is unexpectedly made seaworthy again by its crew).
There was no benefit to the owner of the endangered ship, and so according to the usual
principles no claim in unjust enrichment is possible. A contractual action, however, should
be possible according to the above interpretation of the consent principle. The contract was
fair, and so the consent principle does not apply.

[38] A possible American example is *United States v Bethlehem Steel Corp* 315 US 289, 330
(1942). Justice Frankfurter, in a powerful dissent, held that a situation in which the plaintiff
paid the defendant monopolist an 'extortionate' price for vital war supplies was 'strikingly
analogous' to the salvage and rescue cases. The majority, upholding the contract, did not so
much disagree with Frankfurter's principle, as with his conclusion that the plaintiff had no
alternatives.

the difference is not great. Most cases in which the plaintiff is unaware of the threat involve substantively fair contracts for the simple reason that most contracts are substantively fair.[39] Of course, the opposite does not follow. That a person knows of a third party's threat does not mean he will try to take advantage of this threat. But it can be questioned whether the common law would apply the 'knowledge' rule strictly to cases in which the plaintiff was not attempting to take advantage of the defendant's predicament by asking for unfair terms. In civil law systems that have addressed this issue directly, an exception is made for just such a case.[40]

9.1.3. CONCLUSION TO DURESS

A number of conclusions are suggested by the above discussion. The first is that both the wrongdoing principle and the no consent principle can individually account for most of the law of duress. The second conclusion is that each of these principles is distinct, conceptually coherent, and normatively justified—albeit on quite different grounds (dissuading wrongdoing, reversing unjust enrichments). The final conclusion, which follows from the first two, is that the law would be clearer if these two principles were separated, such that each becomes recognized as the basis for a distinct legal doctrine. More specifically, the label 'duress' should be reserved to claims based on the wrongdoing principle. As we have seen, nearly all duress cases are already explicable on this basis. The word 'duress' is also closer, linguistically, to a wrongful threat than it is to a state of necessity. Finally, the alternative of associating duress exclusively with claims of no consent would involve a much larger shift in meaning. The consent principle applies to pure states of necessity (which have never been considered part of the law on duress, even where the law has recognized such a defence) and, in addition, it applies only to substantively unfair contracts (which requirement has never been part of the law of duress). For these reasons, the consent principle seems the better choice as the basis for a newly named doctrine.

Finally, I note that a plausible name for a new 'no consent' doctrine is 'state of necessity'. Admittedly, the consent principle applies not just to states of necessity, strictly defined, but also to cases involving threats. But

---

[39] It is interesting in this regard that recent common law cases have made the 'knowledge' requirement easier to satisfy by expanding the concept of 'constructive notice' of wrongdoing. Significantly, this expansion is limited to cases in which the resulting contract was substantively unfair: *Barclays Bank v O'Brien* [1994] 1 AC 180.

[40] e.g. Art. 1404, *Civil Code of Quebec*.

from the perspective of the consent principle, a threat is equivalent to a state of necessity. Once the issue of wrongdoing is put aside, a threat is analogous to an impending natural disaster. Each leaves the relevant party with no choice but to enter the contract in question. But before this label can be confirmed it is necessary to examine our next topic—unconscionability. The same state of necessity cases that has been discussed in this section are also central in any discussion of unconscionability.

9.2. UNCONSCIONABILITY

The term 'unconscionability'[41] does not have a fixed meaning in law. In the context of contractual obligations, however, it is typically applied to contracts (or clauses in contracts) that are thought to have two characteristics. First, the contract's terms are unfair. Second, the party disadvantaged by the contract would not have entered it had he not been vulnerable in some respect.[42] Thus, the label is commonly applied to 'extortionate' rescue-at-sea contracts (of the kind discussed in the previous section), in which the only possible rescuer of an endangered ship agrees to perform a rescue, but only for a very high fee. The term is also commonly applied to contracts in which a promisor agrees to unfair terms because he is either unaware of the terms or does not understand their meaning.[43] An example might be a credit arrangement between a sophisticated creditor and an unsophisticated debtor that contains, in small print, an unexplained and complex acceleration-of-debt clause, the effect of which is that the cost of the loan is far greater than comparable loans.

Unlike the other 'excuses' discussed in this chapter, unconscionability has not traditionally been recognized as a general defence to a claim for breach of contract in the common law. In the United Kingdom, and despite the best efforts of Lord Denning,[44] this traditional position remains the law today.[45] With rare exceptions, the notion of unconscionability is

---

[41] In the United Kingdom, the phrase 'inequality of bargaining power' is sometimes used as a substitute for 'unconscionabilty': *Lloyd's Bank Ltd v Bundy* [1975] QB 326.

[42] Chitty (1999) 452; Treitel (1995) 381; Farnsworth (1999) 311–14; Waddams (1976); Epstein (1975).

[43] I leave to the side cases in which the promisor is aware of, and understands, the terms, but is mistaken about the value or nature of the thing promised. Though sometimes described as raising issues of unconscionability, such cases are more typically thought to raise issues relating purely to the law of mistake. Related to this point is that there is much less support for extending a defence of unconscionability to such cases, even among scholars who support the defence generally.

[44] *Lloyd's Bank Ltd v Bundy* [1975] QB 326.

[45] *National Westminister Bank plc v Morgan* [1985] AC 686.

discussed explicitly in English decisions only as part of the background for the application of a small number of narrowly defined defences. Other common law regimes have been more receptive to introducing a general and explicit defence of unconscionability. Australia,[46] the United States,[47] and, to a lesser extent, Canada,[48] allow for unconscionability, although in each of these regimes the courts have applied the defence cautiously.

But notwithstanding the mixed support it has received in law, the concept of unconscionabilty is of considerable theoretical interest to contract scholars. There are two main reasons for this interest. First, it is often argued that a number of specific contract law rules and decisions are best *explained* using the concept. Views differ as to the number of such rules and decisions. The short list might include only those rules that the courts themselves typically explain on the basis of a concern for unconscionability. In the United Kingdom, the main examples are the rules providing for the possible invalidity of rescue and salvage contracts,[49] contracts with expectant heirs,[50] and contracts with 'poor and ignorant persons' (usually translated today as 'poorly educated' or something similar)[51]. The medium-length list might add the rules governing the validity of stipulated damages clauses,[52] forfeiture clauses,[53] exclusion and limitation clauses,[54] restrictive covenants,[55] clauses in consumer contracts,[56] contracts in which one party was subject to undue influence,[57] and consumer credit arrangements.[58] Finally, the long list would add, *inter alia*, a number of specific decisions ostensibly based on doctrines such as offer and acceptance, consideration, incorporation of terms, interpretation, mistake, frustration, and so on. Scholars defending the long list thus believe that a concern for unconscionability influences—typically

[46] *Commercial Bank of Australia v Amadio* (1983) 151 CLR 447.

[47] See in particular s.2–302 of the *Uniform Commercial Code* and s.208 of the Restatement of Contracts (second).

[48] *Harry v Kreutziger* (1978) 95 DLR (3d) 231.

[49] *Akerblom v Price* (1881) 7 QBD 129.

[50] *Aylesford v Morris* (1873) LR 3 Ch App 484.

[51] *Fry v Lane* (1888) 40 Ch D 312. In *Craswell v Potter* [1978] 1 WLR 255, the concept of 'poor and ignorant' was extended to 'member of the lower income group' and 'less highly educated'.

[52] *Dunlop Pneumatic Tyre Co Ltd v New Garage and Motor Co Ltd* [1915] AC 79.

[53] *Workers Trust & Merchant Bank Ltd v Dojap Investments Ltd* [1993] AC 573.

[54] *Unfair Contract Terms Act* 1977.

[55] *Maxim Nordenfelt Guns and Ammunition Co v Nordenfelt* [1893] 1 Ch 630.

[56] *Unfair Terms in Consumer Contracts Regulations 1994*, esp. Regs 3 & 4.

[57] *National Westminister Bank plc v Morgan* [1985] AC 686.

[58] *Consumer Credit Act* 1974.

without acknowledgement—the courts' approach to nearly every aspect of contract law.[59]

A second reason unconscionability is of theoretical interest is that it is often argued that courts *should* recognize a general defence of unconscionability—or at least that they should explicitly use the concept when applying the just mentioned rules.[60] The primary focus of this book, of course, is arguments about how best to understand the existing law—not arguments about how the law should be reformed (1.1). But as is frequently the case, the interpretive and prescriptive inquiries are related (1.5). In seeking to determine if particular rules (and decisions) are explicable on the basis of a concern for unconscionability, a recurring question is whether unconscionability is a coherent and morally attractive notion, either as a general defence or as applied to specific situations. The idea that a concern for unconscionabilty explains various legal rules is more plausible, in other words, if it can be shown that law-makers *should* be so concerned.

The discussion that follows is in three parts. First, I expand on the above definition of unconscionability by describing in more detail the kinds of contracts to which the label is typically applied. Next, I briefly examine the extent to which the courts appear to care about unconscionability, thus defined. Finally, the third and longest part discusses normative justifications for caring about unconscionability. It is in this part that the no consent principle that I discussed in connection with duress makes a second appearance.

9.2.1. DEFINING UNCONSCIONABILITY

The term 'unconscionability' does not, as I said, have a fixed meaning. Nevertheless, there is a reasonable degree of consensus about certain general characteristics of unconscionable contracts. Identifying these characteristics does not commit one to deciding that courts do, or should, care about unconscionability, or even to the view that the term is a useful one in legal discussions. But it is a necessary preliminary to addressing such issues.

I noted above that, in contractual situations, the term unconscionability is most commonly applied to contracts whose terms are thought to be unfair, *and* to which the disadvantaged party would not have agreed

---

[59] Collins (1997) 251–282; Farnsworth (1999) 302; Atiyah (1986) 329–54; Llewellyn (1939) 702.

[60] Benson (2001); Waddams (1976). Lord Denning in *Lloyd's Bank Ltd v Bundy* [1975] QB 326.

but for his vulnerable position (however defined). This meaning is often expressed by stating that unconscionability arises from the combination of a substantive 'defect' (the substantive unfairness of the terms) and a procedural 'defect' (the vulnerability of the defendant).[61] In addition, it is sometimes (though not always) stated that the advantaged party must be morally blameworthy.[62]

Each of these elements of unconscionability is examined separately below. A general observation, however, is that none of them satisfy (individually or collectively) the standard requirements for fraud, duress, or incapacity. If they did, there would be no reason to invoke unconscionability to explain why the contract in question should not be enforced.

The first requirement, that the contract be substantively unfair, is satisfied if the parties' obligations are unequal in value (and there was no intent to make a gift or to fulfill what civil law lawyers sometimes call a 'natural obligation', such as a pre-existing debt or a duty of honour—say to support one's parents).[63] As regards the meaning of 'unequal in value', insofar as their exists an orthodox view it would appear to be that an exchange is unequal if it is made at a price significantly different from the market price. Thus, the fairness of the rescue contract and the loan agreement would be determined by the normal market price for a comparable rescue or loan. Where a comparable market does not exist (which is arguably the case in the rescue example), the fair price appears to be determined by estimating the price that would have been set if such a market existed, which in practice means cost plus normal profit.[64]

The second requirement, the procedural aspect of unconscionability, is satisfied, in the standard view anyway, if the circumstances in which the contract was entered into fall into either of two categories. The first is that the defendant was in a 'state of necessity'. As I explained when discussing duress, a contract is made in a state of necessity if, through no fault of the plaintiff, the defendant needed a particular good or service in order to avoid a serious loss or injury, and the only possible provider was the plaintiff. A rescue-at-sea contract is the classic example of a contract made in a state of necessity: the captain of the endangered ship needs rescue services to avoid a serious loss, and the sole possible provider of such services is the passing ship.

The other situation that satisfies the procedural element for a finding of unconscionability is one in which there exists a cognitive asymmetry

---

[61] Leff (1967).　　[62] Chitty (1999) 452; Burrows (1993) 204.
[63] Ghestin and Goubeaux (1994) 728ff.　　[64] *The Medina* (1876) 1 PD 272.

between the plaintiff and the defendant, which results in an advantage to the plaintiff. A cognitive asymmetry, in the sense intended here, is established by showing that there was a significant risk that the defendant was not aware of, or did not understand the meaning of the relevant terms. Cognitive asymmetries can arise from circumstances peculiar to the contracting party (e.g., little education, low intelligence, lack of knowledge, lack of independence) or from circumstances peculiar to the contract (e.g., the contract was difficult to understand, was in fine print, or dealt with difficult-to-estimate probabilities). The loan contract example involved both of these kinds of cognitive asymmetries. The debtor was inexperienced, and the acceleration-of-debt clause was both easily missed and difficult to understand.

Finally, the third 'requirement', moral blameworthiness, is not, as I said, consistently recognized as a necessary element of unconscionability. In any event, it is rarely an issue in cases in which the procedural and substantive requirements described above are satisfied. This is because blameworthiness is thought to be established (merely) by showing that the defendant had *knowledge* of the plaintiff's circumstances and of the unfairness of the terms.[65] Blameworthiness, in this sense, will almost always exist in cases in which the first two requirements are satisfied.

A number of questions are raised by the above definitions. But they are best addressed in the context of examining those specific rules or decisions that are said to express a concern for unconscionability.

9.2.2. DO COURTS CARE ABOUT UNCONSCIONABILITY?

To what extent do courts appear to care about unconscionability, thus defined? Do courts refuse to enforce unconscionable contracts? And do they do this *because* the contracts are unconscionable?

I noted above that common law courts have not traditionally recognized a general defence of unconscionability, and that in the United Kingdom this remains the position today. This does not establish, however, that English law attaches little importance to the concept of unconscionability. There are two ways that a concern for unconscionability might be expressed. One is by introducing a general defence of unconscionability. The other (which may be combined with the first) is by introducing a number of situation-specific unconscionability-based rules. That a legal regime limits itself to the second method does not mean that it regards unconscionability as unimportant. The choice might instead be

---

[65] Chitty (1999) 452; Burrows (1993) 204.

based on a conclusion that, however serious unconscionability is in principle, a concern for unconscionability is not appropriately expressed by means of a general defence.

Assuming that English courts care about unconscionability, it would be understandable if they chose to express such concern through situation-specific rules. The requirements for establishing unconscionability—procedural unfairness in the sense of a state of necessity or a cognitive asymmetry, substantive unfairness, and moral blameworthiness—are difficult to apply in the abstract. As I explained when discussing duress, there is no simple test for identifying a state of necessity—situations are 'more or less' states of necessity. The same is true of cognitive asymmetries—contracting parties are 'more or less' sophisticated, contracts are 'more or less' complex, and so on. As for 'substantive fairness', there is no need to adopt the extreme view (rejected in 9.2.4) that it is meaningless in a market economy to acknowledge that judges will often have difficulties applying such a standard.

For these reasons, recognizing a general defence of unconscionability would almost certainly introduce a significant degree of uncertainty into the law. To that extent, a general defence conflicts with the ideal of the rule of law. According to this ideal, the law should be clear and predictable.[66] Of course, certainty is not the only virtue of good law; the law should also be substantively just. It may well be, therefore, that the substantive benefits of introducing a general defence outweigh its negative effects on the rule of law. But whether this is the case with respect to a particular legal regime cannot be answered in the abstract. The extent to which apparently open-ended standards will lead to unpredictable results depends, in large part, on regime-specific features, in particular the judicial culture of that regime. It is difficult to say whether, assuming that unconscionability matters in principle, such a concern is appropriately pursued in England by situation-specific rules. But what can be said confidently is that the extent to which a general defence is recognized (assuming, again, that unconscionability matters in principle) should vary between legal regimes—which is what happens in practice.

The question I turn to now is whether, and to what extent, English law expresses a concern for unconscionability through situation-specific unconscionability based rules. To begin, it is clear there exist a number of contract rules that appear, on their face, to be concerned with exactly the combination of procedural and substantive defects described above.

---

[66] Raz (1979) 212–19.

So far as English law is concerned, perhaps the clearest demonstration of a concern for unconscionability is seen in the rules on the 'short list' given earlier. These rules, recall, provide for the invalidity of substantively unfair contracts that are made in a marine rescue or salvage context, or that are made with either expectant heirs or 'poor and ignorant persons'. The rescue and salvage contracts are made in a classic state of necessity situation, while contracts made with expectant heirs or poor and ignorant persons are made in cognitive asymmetry situations. There is a clear risk that expectant heirs or poor and ignorant persons may not fully understand any contracts that they enter.

Many (but not all) of the doctrines described in the 'medium-length list' of unconscionability are similar to those in the 'short list' in that they reflect a concern for both cognitive asymmetry and substantive unfairness. Thus, the rules on 'presumed undue influence' provide that parties in a situation of cognitive asymmetry (because of the defendant's dependence on the plaintiff, together with the absence of independent legal advice) may set aside their contracts if they are substantive by unfair ('manifestly disadvantageous').[67] Most of the legislation in the medium list also appears to reflect a concern for cognitive asymmetries and substantive fairness. For example, the *Unfair Contract Terms Act* 1977 provides for the invalidity of substantively unfair ('unreasonable') exclusion and limitation of liability clauses. In this case, the cognitive asymmetry arises because of the very nature of such clauses. The consequences of exclusion and limitation clauses are often not fully appreciated, either because the background liability rules (which they qualify) are themselves not well understood, or because of the tendency to discount the importance of low-probability events (i.e., a future breach of the contract).[68] Admittedly, the mere fact that a contract contains such a clause does not prove the existence of an information asymmetry. The defendant might be a sophisticated commercial party who has read the contract carefully. It is therefore appropriate, insofar as a concern for cognitive asymmetry is valid, that the act directs courts to examine not just the nature and fairness of the clause, but also the 'strength of the bargaining positions' of the parties (schedule 2).

An underlying concern for both cognitive asymmetry and substantive unfairness cannot, on the other hand, be said to explain all the rules on the medium list. More specifically, it cannot explain the rules providing

---

[67] *CIBC Mortgages plc v Pitt* [1994] 1 AC 200.
[68] Ulen (1989); Weinstein (1980); Arrow (1982).

for the invalidity of 'unreasonable' restrictive covenants, stipulated damages clauses, and forfeiture clauses. To be sure, the clauses that are the focus of such rules are similar to the clauses examined in the previous paragraphs in that their legal significance is often difficult to understand or appreciate. Restrictive covenants, stipulated damages clauses, and forfeiture clauses qualify legal responsibilities or liabilities attendant to the occurrence of a low-probability future event (termination or breach of the contract). In addition, courts sometimes state that they will hesitate to set aside such clauses when they are entered into by sophisticated commercial parties.[69] Thus, the cognitive asymmetry requirement seems satisfied. But there is a difference between these rules and the other rules on the medium list as regards the other requirement for unconscionability —substantive unfairness. More specifically, the 'unreasonableness' standard that is applied to these clauses is not (despite initial appearances) a substantive fairness standard. Rather, unreasonableness is determined by asking if the clause is more extensive than is necessary to protect a proprietary interest (in the case of restrictive covenants) or a contractual interest (in the case of stipulated damages clauses and forfeiture clauses).[70] In principle, therefore, a restrictive covenant, etc. can be invalidated even if the clause (and the contract generally) is substantively fair. An unreasonable restrictive covenant remains unreasonable even if the party subject to it receives a large sum of money in compensation.

One respone to the above characterization of the rules on restrictive covenants, stipulated damages clauses, and forfeiture clauses is to argue that, regardless of the orthodox description of these rules, *in practice* courts apply them in a way that is consistent with a concern for unconscionability.[71] Courts are said to do this either by misdescribing the facts of the case or by misapplying the rules—with the result that unconscionable contracts are not enforced. This argument is, of course, part of a larger argument to the effect that courts generally manipulate facts or rules so as to ensure that unconscionable contracts are not enforced. They do this, according to the larger argument, not just when applying the rules on restrictive covenants, etc., but when applying all or nearly all contract law rules.

There can be no doubt that certain contract law decisions are best explained on the basis that the court was influenced by an unexpressed concern for unconscionability. Given that many lawyers, scholars, and

---

[69] *Philips Hong Kong Ltd v Att. Gen. of Hong Kong* (1993) 61 Build LR 49.
[70] Smith (1995) 578.   [71] Waddams (1976).

judges have argued openly for introducing an explicit defence of unconscionability into English law, any other conclusion would be surprising.
But to determine just how often courts act in this way is outside the scope
of this book. Even if the inquiry were limited to, say, restraint of trade
cases, a detailed analysis of hundreds of individual decisions would be
required. Instead, what can be done here is to examine in more detail
arguments for why courts *should* take unconscionability into account. The
more convincing such arguments are, the more likely it is that courts
actually do what they prescribe.

9.2.3. NORMATIVE JUSTIFICATIONS FOR UNCONSCIONABILITY: INTRODUCTION

Three different explanations for why courts should care about unconscionability are examined below: the procedural fairness explanation, the
substantive fairness explanation, and the orthodox (or 'non-reductionist')
explanation. It may be useful to mention in advance that what primarily
distinguishes the explanations is the manner in which they understand
the relationship between the substantive and procedural aspects of
unconscionability. As its name suggests, the procedural fairness explanation regards procedural fairness as the underlying or true concern, with
substantive fairness being merely of evidentiary interest. The substantive
fairness explanation reaches the opposite conclusion. Finally, the orthodox (or non-reductionist) explanation supposes that *both* the procedural
and substantive aspects of unconscionability are important in principle.

9.2.4. UNCONSCIONABILITY AS PROCEDURAL UNFAIRNESS

According to the procedural fairness explanation, the reason courts
should worry about unconscionable contracts is that such contracts may
be tainted by one of the 'ordinary' and well-established procedural
defects, such as duress, fraud, or undue influence.[72] In this view, what
makes unconscionability cases special—why, in other words, they cannot
be decided merely on the basis of the ordinary rules regarding duress,
fraud, and so on—is that the available evidence regarding the contract's
formation supports no more than a suspicion of the relevant procedural
defect. Unconscionability cases are therefore cases of what might be
called 'presumed' duress, fraud, and so on. The role of the substantive
element of unconscionability, in this explanation, is to confirm the

---

[72] Epstein (1975).

suspicion of an invalidating procedural defect. If the contract is substantively unfair, it can be assumed that the suspected procedural defect actually occurred. But substantive unfairness matters only as evidence. The underlying reason for refusing to enforce the contract is purely procedural.

From a theoretical perspective, the procedural fairness explanation of unconscionabilty has one obvious attraction: it is consistent with the traditional view that, in principle, courts should care only about the formation of contracts. It is consistent, in other words, with the idea that the content of a contract and, in particular, the fairness of its terms, is a matter for the parties. The procedural fairness explanation reduces the 'problem of unconscionability' to nothing more than the familiar problem of insufficient evidence of a (standard) procedural defect. The response to this problem is also explained in familiar terms: the courts should rely on indirect evidence as a substitute for direct evidence.

But how well does this explanation account for the kinds of cases that (I have argued) are thought to raise unconscionability concerns? The first point to make is that the procedural fairness explanation offers a natural explanation for why courts should care about the substantive fairness of contracts formed in three kinds of cognitive asymmetry situations. The first of these cognitive asymmetry situations is characterized by close dealings between parties with significantly unequal cognitive abilities. Examples here include contracts concluded following face-to-face dealings between sophisticated commercial parties and unsophisticated consumers (e.g., a door to door sale) or between parties in a relationship of trust and dependence (e.g., lawyer-client, doctor-patient). Situations of this kind undoubtedly raise a risk of fraud. Evidence that the resulting contract was substantively unfair can plausibly be regarded as providing indirect proof that this risk materialized. Of course, it would be preferable if the courts could focus, in such cases, solely on direct evidence of fraud. But this is often impossible to do, either because it cannot be proven that the relevant statements were actually made, or because the statements could be given more than one interpretation. Many of the legislative provisions found in the 'fair trading' legislation that I noted earlier (e.g. *Unfair Terms in Consumer Contracts Regulations* 1994), together with certain undue influence cases, can be explained on this basis.

The second kind of cognitive asymmetry case that fits well with a procedural fairness explanation is one in which the defendant was in a dependant relationship with the plaintiff. In such cases, the relevant procedural risk is undue influence, understood here as a dependant's incapacity to act independently because her judgment has been 'surrendered' to another.[73] In situations in which the defendant is dependant, there is an obvious risk that she may act in just this way. In such cases, evidence that the relevant contract was substantively unfair can be regarded, again, as confirming that the risk materialized. In common law systems, cases of this kind are usually described as cases of 'presumed undue influence', but they are also sometimes described as unconscionability cases.[74] According to the procedural fairness explanation, both of these descriptions are correct. These cases fall within the general category of unconscionability because they are cases in which the procedural history gives rise to a risk of procedural defect. But because the relevant procedural defect is undue influence, it is also appropriate to describe this sub-category as that of presumed undue influence.

The third and final cognitive asymmetry situation that is thought to raise concerns for unconscionability and in respect of which such concerns are explicable using a procedural fairness account is one in which the defendant may have either been unaware of, or failed to understand the meaning of, the relevant contractual terms. An example might be a case in which an inexperienced consumer does not read, or does not understand, a clause in his contract of sale that grants the vendor the right to repossession if the purchaser is late with one payment. In such cases, there is a risk that the defendant may have made an invalidating mistake. More specifically, there is a risk that the defendant may have made a mistake as regards the *terms* of the contract (as opposed to a mistaken assumption about the value or nature of what was promised: 9.3). In the example, the relevant risk is that the consumer either thought the terms were different than they were or that they meant something other than what they actually meant. The first kind of situation is similar to the mistake made when a contractor intends to write 'plus expenses' into in a contractual document, but then forgets to do so. The second kind is similar to the mistake made when a purchaser thinks 'the painting in storage bin X' is the Rembrandt he earlier saw on the wall, when it is actually a different painting. In cases of this kind, the court would, if it had clear evidence of the facts, and if the mistake was known to the other party, either rectify the contract or set it aside. As I discuss elsewhere, such decisions are properly regarded as applying the rules of offer and acceptance law; the reason that a contract formed in these circumstances is set aside (or rectified) is that, despite outward appearances, the mean-

---

[73] Birks and Chin (1995b).
[74] Lord Denning in *Lloyd's Bank Ltd v Bundy* [1975] QB 326.

ing of the parties' agreement is different from what the parties say they said or wrote (8.3; 9.3). In other words, there was no agreement. On this basis, this third group of cognitive asymmetry cases can be regarded as cases of 'presumed non-agreement'. In these circumstances, there is a risk that the defendant did not know or understand the meaning of the relevant terms—that is, that there was a failure to agree. But the court lacks direct proof of this failure. Evidence that the contract was substantively unfair confirms that this risk materialized. The only other requirement for establishing a failure to agree is that the plaintiff be aware of the defendant's mistake. Interestingly, the 'moral blameworthiness' requirement appears to fulfill just this role; as I noted, the requirement is satisfied, in practice, by showing the plaintiff was aware that the defendant's cognitive defect meant he was vulnerable or weak.[75]

The procedural fairness explanation of unconscionability explains neatly, then, why certain situations involving cognitive asymmetries are thought to raise unconscionability concerns. With respect to such cases, this explanation accounts for both the procedural and substantive elements of unconscionabilty (albeit on very different grounds). For similar reasons, this explanation therefore also explains neatly those rules (noted above) that appear to focus on just such asymmetries. But it also seems clear that the procedural fairness explanation cannot account for all the cases to which the label unconscionable is typically applied. More specifically, the explanation does not explain state of necessity cases. From a procedural fairness perspective, the difficulty posed by such cases is explaining why it should matter whether the contract was concluded at a fair price. Evidence concerning the substantive fairness of a contract formed in a state of necessity does not tell a court anything significant about the contract's procedural history. From a procedural perspective, the relevant facts are already known—namely that the defendant agreed to the plaintiff's terms because she was in a state of necessity. This is not to deny that the existence of a state of necessity might be sufficient, without more, to negate consent (as I argued when discussing duress and will suggest again later in this section). But an argument along these lines cannot be adopted by the procedural fairness explanation of unconscionability. The procedural fairness explanation supposes that courts care about substantive unfairness because it provides indirect evidence of the relevant procedural defect. But, again, in a state of necessity case the court already knows everything it needs to know about such a defect.

---

[75] Of course, the general rule is that if you have signed a contractual document you are presumed to have agreed to all the terms therein. But this is merely a rule of evidence.

Indeed, it is only because a state of necessity has been proven that the court examines the fairness of the contract's terms.

For this reason, I conclude that a concern for unconscionability can *sometimes* be explained as nothing more than a concern for (ordinary) procedural defects such as fraud, duress, undue influence, or lack of agreement. Stated differently, the procedural fairness explanation provides a plausible argument for why, in principle, it would be appropriate to add to the existing category of 'presumed undue influence' categories such as 'presumed duress', 'presumed fraud', and 'presumed lack of agreement'. But as a general justification for caring about unconscionability, the procedural fairness explanation is incomplete.

9.2.5. UNCONSCIONABILITY AS SUBSTANTIVE UNFAIRNESS

As its name suggests, the substantive fairness view supposes that the underlying problem with contracts thought to be unconscionable is that the contracting parties' obligations are unequal in value.[76] In this view, the fact of an unequal exchange is itself regarded as a sufficient reason to set aside a contract.

The first hurdle facing the substantive fairness view is to explain why unconscionability is generally understood to include a procedural element (cognitive asymmetry, state of necessity). If all that matters is substantive fairness, why is the concept not expressed solely in substantive terms?

One explanation that must be rejected is that evidence of a procedural defect provides indirect evidence of substantive unfairness. Admittedly, a substantively unfair contract will, by definition, have been formed in procedurally imperfect circumstances (e.g., cognitive asymmetry, state of necessity). But it is not clear why a court would want indirect evidence of substantive unfairness when direct evidence is readily available; the contract's terms are known to the court. A second reason for rejecting this explanation is that if it were correct, we would expect the law to allow for a straight defence of 'substantive unfairness' for cases in which the evidence *is* clear. But the law does not recognize such a defence, either generally or in specific circumstances.[77] There exists at most only a few

---

[76] Gordley (1981); Benson (2001).

[77] Apparent counter-examples can be dismissed on the grounds either that they do not focus explicitly on the *fairness* of contract terms (e.g. the rules regarding penal clauses, restrictive covenants) or that they require courts to take into account procedural factors (e.g. *Consumer Credit Act* 1974, s.134.3). A clear (but isolated) counter-example in the civil law is the French rule that a contract for the sale of land at 5/12ths its value may be set aside: *Code Civil* art. 1674.

decisions (not rules), mostly in the United States, in which courts have set aside a contract explicitly on the sole basis that the terms were unfair.[78]

In the end, there appear to be two possible arguments for those who would defend the substantive fairness explanation of unconscionability. The first is to acknowledge the lack of fit, but then to present the substantive fairness explanation as a bluntly prescriptive claim about how unconscionability should be understood. The second, which may be combined with the first, is to argue that, regardless of what courts *say they are doing*, in practice, courts apply unconscionability (and those doctrines that are alleged to implement the concept) as the substantive fairness explanation says it should be applied. In this view, courts do not openly support a pure substantive fairness standard because, essentially, it is politically unfashionable; support for substantive fairness is regarded as inconsistent with modern notions of freedom of contract that (as I explain below) are thought to underlie both market economies and the modern liberal state. But, despite this orthodoxy, what courts actually do, it is said, 'is remarkably consistent with the principle of equality in exchange'.[79]

As I have noted elsewhere, claims to the effect that courts are doing something different than what they say they are doing are difficult to evaluate within the scope of this book. A detailed examination of a large number of individual decisions is required. This difficulty is exacerbated in the case at hand because substantive unfairness is invariably linked to a procedural defect. Because of this linkage, it is difficult to find cases that fit the substantive fairness explanation without at the same time fitting one or both of the alternative explanations.

For this reason, the persuasiveness of claims that, in practice, courts are concerned about substantive fairness depend to a large degree on the validity of the essentially prescriptive argument that courts should be so concerned. If good arguments can be presented for why courts should care about substantive fairness, the argument that this is what they actually do is more plausible. I turn, then, to examine normative justifications for caring about substantive fairness.

---

[78] *American Home Improvement v MacIver* 105 NH 435 (1964); *Cityland and Property (Holdings) Ltd v Dabrah* [1968] Ch 166.

[79] Gordley (1981) 1588; Atiyah (1976) 179–243, 320–54. Gordley and Atiyah also believe that courts often act on the basis of a concern for pure substantive fairness when applying other legal doctrines, such as consideration, mistake, and so on. In this view, unconscionability cases are special merely in that in these cases courts have come closest to admitting the truth.

Normative arguments for caring about substantive fairness

The idea that substantive unfairness should be a sufficient reason, in itself, to set aside a contract is not embraced by many modern contract scholars. One reason for this rejection is that the very concept of a 'fair price' is thought to be meaningless in a market economy. Value is subject-ive.[80] A second, perhaps more fundamental reason, is that a substantive fairness standard is thought to be inconsistent with the ideal of freedom of contract. According to the orthodox understanding of this ideal, the courts' role is merely to ensure that the process by which agreement is reached is fair and voluntary. The content of contracts is up to the parties.

The first of these objections is the less serious. To be sure, the idea that there is an unchanging 'natural' or 'just' price for an object is implausible. But as James Gordley explains, those defending substantive fairness have never adopted this formulation of the concept.[81] Rather, their view is that a contract is substantively fair when the purchasing power of the parties is left relatively unchanged by the bargain. What this means, in practice, is that substantive fairness requires that goods be sold at approximately their standard market price. Within this framework, it is understood, of course, that for certain unique goods, say a family heirloom, it makes no sense to speak of a market price. The same may be true of goods in respect of which the market price is fluctuating severely (for example, oil prices during the 1973 oil crisis). As well, the existence of monopolies, whether situational or non-situational, raises particular problems for the concept of a market price. Finally, even in respect of goods that are easily obtained in a stable competitive market, there usually exists a range of available prices. But even with these qualifications, it is often possible to speak confidently of the market price for a particular good or service. Admittedly, courts are not always in a good position to identify such prices. But these are reasons only for limiting the practical scope of a substantive fairness standard.

The objection that regarding substantive fairness as a criterion of con-tractual validity is inconsistent with freedom of contract is more difficult to rebut. In Chapter 7, I argued that support for freedom of contract is consistent with a variety of substantive limitations on enforceability (e.g.,

---

[80] Thus, Frederick Pollock, quoting Hobbes, wrote, 'The value of all things contracted for is measured by the appetite of the contractors, and therefore the just value is that which they be contented to give': (1885) 208.

[81] Gordley (1981) 1604–17. I discuss the meaning of substantive fairness in Smith (1996) 140–44.

contracts to commit a crime, prostitution contracts). But the arguments in that chapter focused exclusively on reasons pertaining to the nature of the activity required by, or facilitated by, the contract (e.g., that the contract involved a legal wrong or an immoral activity). Nothing in Chapter 7 supported the conclusion that a contract should be set aside simply on the ground that it is substantively unfair.

Significantly, the leading modern defender of the importance of substantive fairness, James Gordley, offers little in the way of a normative justification for the concept. Gordley traces (what he calls) 'equality in exchange' to Aristotle's notion of commutative (or corrective) justice.[82] But aside from observing that, everything else being equal, disturbing the existing allocation of resources seems like a bad thing, Gordley offers almost no arguments in defence of equality in exchange (nor can any be found in Aristotle's discussion). To the contrary, Gordley's normative arguments focus more on explaining why certain *limits* should be placed on equality in exchange, so as to ensure that goods and resources flow smoothly in the economy.[83]

One suggestion, which draws on Gordley's comment about disturbing the existing allocation of resources, is that substantive fairness is important because it helps to maintain a just distribution of resources. If contracts are substantively fair, the existing scheme of distributive justice will not be disturbed by contractual reallocations of purchasing power. The obvious objection to this suggestion is that it is not clear why we should care about maintaining the existing distribution of resources in societies, like our own, in which the existing distribution does not conform to any known criteria of distributive justice. Why worry about upsetting an unjust distribution? From the perspective of distributive justice, the most that might be claimed is that a standard of substantive fairness is useful in preventing distributively unjust societies from becoming yet more unjust. But even this (weak) justification applies only in the case that most substantively unfair contracts favour the better off in society at the expense of the worse off—a debatable proposition.

A second suggestion, which can also be inferred from Gordley's comments, is that substantively unfair contracts should not be enforced because a person who benefits from an unequal exchange has acted wrongly, or at least badly. In a substantively unfair contract, one party's purchasing power increases and the other's decreases by an equal amount. The advantaged person has acted wrongly, according to this suggestion,

[82] Aristotle (1962) V.4, V.5.   [83] Gordley (1981).

because she has treated the disadvantaged person as less deserving of an equal share of the resources that is the object of their trade. This is a difficult proposition to assess. It is undeniable that we ordinarily regard those who knowingly and intentionally benefit at another's expense—for whatever reason—as deserving of censure and criticism. To adopt Gordley's language, they seem less virtuous than those who make equal exchanges. But like many other virtues—charity, courage, wisdom—it is not clear that the virtue of 'substantive fairness' is one that courts should care about in a private law suit. Rather, such a virtue seems more like charity or courage; it is something we care about in judging people's characters, but not something that should matter in deciding whether a person is liable under a contract. What is wrong in making an offer at a high price? The offeree is free to accept the offer or not. Of course, in some cases the other party is not truly free, either because of a state of necessity or a cognitive asymmetry. We may conclude that it is wrong to make a high offer in such a case. But if one thinks that procedural considerations of this kind should matter when determining the 'morality' of making a high offer, then one is no longer arguing that substantive fairness matters in and of itself. Rather, one is arguing that substantive unfairness matters only when the contract is also procedurally imperfect. This is the orthodox explanation of unconscionability that I discuss below.

A final suggestion put forth to justify the substantive fairness view focuses on the defendant's position. It proposes that substantively unfair contracts are bad because they harm autonomy, and more specifically, because they harm the defendant's ability to plan his or her life.[84] Unintended decreases in wealth upsets one's ability to plan one's life; we plan our lives on the assumption that our purchasing power will not be decreased, or at least not decreased by voluntary transactions. Substantively unfair contracts can defeat these expectations. Like the distributive justice argument, this idea provides, at best, a weak justification for caring about substantive unfairness. Substantively unfair contracts have a small effect on our ability to lead autonomous, self-directed lives in comparison with many other limits on autonomy that we live with all the time.[85]

---

[84] Smith (1995).

[85] I also note that, although I once defended such an argument (1995), it fits poorly with the rights-based approach to contract that I have generally defended in this book. The argument supposes that a contract that has met the usual procedural requirements, and in which there has been no wrongdoing, may be set aside simply because one party's expectations are upset.

The conclusion suggested by these observations is that it is difficult to defend the idea that substantive fairness matters, in and of itself, on the basis of any well-recognized moral theory.[86] This conclusion should not be surprising. As I noted earlier, support for substantive fairness is not part of the official discourse of contract law, nor is it defended by many contract law scholars. But at the same time, the idea that contracts can be substantively unfair, and that this can be a bad thing, is commonplace in ordinary thinking. It would therefore be surprising to find that courts never acted on this idea. Moreover, it may be the case—though this is not my view—that substantive fairness is one of those concepts, like 'consent' or 'fairness' generally, that is so basic to our ideas of morality that it cannot be explained using other moral notions (such as distributive justice or wrongdoing). Such concepts are not derived from moral theories, but are rather the bedrock facts (of morality) against which we test such theories. This possibility cannot be denied, but it seems inconsistent with ordinary intuitions about substantive fairness. For these reasons, I conclude that the substantive fairness explanation of unconscionability is unconvincing.

9.2.6. THE ORTHODOX ('NON-REDUCTIONIST') VIEW: UNCONSCIONABILITY AS A COMBINATION OF PROCEDURAL AND SUBSTANTIVE FAIRNESS

The third and final explanation for why courts should care about unconscionability is what I shall call the orthodox view. In this view, *both* the procedural and substantive elements of unconscionability (as defined above) are important in principle, and not merely as evidence of 'something else that matters'. The combination of procedural and substantive factors that are thought to give rise to an unconscionable contract are therefore regarded as giving rise also to a distinct 'combination' defect, one that cannot be explained in either purely procedural or purely substantive terms.

As might be expected, this understanding of unconscionability fits well with how the term is normally used and understood. In ordinary legal

---

[86] One justification for caring about substantive fairness that I have not discussed is the 'Hegelian' justification defended by Benson (1989; 1992; 2001) and Brudner (1993). I find this justification unconvincing, but this is not the reason I do not discuss it. Rather, it is because it is not possible—in my view anyway—to present a comprehensible explanation of this justification other than as one element in a long and highly abstract discussion of Hegelian philosophy (and even then, I am not sure the explanation is comprehensible). The difficulty, it should be stressed, is not so much the complexity of the justification, but the utter unfamiliarity of the organizing ideas.

usage, both the substantive and the procedural elements of unconscionability are regarded as important in principle. Indeed, this understanding is reflected in the very existence of the term. The term is needed because (in this view) unconscionability is *sui generis*. By contrast, if either of the views described above represented the orthodox understanding, then we would expect the term to be replaced with something along the lines of either 'presumed duress/fraud/incapacity' or 'substantive unfairness'.

But the main question for this explanation is whether a concern for unconscionability, thus understood, is normatively justified. More specifically, what is the nature of the 'substantive-procedural' defect or problem that is (allegedly) characteristic of unconscionable contracts? And why, if at all, should courts worry about it? Three possible answers to these questions are examined below.

The 'facilitating contracting' explanation of unconscionability

The first suggestion, which is grounded in efficiency-based and other utilitarian approaches to contract law, justifies an unconscionability principle (whether expressed as a general defence or by situation-specific rules) on the basis that it facilitates contracting. More specifically, it is argued that refusing to enforce unconscionable contracts helps contracting parties to reach mutually beneficial agreements in certain situations in which such agreements might not otherwise be reached (or reached only after incurring extra costs).[87]

According to this explanation, the significant feature of state of necessity situations and cognitive asymmetry situations is that in both situations there is a significant risk that potential contracting parties may fail to reach agreement, or do so only after incurring extra costs. As regards states of necessity, this is the case because, by definition, there exists a wide range of potential contract prices at which the parties could strike a mutually beneficial agreement. In the typical rescue-at-sea scenario, for example, there is a significant difference between the rescue's cost and its value. The parties therefore have an incentive to engage in hard bargaining over how this difference will be split between them. It further follows that there is a risk that no agreement will be reached; the rescuer may call the other captain's bluff—or vice versa. Or if an agreement is reached, it may happen only after much time (and perhaps some cargo) is lost. Thus, the explanation concludes, the process of making it known *in advance* that the rescuer will receive only a fair market price (including a percentage

---

[87] Buckley (1990).

for profits) serves to eliminate needless and potentially detrimental bargaining. The contract at a fair price is still a mutually beneficial contract.

As regards cognitive asymmetry cases, the explanation is that parties may fail to reach agreement because of worries on the part of the less knowledgeable or less experienced party that he is not getting a fair price.[88] In situations in which one party is unsure if he is getting a fair market price, that party may either refuse to contract at all, or do so only after incurring significant extra costs (e.g., asking for outside expertise, consulting a lawyer, etc.). This failure to reach agreement may happen despite the potential for a mutually beneficial bargain. The conclusion to this explanation is, again, that applying a substantive fairness standard to transactions involving cognitive asymmetries will cure the above problem. The purchaser, who has a guarantee that the price will be fair, can contract with confidence.

It seems clear that applying a substantive fairness standard in the situations just described can indeed facilitate contracting. But it is difficult to say how significant such assistance will prove. Recall that it is a starting assumption of efficiency-based (and other utilitarian) theories of contract that, in general, the best way to facilitate mutual beneficial contracts is to leave the terms of contracts up to the parties (4.1). The parties are assumed to know better than the courts what is in their best interests. It follows that, while the facilitating contracts explanation is based on a normative value shared by efficiency theories (promoting utility), the explanation supposes that a major exception should be made to the general idea, also shared by such theories, that freedom of contract is the best way to achieve this value. To determine if this exception is justified, empirical data on the likelihood of contract breakdown is needed, as well as information about the relevant individuals' knowledge of the legal rules. Contracting parties cannot be influenced by rules of which they are unaware. This caveat is particularly important for understanding those cognitive asymmetry cases in which the disadvantaged parties' inexperience is such that they are also unlikely to be aware of their legal rights. Evidence of the likelihood that judges will apply unconscionability improperly is also required. So far as I am aware, there is no data available on these questions.

A second, and in my view more important objection to the facilitating contracts explanation is that it is inconsistent with what judges think they are doing when they strike down unconscionable contracts. Judges do not

---

[88] Belley (2003).

regard such cases as merely presenting an occasion for them to stipulate terms so as to facilitate future contracting. Instead, judges regard the dispute as requiring them to determine if something went wrong as between the parties before them, and then to try to resolve *that* problem. In other words, they regard the problem as one of justice, not utility. For theorists who think a good explanation of the law should be at least minimally consistent with how legal actors themselves understand what they are doing (a position I defend in 1.6), this is a serious objection. The one caveat is that this objection applies less strongly to certain of the legislative enactments in this area. Legislation is often understood by those passing it to be designed not to solve disputes, but instead to facilitate the smooth functioning of the economy. Certain of the legislation discussed above arguably fits this description (e.g., the *Unfair Terms in Consumer Contracts Regulations* 1994). Even in such cases, however, it may be queried whether judges who apply the legislation adopt this same perspective.

The wrongdoing explanation of unconscionability

In considering the remaining orthodox justifications for unconscionability, the distinction between plaintiff-based 'wrongdoing' justifications and defendant-based 'consent' justifications that I adopted in the earlier discussion of duress is again useful. As applied to unconscionability, the former justifications suppose that the courts' concern is, and should be, unconscionable *behaviour*. By contrast, the latter justifications suppose that the concern is, and should be, unconscionable *contracts*.

More specifically, the wrongdoing justification supposes that contracting parties who take advantage of other contracting parties' weaknesses or vulnerabilities have acted 'unconscionably', and are therefore wrongdoers. As such, they may legitimately be denied the court's assistance in enforcing their contractual claims (for reasons I explained earlier: 9.1.1).

This justification fits well with our ordinary reactions to unconscionable contracts. As I noted above, we normally condemn people who obtain advantages from others by means of unconscionable contracts. The very term 'unconscionable' implies as much. The same is true of the other terms typically used to describe such contracts, such as 'extortionate' or 'exploitative'. But the justification fits less well when we shift from considering our visceral reactions to unconscionable contracts to examining the actual behaviour that gives rise to such contracts. With respect to state of necessity cases, the objection to the wrongdoing explanation is that it is inconsistent with the common law principle that there is no obligation to assist persons in a state of necessity. Given this baseline, on what basis can it be concluded that a person who does offer assistance (even if at a high price) is a wrongdoer? An offer at a high price is preferable to no offer at all. Moreover, even if the common law did enforce a duty to assist (as is the case in certain civil law regimes),[89] this duty would almost certainly apply only to situations in which a person's life was endangered. It would not apply to cases in which the risk was to property rather than to persons (for example, where a house in a remote town is at risk of being flooded because of a broken pipe, and there is only one plumber in town). Yet situations of this kind qualify as states of necessity. The difference between them and rescue-at-sea cases is of degree, not kind.

Cases involving cognitive asymmetries differ from state of necessity cases in that the disadvantaged party is actually left worse off after contracting than they were before. But, again, it is difficult to regard the making of the offer—which is the only act that the advantaged party does—as a wrongful act. There is no duty to not make offers at a high price. I commit no wrong by offering my paperback copy of *Hamlet* for sale at a price of £1,000; no one is obliged to take up my offer. Just as there is no general duty to assist others in danger, so too there is no general duty to make only beneficial offers.

In response to these observations, it might be argued that, while there is no general duty to make offers at reasonable prices, it is wrong to make a high price offer when part of the very reason for doing so is the offeror's knowledge that the offeree is vulnerable. Thus, it might be said, while it is normally not wrongful to offer a paperback copy of *Hamlet* for £1,000, it is wrongful to do this in situations in which one knows that the offeree may mistakenly believe that £1,000 is the usual market price. In this view, the purpose of the blameworthiness requirement is precisely to establish that the defendant had such knowledge. As I noted above, this requirement is generally understood to be satisfied by the offeror's mere knowledge of the price and of the offeree's vulnerability.

The idea that an otherwise blameless act can be a legal wrong because of an 'unconscionable' motive raises difficult issues. On the one hand, it is uncontroversial that we take people's motives into account when we assess their characters. We say, for example, that the person who performs his contracts because he thinks he has a moral obligation to do so is a better person than one who performs only because he is worried

---

[89] Quebec Charter of Human Rights and Freedoms, Art. 2(2).

about his commercial reputation. Moreover, there exists an entire school of moral philosophy—'virtue ethics'—in which such assessments occupy a central role.[90] In broad terms, virtue ethics assesses actions in terms of their significance for the actor's attainment of virtues such as courage, wisdom, charity, honesty, and so on. On the other hand, questions of virtue (and motive) are generally disregarded by utilitarian and rights-based moral theories (4.1; 4.6). More importantly, they are generally disregarded by private law. Performance of a contract is performance regardless of the performer's motivations. The same is true of breach of contract. Indeed, contract law is generally indifferent even to the deliberateness of a breach (Chapter 10). In broad terms, this must be right: the role of the courts is not to provide general evaluations of peoples' characters. It is to dispense justice. And even if acting justly is itself a virtue (which seems plausible), the *content* of justice itself cannot easily be explained in these terms (11.1.1).

I conclude, then, that explaining a concern for unconscionability as a concern for unconscionable *behaviour* fits poorly with both positive contract law and the moral foundations of that law. This does not mean that courts are never influenced by such a concern. The view that people who take advantage of others deserve condemnation is widespread. More significantly, my brief comments about the difficulty of finding a clear normative foundation for such a concern cannot be regarded as determinative of the issue. The role, if any, for virtue ethics in private law is as yet a relatively unexplored topic. What can be said, however, is that the burden of explaining unconscionability on the basis of a concern for unconscionable behaviour lies upon those defending this view.

The consent-based explanation of unconscionability

The final justification to be considered is a consent-based justification. My explanation of this justification will be brief as it relies upon arguments that I presented, and defended, in my discussion above of duress.

The idea underlying the consent-based justification for unconscionability is that unconscionable contracts should not be enforced because the disadvantaged party did not consent *and* because the contract was substantively unfair. When these two conditions are satisfied, the result is that the contract unjustly enriches the plaintiff (in the form of an unjustly obtained contractual *right*)—which enrichment the courts

---

[90] e.g. Hursthouse (1999).

should reverse by refusing to enforce the contract. Unconscionability, in other words, is ultimately about the reversal of unjust enrichments.

The explanation of how this justification applies to state of necessity unconscionability cases was provided in the discussion of duress earlier in this chapter (9.1.2). My conclusion, recall, was that contracts entered into in a state of necessity are properly regarded as non-consensual. The same rescue-at-sea example that I have employed to illustrate state of necessity unconscionability cases was used in making this point. The argument, in brief, was that a rescue-at-sea contract is not consensual for the simple reason that the captain of the distressed ship had no choice. It was further argued that a non-consensual contract should be refused enforcement if —and only if—it is substantively unfair. The idea underlying this argument was that, while consent is not properly regarded as a prerequisite to a valid contract, the non-consensual creation of contractual rights can give rise to an unjust enrichment when those rights benefit one party at the expense of another—which happens when the rights are not equivalent in value. Assuming that these arguments are valid (as I concluded), a concern for consent and, ultimately, for reversing unjust enrichments, explains why courts should be concerned about state of necessity cases.

In the earlier discussion of duress cases, I focused exclusively on contracts made under pressure. Cognitive asymmetry cases were therefore not examined. But it seems possible, in theory at any rate, that a consent-based explanation of cognitive asymmetry cases might be constructed. The argument would be similar to the procedural fairness explanation of unconscionability presented above. Thus, it might be argued that evidence of substantive unfairness in cognitive asymmetry situations proves that the disadvantaged party did not truly consent to the agreement— say, because they did not understand, or were not aware of, the agreement's terms. The same substantive unfairness might then be used (as in the above explanation of state of necessity cases) to show that the non-consensual contract led to an unjust enrichment.

I will not explore this suggestion further. It is unnecessary to do so because insofar as disadvantaged parties did not consent in this way, it will also be the case that they did not actually *agree* to the relevant contracts (for reasons I explained in examining the procedural fairness explanation). And if they did not agree to the contract, then there is no contract to which they could consent or not consent. In short, the very arguments that might support a consent-based explanation of cognitive asymmetry cases make this explanation redundant. Insofar as these arguments are persuasive, they show that the relevant contracts should be set aside because they were not agreed to.

9.2.7. CONCLUSION TO UNCONSCIONABILITY

The main conclusion suggested by this discussion of possible justifications for setting aside unconscionable contracts is that no single justification can be applied to all such contracts. More specifically, I argued, first, that the best explanation for why courts should care about the category of cognitive asymmetry unconscionabilty cases is that these are cases of presumed procedural defects. These are cases, in other words, in which courts have good reason to be concerned about fraud, undue influence, duress, or a simple failure to agree, but in which they lack direct evidence of the defect. Evidence of substantive unfairness provides indirect confirmation that the relevant risk materialized.

My second main argument was that the best explanation for why courts should care about the other category of unconscionability cases, state of necessity cases, is that the combination of lack of consent and unfair terms exhibited by such contracts gives rise to unjust enrichments. Such contracts should therefore be set aside in order to reverse unjust enrichments. Confirming a conclusion I reached in my discussion of duress, this idea could be expressed in law by introducing a distinct defence of 'state of necessity'. Alternatively, it could be expressed by making clear that such relief as is now provided by situation-specific state of necessity doctrines (e.g., the rules on marine rescue contracts) is based on such a principle. The main point, however, is that 'no consent' should be recognized as a distinct explanation for why certain kinds of contracts should not be enforced.

A third and final conclusion is that, even accepting that there are good reasons for courts to carefully scrutinize contracts made in a state of necessity or in circumstances involving a cognitive asymmetry, courts should be cautious to act on such reasons. As we have seen, the extent to which either a 'state of necessity' or a 'cognitive asymmetry' exists is a matter of degree. In addition, the notion of substantive unfairness is not an easy one for a court to apply. These considerations help to explain why common law regimes have given mixed support to the idea of a general defence of unconscionability. But they also explain why even the application of situation specific defences based on the above concerns should be introduced, and applied, carefully.

9.3. MISTAKE

In Chapter 8, I argued that the rules on mistake can be explained as one part of the general rules for establishing the content of a contract. Understood in this way, these rules do not constitute a distinct law or excuse of 'mistake', properly speaking (which is why this explanation is not discussed in this chapter). Instead, when a contract is set aside for mistake it is because the contract contains an implied term stipulating that this should happen. From the perspective of this explanation of mistake, the main issue is whether such implied terms are *implied-in-law* (as the fairness and efficiency explanations assert) or *implied-in-fact* (as the interpretation explanation asserts).

But I also stated in Chapter 8 that none of the above explanations of mistake should be accepted before considering the alternative 'non-implied term' explanations. That task is taken up at this point. Specifically, the two most important non-implied term explanations for mistake are examined in this section: (1) the no-agreement explanation and (2) the no-consent explanation. In addition, I will also say something about misrepresentation, changed circumstances, and discharge for breach.

Before examining the no-agreement and no-consent explanations, something must be said briefly about the rules they seek to explain. As in Chapter 8, the law relating to mistake is defined here as that which applies to cases involving 'mistaken assumptions', in particular, to mistaken assumptions not caused by the other party's misrepresentation. Mistaken assumptions, in turn, are mistakes that relate to the existence, quality, or characteristics of the object of a contractual obligation. Examples of mistaken assumptions might therefore include a belief that a piece of land for sale was zoned commercial when in fact it was zoned residential or a belief that a particular painting for sale was by a minor artist when in fact it was by an old master (as in Chapter 8, I limit myself to sale contracts, but the analysis can be generalized). Cases involving mistaken assumptions (not caused by the other party) are decided in the common law according to the rules regarding 'common' (or 'mutual') mistake. The basic rule is that a contract can be set aside only if the relevant mistake was shared and of fundamental importance.[91] This test is rarely satisfied.

The primary significance of defining mistake cases in this (traditional) way is that three categories of cases that are sometimes thought to raise

---

[91] *Bell v Lever Bros Ltd* [1932] AC 161.

similar issues are not included: cases involving changed circumstances (frustration), cases involving agreement mistakes, and cases involving mistakes caused by misrepresentations. Cases involving changed circumstances are discussed later in this chapter. The other two categories——cases involving agreement mistakes and cases involving mistakes caused by misrepresentations—are discussed briefly below. Aside from being important in their own right, the issues raised by these two categories are important in understanding the law relating to mistaken assumptions.

9.3.1. AGREEMENT MISTAKES

Agreement mistakes fall into three main categories: (1) mistakes as to whether one is entering a contract at all (e.g., thinking that an offer to sell is a mere invitation to negotiate), (2) mistakes as to the terms included in the contract (e.g., thinking a contract term says '£1,000' when it actually says '£100'),[92] and (3) mistakes as to the identity of the subject matter of a contract (e.g., thinking that an agreement to purchase 'the painting in the front window of Mr. Jones' store' was actually an agreement to purchase the painting in the front window of the store next door).

The rules regarding agreement mistakes are sometimes portrayed as one part of a distinct 'law of mistake',[93] but this seems misleading. Although one or both of the parties in a case involving an agreement mistake may have been mistaken as to the intentions of the other party, or the meaning of a particular statement or action, what matters from the law's perspective is not whether a mistake has happened, but whether the parties have reached an agreement. The relevant question (as I explained in 5.2.1) is whether an offer was made, and, if so, whether it was matched by an acceptance. That a mistake was made may explain *why* a particular offer and acceptance did not match, but no legal principles aside from those pertaining to offer and acceptance are needed to explain why courts sometimes refuse to enforce 'agreements' that involve agreement mistakes. Consistent with this conclusion, agreement mistakes are discussed in more detail in Chapter 5.

---

[92] Although I cannot defend the claim here, it is suggested that cases involving mistaken identities also fall into this category. The personal nature of promissory liability (3.1.1) means that a mistake as to the promisee's identity precludes a promissory obligation arising at all. This conclusion is consistent with the rule that a mistake as to identity, where operative, renders a contract void *ab initio*, that is to say, it prevents a contract from being formed at all: Treitel (1995) 274.

[93] e.g. Treitel (1995) 274.

From the perspective of this chapter's concerns, the main issue concerning agreement mistakes is whether a mistaken assumption can be understood as just another example of an agreement mistake—and so explained on similar grounds. As we shall see, this is precisely the argument made by the no-agreement explanation of mistaken assumptions, which I discuss below.

9.3.2. MISTAKES CAUSED BY MISREPRESENTATIONS

In contrast to agreement mistake cases, misrepresentation cases typically do involve mistaken assumptions. The difference between misrepresentation cases and ordinary mistaken assumptions cases is that in the former the mistaken assumption is caused by the other contracting party, while in the latter it is self-induced. The common law draws a clear distinction between these two categories. In contrast to the narrow grounds on which relief is granted in cases involving ordinary mistaken assumptions, the general rule in cases in which a person is induced to enter a contract by a misrepresentation is that the contract may be set aside.[94] Significantly, it does not matter whether the misrepresentation was intentional, negligent, or innocent; nor does it matter whether the mistake was related to an essential feature of the contract.[95]

For present purposes, the main point to make about misrepresentation cases is that, with one exception, they are explicable on the basis of the same wrongdoing principle that I argued helps to explain the law of duress (9.1.1). To fraudulently or negligently mislead another is, and is clearly recognized by tort law to be, wrongful. On this basis, a court may deny a plaintiff's request to enforce a contractual right that was obtained by a fraudulent or negligent misrepresentation on the same basis that it may deny such a request when the contractual right was obtained by the plaintiff's wrongful threat. In each case, the plaintiff is a wrongdoer.[96]

The exception is where the misrepresentation is caused by a non-intentional and non-negligent misrepresentation (an 'innocent' misrepresentation). The mistaken party's right to rescind the contract in such cases cannot be explained using the wrongdoing principle because the plaintiff is not a wrongdoer. Indeed, there is no straightforward explanation of this area of the law. The relevant mistake is not typically serious enough, *qua* mistake, to justify setting aside the contract for this

---

[94] *Edgington v Fitzmaurice* (1885) 29 Ch D 459.

[95] The right to rescission for innocent misrepresentation has been limited in the UK by the *Misrepresentation Act* 1967, s.2 (2).

[96] For judicial support, see e.g., *Redgrave v Hurd* (1881) 20 Ch D 1, 12–13.

reason. Admittedly, it was the plaintiff who *caused* the mistake. It might seem to follow that, as between the two innocent parties (the plaintiff and the defendant), the plaintiff should be responsible for any harm caused by the mistake. But if this argument is valid here, why is it rejected elsewhere in the law? The general rule is that, absent wrongdoing, losses are left to lie where they fall.

I offer no solution to the above puzzle. But I will suggest that insofar as a solution can be found, it will be grounded in the difference between making persons *liable* for the consequences of their innocent actions (i.e., liable to pay damages or to perform) and *denying* to persons benefits that were obtained by virtue of their innocent actions (i.e., denying enforcement). Without going into detail, it seems clear that the kind of argument needed to justify the former is different than that needed to justify the latter. Ordering damages is more serious than refusing to enforce a contract.[97] Indeed, given that respectable arguments can be made for general strict liability in tort law,[98] it would be surprising if strong arguments could not be developed for 'strict loss-of-benefits'.

9.3.3. MISTAKEN ASSUMPTIONS

Aside from the efficiency, fairness, and interpretation explanations examined in Chapter 8, the main explanations of the rules relating to mistaken assumptions are what I have called the no-agreement and the no-consent explanations. Each is examined below.

The no-agreement explanation

One possible explanation of mistake cases is that relief is granted when, and because, the parties did not reach an actual agreement. In this view, mistaken assumptions are a kind of agreement mistake. More specifically, the parties are regarded as not reaching agreement because, despite superficially appearing to agree to sell a particular thing, they were actually agreeing to sell a different thing. According to this explanation, therefore, a painting that is the subject of a sale contract may be counted as a 'different thing' from what the parties supposed they were buying

---

[97] The discretion given to English judges by the *Misrepresentation Act* 1967 s.2 (2) to substitute damages for recission in cases of innocent misrepresentation might be thought to contradict this point. But on closer inspection s.2 (2) confirms the point. Damages are given in lieu of rescission precisely in those case in which rescission would effectively penalize the plaintiff's behaviour because, say, the plaintiff had incurred significant reliance expenses. By awarding damages, the court therefore reduces the penalty.

[98] Epstein (1973).

and selling if, contrary to their assumptions, it was by a minor artist rather than by Rembrandt. Judicial support for this view can arguably be found in Lord Atkin's famous statement in *Bell v Lever Bros*[99] that an operative mistake must make the thing contracted for 'essentially different' from that which the parties had assumed.

Insofar as the no-agreement explanation is meant to explain the law actually in force, an immediate objection is that it is inconsistent with the rule that a mistaken assumption must be shared to ground relief. From the perspective of the no-agreement explanation, a unilateral mistake as to the identity of the very thing that is the subject of the contract should be operative, at least in cases in which the mistake was known to the other party. This is the rule that is applied to ordinary agreement mistakes (5.2.1), and if mistaken assumptions are equivalent to agreement mistakes, there is no reason to apply a different rule.

But the more important objection to the no-agreement explanation is a substantive objection. According to the no-agreement explanation, contracting parties may be agreed as to the terms of their contract, that is to say, as to the descriptions of their respective obligations, yet still not be agreed about what those obligations are. The explanation therefore supposes that, even though, say, a purchaser and a vendor agreed that the purchaser is buying *this* painting (identified by its location on a gallery wall), because they were mistaken about the painting's provenance, they may not have agreed to the sale of the painting on wall. The obvious difficulty with this suggestion is that it flies in the face of the common sense view that the parties were actually agreed as to which painting was the object of their contract. Agreement mistakes and mistaken assumptions, in other words, just *are* different. Agreement mistakes (in this context) are mistakes about the identity of a thing; mistaken assumptions are mistakes about a thing's attributes. While recognizing that in some cases this distinction is difficult to draw,[100] it is a basic assumption of ordinary language and thinking that the distinction exists. A purchaser who agrees 'to buy the painting on the wall' might think she should not be bound by her agreement if the painting turns out to be a fake rather than the Rembrandt she had thought it was. But her argument would not be that she did not agree to buy 'the painting on the wall'. The painting on the wall is the same painting regardless of whether or not Rembrandt painted it.

---

[99] *Bell v Lever Bros* [1932] AC 161, 218.
[100] e.g. *Smith v Hughes* (1871) LR 6 QB 597

I conclude, therefore, that the no-agreement explanation has difficulty explaining both mistake cases in which relief is refused and mistake cases in which relief is granted. The explanation must be rejected.

The no-consent explanation

The no-consent explanation of mistake cases supposes that when contracts are set aside for mistake it is because the parties did not consent to the contract. In contrast to the no-agreement explanation, which analogizes mistake cases to cases involving agreement mistakes and, more broadly, to offer and acceptance cases, the no-consent explanation thus analogizes mistake cases to cases involving duress, undue influence, and other so-called 'defects of consent'. More specifically, and drawing on the same reasoning that distinguishes duress issues from offer and acceptance issues (namely the idea that duress is not inconsistent with true agreement: 9.1.2), this explanation supposes that parties who have reached an agreement (i.e., matching offers and acceptances) should be released from their agreement if those offers or acceptances were not made consensually. It further supposes (here following orthodox French legal doctrine)[101] that one way consent may be vitiated is by a mistaken assumption.

Of the five main explanations of the law relating to mistake, the no-consent explanation is unique in providing a straightforward explanation for the orthodox view that mistake is a distinct legal excuse and, more generally, for the view that there exists a 'law of mistake'. According to the no-consent explanation, a law of mistake is needed for the same reason that a law of duress is needed. Each focuses upon a distinct way in which consent may be vitiated. Neither can be reduced to offer and acceptance rules, or rules relating to implied terms.

But in other respects the no-consent explanation is less persuasive. One obvious difficulty is that like the no-agreement explanation, the no-consent explanation cannot explain why the common law refuses relief for unilateral mistakes, even when the mistake is known by the other party. If consent matters, lack of consent by just one party should be a sufficient ground for relief. The law does not require that duress or undue influence be shared.

A second, more basic, objection to the no-consent explanation is that regarding consent to a promise (or an agreement) as conditional on the consent being 'informed' seems inconsistent with the very notion of a

---

[101] Ghestin (1993) 455ff.

promise.[102] As we have seen (3.1.1.), it is of the essence of a promise that it replaces the ordinary reasons for and against doing the promised act (e.g., that the promise is or is not useful or valuable, etc.). The promised act should be performed simply because the promise was made. It follows that the fact that a promisor later regrets the promise (say because she had made a mistake) is, by definition, not a valid reason not to do the promised act. If I have promised to lend my car to Ann next Saturday, I should lend Ann the car even if I later regret the promise. Permitting a no-consent excuse is inconsistent, then, with the very meaning of promises. Stated differently, promisors are aware when they promise that they have limited knowledge, and they necessarily regard this knowledge as sufficient; promisors effectively waive the need for their consent to be informed. To deny this is to deny the very possibility of promissory obligations.

For these reasons, I conclude that the no-consent explanation of mistake must also be rejected. The explanation is inconsistent both with the nature of promises and with the basic requirements of a defence of mistake.

9.3.4. CONCLUSION TO MISTAKE

The conclusion of this section—that the no-agreement and no-consent explanations are unpersuasive—confirms the conclusion I tentatively reached in Chapter 8 regarding the fairness, efficiency, and interpretation explanations of mistake. While acknowledging that none of these explanations explain the law perfectly, I argued that each provides a prima facie plausible explanation of the law's main features. Lacking a superior alternative, those explanations now stand out as the most persuasive. The overall conclusion to this and the previous chapter with respect to mistake cases is therefore that mistake cases are best explained on the basis of rules for establishing the content of a contract.

9.4. CHANGED CIRCUMSTANCES (FRUSTRATION) AND DISCHARGE FOR BREACH

From a theoretical perspective, claims that a contract should be set aside for changed circumstances ('frustration') or because the other party

---

[102] I note that the special role promises and agreements play in contract law helps to explain why consent is understood differently in unjust enrichment law, as well as in the law regarding consent to medical operations.

committed a breach ('discharge for breach') raise similar issues to claims of mistake. In each case, the claim appears to be one to set aside a prima facie valid contract for reasons unrelated either to the content of the contract or to the way in which it was created.

Consistent with this observation, explanations of the theoretical foundations of the law of frustration and discharge for breach are similar to those that have been given for the law on mistake. Thus, one explanation is that cases in which contracts are set aside for changed circumstances or breach are explicable on the basis that the contracts contained implied terms to this effect. The different variants of this explanation that exist (e.g., efficiency-based, fairness-based, and interpretation-based) were discussed in Chapter 8. I will say nothing more about them here.

As regards 'non-implied term' explanations of frustration and discharge for breach, there is nothing directly equivalent to the no-agreement and no-consent explanations of mistake; the rules on frustration and discharge for breach focus on post-formation events and agreement and consent are determined at the time of formation. But there are explanations of frustration and discharge for breach that are similar to the no-agreement and no-consent explanations in that they suppose the relevant rules are rules for establishing the validity, rather than the content, of a contract. I briefly examine two such explanations below.

9.4.1. FRUSTRATION AND BREACH AS 'DESTROYING THE FOUNDATIONS' OF A CONTRACT

It is sometimes said that the effect of a frustrating event is to remove or 'destroy' the very foundations of a contract. Though often presented merely as a *test* for frustration (e.g., as one part of a test for establishing implied-in-fact terms), this idea is sometimes thought to provide a *justification* for the doctrine. Thus, in one leading case the court explained its decision to set aside a contract on the basis that 'the foundation of what the parties are deemed to have had in contemplation has disappeared, and the contract itself has vanished with that foundation'.[103] This same idea might also be applied to discharge for breach cases; substantial non-performance by one party could be said to destroy the foundation of the contract.

As a metaphor or image, the idea of a contract's foundations being destroyed is interesting. But as a justification, it begs the question: what

---

[103] *Tamplin SS Co v Anglo-Mexican Petroleum Co* [1916] 2 AC 397, 406; see also *W. J. Tatem Ltd v Gamboa* [1939] 1 KB 132, 137.

does it mean, in concrete terms, for a contract's 'foundations' to be destroyed? Contracts do not have foundations in any usual sense of this term. More specifically, there is nothing in the tests for the formation of a contract that refer to a foundation or anything similar. In the common law, contracts do, of course, require consideration. But with the exception of unilateral contracts, consideration is shown by making a promise, not by doing something. Moreover, a frustrating event or serious breach often only causes the loss of part of the benefit of a contract (and so the consideration requirement would still be fulfillled). Finally, given that the most plausible rationalia for the consideration doctrine focus upon the formation and initial validity of a contract (the 'formal' justification: 6.3), its purpose is served regardless of whether a frustrating event or serious breach occurs.

9.4.2. BREACH AS AN OFFER TO TERMINATE

The theoretical foundations of the rule that a contract may be set aside on the basis that one party committed a serious breach has been little explored in common law legal scholarship. But one explanation sometimes advanced is that a party that commits a significant breach has, in effect, made an offer to terminate the contract.[104] If this offer is accepted, the contract is then terminated by agreement. The breaching party has offered to end the contract, and the victim of breach accepts this offer by declaring the contract over (or simply refusing to perform). This explanation of discharge for breach may be regarded as the converse of the no-agreement explanation of mistake. The latter supposes that mistake cases are explicable on the basis that the parties failed to reach an agreement at all; this explanation supposes that discharge for breach cases are explicable on the basis that the parties made a subsequent agreement to set aside their contract.

From a normative perspective, this suggestion is unimpeachable. It is clear that a contract may be set aside on the ground that the parties agreed to set it aside. But the question is whether such agreements have, as a matter of fact, been reached in cases in which contracts are set aside for breach. The short answer would appear to be that in many, if not most, such cases no such agreement has been made. It is just not true, as a matter of fact, that parties who commit breaches of the kind sufficient to support termination (i.e., serious breaches) are always offering to terminate the contract. Rather, it seems clear that such parties often wish the

---

[104] Cheshire, Fifoot and Furmston (2001) 601.

contract to stay alive. We know this because such parties often dispute the innocent party's right to terminate. For this reason, I conclude that, like the idea of a breach destroying a contract's foundations, the idea that a breach is an 'offer to terminate' is a kind of metaphor. From the law's perspective, the breach is regarded *as if* it were an offer to terminate. But it is not actually such an offer.

9.4.3. CONCLUSION TO FRUSTRATION AND DISCHARGE FOR BREACH

The conclusion suggested by these admittedly brief comments on frustration and discharge for breach is the same one that I reached with respect to the law of mistake; it is that implied term explanations of this area of law (which explanations I discussed and defended in Chapter 8) are more persuasive than the alternatives. A further conclusion is that mistake cases, frustration cases, and discharge for breach cases all raise substantively similar issues.[105] In contrast to the explanations discussed in this chapter, which draw a clear distinction between mistake, frustration, and discharge for breach (on the basis that the first is about formation and the latter two about termination), the implied term explanations defended in Chapter 8 explain all three categories on the basis of similar concerns about either fairness, efficiency, or interpretation.

9.5. CONCLUSION

In the introduction to this chapter, I stated that what the doctrines of duress, unconscionability, mistake, frustration, and discharge for breach have in common is that each is potentially explicable on the basis that it provides for setting aside a contract for reasons unrelated either to the existence or content of the relevant agreement. Each of these doctrines, in other words, is potentially a true excuse doctrine. But I also noted that one of the main tasks of the chapter would be to determine if all of these doctrines are, in the end, best explained in this way. The conclusion to that inquiry, it should now be clear, is a mixed one. On the one hand, I have argued that duress does, indeed, qualify as a clear excuse doctrine. Duress cases can, in general, be explained either on the basis of an external-to-contract wrongdoing principle or an external-to-contract consent principle (though certain duress cases are explicable only on the basis of one of these principles). On the other hand, mistake, frustration,

---

[105] McKendrick (1997) 282–84; Trebilcock (1993) 127–46; Collins (1997) 277–78.

and discharge for breach, cannot easily be explained on the basis of these or any other external principles. Rather, the internal-to-contract explanation of these doctrines that I defended in Chapter 8—namely that they give effect to implied-in-fact or implied-in-law contractual terms—was confirmed as the most persuasive explanation.

As for the difficult notion of unconscionability, I concluded that there are important differences between the kinds of contracts to which this label is typically applied. In particular, what I described as 'state of necessity' unconscionability cases are best explained in terms of the same consent-based concerns that also arise (I argued) in most duress cases, which concerns are themselves grounded in a deeper principle of reversing unjust enrichments. I further concluded that it might be clearer if such concerns were understood as flowing from a distinct 'state of necessity' principle as opposed to being given expression, as happens now, under the labels of duress and unconscionability. If this were done, duress would henceforth be understood as grounded exclusively in a concern for wrongdoing. The other main category of unconscionability cases, cognitive asymmetry cases, raises a variety of concerns. In some cases in this category, the issue is whether an agreement was reached at all; in others, the issue is whether there was duress, fraud, or undue influence. These are cases, in other words, of either 'presumed' failure of agreement (i.e., offer and acceptance cases), or of presumed duress, fraud, or undue influence (i.e., cases about wrongdoing or lack of consent). In the end, the only thing that links the various categories of (so-called) unconscionable contracts is that it is difficult to formulate clear principles to explain when relief is appropriate. The main reason for this difficulty is that the extent to which a contract was formed in a state of necessity or in a situation of cognitive asymmetry is a matter of degree.

10

Breach of Contract: The Puzzle of Strict Liability

The topic of 'breach of contract' has received relatively little attention in contract textbooks and even less attention in theoretical discussions of contract law. In the case of contract textbooks, this is not surprising. According to the orthodox view, the law in this area can be summarized in one sentence: contracts must be performed strictly according to their terms.[1] Assuming the contract or contractual obligation is valid, the only legal issue raised by an alleged breach of contract is whether the contract actually requires the defendant to do what it is alleged she should have done. This is a question of contract interpretation, the answer to which is determined primarily on the basis of factual evidence.

The silence on this topic on the part of contract theorists *is* surprising. This is mainly because it is far from obvious why contractual liability is strict. In tort law, the general rule is that liability is fault-based. The defendant is required to pay compensatory damages only if he caused the relevant loss intentionally or by acting carelessly. If the defendant is blameless, the loss is left to lie where it falls. Why, then, is a different standard applied to contractual obligations?[2] A related point is that a strict liability standard is inconsistent with what courts say about the morality of breaching a contract. If breaching a contract is considered to be a wrong and plaintiffs are regarded as presenting complaints against defendants in contract cases, then the standard for liability should not be

---

[1] 'It is axiomatic that, in relation to a claim for damages for breach of contract, it is, in general, immaterial why the defendant failed to fulfill his obligations, and certainly no defence to plead that he has done his best': Lord Edmund Davies in *Rainieri v Miles* [1981] AC 1050, 1086.

[2] In this regard, it is interesting that in civil law systems liability for breach of contract typically is subject, in principle anyway, to the same fault standard as liability in tort: e.g. Art. 276 German Civil Code (BGB); Nicholas (1992) 31. In practice, the results are similar to those seen in common law systems because civil law systems typically go on to state that in many categories of contracts a failure to achieve the promised result constitutes 'fault'. This approach thus gives rise to the same puzzle described above because it is not clear how a (mere) failure to achieve a result can count as a fault.

strict. To state that someone is a wrongdoer is to find some degree of fault in that person's behaviour—to regard the breacher as blameworthy. But neither fault nor blame is required by a strict liability standard.

This chapter considers possible answers to the question of why courts apply a different standard of liability in contract cases than in tort cases (if this is indeed what they do). The chapter is organized around two broad categories of such answers: (1) explanations that challenge the question's normative premises, and (2) explanations that challenge the question's factual premises. Explanations in the first group argue that the question's normative premise that a strict liability standard is prima facie unjustified (i.e., that strict liability is normatively suspect) is incorrect. By contrast, explanations in the second group argue that question's factual premise (i.e., that contract and tort law actually apply different standards of liability) is incorrect. I conclude that only one of the explanations in the second group—the 'conjunctive obligation' explanation— provides a satisfactory solution to the puzzle of strict liability.

10.1. DEFENDING STRICT LIABILITY

Explanations of strict liability within the first group argue that it is wrong to assume that just because tort law applies a fault standard there is something normatively puzzling about strict liability in contract law. More specifically, this group of explanations argues that strict liability is, in principle, morally appropriate. In theory, both a radical and a moderate version of this argument are possible. The radical version states that strict liability is appropriate *generally* in the law of obligations (i.e., both in contract law *and* in tort law). In this view, and contrary to the assumption of my initial question, there is nothing odd about strict liability in contract. Rather, what is odd is that tort law has not followed the lead of contract. I will not discuss this argument further. Though a theoretical possibility, it has rarely been defended,[3] or even seriously examined except as a position to attack.[4] Most tort theorists defend the standard of reasonable care, and they do this regardless of their broader moral commitments (e.g., whether they generally defend rights-based[5] or utilitarian[6] moralities).

The moderate, and more common, version of this argument accepts that a fault standard is appropriate for tort cases, but then argues that a

---

[3] Epstein (1973).   [4] e.g. Perry (1988); Weinrib (1995) 171–203.
[5] e.g. Weinrib (1995) 171–203.   [6] e.g. Posner (1998) 179–84.

strict liability standard is appropriate in contract cases because they are different from tort cases. Two sub-versions of this argument are possible; each is examined below.

IO.I.I. CONTRACT LAW VINDICATES PROPERTY RIGHTS

One possible explanation for why strict liability is, in principle justified in contract law is that contract law is essentially about *directly enforcing* (or 'vindicating') property rights.[7] According to this view, courts are essentially determining who owns what in contract cases, and then telling non-owners to give the owners what they own. That the non-owner may not be at fault is therefore irrelevant. If I accidentally take your umbrella, I have to give it back; it is no defence that I made an entirely innocent mistake or even that you were at fault for leaving your umbrella where you did. On the same basis, it might be argued that if I have sold goods to you and failed to deliver them, regardless of the reason for non-delivery, the goods belong to you and I must give them to you. It makes no difference that I am at fault for the non-delivery.

The vindication of property rights explanation raises interesting conceptual issues about the extent to which contractual rights resemble ordinary property rights (3.1.3; 3.4). But these issues may be sidestepped here, because, even it is accepted that contractual rights are just like ordinary property rights, the vindication of property rights explanation of strict liability is vulnerable to an obvious objection. The objection is that this account explains only why fault should not be a pre-condition to an order of specific performance; it does not explain why fault should not matter when courts are ordering damages. When courts order specific performance, at least in cases involving sale contracts, they can plausibly be regarded as doing just what this explanation supposes courts do in contract cases—vindicating property rights. The court is ordering the defendant to give the plaintiff a specific object or a specific piece of property. Assuming this understanding of specific performance is correct, then fault should not be a pre-condition to the making of such awards; the plaintiff is not being asked to repair the consequences of her wrongdoing, but merely to perform her primary contractual obligation. But damages orders are different; an order of damages *is* an order that the

---

[7] It is difficult to find authors who advance this argument explicitly, although hints of it can be seen in authors who adopt the 'transfer' theory of contract (the view that contracts are transfers of existing property rights): e.g. Benson (2001) 134. A version of this argument is, however, the usual explanation for why the duties enforced by unjust enrichment law are strict: Birks (1999; 2000); Smith (2001b)

defendant repair the effects of her breach (by paying compensation). Damages are a personal, not proprietary, remedy. The vindication of property rights explanation cannot explain, therefore, why it is not a pre-condition to the making of such orders that the defendant be found to have been at fault in failing to perform. Compensatory orders serve the same basic function regardless of whether the underlying duty was created by agreement (contract) or imposed by the general law (tort).

The vindication of property rights explanation of strict liability is relatively easy to dismiss. But examining it is useful because it makes clearer the precise nature of the puzzle posed by strict liability. The puzzle relates specifically to the apparent difference between contract and tort with respect to the standards of care applied in evaluating a claim for *damages*. Thus, the puzzle does not arise (or at least it is not obvious that it arises) in cases in which breach is pleaded in support of a claim for specific performance. As we have just seen, specific performance is argu-ably explicable as a method of vindicating property rights, and as such is, in principle, consistent with strict liability (whether specific performance should actually be regarded in this way, and whether fault is in practice irrelevant, are issues that I discuss in 11.2).[8] Nor, it may be added, does a puzzle arise in those cases in which it is claimed that a breach gives grounds for the termination or rescission of a contract. In such cases, it is prima facie appropriate to define breach using a strict liability standard because the party claiming that a breach has occurred is not requesting compensation for the breach; rather, she is arguing that a condition precedent to her own performance has not been fulfilled (i.e., perform-ance of the other party's contractual obligation). In assessing such an argument, it is irrelevant why the condition is not fulfilled.

10.1.2. STRICT LIABILITY IS SELF-IMPOSED (THE 'IMPLIED AGREEMENT' EXPLANATION)

The more common justification for a strict liability standard in contract explains the standard on the ground that contracting parties themselves have implicitly agreed to it. According to what I shall call the 'implied agreement explanation' of strict liability, it is fair, in principle, to impose such a standard because, aside from contracts with professionals, etc., contracting parties understand and intend that their liability should be

---

[8] In this regard, it is important to keep in mind that certain monetary awards are arguably best understood as a form of specific performance. I discuss this possibility further below and in Chapter 11. For present purposes, it is sufficient to note that not all monetary awards can be interpreted in this way.

strict. One way this explanation is expressed is through the idea that contractual liability is strict because one of the functions of a contract is to allocate risk. A rule of strict liability, it is said, respects the parties' decision as to how to allocate the risk of a particular event happening or not happening. A second way this explanation is expressed is through the idea that contractual liability is strict because it is based on a promise. The defendant promised that a certain thing would be done. It follows that if the promised thing is not done, the defendant is at fault and should be liable for the consequences.

The implied agreement explanation of strict liability has an obvious attraction; it grounds strict liability in the familiar and broadly accepted idea that contractual obligations are determined by the parties' intentions. But the explanation is vulnerable to two objections.

The first, less important, objection is that this explanation does not explain why courts describe breach of contract as a wrong. The fact that a defendant may have agreed to a strict liability standard does not change what would otherwise be an innocent non-performance into a faulty non-performance. If the defendant acted blamelessly when he failed to perform, then he acted blamelessly even if he signed a contract that stated 'liability under this contract is strict.' My saying 'any innocent mistakes that I make in the future are my fault' does not make this true. Indeed, the statement is conceptually incoherent. I can consent to be treated *as if* I was at fault, but I cannot actually change the meaning of 'fault' (or 'blameworthy', 'wrong', etc.). If defendants in breach of contract cases are not at fault, why are they described (and treated) as wrongdoers?

This question leads me to the second, and more fundamental, objection to the idea that strict liability is justified, in principle, because contracting parties have impliedly agreed to strict liability. The objection is that it is not actually possible to agree to be strictly liable for non-performance. Let me explain. The idea that contracting parties implicitly agree to a strict liability standard could mean either of two things. One possible meaning is that the parties have agreed to change the very meaning of what counts as 'fault', such that innocent non-performance is regarded as faulty non-performance. This interpretation, as I have already noted, is conceptually incoherent. The meaning of fault cannot be changed by agreement. Of course, it is possible to change the *content* of our obligations by agreement. We can agree, for example, that I should deliver promised goods on Friday rather than Wednesday. But it is conceptually impossible to agree that, say, if I am late in delivering on Friday *despite* using all reasonable care, etc., I am at fault for this non-performance. If contracting parties use reasonable care, etc., in attempting to fulfill their obligations, then nothing they said previously can make their failure to perform a faulty act.

A second possible interpretation of what it means to agree to strict liability is that it means to agree to be treated *as if* non-performance implied fault. Agreeing to strict liability means, in other words, that contracting parties have agreed that they will compensate one another in the event of innocent non-performance. This interpretation raises no conceptual difficulties. It regards contracting parties as promising, in effect, to act as insurers for any losses that might arise through their own innocent non-performance. Whether made explicitly or implicitly, this kind of contractual undertaking is unproblematic. Moreover, and as I explain in more detail below (10.2.2), it is reasonable to conclude that promissory obligations, in general, are actually understood in this way (i.e., as including a 'secondary' obligation to compensate in the case of innocent non-performance of the 'primary' obligation).

But this second way of explaining the implied agreement justification is also open to a serious objection: it is that the explanation does not actually provide a justification of *strict liability*. To justify strict liability it must be shown that a failure to perform a contractual undertaking is, regardless of the reason, a sufficient ground to require the non-performing party to pay compensatory damages. But according to the explanation now being considered, the justification for requiring defendants to pay compensation in cases in which their non-performance was innocent is that they actually *agreed* to make such a payment. Yet if they agreed to such payments, then requiring them to actually make the payments cannot be explained as damages for *breach* of contract. Rather, the payment is simply performance of the second part of the defendant's contractual undertaking. Of course, the defendant might also fail to perform this second contractual obligation. A court order to pay damages might therefore be explained on the ground that damages are being awarded in order to compensate for the consequences of the defendant's failure to perform a contractual undertaking to compensate. This is a plausible argument; indeed, I argue below that it is crucial to understanding damages (10.2.2). But again, it is not a justification for strict liability. In the context of a contractual obligation to compensate, such a justification would need to show why *that* obligation should be subject to a strict liability standard. The only justification the implied agreement approach can offer is the same one I just rejected—namely that the parties have agreed to this standard.

The implied agreement justification for strict liability introduced a number of interesting arguments. Some of these arguments turn out to be important (I will argue below) in explaining strict liability. Overall, however, my conclusion is that this second approach to justifying strict liability is also unconvincing. Strict liability cannot be self-imposed.

10.2. CHALLENGING THE ASSUMPTION OF STRICT LIABILITY

Recall that the puzzle of strict liability is why courts apply this standard to contractual obligations when they do not apply it to tort obligations. The first attempt to solve this puzzle argues that strict liability is appropriate in contract law because contractual obligations are different from tort obligations. As we have just seen, this argument is not convincing. The second attempt, which I consider now, focuses on the *factual* premises of the puzzle. More specifically, explanations in this second category argue that it is wrong to assume that a different standard of liability is actually applied in contract than in tort.

In theory, two versions of this explanation—a tort centered version and a contract centered version—are possible. The tort centered version argues that, from the perspective of tort law, strict liability is not a puzzle because tort law itself often imposes strict liability. Strict liability is applied, for example, in claims based on vicarious liability, liability under *Rylands v Fletcher*, and in certain instances of products liability. Thus, the argument concludes, there is nothing odd about contract also doing this (or if there is something odd, it is an oddity that tort law shares equally). This argument provides a useful reminder that tort law is not uniform in its treatment of liability issues. But as an attempt to explain away the apparent anomaly of contractual strict liability, it can be dealt with quickly. The instances of strict liability in tort, though not insignificant, are exceptional, and are recognized as such. There is nothing comparable in tort law to the general standard of strict liability allegedly applied in contract law. In addition, it seems clear, without going into detail, that the particular circumstances that are alleged to justify such exceptions to the general rule in tort (e.g., the relevant activity is abnormally dangerous, the defendant is better able to spread or absorb the risk, the defendant is a commercial enterprise, the defendant is more experienced in litigation, or the defendant controls the relevant evidence)[9] only sometimes arise in

---

[9] e.g. Calabresi and Hirschoff (1972); Epstein (1973); Fletcher (1972).

contract cases.[10] None of these circumstances are a general feature of contractual relations—as would be necessary to justify a general rule of strict liability.

The contract centered version of this explanation is the more important one. It argues that the puzzle of strict liability disappears once it is recognized that contractual liability is not actually strict; rather contractual liability, like tort liability, is fault-based. There are (yet again) two sub-versions of this argument.

10.2.1. LEGAL LIMITS ON STRICT LIABILITY

The more common version of this argument is that contractual liability is not strict, or at least not always strict, because there exist the excuses of frustration and impossibility, and more importantly, because many contractual obligations are, in practice, obligations to use reasonable care.[11] For example, contractual obligations entered into by lawyers, doctors, and other professionals are, in the usual case anyway, said to be obligations to use reasonable care. The doctor is not liable in contract for failing to fix the plaintiff's nose unless she either failed to do the promised operation altogether or did it carelessly. In such cases, the standards applied in tort and in contract appear to be identical.

In assessing this argument, one could debate the extent to which frustration and impossibility are based on a notion of fault (very little in my view: 8.3.8). One could also debate the extent to which contractual duties to use reasonable care derive from the court's concern for fault considerations as opposed to merely reflecting the content of the parties' (actual) agreement for which they are then held strictly liable (see 8.1.2 for arguments supporting the latter view).[12] But it is not necessary to enter these debates because it is clear that, however they are resolved, the excuses of frustration and impossibility, together with the existence of contractual duties to use reasonable care, do not establish that a fault standard is generally or even widely applied in contract law. Pleas of frustration or impossibility are rarely successful. More to the point, it is clearly insufficient in order to establish such a plea, merely to show that the defendant was not at fault for non-performance. As for contractual duties to use reasonable care, while such duties are found in respect of certain

---

[10] More precisely, none of these arguments could justify general strict liability in contract without at the same time justifying general strict liability in tort—which would lead us back to the normative argument (considered and rejected above) that strict liability is the appropriate standard generally in private law.
[11] Nicholas (1995).   [12] On which, see Nicholas (1995).

contracts, this is the exception rather than the rule. The standard contract of sale or loan, for example, is regarded as subject to a strict liability standard.

10.2.2. CONTRACTUAL OBLIGATIONS AS CONJUNCTIVE OBLIGATIONS

The second way of challenging the assumption that contractual liability is strict is more far-reaching. According to what I shall label the 'conjunctive obligation' explanation of strict liability, contractual liability is *never* actually strict (despite what courts say).

The starting point for this explanation is the insight (first introduced when discussing the implied agreement explanation) that, while it is not possible to agree to change the meaning of fault, it is possible to agree to compensate another in the case that one innocently fails to perform a contractual undertaking. The conjunctive obligation explanation supposes that this is what contracting parties actually do. More specifically, this explanation supposes that contracting parties (and promisors generally) agree to a two-part (or 'conjunctive') obligation when they make contracts. The first, or 'primary', obligation is the obligation to bring about the promised result (e.g., delivery of goods, payment of the price). The second, or 'secondary', obligation, which will arise only in cases of innocent non-performance of the primary obligation, is an obligation to compensate the promisee for losses arising from such non-performance. Each of these obligations are assumed to be subject to a fault standard.

The assumption that, as a matter of fact, contracting parties actually agree to secondary obligations to compensate seems robust. In principle, there are three ways in which promisors might understand the liability conditions that are attached to their (primary) promissory undertakings. First, these undertakings might be regarded as giving rise to strict obligations to achieve the promised (primary) result—with the implication that a failure to achieve this result is always blameworthy. This understanding must be rejected for reasons already explained (10.1.2). It is not actually possible to agree that innocent non-performance is blameworthy. Second, a promissory undertaking might be understood as giving rise to an obligation to use reasonable care to attempt to achieve the promised result, and nothing more. This understanding is conceptually possible, but is inconsistent with the ordinary understanding of promising. No one supposes that promisors' obligations are limited simply to using reasonable care to achieve the promised result. 'I did my best' is not a sufficient response. This leaves only the third possibility, which is that promises are conjunctive obligations. This possibility is both conceptually coherent, and consistent with how promises are ordinarily understood. In ordinary life, promises, agreements, and other kinds of voluntary undertakings are understood in just the way the conjunctive obligation explanation supposes. There is room for the innocent non-performance of a primary promissory obligation—but it is assumed to give rise to a secondary obligation to remedy the non-performance.

On the assumption that contracting parties agree to conjunctive obligations of this kind, the next question is whether this explanation is consistent with the law. In considering this question, two kinds of cases in which damages are awarded must be distinguished. In the first, more common, category, the defendant was at fault in failing to perform her primary contractual undertaking. In such cases, the explanation for awarding damages is straightforward: the defendant was at fault, thus his breach is wrongful. Aside from the origin of the underlying duty, such a case is no different from an ordinary tort case. In each, the defendant is required to pay damages for a fault-based breach of duty.

The second, less common, category of cases are those in which the defendant was *not* at fault in failing to perform her primary undertaking; the explanation here is more complex. The first point to make is that the defendant's innocent non-performance of her primary undertaking will have given rise to a secondary obligation to compensate. This obligation, as I have already indicated, is not imposed by law. It is not 'damages'. Rather, it is an ordinary, self-imposed (though typically not explicit), contractual obligation. If the defendant performed this obligation, then the plaintiff has no complaint. But assuming that the defendant failed to perform this secondary obligation, a court deciding such a dispute has two options. The first option is to order specific performance of the secondary obligation. There seems to be no reason for courts to refuse such a request; the obligation is a monetary one, thus the usual arguments against specific performance do not apply (11.2). The second option is to order the defendant to pay compensatory damages for the losses arising from their failure to perform the secondary obligation. Since this obligation is itself subject to a fault-standard, a pre-condition to making such an order is that the defendant is at fault in failing to make a payment. But— an important point—in such cases, fault is automatic. It is automatic because, in principle, the only valid excuse for a failure to satisfy a monetary obligation is insolvency. Unless one is bankrupt, payment is always possible. Of course, *lateness* in paying can sometimes be excused. A cheque might get lost in the post. But by the time a case reaches the courts such excuses will not work. At this stage, the only excuse for failing to pay is that one is bankrupt.

In this second, less common, category of breach cases, monetary awards can be explained, then, either as the specific performance of a secondary obligation to compensate *or* as damages for the faulty non-performance of that obligation. The actual content of the order will be the same in either case, since damages will be equal to the amount of money originally owed. Given that courts typically describe such orders as damages, it probably makes sense to regard them in this way. But from the perspective of the conjunctive obligations explanation, it does not matter whether they are regarded as damages or specific performance. It is sufficient that they can be explained without invoking any notion of strict liability.

10.3. CONCLUSION

I conclude that, of the various explanations of strict liability examined above, the conjunctive obligation is the most persuasive. This explanation resolves the apparent inconsistency between standards of liability in tort and contract on the basis that contractual liability is actually fault-based. It is consistent, therefore, with the legal view that breach of contract is a wrong. It is also consistent with the ordinary understanding of what promisors agree to when they make a promise, and with what it is conceptually possible for them to agree to. Finally, it is consistent with what courts actually do (though not always with what they *say* they do)[13] when they order defendants to pay damages.[14]

---

[13] As for why courts *say* that contractual liability is strict, the explanation, I suggest, lies in contract law's roots in the proprietary action of debt: Ibbetson (1999) Chapters 1–3.

[14] A complete explanation of this area of the law must also take into account various rules regarding the commencement of interest payment periods and limitation periods, as well as the possibility of claims for damages for late payment of secondary monetary obligations. Space precludes examining these issues here, but I note that it is unlikely they will prove significant in the above debate. Damages and interest payments are difficult to distinguish in the case of monetary obligations; in addition, many of the relevant rules arguably are explicable, in part, on the basis of non-contractual unjust enrichment principles or simply on administrative grounds (e.g. starting dates for limitation periods).

Remedies for Breach

Common law contract theorists have devoted particular attention to examining remedies for breach of contract. Part of the explanation for this attention is that remedies have played a crucial role in the development of the common law. In the medieval writ system from which the modern law evolved, causes of action were framed primarily in terms of remedies sought.[1] The common law lawyer has thus traditionally approached contract issues through a remedial lens—a tradition kept alive in the practice of many common law faculties by starting contract courses with remedies. In addition, remedial issues are frequently of decisive importance in litigation—and it is from litigation, of course, that the common law has developed.

But the main reason contract theorists have devoted special attention to remedies is that thinking about remedies raises important theoretical questions. Thus, what I described earlier in this book as the analytic debate about whether contractual obligations are best understood as promises, reliance-based obligations, or something else (2.1), has been conducted, to a significant degree, as a debate about remedies.[2] So too, what was earlier described as the normative debate about whether contractual obligations are justified on the basis of individual rights or social utility (2.1), has frequently also been conducted, particularly in recent years, as a debate about remedies.[3]

Consistent with these observations, in this chapter I examine remedies primarily (though not exclusively) from the perspective of what they tell us about broader theories of contract—and vice versa. More specifically, in the first section of the chapter, I will describe in broad outline how the leading general theories of contact law (as described in Part II of the book) approach remedial issues. The main focus here will be on the different approaches to remedies taken by theories that justify contract

---

[1] Ibbetson (1999) Chapter 1.
[2] e.g. Fuller and Purdue (1936); Gilmore (1974); Atiyah (1979).
[3] e.g. Polinsky (1983) 29–36; Posner (1998) 145–46; Friedman (1989).

law on the basis that it protects individual rights ('rights-based theories') and theories that justify contract law on the basis that it promotes social welfare ('utilitarian' theories, in particular 'efficiency' theories). In this section, I also discuss the different approaches to remedies taken by theories that regard contracts as essentially promissory obligations and theories that regard contracts as reliance-based obligations. Subsequently, in the second and third sections of the chapter, I turn to examine in more detail the rules relating to, respectively, specific performance and damages in the light of the observations made in the first section.

Given that this is a book about contract law, it may be useful to mention at the outset that it is not assumed that the rules regarding remedies for breach of contract are a part of 'contract' law, strictly speaking. To the contrary, it will be a theme of this chapter that, while remedial rules tell us important things about contractual obligations, they are separate from such obligations, strictly speaking. Consistent with arguments that I have made elsewhere in this book (9.1; 10.1.1), the arguments of this chapter suggest that contract law, properly understood, is limited to the rules that govern the creation and content of contractual obligations.

Finally, a word must be said about terminology. In its ordinary meaning, a 'remedy' is something that is designed to heal or cure a loss or injury. As we shall see, certain judicial orders discussed in this chapter are arguably not remedies in this sense (indeed, from the perspective of efficiency theories none of the orders discussed in this chapter are true remedies). Unfortunately, there is no other convenient English word to describe the kinds of orders examined in this chapter; I therefore (reluctantly) follow conventional usage in describing all such orders as 'remedies'.

11.1. AN OUTLINE OF GENERAL APPROACHES TO REMEDIES

By way of introduction, recall that in Chapter 2 it was suggested that general theories of contract law can be distinguished according to how they answer two related questions: a *normative* question about the justification for contractual obligations and an *analytic* question about the nature or essential characteristics of such obligations. With respect to the normative question, the main distinction is between theories that justify contractual obligations on the basis that they give rise to individual rights to performance ('rights-based theories') and theories that justify contractual obligations on the basis that they promote social welfare ('utilitarian' theories). As regards the analytic question, theories were distinguished according to whether they regarded contractual obligations as created by self-imposed obligations ('promissory theories'), reliance-inducing statements ('reliance theories'), or transfers of already existing rights ('transfer theories').

It may also be recalled that different combinations of answers to the analytic and normative questions are possible (e.g., rights-based promissory theories and rights-based reliance theories). In addition, at a certain point the answers to these questions overlap with one another. Each of these complexities resurfaces in discussions of general approaches to remedies. There is no way to eliminate them entirely, but in the hopes of making this section easier to follow, the discussion will be structured primarily in terms of the distinction between the approaches taken by rights-based theories and utilitarian theories. For the most part, it is this distinction that is important when discussing remedies. The distinctions between promissory, reliance, and transfer theories are discussed at the end.

II.I.I. RIGHTS-BASED APPROACHES[4]

Rights based theories of contract suppose that contracts create individual rights to performance and corresponding duties on other individuals to fulfill those rights (4.6). In this traditional and probably still orthodox view, breach of contract is a wrong done to a particular individual—the promisee. The duty to perform is explained and justified entirely on the basis of considerations specific to the contracting parties. That breaching a contract may dissuade others from contracting in the future, or in any other way that has negative consequences for social welfare, is irrelevant.

To understand how rights-based theories approach remedial issues, it is useful to begin by considering the different kinds of requests that, consistent with such theories, we might imagine a victim of breach (for the purposes of this chapter, the 'plaintiff') bringing before a court. There are four main possibilities. First, plaintiffs might ask courts to order defendants to do what, from a rights-based perspective, they were meant to do in the first place—namely, to perform their contractual obligations (e.g., deliver goods, make a payment, perform a service). Second, plaintiffs might ask courts to order defendants to compensate them for any losses they suffered as a result of those defendants breaching their

---

[4] My discussion here repeats parts of 4.3.3.

contractual duties. Third, plaintiffs might ask courts to order defendants to return to them benefits that they conferred on those defendants in anticipation of performance. Fourth, and finally, plaintiffs might ask courts to punish defendants (or alternatively a public prosecutor might make such a request).

In analysing such requests from the perspective of rights-based theories, the first point to make is that the concepts such theories use to explain the creation and content of contractual obligations do not explain why courts should ever grant such requests. The idea that contracts create individual rights and that rights should be respected, do not imply any particular view about how courts should respond to claims that contractual rights have been breached. In order to explain why and when courts might be justified in granting requests of the kind just described, rights-based theories must therefore be supplemented by other justificatory arguments. Two such arguments—one that applies to direct enforcement and a second that applies to compensatory orders—are examined below. Orders to return benefits and punitive orders are discussed later in the chapter (11.3).

Direct enforcement

A request for what I have called 'direct enforcement' is a request that the defendant be ordered to perform the contractual obligations that he has thus far failed to perform—to deliver goods, make a payment, etc. An order of specific performance is usually regarded in this way in rights-based theories—it is regarded as the direct enforcement of a primary contractual right. Rather than attempting to remedy the harm that a breach has caused, such an order is regarded (in such theories) as an attempt to ensure that the contract is performed.

The content of direct enforcement orders is easily explained from a rights-based perspective; such orders merely require defendants to do what rights-based theories say they should do—perform their contractual undertakings. But an explanation for why courts are justified in *ordering* defendants (on pain of punishment)[5] to perform these duties is still required. That I have a duty to perform does not, in itself, justify a court in ordering me to perform. I also have a duty to drive carefully, but no one would imagine that this fact justifies a court in ordering me to

---

[5] It is a crucial feature of specific performance orders that their non-performance can lead to criminal sanctions. Otherwise, such orders are merely declaratory.

drive carefully. Consistent with the harm principle[6] (3.1.4), a pre-emptive strike—in the form of the court *anticipating* the violation of a contractual right and then acting to prevent that violation—requires special justification.

A complete explanation of why and when the state (through the courts) is justified in ordering individuals to act in certain ways is one part of a general theory of the state. But for present purposes, it is sufficient to make the (uncontroversial) point that direct enforcement orders are justified when defendants have shown themselves unwilling to perform their legal obligations. In such cases, direct enforcement is justified on the basis that it is the only way to prevent a wrong from happening or continuing to happen. In practice, unwillingness to perform will be established by the fact that the defendant is in court and has thus far failed to perform. But it must be stressed that the justification for the order is not, fundamentally, that there was a breach, but rather that the breach (together with the fact that the dispute is now in court) establishes the defendant's unwillingness to perform. In principle, therefore, direct enforcement might be justified in a case in which a defendant made clear prior to the date of performance that he was unwilling to perform. The last point underscores the fact that, understood in this way, a direct enforcement order is a pre-emptive interference with individual liberty. In principle, it is justified because the court is convinced of the certain wrong that will occur (or continue to occur) unless it acts. But like other pre-emptive actions by the state (e.g., prohibitions against publishing defamatory material), such orders might legitimately be subject to further conditions. This qualification is important when explaining the actual rules on specific performance.

Compensation

A second way that a legal system might give force to rights-based contractual obligations is by requiring those who breach them to pay compensation to their victims. Thus, an order of damages is typically regarded in rights-based theories as an order that the defendant compensate the plaintiff for the harm caused by infringing the plaintiff's contractual rights.

From a rights-based perspective, compensatory orders raise two issues. The first is the same issue I discussed a moment ago: why is the state

---

[6] 'The only purpose for which power can rightly be exercised over any member of a civilized community against his will is to prevent harm to others': Mill (1859) Chapter 1.

justified in *ordering* the defendant to make such payment? Nothing further needs to be said about this issue; assuming that compensation should be paid, courts will be justified in ordering its payment on the same grounds that they are justified in ordering performance of the defendant's primary obligation—namely that the defendant is unwilling to perform. The only difference between primary and secondary obligations in this respect, is that the latter are always possible. It is never too late to pay compensation. The second, and more fundamental issue raised by compensatory orders concerns the content of the obligation: why should the defendant pay compensation? This question must be addressed because, unlike in the case of direct enforcement orders, compensatory orders cannot be justified on the ground that they merely enforce the original obligation. Compensation is not performance.

The explanation of why and when compensatory orders may legitimately be made is grounded in a different concept—the concept of justice. Non-justice-based explanations of damages do indeed exist—the utilitarian explanation discussed later in this chapter is the leading example —but they cannot be adopted by rights-based theories without undercutting the justification that such theories offer for contractual obligations generally. Justice takes various forms (e.g., distributive, retributive, corrective). The particular form that is appropriate to explaining judicial orders depends on the nature of the order in question. In respect of contract law, and focusing here on the usual remedy of compensatory damages, the obvious candidate for a justificatory explanation is *corrective* justice. Corrective justice is concerned with the justice of duties to repair or to rectify harms, and in particular, with duties to repair harms caused by one's wrongful actions. Corrective justice might thus be described as individual or personal justice.[7]

The general idea underlying corrective justice is that individuals have a duty to repair or 'correct' wrongful losses they have caused. What counts as wrongful is not specified by the concept of corrective justice; corrective justice is meant to explain (secondary) duties to repair rather than (primary) duties not to cause wrongful losses. Primary duties must be explained on other grounds. In a rights-based theory of law, those grounds are individual rights: a wrongful loss is a loss that arises from

---

[7] Corrective justice can therefore be contrasted with both distributive justice—the justice of schemes for distributing goods, income, and other resources—and retributive justice—the justice of punishment: see generally Aristotle (1962) Book V; Finnis (1980) Chapter VII; Miller (1987) 260–63; Perry (2000).

rights-infringing behaviour—which category includes breach of contract (4.3.2).

The concept of justice thus provides a normative basis that is compatible with (though not required by) rights-based theories of private law for explaining why and when compensatory orders should be made. Of course, it might still be asked if justice is intrinsically valuable in the way just described. Does the value of justice actually *justify* compensatory orders? No attempt will be made to answer this question here. Indeed, it may be doubted whether it is actually possible to 'justify' justice. Justice would appear to be a basic or bedrock concept (like consent: 9.1.2), the value of which cannot be reduced to (and thus explained in terms of) any other concept. Like friendship, knowledge, and other basic values, there is little that can be said to explain why it is valuable beyond explaining its meaning.[8]

The content of remedial orders

Up to this point, I have said nothing about how rights-based approaches regard the content of direct enforcement orders and compensatory orders. Nothing was said, for example, as to whether compensation should be set at the value of the contractual undertaking ('expectation' damages) or at the value of the plaintiff's detrimental reliance on that undertaking ('reliance' damages). This silence was intentional. The idea that rights-based obligations are given legal recognition by direct enforcement orders and compensatory orders does not tell us what contractual obligations oblige people to do. It does not tell us, in other words, which of the different theories about the nature of contractual obligations —promissory theories, reliance theories, and transfer theories—is more persuasive. (Though elsewhere in this book I have offered different reasons, consistent with rights-based theories, for preferring the promissory account: 3.1.)

But while adopting this view of remedies does not presume a position in the debate between promissory, reliance, and transfer theories of contract, it does suggest that remedies are important when thinking about which of these theories best fits the law. As described above, remedial orders, whether in the form of direct enforcement or compensation, are meant to reflect the underlying obligation. Direct enforcement orders, for

---

[8] Thus, most justifications for corrective justice (beginning with Aristotle's original discussion) are largely or exclusively explanations of the concept's meaning: Aristotle (1962) Book V; Finnis (1980) Chapter VII; Weinrib (1995) 56–84; Coleman (1992); Fletcher (1972); Perry (1990; 1992).

example, are meant to actually duplicate the underlying obligation. Compensatory orders, for their part, are meant to compensate for the loss caused by the non-performance of the underlying obligation; the level of compensation should thus reflect the content of that obligation.

It is because of this link between remedies and rights that (as I said earlier) remedial rules are important in the debate between those who think contracts are promises and those who think they are reliance-induced obligations or mere transfers of existing rights. I will consider this debate when I examine the remedies of specific performance and damages in more detail below.

11.1.2. UTILITARIAN ('EFFICIENCY') APPROACHES

The main alternative to rights-based justifications for contract law is provided by utilitarian theories. Utilitarian theories (in the sense this term is used in this book) justify contract law on the basis that it promotes human well-being or 'utility', broadly understood (4.1). The best known example of a utilitarian theory (and the model for the discussion that follows) is the efficiency theory, which justifies contract law on the basis that it promotes the 'welfare', subjectively understood, of all members of society (4.1). Contract law, in this view, is an instrument for helping citizens satisfy what they regard as their needs and wants.

Defenders of efficiency-based theories of contract law have devoted particular attention to explaining remedial orders. This is not surprising. In such theories, remedial orders are regarded as the specific means by which the state (through the courts) promotes social welfare in the context of contractual transactions. Unlike in rights-based theories, therefore, the normative value underlying efficiency theories ('efficiency' or 'utility') is used to explain not just the rules regarding the creation and content of contracts, but also the rules stipulating how courts should respond to claims that a contract has been breached. Indeed, at a conceptual level, efficiency theories do not draw a clear distinction between remedial rules and non-remedial rules. They are both explained using the same basic idea of promoting welfare.

Two models of remedies

In principle, there are two ways that remedial orders might be used to promote efficiency, and thus two ways that efficiency theories might explain such orders. First, remedial orders might be used to order individuals to behave in ways that *directly* increase welfare. For example, a court might order Jane to deliver a car in her possession to Susan, on the basis that Susan will obtain more welfare from the car than will Jane. In this example, the required act (delivering the car) directly increases welfare because the result of the act (Susan owning the car) increases the level of welfare in the world. Second, remedial orders might be used to create *incentives* for individuals so that in the future individuals will act in ways that (directly) increase welfare. Thus, a court might rule that persons in Jane's position who fail to deliver their cars to those, like Susan, who value them more highly must pay a sum of money. The idea underlying this second approach is that the threat of being subject to such an order will encourage individuals in Jane's position to make the requisite efficient transfers.

The literature on efficiency theories of contract does not always distinguish these two ways of promoting efficiency. But, in practice, most theorists assume that the second method better explains how courts do and should operate.[9] This assumption seems plausible, but it requires explanation. Recall that it is a basic assumption of efficiency theories that voluntary exchanges are presumptively efficient (4.1.1). If I agree to give you my cow for your horse, the assumption is that you value my cow more than your horse, and vice versa. The exchange is thus mutually beneficial, and efficient. On this basis, it might be thought that the first way of promoting efficiency—ordering defendants to act in a way that directly increases welfare—is the appropriate response to claims of breach of contract. The courts increase welfare simply by ordering the parties to do what they have already agreed to do. But this conclusion does not follow. This is because sometimes it is efficient *not* to perform a contract. In particular, performance may be inefficient if circumstances have changed since the contract was made, or if one or both of the parties made an error when they entered the contract. For example, if subsequent to agreeing to sell you my cow, I discover that I desperately need a cow then our contemplated exchange is probably inefficient. I need the cow more than you do. In such a case, therefore, forcing me to perform my contractual obligation will decrease, not increase, welfare.[10] Of course, one possible response to the existence of such cases might be to design the rules on

---

[9] See Craswell (2001).

[10] Although this argument is related to the efficiency-based explanation for why specific performance is not the primary remedy for breach, it is not actually an explanation of that rule. As we shall see, orders of specific performance can be understood (and typically are so understood in efficiency theories) as setting up incentives rather than as attempts to increase welfare directly. Consistent with this view, specific performance of an inefficient contract may not actually lead to inefficient performance; this would be the case, for example, if the plaintiff agreed to waive the right to performance: 11.1.4.

frustration and mistake so that contracts could be set aside when changed circumstances or errors make their performance inefficient. If this were done, then direct enforcement could never lead to inefficient performance, since valid contracts, by definition, would always be efficient. But such orders would be inefficient in other ways. Specifically, broadening the excuses of mistake and frustration would make people more hesitant to enter and to rely upon contracts generally. From an efficiency perspective, a basic function of contract law is to facilitate making, and relying upon, contracts (4.1.1).

The problems just described do not arise, however, if, rather than attempting to increase welfare directly, courts limit themselves to providing incentives for efficient (future) behaviour. If the aim of the law is to provide incentives, then the various decisions that might be influenced by remedial orders (e.g., to perform a contract, to enter a contract, to rely on a contract) can all be taken into account when fashioning remedies (in theory anyway). On this basis, efficiency-based explanations of remedial orders generally regard such orders as creating incentives for future contracting parties to act in efficient ways. In particular, remedies are explained on the basis that they facilitate not only efficient performance, but also efficient contract making, efficient reliance on contracts, and so on.

Remedies as incentives: three observations

As I will explain in the next two sections, difficult factual questions arise when one tries to determine if the orders that courts actually make produce efficient incentives with respect to the above range of behaviour. But, for the moment, I will limit myself to three general observations about efficiency-based explanations of remedies.

The first observation is that the basic idea underlying the efficiency explanation is a simple one: undesirable (i.e., inefficient) behaviour should be deterred and desirable (i.e., efficient) behaviour should be promoted. This same idea underlies, for example, deterrence justifications for punishment (penalizing undesirable behaviour will dissuade others from acting in a similar way) and the usual justifications for tax breaks (subsidizing an activity will encourage participation). It may be asked, of course, whether remedial rules actually have a significant influence on how contracting parties behave. Numerous studies have concluded that individuals often act irrationally (in the sense of not responding to incentives), are heavily influenced by non-legal norms, are ignorant about or unable to afford the use of legal sanctions, and, more generally, carry on their affairs with little apparent regard for legal penalties or rewards (4.3.3). But as I argued in Chapter 4, contract law is one field in which the assumption that legal incentives make a difference seems relatively robust (4.3.3).

The second observation is that, from an efficiency perspective, what the law calls 'remedies' are not, strictly speaking, true remedies. In the ordinary understanding, a remedy is designed to cure or repair a wrong, loss, or other problem; remedies are backwards-looking. But from an efficiency perspective, what the law calls remedies are forward-looking; they are designed to avoid undesirable things happening in the future. This observation does not deny that the best way to influence future behaviour might be for courts to make orders that *look like* true remedial orders. Nor does it deny that it might be efficient for judges to actually think they are ordering true remedies (on the basis that judges are more likely to set appropriate incentives if they approach their job in this way: 4.4.1). The point is simply that, at the level of principle, there is no role for (true) remedies in efficiency theories. From an efficiency perspective, what happened in the past is just that—in the past.

The third, related observation is that, from an efficiency perspective, remedial orders have little to do with justice, as conventionally understood. Recall that remedial orders are just if they require defendants to give to plaintiffs what is fitting or appropriate or due to them. But efficiency theories explain remedies not in terms of what is due to a particular individual, but in terms of what will produce the greatest welfare in society generally. Damages are ordered not because they are due to the plaintiff as a matter of justice; rather, they are ordered to send a signal about how future contracting parties should behave. Moreover, from an efficiency perspective, the link between the defendant and the plaintiff is merely one of administrative convenience. In principle, the goal of ensuring that contracting parties face the correct mix of penalties and rewards (so that they act efficiently) could be achieved by ordering defendants to pay damages to the state, and by allowing plaintiffs to collect compensation from the same source. The efficiency theories' explanation for why the law requires defendants to pay plaintiffs is that this is administratively cheaper than the alternatives. In a system in which plaintiffs are compensated by defendants, plaintiffs have incentives to bring forth the information that courts require to make remedial orders. In effect, the plaintiff is bribed to act as the equivalent of a public prosecutor.

In light of these three observations, it is not surprising to learn that efficiency explanations of remedies (and of contract law generally) are often criticized on the ground that they are morally unattractive, or that they are inconsistent with what judges say and understand themselves to be doing. In my view, these are significant objections, particularly the second one. But as they were examined in Chapter 4's general discussion of efficiency theories (4.1.5; 4.1.6), I will say nothing more about them here.

In the next two sections, the rules regarding, respectively, specific performance orders and damages orders are examined against the background of the two general approaches to remedies described above.

11.2. SPECIFIC PERFORMANCE

Orders of specific performance are orders that defendants do the very thing they had promised to do under their contracts. In the common law, specific performance is described as a supplementary remedy; it is available only when damages are 'inadequate'.[11] In practice, damages are found to be inadequate primarily in cases involving the sale of unique goods or land. Specific performance is not traditionally available for personal service contracts, though injunctions (that is, orders not to do something) are routinely awarded. Finally, orders that defendants pay to plaintiffs an 'agreed sum' (e.g., the price in a sale contract), which are routinely awarded, are usually described as specific performance orders.

The rules on specific performance have played an important role in debates about the justification of contractual obligations. In particular, it is often argued that the common law's approach to specific performance is inconsistent with the traditional view (defended in rights-based theories) that valid contractual undertakings should be performed. The rule that specific performance is a secondary remedy is said to fit better with the view (defended by efficiency theories) that the law encourages performance when, but only when, it is efficient. In the discussion that follows, I question this conclusion. More specifically, I will suggest that although rights-based theories and efficiency theories offer radically different explanations of the common law's approach to specific performance, each is equally able to account (or not account) for this approach.

11.2.1. RIGHTS–BASED EXPLANATIONS

As we have seen, the traditional, rights-based understanding of contract law supposes that valid contractual undertakings should be performed

---

[11] Chitty (1999) 1357.

(4.6). This view further supposes that courts are prima facie justified in directly enforcing legal duties, contractual or otherwise, when it is clear that those duties will not otherwise be performed—a condition fulfilled in most breach of contract cases by the defendant having been found to be in breach.[12] The following question then arises: if this traditional view is correct, why is specific performance available only when damages are inadequate?

The response of many defenders of the traditional view to this question is, in effect, to admit that rights-based approaches are unable to justify the common law's rules on specific performance, but then to argue in partial defence that these rules are explicable (though not justifiable) on historical grounds. The main such historical ground is that specific performance orders were originally available only in courts of equity, which courts were themselves regarded as supplementary to the common law courts. But this admission may be unnecessary. Three possible justifications exist for the common law's approach to specific performance. Each is consistent with the assumption that contracting parties have a legal obligation to perform their contractual undertakings. I will describe each below, and then consider which, if any, are convincing.

Specific performance is impossible

The first possible justification claims that the entire debate about specific performance is based on a mistaken assumption—the assumption being that it is still possible for a contract to be performed once it has been broken. The assumption is mistaken because, aside from cases involving anticipatory repudiations (i.e., where defendants have indicated *in advance* that they will not perform),[13] defendants who have breached are, by definition, no longer able to perform their primary contractual obligation—it is too late. If performance was meant to happen on May 1, then ordering the defendant to perform on September 1 is ordering her to do

---

[12] Strictly speaking, this is not quite right, since in many disputes the defendant is in principle willing to perform; it is just that she disputes, in good faith, the plaintiff's interpretation of what the contract requires her to do. In such a case, a declaration would, in principle, be appropriate. That the common law does not generally make such declarations is explained, I suggest, by its general refusal to allow the excuse of ignorance of the law.

[13] Claims for the specific performance of a restrictive covenant, such as a covenant not to compete, may be included within this category. Although in most such cases, plaintiffs allege that the covenant has already been breached by the defendant, insofar as plaintiffs are asking for specific performance of the covenant *in the future*, they are basically arguing that the defendant has committed an anticipatory repudiation. The defendant's past breach is evidence that the defendant is likely to breach again in the future.

something different than she was originally obliged to do. The defendant is being ordered to do something that is merely *similar* to her contractual obligation. If this is correct, then it follows that the only possible remedy for breach of contract is a compensatory remedy. It further follows, in this view, that cases in which 'specific performance' is ordered are cases in which an order of 'late performance' is the best way to *compensate* the plaintiff. Such orders are not true orders of specific performance. Finally, the explanation for why 'specific performance' is a secondary remedy is that, from the perspective of ensuring compensation, monetary awards are normally satisfactory. It is only exceptionally that ordering (late) performance is the best or only way to compensate the plaintiff.

Contractual obligations are disjunctive obligations

The second possible justification also supposes that the debate about specific performance is based on a misunderstanding—but this time the misunderstanding is said to concern what it is that contracting parties have promised to do. According to this justification, the obligations that contracting parties have agreed to are disjunctive obligations; specifically, they are disjunctive obligations to perform the primary obligation (e.g., deliver goods, perform a service, make payment) *or* to provide compensation in lieu of such performance. The parties therefore have a choice— and they have this choice not because the law says so (as efficiency theories conclude: see below), but because they have, as a matter of fact, agreed to such a choice, even if only implicitly. If this interpretation of contractual obligations is correct, then when a court orders 'damages' it is actually directly enforcing the second half of the defendant's disjunctive obligation—the obligation to provide compensation. In other words (and in stark contrast to the previous justification), this justification regards both specific performance *and* damages as forms of (true) specific performance. What the courts currently call 'specific performance' merely identifies those cases in which the parties have not, as a matter of fact, agreed to a disjunctive obligation.

Specific performance intrudes on personal liberty

The third possible justification for the common law's reluctance to order specific performance is that directly enforcing contractual obligations prima facie intrudes on personal liberty. In contrast to the previous justifications, which focused on specifically contractual issues, this justification is grounded in broader concerns about the proper role of the state and its relations with citizens.

This third justification is essentially an extension of the idea, common to both common and civil law regimes, that directly enforcing personal service contracts is undesirable because it is intrusive of personal liberty. The idea underlying the extension is that nearly *all* contractual obligations involve, in theory at any rate, a form of personal service. This is the case because unlike, say, obligations enforced by tort law, the standard contractual obligation is an obligation *to do something for another person.* The typical contractual obligation is to produce goods, make a delivery, pay a sum of money, etc.—all of which involve positive acts for the benefit of another. In the Western political tradition, directly enforcing obligations of this kind has long required special justification. Direct state enforcement of obligations 'to do' has acquired a symbolic meaning that goes far beyond the practical burdens that such obligations may entail. In such cases, direct enforcement is experienced, rightly or wrongly, as akin to a kind of servitude.

According to this explanation, there is a presumption, then, against ordering specific performance. But certain exceptions to the rule can be justified. In particular, specific performance may be justified in cases in which a monetary award will not provide adequate compensation and/or in cases in which the liberty concerns that specific performance normally raises are not present. The current exceptions are then explained on this basis. Thus, the courts are willing generally to specifically enforce obligations that raise few liberty concerns, such as negative covenants (e.g., restrictive covnenants) and monetary obligations. They are also willing to enforce obligations for which compensation is difficult *and* which are only minimally intrusive of liberty, such as obligations to deliver unique goods or to hand over title to land.

Conclusion

Each of the above explanations for why specific performance is a secondary remedy is prima facie plausible. But of the three, only the third—the liberty-based explanation—seems capable of offering a general justification for the common law's approach. The objection to the first justification—that specific performance is literally impossible—is that while it is true that late performance is not identical to timely performance, in most cases this difference would seem to relate only to the form of the obligation rather than its essence. Late delivery is, in essence, the same thing as timely delivery. The ordinary understanding of specific performance orders supports this conclusion: plaintiffs who request specific performance are understood (and understand themselves) to be asking that the defendant do the very thing he promised to do. The conceptual point on which this first justification turns is inconsistent, in other words, with ordinary understandings of when performance has become impossible. Turning to the second justification—that contractual obligations are disjunctive obligations—the objection is factual rather than conceptual. It just seems implausible, as a matter of fact, to regard contracting parties as having agreed, in the typical case, to disjunctive obligations to perform or compensate. To be sure, contracting parties *could* make such agreements, and undoubtedly some contracting parties do make such agreements (particularly contracting parties who are well-versed in the law), but as a general account of how parties understand their agreements, the suggestion is implausible.

The third justification—that specific performance is intrusive of personal liberty—is not vulnerable to either of these objections. This justification rests on well-established normative grounds (albeit of a kind not generally discussed in this book), and it also neatly explains why specific performance is sometimes granted. Admittedly, the third justification is consistent with courts granting specific performance more often than is actually done. More specifically, if this justification explains the law, it would seem that specific performance should be more widely available than it is in cases in which the defendant is a large or medium sized corporation. The concern for liberty on which this justification rests has little force when the defendant is merely required to ask its employees, or a sub-contractor, to perform a particular task. But this observation is not so much an objection to the basis on which specific performance is awarded as an objection to the general rule (applied throughout private law) that corporate bodies are treated in law as if they were real persons.[14] This rule is indeed difficult to defend when its effect is to preclude an award of specific performance. But for present purposes, the important point is that this rule is not evidence against the liberty-based explanation of specific performance.

I conclude, then, that despite initial appearances to the contrary, the common law's apparent reluctance to award specific performance can be reconciled with rights-based theories of contract law. More specifically, it can be reconciled on the basis that awarding specific performance is prima facie intrusive of personal liberty. On this basis, it is appropriate that plaintiffs seeking specific performance be required to show that their

[14] *Salomon v Salomon* [1897] AC 22.

application does not raise such concerns and/or that the alternative of a monetary order will fail to provide satisfactory compensation.

11.2.2. EFFICIENCY-BASED EXPLANATIONS

The rules on specific performance are often thought to provide the strongest evidence in support of efficiency theories of contract. Such theories are said (by some) to offer a simple explanation for why specific performance is a secondary remedy. In examining the efficiency-based explanation of specific performance, I will begin by describing this simple or basic account which, following conventional usage, I will call the 'efficient breach theory'. Complications are introduced later.

The efficient breach theory

According to the efficient breach theory, the reason specific performance is not the primary remedy in the common law is, simply, that performance is not always efficient.[15] In particular, performance may be inefficient if circumstances have changed since the contract was made or if the parties contracted on the basis of a mistaken assumption. In these cases, the normal presumption that performing voluntary agreements is efficient does not apply—and thus it is preferable, from an efficiency perspective, for performance not to happen. By making specific performance a secondary remedy, the law is then said to encourage this outcome; contracting parties can choose to pay damages rather than to perform.

Two examples that I first discussed in Chapter 4 are useful for illustrating the efficient breach theory—and also for considering some of its limitations. The first involves an actual case, *Tito v Waddell*,[16] in which the inhabitants of Ocean Island granted mining rights to the British Phosphate mining company in 1941 in exchange for a fee and a promise to replant the island to its original state. British Phosphate mined the land, but before they had begun to replant, the island was intensively bombed (during WWII), leaving it permanently uninhabitable (or so it was thought at the time). The islanders were moved to another island 1,500 miles away, and the replanting, which would have been very expensive, was not done. The second example involves a hypothetical contract between a farmer and a merchant, in which the merchant agrees to buy 100 barrels of grain from the farmer for £40 a barrel. The grain costs the farmer £25 a barrel to grow and is worth £50 a barrel to the merchant. Subsequent to entering the contract, but prior to delivery of the grain,

---

[15] Birmingham (1970); Barton (1972).   [16] [1977] Ch 106.

the farmer is approached by a second merchant, who values the grain at £75 a barrel, and who offers the farmer £60 a barrel for all his grain.

On these facts, performance in each case appears prima facie inefficient. In *Tito*, performance is inefficient because it would cost more than it was worth (to the islanders or anyone else). Replanting would add almost nothing to the commercial value of the land (because the island was uninhabitable), and though the islanders may have placed a non-pecuniary value on the island being replanted, it is unlikely that value was anywhere close to the cost of replanting. Stated differently, had the contracting parties known in advance about the bombing and the relocation, they never would have bargained for a replanting clause. The reduction in the contract price that the mining company would have demanded for such a clause would have been more than the islanders would have agreed to.

In the grain example, performance is said to be inefficient because the second merchant values the promised grain more highly than the promisee (the first merchant). Since the efficient allocation of goods is obtained when goods end up with the persons who value them most highly, the efficient result is for the grain to end up in the hands of the second merchant.

The (simple) efficient breach theory therefore concludes that the reason specific performance is not the primary remedy for breach of contract is that such a rule could lead to inefficient performance in cases such as the two just described. British Phosphate, faced with the prospect of an order of specific performance, would have performed (or would eventually have been forced to perform). The same is true of the farmer. But under the existing rules, neither British Phosphate nor the farmer is required to perform. Each can choose to pay damages instead—which is exactly what British Phosphate did in the *Tito* case.

Of course, the efficient breach theory does not suppose that it is generally efficient for contracts to be breached. In most contracts, the presumption that performance is efficient is robust. In such cases, therefore, performance should be encouraged. According to the efficient breach theory, the law provides just such encouragement by means of the rule that contract breakers must compensate their victims for the value of their promised performance. This rule (which I discuss in more detail in the next section) is explained on the basis that it internalizes the costs of breach to promisors. Specifically, the awarding of compensatory damages gives promisors an incentive to breach when, but only when, the cost of performance is greater than its value to promisees. For the purposes of the present discussion, the only point to add is that the explanation then given for why specific performance is exceptionally available is that sometimes it is too difficult (and thus too costly) to assess compensatory damages. This would be the case, for example, if the plaintiff's loss cannot be measured without evaluating her subjective or non-market preferences — as with the breach of a contract to deliver unique goods or the breach of a contract to transfer title to land (land historically being a form of unique good).[17]

Complicating factors

Thus described, the efficient breach theory appears to offer a neat explanation for the common law rule that specific performance is a secondary remedy for breach of contract. Although the explanation differs radically from how courts explain what they are doing, it appears to fit well with what courts are, in fact, doing. But on closer inspection, the link between efficiency and the rules on specific performance is not as close as this explanation suggests. Explaining why and in what ways the slippage arises raises complex issues. But the basic objection to the efficient breach theory is that it is not obvious that a presumptive remedy of specific performance would actually encourage wasteful performance. More specifically, it is not obvious because if the performance of a particular contractual obligation is indeed inefficient, the contracting parties will have incentives to renegotiate or 'bargain around' a rule of specific performance so as to reach the efficient result.[18] In other words, inefficient performance would not actually happen. Thus, in the *Tito* case, described above, it is unlikely that granting the islanders the right to demand specific performance would have resulted in the mining company wastefully replanting the island. Assuming that the court had the facts correct — namely, that replanting cost far more than it was worth to the islanders — it would have been in both parties' interests to reach an agreement whereby the islanders waived their right to replanting in exchange for the company paying them a sum of money in between the cost of replanting and the value of replanting. A payment within this range would have left both parties better off than if performance happened. Given the possibility of making a mutually advantageous bargain, economic theory suggests that the parties, or more likely their lawyers, would have made a deal.

The same reasoning can be applied to the grain example, above, in which the farmer vendor who was contractually obliged to sell his grain

---

[17] Kronman (1978).
[18] This is one application of the 'Coase theorem' — the idea that individuals have an incentive to bargain around (apparently) inefficient legal rules: Coase (1960).

to one merchant received a higher offer from a second merchant. A rule that specific performance is the primary remedy need not lead to an inefficient outcome in such a case. The farmer could use a portion of the profits he would make from selling the grain at a higher price to the second merchant to pay the first merchant to waive his rights to performance. Moreover, even if the original contract of sale were performed, the efficient result could still be achieved. The first merchant could himself resell the grain to the second merchant. If the second merchant does indeed value the grain more than the first merchant, such a deal would leave both of them better off. Thus, they would again have an incentive to conclude just such a bargain.

The possibility of renegotiation or of resale following an order of specific performance shows, therefore, that a presumptive rule of specific performance is not obviously inefficient. But it does not establish the contrary; that is, it does not establish that specific performance is efficient. Rather, what these possibilities show is that, in principle, either a presumptive rule of specific performance or a presumptive rule of damages could be efficient. Both rules are potentially efficient because under both, the relevant resources can still end up with the party that values them most. Given this conclusion, the efficiency of damages as compared to specific performance turns on a range of other factors that I have not yet considered. Three of these factors are examined below. Each adds a layer of complication to the original efficient breach theory.

Transaction costs

One factor is the 'transaction costs' associated with each rule. These represent the costs, in money, time, or other resources associated with any renegotiation or resale. They are the real costs that must be accounted for by any efficiency theory. The lower such costs are, the more efficient the outcome, everything else being equal. In cases like *Tito*, in which the reason performance is inefficient is that the value of performance has dropped, the transaction costs associated with a rule of specific performance will typically be greater than those associated with an order of damages. This is because if damages are ordered in a case such as *Tito*, the parties need not have any further dealings in order to achieve the efficient outcome of no performance (meaning that they incur no further transaction costs—but note the factor of litigation costs discussed below). By contrast, an order of specific performance would typically lead to further transaction costs, as the efficient outcome can be achieved only if parties negotiate a deal whereby the promisee waives the right to specific performance. Thus, a damages rule seems more efficient for such cases. On the other hand, in sale of goods cases (such as our grain example), in which the reason performance (appears) to be inefficient is that a third party values the goods more highly, it is less clear which rule results in lower transaction costs.[19] Given that either the seller or the buyer can resell the goods to the third party, the answer depends on which of them is able to make such a sale at the lower cost. Typically, sellers are better placed to do this, because they are in the business of selling. But it is possible that the original buyer would be better placed—for example, if she was a broker. As such, it is possible that a rule awarding specific performance might yield more efficiency in such cases than one awarding only damages. Overall, however, consideration of transaction costs would appear to support the current rule that specific performance is a secondary remedy.

Dispute resolution costs

A second factor that must be taken into account when comparing the efficiency of specific performance and damages is the dispute resolution costs associated with each rule. These are the court and litigation costs borne by the state and the parties. Again, these are real costs, and so must be accounted for in an efficiency analysis. This factor generally argues in favour of specific performance as a presumptive rule. The reason is that ordering specific performance is usually straightforward, whereas assessing damages is not. With respect to specific performance, the only question the court needs to ask is whether performance is possible. But before ordering damages, judges must engage in the often difficult task of calculating plaintiffs' losses. It should also be noted that if contracting parties are aware that specific performance is the presumptive rule, then, assuming that breach is established and that specific performance is desired and possible, there is little reason for the parties to even go to court. The legal outcome is clear.

The risk of undercompensation

A third, closely related factor, which again argues in favour of a rule of specific performance, is that courts may underestimate the full costs of breach when assessing damages. Evidentiary difficulties associated with determining losses and (a related point) legal limits on the recovery of

---

[19] If the contract involves a *service* that is desired by a third party, then the previous analysis applies because a service cannot be resold once it has been performed.

non-pecuniary and consequential losses (11.3.5) may result in plaintiffs being undercompensated. The likelihood of undercompensation then leads, according to the logic of the efficiency-based explanation of damages, to the encouragement of inefficient breaches. Admittedly, in response to an undercompensatory damages order (or in anticipation of such an order), contracting parties could enter a new contract, thereby ensuring that the efficient performance occurs. In other words, they could renegotiate. But making such an agreement introduces additional transaction costs. Ordering specific performance avoids the possibility of undercompensation (and, for that matter, overcompensation) entirely.

The end result of taking these and other considerations I have not mentioned[20] into account is that it is difficult to say whether a presumptive rule of damages or a presumptive rule of specific performance is the more efficient. From an efficiency perspective, each rule has advantages and disadvantages. In theory, these advantages and disadvantages could be weighed against one another to determine the optimal overall rule. But in practice this cannot be done because it is too difficult to attach figures to the relevant costs. The economic literature on this topic confirms this conclusion. The number and sophistication of the articles debating the merits of damages and specific performance is matched only by the lack of consensus as to which remedy is more efficient.[21]

11.2.3. CONCLUSION TO SPECIFIC PERFORMANCE

The conclusion suggested by the above observations is that, notwithstanding initial appearances, rights-based theories are able to explain the rules on specific performance as well as efficiency theories. Indeed, it is arguable that rights-based theories offer, on balance, the more convincing account—at least so far as fit with the law is concerned. But overall, neither approach is clearly superior so far as the criterion of fit is concerned. It follows that, insofar as one approach is considered superior, this conclusion will be reached on the basis of non-fit criteria of the kind that I discussed in Chapter 4's general examination of efficiency theories (e.g., moral criteria, transparency: 4.1.5; 4.1.6). I will not repeat that discussion here, though I note that one of its conclusions was that rights-based theories generally score better on the fit criteria than do efficiency and other utilitarian theories.

---

[20] For example, the effect of the chosen remedial rule on decisions such as whether to enter a contract at all, who to contract with, how much to spend in reliance on expected performance, and how much to spend on precautions against breach: Craswell (1988; 2001).

[21] A sample includes Kronman (1978); Schwartz (1979); Bishop (1985); Mahoney (1994).

11.3. DAMAGES

According to orthodox law, damages for breach of contract are intended to put plaintiffs in the same position, so far as money is able, that they would have been in had their contracts been performed. This approach is often summarized by saying that the apparent aim of damages is to compensate plaintiffs' 'expectation' interest (on the basis that plaintiffs get the benefit they 'expected' to get from performance).[22] A more useful summary description might be to say that the apparent aim is to compensate the promisee's 'promissory' or 'performance' interests.[23]

The basic damages rule plays an important role in the two main theoretical debates about contract law. The first debate is the same one that I just discussed with respect to specific performance—namely the debate between theories that justify contractual obligations on the basis of individual rights and theories that justify contractual obligations on the basis of welfare or efficiency. The second is the debate between theories that regard contracts as essentially promises (or agreements) and theories that regard some or all contracts as essentially reliance-based obligations. These debates sometimes overlap, but for convenience I will examine them separately. As before, the analysis has a dual focus. On the one hand, I am interested in what the damages rule tells us about the validity of different general approaches to contract law. On the other hand, I am interested in what these different approaches tell us about the damages rule.

11.3.1. THE NORMATIVE DEBATE: RIGHTS-BASED VERSUS EFFICIENCY-BASED EXPLANATIONS

I begin my analysis of the damages rule by comparing, in turn, the explanations of this rule that are offered by efficiency theories and rights-based theories. Efficiency theories are examined first as their explanation of damages is a continuation of their explanation of specific performance.

Efficiency-based explanations of the basic damages rule

From the perspective of an efficiency theory, the fundamental purpose of an award of damages is to establish incentives for *future* potential contracting parties to act efficiently. In the simple or basic version of this explanation (the 'efficient breach theory' that I described when examining

---

[22] Fuller and Purdue (1936).   [23] Friedman (1995).

specific performance), this is said to be achieved by setting damages such that contracting parties have incentives to perform when, but only when, it is efficient to do so. More specifically, the normal damages rule ('expectation damages') is said to encourage efficient performance because it internalizes the costs of breach to promisors. By setting damages at the value of the promised performance, promisors have an incentive to perform when, but only when, that value is greater than the cost of performance. Consider that if damages were assessed at less than the expectation measure, there would be an incentive to breach in some cases in which breach is not efficient (when the cost of performance is less than its value). For example, if damages were assessed at £50 for the breach of a promise that costs £100 to perform but that is valued by the promisee at £200, then promisors in such cases would have a financial incentive to breach—even though performance clearly is efficient. By contrast, if damages were more than the expectation measure (for example, if punitive damages were awarded in contract), parties might be dissuaded from breaching in cases in which the cost of performance is greater than its value.

Thus, as was true of the efficient breach explanation of specific performance, the efficient breach explanation of damages appears to fit neatly with the basic damages rule (though not, of course, with the courts' explanations of that rule). But as was also true in respect of specific performance, closer inspection reveals that the efficiency implications of the damages rule are more complex than the efficient breach explanation suggests. The efficient breach explanation focuses solely on how damage awards influence contracting parties' decisions to perform or not (the 'breach' decision). But a variety of other decisions are also affected by the measure of damages awarded.[24] Thus, to determine if a particular measure of damages is efficient, its effects on these other decisions must also be taken into account. More specifically, it is necessary to consider whether the current rule internalizes the costs of these decisions to the relevant party (in the same way that it internalizes the costs of the breach decision). As I explain below in considering two such decisions, the rule appears not to do this. The end result, I will conclude, is that it is unclear whether the expectation measure of damages actually promotes efficient behaviour.

One additional decision that is affected by the measure of damages awarded is what may be called (albeit awkwardly) the 'contract' decision.

[24] Craswell (1988; 2001).

This is the decision to enter a contract in the first place (i.e., to make an offer or an acceptance). Recall that from an efficiency perspective, a basic function of contract law is to facilitate contracting (4.1.1). In other words, a basic function of contract law is to facilitate the contract decision. According to efficiency theories, the primary way courts facilitate this decision is by protecting persons who enter contracts from the losses that they might suffer if the other party reneges on the agreement.

The significance of this observation for the efficient breach theory is that such protection is achieved by awarding *reliance* damages, not expectation damages. Reliance damages are equal to the costs incurred and profits foregone (from entering a different, but comparable, contract) in reliance on a contract. As such, they fully compensate for the loss suffered as a result of *entering* a contract—and thus they fully protect those who enter contracts. Moreover, granting more than reliance damages (i.e., granting expectation damages) is inefficient from the perspective of facilitating efficient contract making. A rule of reliance damages internalizes to each party the costs of her or his respective contractual promise (i.e., her offer or acceptance). If a contractual promise is not performed, the promisor must bear the losses caused to the other party by virtue of that promise (i.e., her reliance losses). Expectation damages, by contrast, require that the promisor pay a sum *greater* than the value of the losses caused by her promise. So far as the contract decision is concerned, therefore, a rule of expectation damages will have the effect of dissuading some parties from entering beneficial contracts. Another way of making this point is that the measure of damages applied to 'defective' contractual promises should be the same tort measure that is applied generally to statements that provide defective information (i.e., mis-statements). From the perspective of the contract decision, a contractual promise is regarded (in efficiency theories) as a way of conveying potentially valuable information.[25] As such, the measure of damages for the promise being defective should be the same as the measure for defective statements of fact—reliance damages.

A second type of behaviour that efficiency theories must take into account when evaluating the efficiency of expectation damages is the amount of reliance that contracting parties invest in a promised performance (the 'optimal reliance' decision). With respect to this decision, the difference between the efficient measure of damages and the measure awarded by law is even more significant. Recall that promisees often rely on

[25] Goetz and Scott (1980).

promises because doing so increases the value of the promised performance—which is efficient (4.1.1). Indeed, from an efficiency perspective, the value of a promise is precisely that it facilitates such reliance.[26] From this perspective, then, the law should establish incentives for promisees to incur the optimal amount and type of reliance on promises. This, of course, has implications for the type of damages that should be awarded. As the law currently stands, a party may carelessly rely in situations when she knows that the promise is unlikely to be performed; she may do this because she is safe in the knowledge that she will receive her expectation damages regardless of her squandered reliance. Such behaviour is inefficient but there is nothing in the current measure of damages to deter it. To dissuade such behaviour, the measure of damages should actually be set at zero. This is the efficient rule because it internalizes to the relying party both the costs and benefits of their decision to rely.

The conclusion to be drawn from considering the various kinds of behaviour that will be affected by the damages rule is that there is no single measure of damages that will promote efficient behaviour with regard to *all* of these decisions. This conclusion does not mean that there is no measure of damages that will create the most aggregate efficient behaviour—in theory, it might well be that the expectation measure produces the most efficient aggregate behaviour (if it could be proved, say, that the breach decision overwhelms all others). But making the necessary calculation is complex to say the least. I doubt that such a calculation has or even could be attempted. As was true in respect of evaluating the efficiency of specific performance, the relevant quantitative data is not available.

Rights-based explanations of the basic damages rule

Recall that rights-based approaches explain damages on the basis of corrective justice. More specifically, they explain compensatory damages on the basis that such orders require defendants to fulfill their duties, in corrective justice, to repair the harm caused by their wrongful actions. Assuming that breach of contract is a wrong (as rights-based theories assume), such orders are justified in contract cases. This explanation is consistent, in broad terms, with the principle that victims of breach have a right to compensatory damages.

Because damages are meant to compensate for the harm *caused* by the defendant's breach, the specific measure of damages that corrective

---

[26] Goetz and Scott (1980).

justice requires in contract cases depends, of course, on what kind of an obligation a contractual obligation is. In particular, it depends on whether a contractual obligation is an obligation to do the very thing the defendant promised to do (as is assumed in promissory and transfer theories) or whether, instead, it is an obligation to ensure that the plaintiff is not made worse off as a result of relying on the contract (as is assumed in reliance theories). If the first view, which regards the wrong of breach as failing to do what was promised, is correct, compensation should, in principle, be equivalent to the value of the promise. But if the second view, which regards the wrong as failing to ensure that the plaintiff is not left worse off as a result of her reliance, is correct, then compensation should, in principle, be equivalent to the amount of reliance incurred.

In theory, rights-based versions of promissory, transfer, and reliance theories are all possible (2.4). But in Part II, I argued that, in the end, only promissory theories are consistent with both the nature of contract law and the normative commitments of rights-based theories (3.4, 4.6). If this conclusion is correct, it fits neatly with the basic rule that damages are meant to compensate the plaintiff for the value of the *promised* thing or service ('expectation damages').

Of course, certain scholars have argued that, despite appearances, courts actually award damages based on the plaintiff's reliance. Some scholars have also argued that various limits on damage awards (e.g., no punitive damages, mitigation, remoteness, etc.) show that courts neither fully protect plaintiffs' promissory interests nor the rights-based entitlements that, in rights-based theories, are thought to underlie these interests. These arguments raise issues of general concern, and so are examined in separate sections below. It may be useful to mention here, however, that so far as the debate between rights-based theories and efficiency theories is concerned, the most important of these arguments focuses on the non-availability of punitive damages or criminal punishment for even deliberate breach of contract. Of the various so-called limits on contract damages, it is this one that poses the most serious challenge to rights-based theories of contract law.

11.3.2. THE ANALYTIC DEBATE: A RELIANCE-BASED EXPLANATION OF DAMAGES?

Overlapping with the above normative debate between rights-based and efficiency-based explanations of the basic damages rule, is an equally important analytic debate between promissory and reliance-based explanations of this same rule. The latter debate pits those who believe that contract damages protect plaintiffs' interests in having promises performed against those who believe damages protect plaintiffs' interests in not being made worse off by relying on a contract. As such, the analytic debate about remedies is itself one part of a larger analytic debate as to whether contractual obligations generally are best understood as promissory obligations or as reliance-based obligations (3.1.3–3.1.4).

At first blush, the basic damages rule appears to provide clear evidence in support of the traditional view that contractual obligations are promissory obligations. Under the basic rule, damages are assessed according to the value of the relevant contractual performance—the value, that is, of what the defendant promised to do.[27] Assuming that damages are meant to compensate for the loss that was caused by the defendant's breach of duty, the obvious conclusion is that that the defendant's duty was to perform the contractual undertaking—a promissory duty. In other words, damages are based on the value of the defendant's promise because the defendant's contractual duty was to perform that promise.

But in a path-breaking 1936 article, Fuller and Purdue challenged this conclusion; more specifically, they argued that the basic damages rule could be explained on the basis that the law was actually protecting what they called the plaintiff's 'reliance interest' (the interest in not being made worse off as a result of relying on another) rather than the plaintiff's 'expectation interest' (the interest in having a promise performed).[28] The details of this argument are examined below. But first it is important to emphasize that Fuller and Purdue's criticism of the traditional view of damages is linked to a more general *moral* criticism of promissory theories of contract (3.2). Fuller and Purdue's reliance theory of damages was motivated by a belief that courts are only weakly justified in enforcing promises *qua* promises. This is because failure to perform a promise does not, in itself, harm anyone; promises *qua* promises are mere words. It is only if the promise has been relied upon that harm may arise. Fuller and Purdue made this point by observing that to award a disappointed promisee the value of the promised performance is a 'queer kind of compensation', in that it compensates promisees for something they never had.[29] On the basis of this moral criticism, Fuller and Purdue then suggested that perhaps courts were awarding damages not in order to protect the expectation interest, but in order to protect reliance. This latter interest was, in their view, a significant one, since they regarded reliance losses as

---

[27] *Robinson v Harman* (1848) 1 Ex 850, 855.   [28] Fuller and Perdue (1936).
[29] Fuller and Perdue (1936) 53.

genuine harms. If this is the correct view of contract damages, it is but a short step to concluding that contracts themselves are best understood not as promises, but as reliance-inducing statements. If the point of contract damages is to protect induced reliance, it makes more sense to suppose that contractual obligations are triggered by reliance-inducing statements. Admittedly, the most common way of inducing reliance is by a promise. But it is not the only way; reliance can be induced by a mere statement of intention. Nor do all promises induce reliance. To conclude, Fuller and Purdue's explanation of contract damages is important not just for what it says about damages, but for what it says about contractual obligations generally.

Turning to the damages rule, Fuller and Purdue's argument was that the expectation measure can be understood as an indirect means of protecting reliance; in effect, expectation damages are a proxy for reliance damages. They are a proxy because in most contracts the plaintiff's reliance loss is equal to the value of the promise. Consider that in typical commercial contracts plaintiffs rely by, *inter alia*, foregoing opportunities to enter similar contracts with third parties. Had the plaintiffs entered those alternative contracts, they typically would have made the same profits that they expected to make under the contracts that they did enter. For example, in reliance on a supplier's promise to provide a purchaser with widgets, the purchaser will not attempt to obtain widgets from other suppliers. Assuming the market for widgets is reasonably competitive, the economic value of the buyer's lost opportunity is equivalent to the economic value of the original contract. Expectation damages can therefore be explained by reliance theories on the basis that they award to plaintiffs the (reliance) value of foregone opportunities. Courts ostensibly apply a standard of expectation damages rather than directly applying a test for reliance due mainly to evidentiary convenience. It would be difficult and costly to prove the value of contracts that plaintiffs might have, but did not, enter. Additional witnesses would need to be brought before the court and courts would be required to assess market conditions directly —something they are not well-equipped to do.

As Fuller and Perdue acknowledged, this interpretation does not explain why expectation damages are awarded for contracts that are made in markets in which the contracted-for good or service was not available from a third party on similar terms. In such 'non-competitive' markets, it cannot be assumed that the plaintiff's foregone opportunity was equal to the value of the promised performance. If there is only one supplier of widgets, the alternative to buying widgets might be to simply do nothing.

But there are two possible explanations of cases involving non-competitive markets, each of which is consistent with Fuller and Purdue's general approach. The first, which Fuller and Purdue defended, is that there are administrative and evidentiary benefits to having a single general rule. To make exceptions for contracts in non-competitive markets would require courts to define the market for the relevant good or service and then to determine whether it is non-competitive—neither of which are simple tasks. Moreover, even for contracts in non-competitive markets, plaintiffs will often be able to claim that while they did not forego entering a similar contract with a third party, they did forego entering other kinds of equally valuable opportunities. The potential purchaser of widgets might argue, for example, that if he had not entered a contract to buy widgets, he would have invested in employee training or expanded his premises. Proving that these alternatives existed, and then establishing the likely profit that would have arisen from them is, again, a difficult task. The second explanation of damage awards in cases involving non-competitive markets is that there is a distinction between what courts say they are doing in such cases and what they are actually doing. As defended in particular by Atiyah,[30] the argument here is that although courts ostensibly award expectation damages regardless of the nature of the contract, in reality they award reliance damages in cases in which it is clear that reliance losses differ significantly from the value of the relevant promise.

On this basis, it is therefore possible to explain the basic rule in contract damages as a rule that attempts, contrary to appearances, to protect plaintiffs' reliance interests. Significantly, few, if any, contemporary contract theorists have adopted this account as a *general* explanation of contract damages. Fuller and Purdue themselves did not explicitly claim to be explaining all damages awards (though they came close to doing so), and in later writings Fuller distanced himself from the stronger claims of the 1936 article.[31] That said, it is not easy to reject the reliance based interpretation of damages on the grounds that it does not fit what courts actually do. To be sure, Fuller and Atiyah's explanations of cases involving non-competitive markets could be debated, but it seems unlikely such a debate would reach any clear conclusion. The necessary evidence regarding evidentiary/administrative difficulties (on which Fuller's explanation relies) and the disparity between what courts say they are doing and what they are actually doing (on which Atiyah's explanation relies) is either not available or can be interpreted in different ways.

[30] Atiyah (1995) 456–64.   [31] Fuller (1941).

The reluctance of contract theorists, including myself, to adopt the reliance-based interpretation of damages must therefore be explained on other grounds. Two such grounds seem particularly important (3.2). The first is that the reliance-based interpretation is inconsistent with what courts say they are doing; courts do not say that they are awarding expectation damages as a proxy for reliance damages. Moreover, they still do not say this despite the fact that Fuller and Purdue's article was written in 1936, and is well-known by most common law judges. The second reason is that the moral premises that inspired Fuller and Purdue's interpretation are far from self-evident. On the one hand, the moral objection to enforcing promises *qua* promises seems overstated. As I argued in Chapter 3, a strong argument can be made that failing to perform a promise harms the promisee, and that it does this even if the promisee never relied on the promise (3.1.4). If this is correct, there is nothing 'queer' in enforcing promises *qua* promises. On the other hand, a strong argument can also be made that, contrary to what Fuller and Purdue assumed, it is *not* legitimate for courts to protect reliance *qua* reliance (3.2.1). If this argument is correct—and the point is controversial—then what is queer is to enforce reliance *qua* reliance.

For these reasons, I conclude that, although the reliance-based interpretation of contract damages is theoretically interesting, it is ultimately unpersuasive. The traditional view that contract damages compensate for the value of a promised performance remains the most convincing view.

In the remainder of this chapter, three specific features of the basic damages rule are examined in more detail: (1) the non-availability of punitive damages, (2) the limited availability of 'cost of performance' damages, and (3) the exclusion of recovery for losses that are too remote (under which heading mitigation and non-pecuniary losses are discussed). Aside from being interesting in their own right, these features of the damages rule have in common that they are often said to be evidence against the traditional view that contractual obligations are rights-based, promissory duties.

11.3.3. PUNITIVE DAMAGES

It is orthodox law that, with rare exceptions, a contract breaker will not be made to pay punitive damages, nor to face any other form of punishment —even when the breach was deliberate.[32] This rule raises a theoretical

---

[32] *Cassel & Co v Broome* [1972] AC 1027. The exceptions, which I discuss below, are found in common law jurisdictions outside of the United Kingdom (notably the United States).

puzzle. The law, like morality, normally regards intentional wrongdoing differently than unintentional wrongdoing; specifically, intentional wrongdoing is normally punished—either through the criminal law or by punitive damages. Thus, while damaging another's property through lack of care is a tort, damaging the same property deliberately is a crime. Admittedly, certain torts do not have criminal equivalents (e.g., defamation), but these torts typically support awards of punitive damages.[33] The puzzle, then, is to explain why breaches of contractual duties are treated differently in this regard.

Efficiency based approaches to remedies have a ready explanation for this rule. They explain it on the same grounds that they explain the rule that specific performance is a secondary remedy (11.1.4)—namely that it is undesirable to require performance of inefficient contracts. More specifically, efficiency accounts of the law argue that if deliberate breach were penalized, contracting parties would effectively be forced to perform, and this would be the case even when the cost of performance is greater than the value of performance. In the case of *Tito v Waddell* that I discussed earlier, for example, had the British Phosphate mining company faced the prospect of punishment for failing to perform, it likely would have gone ahead and completed the replanting—even though replanting cost far more than it was worth to the islanders. By contrast, under the current rule in which the only penalty for breach is a requirement to pay compensation, British Phosphate had an incentive to breach—which is exactly what it did. As we have seen, setting damages at an amount equal to the value of the promised performance gives contracting parties incentives to perform when, but only when, performance is efficient (11.1.6). A rule permitting punishment for breach changes these incentives.

But from the traditional rights-based view of contract law, the refusal to punish deliberate breach is a genuine puzzle. If breach of contract is a wrong, as this view asserts, why does the law not punish it when it is done deliberately? There is no easy answer to this question. The suggestion that it would be too difficult to distinguish deliberate from non-deliberate breaches is unconvincing. This difficulty could be solved by giving the defendant the benefit of a strong presumption that breach is not deliberate. More promising at first instance is the idea that breach of contract should not be punished because the relevant obligation has been created voluntarily rather than (as in the case of tort obligations) imposed by the state. Private citizens should not be permitted to create new crimes. But

---

[33] *Cassel & Co v Broome* [1972] AC 1027.

on closer inspection, this idea also fails to convince. Contracting parties would not actually 'create' the crime of deliberate breach of contract; they would merely be able to specify the content of the contractual duty whose breach would qualify as criminal. In addition, while this idea might count weakly against making deliberate breach a crime, it has little, if any, force against an award of punitive damages.

In the end, the most plausible explanation of the rule from a rights-based perspective is the traditional one that breach of contract is simply not serious enough to attract punishment. The idea underlying this explanation is not that the kinds of pecuniary harms associated with breach of contract are unimportant; pecuniary losses can, of course, be very serious. In any event, the law is clearly willing to punish wrongs that cause only financial loss—fraud is an obvious example. Instead, the underlying idea is that the kinds of financial losses that are caused by deliberate breaches of contract are different—and so less serious—than the losses that are the focus of tort claims because in a typical case of deliberate breach, the breaching party is willing to pay compensation. In *Tito*, for example, the British Phosphate mining company never denied its liability for the losses caused by its breach. To be sure, the courts would not allow a defendant charged with assault to go unpunished simply because she could prove that she was at all times willing to pay compensation. It is at this point in the argument that the distinction between pecuniary and non-pecuniary harm becomes relevant. Offering to pay compensation for a physical assault does little to reduce the seriousness of the assault. But offering to pay compensation for a purely financial loss has just this effect. The breach remains a wrong—but it is a less serious wrong if the loss is pecuniary *and* the breach is accompanied by an intention to compensate.

Of course, the above explanation does not apply to cases in which defendants not only deliberately breach, but also deliberately try to avoid paying compensation when they know compensation is owed. Sometimes the mere fact that breach was deliberate is evidence of this latter intent. This will be the case where the primary obligation is monetary—say where an insurer fails to pay out on a claim that it knows is valid, in the hopes that the insured will give up trying to collect. In such cases, the seriousness of the wrong is not mitigated by an intent to compensate, and so punishment would seem appropriate in principle. But even here, what is being punished is not so much a breach of contract as the defendant's extra-contractual attempts to deny liability. It is also worth noting that it is in situations of just this kind that courts in some common law jurisdictions have, exceptionally, punished contract breachers.[34]

The idea that breach of contract is not serious enough to justify punishment is more convincing than the alternative rights-based explanations of the common law's approach to punishing breach. But it does not provide a fully satisfactory explanation of this approach. The explanation suggests that breach of contract is merely different in degree, and not in kind, from other wrongs. But this is not how judges and lawyers actually regard such breaches; breach of contract is regarded as qualitatively different from other breaches. This objection might be disregarded if the rule against punishing deliberate breach could be explained as a mere historical quirk or as an administrative convenience. But this is not possible. No Western legal system punishes deliberate breaches as a matter of course. Indeed, so far as I am aware, no judge or legal scholar has ever argued that deliberate breach should, in principle, attract punishment. I conclude, therefore, that the law's refusal to punish deliberate breach remains a puzzle from the perspective of rights-based approaches to contract law.

11.3.4. COST OF PERFORMANCE VERSUS DIMINUTION IN VALUE

A controversial issue in the common law is whether courts should assess monetary awards at the level of 'cost of performance' as opposed to 'diminution in value' in cases in which these amounts differ. Cost of performance (or 'cost of cure') is the cost to the plaintiff of obtaining substitute performance by a third party. By contrast, diminution in value is the value to the plaintiff, in monetary terms, of the performance. Typically, these amounts are the same because the plaintiff usually values performance at least as much as performance costs (which is why the plaintiff was willing to pay the defendant for such performance in the first place). But these two amounts may differ in cases in which circumstances have changed since the contract was made or in which the contract was entered into on the basis of a mistake. More specifically, in such cases the cost of performance may exceed its value to the plaintiff. The case of *Tito v Waddell*[35] can again be used to illustrate the point. In *Tito*, the cost to replant the mined island was in the order of millions of

---

[34] *Whiten v Pilot Insurance Co* [2002] 1 SCR 595; *Freeman & Mills Inc v Belcher Oil Co* 900 P2d 669 (1995).
[35] [1977] Ch 106.

pounds, but the value of replanting to the plaintiff islanders (who no longer lived on the island) was, on the assumed facts, a nominal sum. In the actual decision, the islanders were awarded the latter sum — diminution in value — as compensation for the mining company's failure to fulfill its contractual obligation to replant. The islanders' claim for the cost of performance measure was denied. The decision has been subject to much discussion — and criticism — but most common law courts have followed it.[36]

In debating the merits of cost of performance versus diminution in value, an initial observation is that it is misleading to describe these two forms of monetary awards as alternative measures of *damages*. Damages, in the sense the term is used in this chapter and by which it is ordinarily understood, are a compensatory measure. They are designed to compensate the plaintiff for the loss she suffered as a result of the defendant's breach. By definition, the extent of this loss, when measured in monetary terms, is equivalent to the monetary value that the plaintiff places on performance. The loss is simply the converse, in monetary terms, of the value of performance. It follows that a monetary award assessed at the level of diminution in value is a damages award in this sense; it straightforwardly compensates plaintiffs for the value of the promised performance.[37] In short, so far as a court has chosen to make an award of compensatory damages — and *only* compensatory damages — the appropriate measure of such damages is diminution in value.

By contrast, cost of performance awards clearly have a different function; such awards are assessed not on the basis of the value of performance, but the cost of actually doing the work. They are assessed, in other words, from a performance-based perspective rather than a loss-based perspective. As such, cost of performance is best understood as a form of substitute specific performance; it represents the amount of money needed to obtain substitute performance.[38] Like a standard award of specific performance, the purpose of such awards is not to remedy the loss arising from a breach, but rather to ensure that plaintiffs receive what they were promised.

---

[36] But not all: e.g. *Groves v John Wunder Co* (1939) 205 Minn 163.

[37] This is not to deny that courts sometimes wrongly measure the value of performance entirely in pecuniary terms (as they arguably did in *Tito*). This mistake is attributable to general limits on the recovery of non-pecuniary losses (which limits I discuss below).

[38] Which is how such awards are regarded in most civil law jurisdictions: e.g. Art. 1602 *Civil Code of Quebec*.

If it is correct to regard diminution in value awards as ordinary compensatory damages, such awards should, in principle, be available to plaintiffs on demand—which is the case under the current law. The more difficult question is when should a cost of performance award—understood now as a form of substitute specific performance—be available? In principle, the answer must be that cost of performance should prima facie be available whenever defendants are unwilling, but able, to fulfill their contractual obligations—which in practice means anytime that defendants are found in breach of contract. This conclusion follows from our earlier discussion of (actual) specific performance, in which it was concluded that, in principle, specific performance should be available whenever the defendant is unwilling to perform (11.1.3). The main difference between claims for actual specific performance and claims for substitute specific performance (i.e., cost of performance) is that the concerns for personal liberty that (I argued) justify limiting specific relief, do not apply to claims for substitutional relief. The defendant is merely required to pay a sum of money to the plaintiff.

On this basis, it may be concluded that, prima facie, cost of performance awards should be generally available as a remedy for breach of contract. There are just two situations in which it would seem appropriate to deny requests for such relief; each is important in explaining why cost of performance is not, in practice, routinely awarded. The first situation is where the relevant work will not actually be done, either because it is no longer possible to do it or because the plaintiff does not intend to do it (and has not yet done it). If a cost of performance award is justified on the basis that it is substitute specific performance, such awards must be conditional on the relevant work actually being done. The purpose of the award, as I said a moment ago, is to ensure that the plaintiff receives what was actually promised under the contract. The second situation in which the prima facie argument in favour of cost of performance does not apply is where the plaintiff is seeking the order in bad faith. In this context, 'bad faith' means that the plaintiff is seeking the order in order to punish the defendant or to set a precedent for future bargaining. In such cases, although the plaintiff can honestly state that he intends to do the relevant work, the explanation for this intention is not that the plaintiff actually seeks the desired performance. Rather, the plaintiff's underlying motive is either to punish the defendant (by making the defendant pay a larger sum than he would pay in ordinary damages) or to set a precedent for future bargaining (so as to induce future co-contractors who breach their contracts to settle for a higher figure). Neither of these reasons justify granting specific performance, substitute or otherwise.

The approach of English courts to awarding cost of performance is broadly consistent with the above account. The basic rule is that cost of performance is awarded only when there is a genuine intent to do the work (or the work is already done).[39] Thus, in *Tito v Waddell* the islanders' request for cost of performance was denied because they did not have this intent. The second limitation that I mentioned—that the award must be sought in good faith—has never been articulated explicitly in these words, but it explains certain cases in which cost of performance has been refused. For example, in *Ruxley Electronics v Forsyth*,[40] the court refused the plaintiff homeowner the sum necessary to lower a swimming pool to the contractually specified depth, even though the plaintiff offered to give an undertaking to the court that he would use any award for this purpose. It seems clear from the facts of the case that the court was concerned that the plaintiff was seeking the order in bad faith.

If the above interpretation of diminution in value and cost of performance awards is correct, the decision to award only diminution in value in cases like *Tito v Waddell* is appropriate. But why, then, are such decisions so often criticized? The answer, I suggest, is that in many of these cases —*Tito v Waddell* is a good example—the decision is objectionable for reasons unrelated to the choice between diminution in value and cost of performance awards. In broad terms, the objection to the outcome in *Tito v Waddell* is that the mining company made a windfall profit. Rather than having to pay for the replanting of the island, the company simply kept the money it would have devoted to this purpose. Described in this way, the islanders' claim to that sum of money is properly described not as a claim for either diminution in value or cost of performance, but as a claim for what is sometimes called 'disgorgement' of profits.[41] The objection to the decision in *Tito v Waddell* is that the mining company should have been made to disgorge to the islanders the profits that it made from its breach.

A claim for disgorgement is not a contractual claim. But considering the possible reasons for allowing such a claim helps to explain why it is often thought (mistakenly) that cost of performance is the appropriate award in cases like *Tito*. There are two main possibilities. The first is that defendants should disgorge their profits because they were obtained as a

---

[39] *Radford v De Froberville* [1977] 1 WLR 1262.   [40] [1996] AC 344.
[41] L. Smith (1995).

result of the defendants' wrongdoing.[42] In this view, the plaintiff's claim in a case like *Tito* should be analogized to cases in which tortfeasors are required to pay over any profits made as a result of their wrongful behaviour. A defendant who has profited through his trespass or breach of copyright, for example, may be required to hand over those profits to the owner of the property or copyright, and such an order will be made even if the infringement did not harm the property or prevent the owner from making a similar profit.[43]

Under the traditional rule governing recovery for so-called 'restitution for wrongs', disgorgement of profits is not available for a breach of contract.[44] Considering whether that rule should be changed—as many have argued[45]—is outside the scope of this book. But it should be noted that granting a disgorgement remedy on the basis that the defendant is a wrongdoer does not address the essence of the plaintiff's complaint in cases like *Tito*. The idea that contract breakers should be made to hand over the profits of their breach applies, in principle, not just to cases like *Tito*, in which cost of performance and diminution in value differ, but also to ordinary breach cases, in which these two figures are the same. In addition, although the idea that wrongdoers should not profit from their wrongs explains why the mining company should give up its profits, it does not explain why the islanders should receive that profit. It does not explain, in other words, why the *islanders* have a complaint against the mining company in *Tito*. Finally, if disgorgement is explained on the basis that defendants should give up their wrongfully obtained profits, then such orders could, in some cases, lead to plaintiffs obtaining windfall profits. *Tito* again can be used to illustrate this point. The mining company's 'profit' from breach is the amount of money they saved by not having to replant. Yet this sum might have been much larger than the original cost of replanting; this would be the case, for example, if the destruction of the island (by bombing) that forced the islanders to vacate the island increased the costs of replanting. If the islanders were awarded this larger sum, it is they who would make a windfall profit from the breach.

The second possible reason for awarding disgorgement in a case like *Tito* is on the basis that the plaintiff is making an ordinary claim in unjust

---

[42] Jones (1983).

[43] *United Australia Ltd v Barclays Bank Ltd* [1941] AC 1.

[44] A limited exception (that would not apply to case like *Tito*) was recently introduced in *AG v Blake* [2001] AC 268.

[45] e.g. Jones (1983); L. Smith (1995).

mere probability.[52] Rather, it turns on a complex, multifaceted notion of responsibility. Without going into detail, it is clear that the notion of responsibility, in turn, depends on various difficult-to-quantify factors, including probability of loss, knowledge of the likelihood of loss, the purpose of the underlying duty, and any undertakings or understandings between the parties.[53] The significance of this for the question at hand is that the apparent differences in the remoteness tests in contract and tort are explicable on the ground that contracting parties have, by definition, had prior interactions, which interactions will normally affect conclusions about responsibility. Most obviously, the parties, in their agreement, may have explicitly or implicitly allocated certain risks to one party or the other. The important point, however, is that whether and to what extent this has happened with respect to any particular contract is a question of fact. It is not inherent in a contract that losses are generally intended to lie where they fall. Nor is the opposite conclusion inherent to tort claims. In many situations that give rise to tort claims, the parties will also have had previous interactions (sometimes through contracts), and those understandings will affect (in theory and in law) the application of the remoteness rules, just as if the claim was a contract claim. A contractual undertaking may limit, for example, the scope of recovery in tort law. In short, the apparent difference between the remoteness rules in contract and tort is better explained as a difference in application than a difference in principle. Consistent with this conclusion, judges have sometimes challenged the view that there is actually a difference in the two tests.[54]

Of course, nothing said above explains the normative basis for the remoteness test. Why must losses be 'reasonably foreseeable'; and what does 'reasonably foreseeable' actually mean? I will not attempt to answer these difficult questions here. If my arguments above are correct, the answers will not tell us anything special about contractual obligations (though they may tell us something about obligations generally, or at least about remedies for their breach). The justification and meaning of remoteness is a general question for the law of obligations.

There exist two other remedial rules that, like the remoteness rule, are sometimes presented as evidence that the law gives only weak support to the enforcement of promises: (1) the mitigation rule, and (2) the rule limiting recovery for non-pecuniary losses. The conclusion that the

---

[52] As made clear in the *The Heron* (previous footnote).
[53] e.g. Hart and Honore (1985); Howarth (1995) 108–11.
[54] e.g. *H Parson (Livestock) Ltd v Uttley Ingham & Co Ltd* [1978] QB 791.

remoteness rules are part of the general rules on remedies helps in understanding each of these rules.

The mitigation rule

According to the mitigation rule, plaintiffs are precluded from recovering damages in respect of losses that they could have avoided had they acted reasonably.[55] Thus, if a purchaser rejects goods ordered under a contract, the vendor cannot recover for losses that she could have avoided by selling the goods to a third party.

Even more than the remoteness rule, the mitigation rule is often assumed to be evidence against the traditional view that contract law enforces promissory obligations. Indeed, the mitigation rule is often presented as evidence that contract law is willing to uphold principles directly in opposition to the idea that contractual obligations are self-imposed (i.e., promises)—namely the idea that contracting parties have, in certain circumstances, duties to positively assist the other party. Some scholars thus find within the so-called 'duty to mitigate', support for a principle of altruism or co-operation.[56]

The difficulty with this interpretation is that there is no actual *duty* to mitigate. If such a duty existed, a person who failed to mitigate could be ordered to do so, or at least ordered to pay damages for breaching the duty. But the law is indifferent as to whether a victim of breach mitigates. The mitigation rule simply provides that damages will be calculated *as if* the defendant mitigated. Whether defendants actually mitigate is irrelevant when determining the amount of damages in contract.

Thus described, the mitigation rule is best explained as one aspect of the general concept of remoteness; the reason plaintiffs cannot recover for losses they could have avoided by acting reasonably is that such losses are too remote. They are too remote because when determining which losses are reasonably foreseeable (or which 'naturally flow') as a result of a breach, the background assumption is that the relevant parties will act reasonably. Mitigation is just what (reasonable) people normally do. This conclusion—that mitigation is an aspect of remoteness rather than a special limit on contractual obligations—is consistent with how the courts approach similar issues in tort claims. In functionally similar tort cases, courts apply the same mitigation rule—but they describe the rule (correctly) as a remoteness rule. Imagine, for example, that a plaintiff

---

[55] *British Westinghouse Co v Underground Electric Ry Co* [1912] AC 673.
[56] Fried (1981) 131; Atiyah (1986) 124.

brings a claim, in tort, for damages arising from the defendant painter having ruined the plaintiff's suit by dropping paint on it while the plaintiff was walking beside a building site. Suppose further that, in addition to claiming for the cost of the suit, the plaintiff claims compensation for having lost his job. In support of the latter claim, he explains that he never showed up to work that week because he had been planning to wear the suit that was ruined. This claim would almost certainly be denied; the court would find that damages for the loss of the job were too remote. More specifically, they would find that it was not reasonably foreseeable that the plaintiff would stay at home rather than go to work wearing one of his other suits. The exact same result would be reached if the plaintiff's claim was made in contract (say because the suit was ruined by a painter working under contract with the plaintiff). But rather than saying that the loss was too remote, the court would say that the plaintiff should have mitigated his loss by wearing a different suit. The point I wish to make is that in each case the underlying reason for denying recovery is the same.

Non-pecuniary loss

A final limit on damages for breach of contract in the common law is found in the rule that compensation is not available for non-pecuniary losses except in cases in which the purpose of the contract is to provide (non-pecuniary) enjoyment or pleasure.[57] No such limit is applied, of course, to tort claims. On this basis, the rule is sometimes presented as yet another special limit on the recovery of damages in contract. More specifically, this rule is sometimes thought to be further evidence that contract law does not take seriously the idea of enforcing promises.

Again, however, the assumption seems misplaced. Like mitigation and the (allegedly) narrow test of remoteness in contract, this rule is best explained as an application of the general principles of remoteness to the kinds of facts typically seen in contract claims. The reason a claim in respect of non-pecuniary losses should typically fail in a contract case is that such losses are not reasonably foreseeable. This is the case for the simple reason that most contracts (and especially those that go before the courts) are made between commercial parties for commercial purposes. The parties enter such contracts to obtain pecuniary advantages; as a consequence it is not reasonably foreseeably that they will suffer non-pecuniary harm from a breach. This is not to deny that sometimes

---

[57] *Jarvis v Swan Tours* [1973] QB 233.

commercial plaintiffs in commercial contracts do suffer such harm—the point is just that it is not reasonably foreseeable that this will happen.

Of course, not all contracts are entered into for pecuniary reasons, and, more generally, it is sometimes the case that the non-pecuniary harms that are caused by a breach are reasonably foreseeable. But such contracts are precisely those for which the law allows recovery for non-pecuniary losses. In principle, compensation for non-pecuniary loss is possible where one of the purposes of the contract is, precisely, non-pecuniary. Overall, then, we can see that, again, contractual claims are treated identically to tort claims. In each, non-pecuniary losses may be recovered if they are reasonably foreseeable. The only difference—which is significant in practice—is that as a matter of fact such losses are rarely reasonably foreseeable in contract cases. Admittedly, it might be clearer if the courts adopted the civil law approach of stating that, in principle, the same rule is applied to all damages claims.[58] But as was true with respect to mitigation, the apparent distinctions between the rules in contract and tort turn out, in practice, to have little significance.

I conclude that the various so-called special limits on recovery of damages in contract are, in general, best explained as mere applications of the general principle that remote losses are not compensable.

11.4. CONCLUSION

The main conclusions of this chapter can be summarized under three themes that have been a recurrent focus of this book. The first theme is a concern for the proper classification of legal rules. As regards remedial rules, I have argued that, although these rules are important for understanding contractual obligations, they are not, in the end, a part of contract law, strictly speaking. Contract law is confined to the rules governing the creation and content of contractual obligations. Remedial rules govern claims for the enforcement of such obligations. As such, they comprise one part of a broader legal category ('remedies' for want of a better name), under which category is included the rules governing the enforcement of both contractual and non-contractual obligations.

The second theme concerns the proper understanding of both the nature of, and justification for, contractual obligations. As regards this theme, the arguments in this chapter have sought to dispel the notion that remedies provide strong evidence against the traditional view that

---

[58] e.g. Art. 1607 *Civil Code of Quebec*.

contractual obligations are rights-based promissory obligations. While acknowledging that alternative accounts, in particular the accounts offered by efficiency theories and reliance theories, fit well with most remedial rules, I have argued that, with the possible exception of the rules governing punishment for breach, the traditional view also fits those rules equally well.

This leads to the third and final theme, which is a concern for broader methodological issues in contract theory. In Chapter 1, I argued that it is often not possible to choose between competing accounts of contract law on the basis that one account fits the law better than the alternatives. Rather, such decisions must be made on the basis of other criteria, such as the theories' moral foundations, their coherence, or the extent to which they make intelligible what judges say and think they are doing ('transparency'). In this chapter, I have focused on the fit criterion when assessing competing explanations of remedies. But my conclusion that, broadly speaking, the leading alternatives fit the law equally well, is consistent with the above argument. More specifically, the discussion in this chapter makes evident that in order to fully understand specific contract law topics it is necessary not just to examine the relevant rules and decisions —as I have done throughout Part III—but also to consider broader methodological issues of the kind discussed in Parts I and II of this book.

Bibliography

Abrahmson, Mark (1978). *Functionalism*. NJ: Prentice Hall.

Angelo and Ellinger (1993). 'Unconscionability: A Comparative Study of the Approaches in England, France, Germany and the United States' 14 *Loyola of LA Int'l & Comp LJ* 439.

Aristotle (1962). Book V, *Nicomachean Ethics*, Martin Ostwald (trans). Indianapolis, Ind: Bobbs–Merrill.

Arrow, K. (1982). 'Risk Perception in Psychology and Economics' *J Econ Inquiry* 1.

Ayres, I. and Gertner, R. (1989). 'Filling Gaps in Incomplete Contracts: An Economic Theory of Default Rules' 99 *Yale LJ* 729.

Atiyah, P. (1979). *The Rise and Fall of Freedom of Contract*. Oxford: Clarendon Press.

Atiyah, P. (1981). *Promises, Morals, and Law*. Oxford: Clarendon Press.

Atiyah, P. (1982). 'Economic Duress and the Overborne Will' 98 *Law Quarterly R* 197.

Atiyah, P. (1986). *Essays on Contract*. Oxford: Clarendon Press.

Atiyah, P. (1995). *An Introduction to the Law of Contract* (5th edn). Oxford: Clarendon Press.

Barnett, R. (1986). 'A Consent Theory of Contract' 86 *Columbia LR* 269.

Barnett, R. (1986b). 'Contract Remedies and Inalienable Rights' 4 *Soc. Phil. & Policy* 179.

Barnett, R. (1991). 'Rights and Remedies in a Consent Theory of Contract' in R.G. Frey and Christopher W. Morris (eds.), *Liability and Responsibility: Essays in Law and Morals*. Cambridge: Cambridge University Press.

Barnett, R. (1992). 'The Sounds of Silence: Default Rules and Contractual Consent' 78 *Virginia LR* 821.

Barnett, R. (1996). 'The Death of Reliance' 46 *J of Legal Education* 518.

Barton, J.H. (1972). 'The Economic Basis of Damages for Breach of Contract' 1 *J Legal Studies*. 277.

Beatson, J. (1991). *The Use and Abuse of Unjust Enrichment*. Oxford: Oxford University Press.

Beatson, J. and Friedmann, D. (1995). *Good Faith and Fault in Contract Law*. Oxford: Clarendon Press.

Becker, M. (1987). 'Promissory Estoppel Damages' 16 *Hofstra LR* 131.

Belley, J-G. (2003). 'La *Loi sur la protection du consommateur* comme archetype d'une conception du contrat' in Pierre-Claude Lafond (ed.), *Melange Claude Masse*. Cowansville, Qc.: Yvon-Blais.

Benson, P. (1989). 'Hegel and Contract Law' 10 *Cardozo LR* 1077.

Benson, P. (1992). 'The Basis of Corrective Justice and Its Relation to Distributive Justice' 77 *Iowa LR* 515.

Benson, P. (1995). 'The Idea of a Public Basis of Justification for Contract' 33 *Osgoode Hall LJ* 273.

Benson, P. (1995b). 'The Basis for Excluding Liability for Economic Loss in Tort Law' in D. Owens (ed.), *The Philosophical Foundations of Tort Law*. Oxford: Clarendon Press.

Benson, P. (1996). 'Contract' in D. Patterson (ed.), *A Companion to the Philosophy of Law and Legal Theory*. Oxford: Blackwell.

Benson, P. (2001). 'The Unity of Contract Law' in P. Benson, *The Theory of Contract Law*. Cambridge: Cambridge University Press.

Bentham, J. (1838). "Anarchical Fallacies" reprinted in Melden, A. (ed.). *Human Rights* (Belmont: Wadsworth, 1970) 28.

Bentham, J. (1948). *An Introduction to the Principles of Morals and Legislation*. Wilfred Harrison (ed.). Oxford: Blackwell.

Bentham, J. (1977). *A Comment on the Commentaries and a Fragment on Government*. Burns, J.H. and H.L. Hart (eds.). London: Athlone Press.

Bernstein, L. (1999). 'The Questionable Empirical Basis of Article 2's Incorporation Strategy: A Preliminary Study' 66 *U Chicago LR* 710.

Birks, P. (1985). *An Introduction to the Law of Restitution*. Oxford: Clarendon Press.

Birks, P. (1995). 'The Concept of a Civil Wrong' in D. Owen (ed.), *The Philosophical Foundations of Tort Law*. Oxford: Clarendon Press.

Birks, P. and Chin Nyuk Yin (1995b). 'On the Nature of Undue Influence' in J. Beatson and D. Friedmann (eds.), *Good Faith and Fault in Contract Law*. Oxford: Clarendon Press.

Birks, P. (1996). 'Failure of Consideration' in F.D. Rose (ed.), *Consensus ad Idem*. London: Hart Publishing.

Birks, P. (1997). *The Classification of Obligations*. Oxford: Oxford University Press.

Birks, P. (1999). 'The Role of Fault in the Law of Unjust Enrichment' in W. Swadling and G. Jones (eds.), *The Search for Principle*. Oxford: Oxford University Press.

Birks, P. (2000). 'Rights, Wrongs and Remedies' 20 *Oxford J Legal Studies* 1.

Bishop, W. (1985). 'The Choice of Remedy for Breach of Contract' 14 *J Legal Studies* 299.

Bishop, W. (1983). 'The Contract-Tort Boundary and the Economics of Insurance' 12 *J Legal Studies* 241.

Brandt, R.B. (1979). *A Theory of the Good and the Right*. Oxford: Clarendon Press.

Buckley, F. (1990). 'Three Theories of Substantive Fairness' 19 *Hofstra LR* 33.

Bufnoir, Claude (1924). *Propriété et Contrat: théorie des modes d'acquisition des droits réels et des sources des obligations* (2nd edn). Paris: Rousseau.

Burmingham, R.L. (1970). 'Breach of Contract, Damage Measures, and Economic Efficiency' 24 *Rutgers LR* 273.

Burrows, A. (1993). *The Law of Restitution*. London: Butterworths.

Brudner, A. (1993). 'Reconstructing Contracts' 43 *U of Toronto LJ* 1.

Calabresi, G. (1970). *The Costs of Accidents*. New Haven: Yale University Press.

Calabresi, G. (1991). 'The Pointlessness of Pareto: Carrying Coase Further' 100 *Yale LJ* 1211.

Calabresi, G. and Hirschoff, J. (1972). 'Toward a Test of Strict Liability in Tort' 81 *Yale LJ* 1055.

Cheshire, Fifoot, and Furmston (2001). *Law of Contract*. London: Butterworths.

Chitty, Joseph (1999). *Chitty on Contracts* (28th edn). H.G. Beale (ed.). London: Sweet & Maxwell.

Coase, R.E. (1960). 'The Problem of Social Cost' 3 *J of Law and Economics* 1.

Cohen, F. (1953). 'Transcendental Nonsense and the Functional Approach' 35 *Colombia LR* 808.

Coleman, J. (1980). 'Efficiency, Utility, and Wealth Maximization' 8 *Hofstra LR* 509.

Coleman, J. (1982). 'The Normative Basis of Economic Analysis: A Critical Review of Richard Posner's *The Economics of Justice*' 34 *Stanford LR* 1105.

Coleman, J. (1988). *Markets, Morals and the Law*. Cambridge: Cambridge University Press.

Coleman, J. (1992). *Risks and Wrongs*. New York: Cambridge University Press.

Collins, H. (1997). *The Law of Contract* (3rd edn). London: Butterworths.

Coote, B. (1980). 'Duress by Threatened Breach of Contract' *Cambridge LJ* 40.

Cooter, R. and Ulen, T. (2000). *Law and Economics* (3rd edn). New York: Addison-Wesley.

Corbin, A.L. (1917–18). 'Does a Pre-Existing Duty Defeat Consideration?' 27 *Yale LJ* 362.

Corbin A.L. (1952). *Corbin on Contracts* (one volume edition). St. Paul: West Pub. Co.

Craswell, R. (1988). 'Contract Remedies, Renegotiation, and the Theory of Efficient Breach' 61 *S. Cal. LR* 629.

Craswell, R. (1989). 'Contract Law, Default Rules, and the Philosophy of Promising' 88 *Michigan LR* 489.

Craswell, R. (1993). 'Efficiency and Rational Bargaining in Contractual Settings' 15 *Harvard J Law & Public Policy* 805.

Craswell, R. (2001). 'Two Economic Theories of Enforcing Promises' in P. Benson (ed.), *The Theory of Contract Law*. Cambridge: Cambridge University Press.

Danzig, J. (1975). '*Hadley v Baxendale*: A Study in the Industrialization of the Law' 4 *J of Legal Studies* 241.

Davidson, D. (1986). 'A Nice Derangement of Epitaphs' in R. Grandy and R. Warner (eds.), *Philosophical Grounds of Rationality*. Oxford: Clarendon Press.

Dawson, J.P. (1947). 'Economic Duress — An Essay in Perspective' 45 *Michigan LR* 253.

Dalzell, J. (1942). 'Duress by Economic Pressure' 20 *North Carolina LR* 341.

De Moor, A. (1987). 'Are Contracts Promises' in J. Bell and J. Eekelaar (eds.), *Oxford Readings in Jurisprudence*. Oxford: Clarendon Press.

DeMoor, A. (1990). 'Intention in the Law of Contract: Elusive of Illusory' 106 *Law Quarterly R* 632.

Devlin, Patrick (1959). *The Enforcement of Morals*. London: Oxford University Press.

Dworkin, R.M. (1978). *Taking Rights Seriously*. Cambridge, Mass.: Harvard University Press.

Dworkin, R.M. (1986). *Law's Empire*. Cambridge, Mass.: Belknap Press.

Eisenberg, M.A. (1979). 'Donative Promises' 47 *U Chicago LR* 16.

Eisenberg, M.A. (1982). 'The Bargain Principle and its Limits' 95 *Harvard LR* 741.

Eisenberg, M.A. (2001). 'The Theory of Contracts' in P. Benson (ed.), *The Theory of Contract Law*. Cambridge: Cambridge University Press.

Ellickson, R. (1989). 'Bringing Culture and Human Fraility to Economic

Actors: A Critique of Classical Law and Economics' 65 *Chicago-Kent LR* 23.

Ellickson, E. (1991). *Order Without Law: How Neighbours Settle Disputes*. Cambridge, Mass.: Harvard University Press.

Elster, J. (1993). 'Some Unresolved Problems in the Theory of Rational Behaviour' 36 *Acta Sociologica* 179.

Endicott, T. (2000). *Vagueness in Law*. Oxford: Oxford University Press.

Endicott, T. (2000b). 'Objectivity, Subjectivity, and Incomplete Agreements' in J. Horder ed. *Oxford Essays in Jurisprudence* (4ᵗʰ Series). Oxford: Oxford University Press.

Epstein, R.A. (1973). 'A Theory of Strict Liability' 2 *J Legal Studies* 151.

Epstein, R.A. (1975). 'Unconscionabilitiy: A Critical Reappraisal' 18 *J of Law and Economics* 293.

Farber, D.A. and Matheson, J.H. (1985). 'Beyond Promissory Estoppel: Contract Law and the "Invisible Handshake" ' 52 *U. Chicago LR* 903.

Farnsworth, E.A. (1999). *Contracts* (3ʳᵈ edn). New York: Aspen Law & Business.

Feinberg, J. (1986). *Harm to Self*. Oxford: Oxford University Press.

Finnis, J. (1980). *Natural Law and Natural Rights*. New York: Oxford University Press.

Finnis, J. (1984). 'The Authority of Law in the Predicament of Contemporary Social Theory' 1 *Notre Dame J of Law and Social Policy* 116.

Fletcher, G. (1972). 'Fairness and Utility in Tort Theory' 85 *Harvard LR* 537.

Frank, J. (1930). *Law and the Modern Mind*. New York: Bretano's.

Frank, J. (1931). 'What Courts Do in Fact' 26 *Illinois LR* 653.

Frankfurt, Harry G. (1988). *The Importance of What We Care About: Philosophical Essays*. Cambridge: Cambridge University Press.

Fried, C. (1981). *Contract as Promise*. Cambridge Mass.: Harvard University Press.

Fried, C. (1981). 'Is Liberty Possible?' The Tanner Lectures on Human Values.

Friedman, D. (1989). 'The Efficient Breach Fallacy' 18 *J of Legal Studies*.

Friedman, D. (1995). 'The Performance Interest in Contract Damages' 111 *Law Quarterly R* 628.

Fuller, L. and Purdue, W. (1936). 'The Reliance Interest in Contract Damages' 46 *Yale LJ* 53.

Fuller, L. (1941). 'Consideration and Form' 41 *Columbia LR* 799.

Fuller, L. (1969). *The Morality of Law* (2ⁿᵈ edn). New Haven: Yale University Press.

Gardner, G. (1931). 'An Inquiry into the Principles of the Law of Contracts' XLVI *Harvard LR* 1.

Gardner, S. (1992). 'Trashing with Trollope; A Deconstruction of the Postal Rules in Contract' 12 *Oxford J Legal Studies* 170.

George, R. (1993). *Making Men Moral*. Oxford: Oxford University Press.

Ghestin, J. and Goubeaux, G. (1977). *Traité de Droit Civil (Introduction Générale)*. Paris: LGDJ.

Ghestin, Jacques (1988). *Les Obligations — Le Contrat: Formation* (2nd edn). Paris: L.G.D.J.

Ghestin, Jacques (1993). *Les Obligations — Le Contrat: Formation* (3rd edn). Paris: L.G.D.J.

Gilles, S.G. (1992). 'Negligence, Strict Liability, and the Cheapest Cost Avoider' 78 *Virginia LR* 1291.

Gilmore (1974). *The Death of Contract*. Columbus, Ohio: Ohio State University Press.

Goddard, D. (1987). 'The Myth of Subjectivity' 7 *Legal Studies* 263.

Goetz, C.J. and Scott, R.E. (1980). 'Enforcing Promises: An Examination of the Basis of Contract' 89:7 *Yale LJ* 1261.

Goetz, C.J. and Scott, R.E. (1983). 'The Mitigation Principle: Toward a General Theory of Contractual Obligation' 69 *Virginia LR* 967.

Goff, R. and Jones, G. (1998). *The Law of Restitution*. London: Sweet & Maxwell.

Goodman, J.C. (1978). 'An Economic Theory of the Evolution of the Common Law' 7 *J of Legal Studies* 393.

Gordley, James (1981). 'Equality in Exchange' 69 *California LR* 587.

Gordley, James (1991). *The Philosophical Origins of Modern Contract Doctrine*. Oxford: Clarendon Press.

Gordely, James (1995). 'Enforcing Promises' 83 *California LR* 547.

Gordley, James (2001). *The Enforceability of Promises in European Contract Law*. Cambridge: Cambridge University Press.

Gordon, R. (1985). 'Macauley, Macneil, and the Discovery of Solidarity and Power in Contract Law' *Wisconson LR* 565.

Grotius, H. (1933). *The Rights of War and Peace, including the Law of Nature and of Nations* (trans. A.C. Campbell). Hyperion.

Gutmann, A. (1980). *Liberal Equality*. New York: Cambridge University Press.

Hale, R. (1923). 'Coercion and Distribution in a Supposedly Non-Coercive State' 38 *Political Science Quarterly* 470.

Hale, R. (1943). 'Bargaining, Duress and Economic Liberty' (1943) 43 *Columbia LR* 603.

Halston, R. (1991). 'Opportunism, Economic Duress, and Contractual Modifications' 107 *Law Quarterly R* 649.

Hamson, C.J. (1938). 'The Reform of Consideration' 54 *Law Quarterly R* 233.

Hare, R. (1982). *Moral Thinking*. Oxford: Clarendon Press.

Hart, H.L.A. (1968). *Punishment and Responsibility*. Oxford: Clarendon Press.

Hart, H.L.A. and Honore, T. (1985). *Causation in the Law* (2nd edn). Oxford: Clarendon Press.

Hart, H.L.A. (1994). *The Concept of Law* (2nd edn). New York: Oxford University Press.

Hayek, F. (1982). *Law, Legislation and Liberty: Volume 1*. London: Routledge & Keegan Paul.

Hempel, Carl Gustav (1965). 'The Logic of Functional Analysis' in *Aspects of Scientific Explanation, and Other Essays in the Philosophy of Science*. New York: New York Free Press.

Hesselink, M. (1998). 'Good Faith' in Hartkamp and Hesselink (eds.). *Towards a European Civil Code* (2nd edn). The Hague: Kluwer Law International.

Hohfeld, W.N. (1913). 'Fundamental Legal Conceptions' 23 *Yale LJ* 29.

Holmes, Oliver Wendell (1897). 'The Path of the Law' 10 *Harvard LR* 457.

Honoré, T. (1988). 'Responsibility and Luck' *Law Quarterly R* 530.

Honoré, T. (1996). 'The Morality of Tort Law — Questions and Answers' in D. Owen (ed.), *Philosophical Foundations of Tort Law*. New York: Oxford University Press.

Horowitz, Morton J. (1977). *The Transformation of American Law*. Cambridge, Mass.: Harvard University Press.

Hovenkamp, A. (1990). 'Positivism in Law and Economics' 78 *Calif. LR* 815.

Howarth, D. (1995). *Textbook on Tort*. London: Butterworths.

Hudson (1968). '*Gibbons v Proctor* Revisited' 84 *Law Quarterly R* 503.

Hume (1739). *A Treatise of Human Nature*, reprinted (1978) Selby-Bigge, ed. Oxford: Clarendon Press.

Hunt, Alan (1996). 'Marxist Theory of Law' in D. Patterson (ed.), *A Companion to the Philosophy of Law and Legal Theory*. Oxford: Blackwell.

Hurst, James Willard (1964). *Law and Economic Growth: The Legal History of the Lumber Industry in Wisconsin, 1836–1915*. Cambridge, Mass.: Harvard University Press.

Hursthouse, R. (1999). *On Virtue Ethics*. Oxford: Oxford University Press.

Ibbetson, D. (1999). *An Historical Introduction to the Law of Obligations*. Oxford: Oxford University Press.

Johnston, J.S. (1990). 'Strategic Bargaining and the Economic Theory of Contract Default Rules' 100 *Yale LJ* 615.

Jones, G. (1983). 'The Recovery of Benefits Gained From a Breach of Contract' 99 *Law Quarterly R.* 443.

Kahneman, D. and Tversky, A. (1984). 'Choice, Values, and Frames' 29 *Am. Psycho.* 341.

Kahneman, D. and Tversky, A. (1986). 'Rational Choice and the Framing of Decisions' 59 *J of Business* 251.

Kant, Immanuel (1991). *The Metaphysics of Morals* (trans. Mary Gregor). Cambridge University Press.

Kant, Immanuel (1974). *The Philosophy of Law* (trans. W. Hastie). Clifton, NJ: A.M. Kelley.

Kaplow and Shavell, S. (2001). 'Fairness v Welfare' 114 *Harvard LR* 961.

Kelsen, H. (1991). *General Theory of Norms* (trans. Michael Hartney). Oxford: Oxford University Press.

Kennedy, D. (1976). 'Form and Substance in Private Law Adjudication' 89 *Harvard LR* 1685.

Kennedy, D. (1986). 'Freedom and Constraint in Jurisprudence: A Critical Phenomenology' 36 *J of Legal Education* 518.

Kessler, F. and Fine, E. (1964). '*Culpa in Contrahendo*, Bargaining in Good Faith, and Freedom of Contract: A Comparative Study' 77 *Harvard LR* 401.

Kreps, David (1990). *A Course in Microeconomic Theory*. Princeton, NJ: Princeton University Press.

Kronman, A.T. (1978). 'Specific Performance' 45 *U Chicago LR* 351.

Kronman, A.T. (1978b). 'Mistake, Disclosure, Information and the Law of Contracts' 7 *J Legal Studies* 1.

Kronman, A.T. and Posner, R. (1979). *The Economics of Contract Law*. Boston: Little Brown & Co.

Kronman, A.T. (1980). 'Contract Law and Distributive Justice' 89 *Yale LJ* 472.

Lamond, G. (1996). 'Coercion, Threats, and the Puzzle of Blackmail' in A. Simester and A.T.H. Smith (eds.), *Harm and Culpability*. Oxford.

Lando, O. and Beale, H. (1995). *The Principles of European Contract Law*. Boston: Dordrecht.

Langille, B. and Ripstein, A. (1996). 'Strictly Speaking, It Went Without Saying' 2 *Legal Theory* 63.

Law Revision Committee (1937). Sixth Interim Report (Statute of Frauds and the Doctrine of Consideration) Cmd 5449.

Lawson, F.M. and Rudden, B. (1982). *The Law of Property* (2nd edn). Oxford: Clarendon Press.

Leff, A. (1967). 'Unconsconability and the Code — The Emperor's New Clause' 115 *U. Pennsylvania LR* 485.

Leff, A. (1970). 'Contract as Thing' 19 *American U LR* 131.

Leff, A. (1979). 'Unspeakable Ethics, Unnatural Law' (1979) 6 *Duke LJ* 1229.

Leiter, B. (1996). 'Legal Realism' in Patterson, D. *A Companion to Philosophy of Law and Legal Theory*. Oxford: Blackwell.

Lindgren, J. (1984). 'Unravelling the Paradox of Blackmail' 84 *Columbia LR* 670.

Llewellyn, K.N. (1931). 'What Price Contract' *Yale LJ* 704.

Llewellyn, K.N. (1938). 'Reassessing Unilateral Contracts: the Role of Offer and Acceptance' 48 *Yale LJ* 1.

Llewellyn, K.N. (1939). 'Book Review' 52 *Harvard LR* 700.

Locke, J. (1988). *Two Treatises of Government*. New York: Cambridge University Press.

Macauley, S. (1963). 'Non-contractual Relations in Business: A Preliminary Study' 28 *American Sociological R* 55.

MacKinnon, Katherine (1995). 'Feminism, Marxism, Method, and the State: Toward Feminist Jurisprudence' in *Feminist Legal Theory* (Vol. 1). New York: New York University Press.

Macneil, Ian R. (1980). *The New Social Contract: An Inquiry into Modern Contractual Relations*. New Haven: Yale University Press.

Mahoney, P.G. (1994). 'Contract Remedies and Optimal Pricing' 24 *J Legal Studies* 139.

McBride, N.J. (1994). 'A Fifth Common Law Obligation' 14 *Legal Studies* 35.

McBride, N.J. (1995). 'A Case for Awarding Damages in Response to Deliberate Breach of Contract' 24 *Anglo-American LR* 369.

McCormick, N. (1972). 'Voluntary Obligations and Normative Powers: Part 1' *Proceedings of the Aristotelian Society* Suppl. 46.

McKendrick, E. (1995). 'Frustration and Force Majeure — Their Relationship and a Comparative Assessment' in McKendrick (ed.), *Force Majeure and Frustration of Contract* (2nd edn). London: Lloyd's of London.

McKendrick, E. (1997). *Contract Law*. London: Macmillan.

Mill, J.S. (1974). *On Liberty*. London: Penguin Books.

Mill, J.S. (1979). *Utilitarianism.* Indianapolis, Ind.: Bobbs-Merrill.

Miller, D. (1987). *The Blackwell Encyclopedia of Political Thought.* Oxford: Blackwell.

Morris, A. (1997). 'Practical Reasoning and Contract as Promise: Extending Contract-Based Criteria to Decide Excuse Cases' 56 *Cambridge LJ* 147.

Munzer, S. (1990). *A Theory of Property.* New York: Cambridge University Press.

Nicholas, B. (1992). *The French Law of Contract.* Oxford: Oxford University Press.

Nicholas, B. (1995). 'Fault and Breach of Contract' in Beatson and Friedmann (eds.), *Good Faith and Fault in Contract Law.* Oxford: Oxford University Press.

Nozick, R. (1969). 'Coercion' in Sidney Morgenbesser, Patrick Suppes, and Morton White (eds.), *Philosophy, Science and Method: Essays in Honor of Ernest Nagel.* New York: St. Martin's Press.

Nozick, R. (1974). *Anarchy, State, and Utopia.* Oxford: Blackwell.

Olivecrona, K. (1971). *Law as Fact* (2nd edn). London: Stevens.

Patterson, D. (1943). 'Compulsory Contracts in the Crystal Ball' 43 *Columbia LR* 731.

Patterson, D. (1996). *A Companion to Philosophy of Law and Legal Theory.* Oxford: Blackwell.

Penner, J.E. (1996). 'Voluntary Obligations and the Scope of Law of Contract' 2 *Legal Theory* 325.

Penner, J.E. (1997). 'Basic Obligations' in P. Birks (ed.), *The Classification of Obligations.* Oxford: Oxford University Press.

Perry, S. (1988). 'The Impossibility of General Strict Liability' 1 *Canadian J of Law & Jurisprudence* 147.

Perry, S. (1992). 'The Moral Foundations of Tort Law' 77 *Iowa LR* 449.

Perry, S. (1995). 'Risk, Harm, and Responsibility' in D. Owen (ed.), *The Philosophical Foundations of Tort Law.* Oxford: Oxford University Press.

Perry, S. (2000). 'Corrective v Distributive Justice' in J. Horder (ed.), *Oxford Essays in Jurisprudence* (4th series). Oxford: Oxford University Press.

Polinsky, A.M. (1983). *An Introduction to Law and Economics.* Boston: Little Brown & Co.

Pollock, F. (1885). *Principles of Contract: Being a Treatise on the General Principles Concerning the Validity of Agreements in the Law of England, and America* (4th edn). Philadelphia: Blackstone.

Pollock, F. (1950). *Principles of Contract: A Treatise on the General Principles Concerning the Validity of Agreements in the Law of England* (13th edn.) Stevens (ed.). London: Stevens. — just insert previous/more recent publisher, etc. as it will not have changed.

Posner, Eric A. (2000). *Law and Social Norms*. Cambridge Mass.: Harvard University Press.

Posner, R. (1977). 'Gratuitous Promises in Economics and Law' 6 *J Legal Studies* 411.

Posner, R. (1981). *The Economics of Justice*. Cambridge, Mass.: Harvard University Press.

Posner, R. (1990). *The Problems of Jurisprudence*. Cambridge, Mass.: Harvard University Press.

Posner, R. (1998). *Economic Analysis of Law* (5th edn). New York: Aspen Law & Business.

Posner, R. and Rosenfield, A. (1977). 'Impossibility and Related Doctrines: An Economic Analysis' 6 *J Legal Studies* 39.

Priest, G. (1977). 'The Common Law Process and Selection of Efficient Rules' 6 *J Legal Studies* 65.

Priest, G. (1977). 'The Common Law Process and the Selection of Efficient Rules' 6 *J Legal Studies* 65.

Putnam, H. (1973). 'Meaning and Reference' 70 *J of Philosophy* 699.

Radin, M. (1987). 'Market-Inalienability' 100 *Harvard LR* 1849.

Rawls, J. (1971). *A Theory of Justice*. Cambridge, Mass.: Belknap Press.

Raz, J. (1979). *The Authority of Law*. Oxford, Oxford University Press.

Raz J. (1982). 'Promises in Morality and Law' 95 *Harvard LR* 916.

Raz, J. (1986). *The Morality of Freedom*. Oxford: Clarendon Press.

Raz, J. (1972). 'Voluntary Obligations and Normative Powers' in *Proceedings of the Aristotelian Society* Suppl. 46.

Raz, J. (1977). 'Promises and Obligations' in P.M.S. Hacker and J. Raz (eds.), *Law, Morality and Society*. Oxford: Clarendon Press.

Raz, J. (1994). *Ethics in the Public Domain*. Oxford: Clarendon Press.

Rose, C. (1994). 'Possession as the Origin of Property' in C. Rose, *Property and Persuasion*. Boulder, Co.: Westview Press.

Ross, Alf (1968). *Directives and Norms*. London: Routledge & Kegan Paul.

Rubin, P. (1977). 'Why is the Common Law Efficient?' 6 *J Legal Studies* 51.

Scanlon, T.M. (1998). 'Promises and Contracts' Paper for Presentation at Conference on Philosophy of Law, University of California, San Diego.

Scanlon, T.M. (1990). 'Promises and Practices' 19 *Philosophy and Public Affairs* 199.

Schubert, G. and Danelski, D. (eds.) (1969). *Comparative judicial behaviour cross-cultural studies of political decision-making in the East and West.* New York: Oxford University Press.

Schwartz, A. (1979). 'The Case for Specific Performance' 89 *Yale LJ* 271.

Schwartz, A. (1998). 'Incomplete Contracts' in Peter Newman (ed.), *The New Palgrave Dictionary of Economics and the Law.* London: Macmillan Reference.

Seavey, W.A. (1951). 'Reliance Upon Gratuitous Promises or Other Conduct' 64 *Harvard LR* 913.

Shavell, S. (1980). 'Damage Measures for Breach of Contract' 11 *Bell J of Economics* 466.

Sidgwick, H. (1874). *The Methods of Ethics.* London: Macmillan.

Simmons, A.J. (2001). *Justification and Legitimacy.* Cambridge: Cambridge University Press.

Simpson, B. (1975). 'Innovation in 19th Century Contract Law' 19 *Law Quarterly R* 247.

Smart, J.J.C. and Williams, B. (1973). *Utilitarianism: For and Against.* Cambridge: Cambridge University Press.

Smith, J.D. (1994). 'Contracts — Mistake, Frustration and Implied Terms' 110 *Law Quarterly R* 400.

Smith, L.D. (1995). 'Disgorgement of the profits of Breach of Contract: Property, Contract and 'Efficient Breach' 24 *Canadian Business LJ* 121.

Smith, S.A. (1995). 'Reconstructing Restraint of Trade' 17 *Oxford J Legal Studies* 565.

Smith, S.A. (1996). 'Future Freedom and Freedom of Contract' 59 *Modern LR* 167.

Smith, S.A. (1996b). 'In Defence of Substantive Fairness' 112 *Law Quarterly R* 138.

Smith, S.A. (1996c). 'Review of Weinrib, *The Idea of Private Law*' 112 *Law Quarterly R* 363.

Smith, S.A. (1997). 'Performance, Punishment, and the Nature of Contractual Obligation' 60 *Modern LR* 360.

Smith, S.A. (1997b). 'Contracts for the Benefit of Third Parties: In Defence of the Third Party Rule' 17 *Oxford J Legal Studies* 643.

Smith, S.A. (1999). 'Concurrent Liability in Contract and Unjust Enrichment: The Fundamental Breach Requirement' 115 *Law Quarterly R* 245.

Smith, S.A. (2000). 'Taking Law Seriously' 50 *U of Toronto LJ* 241.

Smith, S.A. (2000b). 'Towards a Theory of Contract' in J. Horder, ed.,

Oxford Essays in Jurisprudence (4th Series). Oxford: Oxford University Press.

Smith, S.A. (2001). ' "The Reliance Interest in Contract Damages" and the Morality of Contract Law' *Issues in Legal Scholarship, Smposium: Fuller and Perdue (2001)*: Article 1. http://www.bepress.com/ils/iss1/art1.

Smith, S.A. (2001b). 'Justifying the Law of Unjust Enrichment' 79 *Texas Law Review* 2177.

Smith, S.A. (2003). 'The Structure of Unjust Enrichment Law: Is Restitution a Right or a Remedy?' 36 *Loyola of Los Angeles LR* 1037.

Spence, M. (1997). 'Australian Estoppel and the Protection of Reliance' 1 *Journal of Contemporary L* 1.

Spence, M. (1999). *Protecting Reliance*. Oxford: Hart.

Stapelton, J. (2000). 'Perspectives on Causation' in J. Horder (ed.), *Oxford Essays in Jurisprudence* (4th series). Oxford: Oxford University Press.

Stoljar, S. (1988). 'Promise, Expectation, and Agreement' 47 *Cambridge LJ* 193.

Thaler, Richard (1991). *Quasi-Rational Economics*. New York: Russell Sage Foundation.

Tiersma, P.M. (1992). 'Reassessing Unilateral Contracts: The Role of Offer Acceptance and Promise' 26 *U of California at Davis LR* 1.

Titmuss, R. (1970). *The Gift Relationship: From Human Blood to Social Policy*. London: Allen.

Trebilcock, M.J. (1980). 'An Economic Approach to Unconscionability' in Barry J. Reiter and John Swan (eds.), *Studies in Contract Law*. Toronto: Butterworths.

Trebilcock, M.J. (1986). *The Common Law of Restraint of Trade: A Legal and Economic Analysis*. Toronto: Carswell.

Trebilcock, M.J. (1993). *The Limits of Freedom of Contract*. Cambdrige, Mass.: Harvard University Press.

Treitel, G.H. (1995). *The Law of Contract*. London: Sweet & Maxwell.

Triantis, G.G. (1992). 'Contractual Allocations of Unknown Risks: A Critique of the Doctrine of Commercial Impossibility' 42 *U of Toronto LJ* 450.

Tversky, A. and Kahneman, D. (1986). 'Rational Choice and the Framing of Decisions' 59 *J of Business* (Suppl) 251.

Ulen, T. (1989). 'Cognitive Imperfections and the Economic Analysis of Law' 12 *Hamline LR* 385.

Unger, R. (1983). 'The Critical Legal Studies Movement' 96 *Harvard LR* 561.

Veljanovski, C. and Harris, D. (1986). 'The Use of Economics to Elucidate Legal Concepts: The Law of Contract' in T. Daintith and G. Tuebner (eds.), *Contract and Organisation*. Berlin: De Gruyter.

Waddams, S. (1976). 'Unconscionability in Contracts' 39 *Modern LR* 369.

Waldron, J. (1988). *The Right to Private Property*. Oxford: Clarendon Press.

Wangerin, P. T. (1986). 'Damages for Reliance Across the Spectrum of Law: Of Blind Men and Legal Elephants' 72 *Iowa LR* 47.

Weinrib, E.J. (1995). *The Idea of Private Law*. Cambridge, Mass.: Harvard University Press.

Weinstein, (1980). 'Undue Optimism About Future Life Events' 39 *J Personality and Social Psychology* 806.

Williamson, O. (1985). *The Economic Institutions of Capitalism*. New York: Free Press.

Wittgenstein, L. (1972). *Philosophical Investigations* (trans G.E.M. Anscomb). Oxford: Blackwell.

Whish, R (2001). *Competition Law*. London: Butterworths.

Wolcher, L.E. (1989). 'Price Discrimination and Inefficient Risk Allocation under the rule of *Hadley v Baxendale*' 12 *Research in Law and Economics* 9.

Wright, R. (1939). *Legal Essays and Addresses*. Cambridge: Cambridge University Press.

Yorio, T. and Thel, S. (1991). 'The Promissory Basis of S.90' 101 *Yale LJ* 111.

Zimmerman, R. and Whittaker, S. (2000). *Good Faith in European Contract Law*. Cambridge: Cambridge University Press.

Index

Printed in the United Kingdom
by Lightning Source UK Ltd.
129974UK00001B/40-42/A

9 780198 765615